In the Minds
and Hearts of the People

Prologue to the
American Revolution:
1760-1774

Text by LILLIAN B. MILLER,

HISTORIAN, NATIONAL PORTRAIT GALLERY,

and the staff of the Historian's Office:

Barbara S. Kraft, RESEARCH HISTORIAN

Frederick S. Voss, RESEARCH HISTORIAN

Jeannette M. Hussey, RESEARCH ASSISTANT

Illustrations selected by

the Curatorial Department, National Portrait Gallery:

Robert G. Stewart, CURATOR

Monroe H. Fabian, ASSOCIATE CURATOR

Richard Kenin, CONSULTANT IN THE BRITISH ISLES

Russell Bourne, EDITOR

Marvin Sadik, DIRECTOR, NATIONAL PORTRAIT GALLERY

In the Minds and Hearts of the People

Prologue to the American Revolution: 1760-1774

NEW YORK GRAPHIC SOCIETY

Greenwich, Connecticut

International Standard Book Number: 0-8212-0496-3 (cloth)
International Standard Book Number: 0-8212-0621-4 (paper)

Library of Congress Catalog Card Number: 73-89950

First published 1974 by New York Graphic Society Ltd.
140 Greenwich Avenue, Greenwich, Conn. 06830
First printing 1974

DESIGNED BY PHILIP GRUSHKIN

Manufactured in the United States of America

CONTENTS

FOREWORD by Marvin Sadik   *page 9*

INTRODUCTION: The Spark that Fired   *13*

I. The King and His Men   *23*

II. Colonial Stirrings   *31*

III. Indians, Land, and the Proclamation of 1763   *51*

IV. The Cost of Empire and the Sons of Liberty   *81*

V. Bloodshed on Boston Common   *113*

VI. Quiet Rumblings   *127*

VII. A Tempest Over Tea   *157*

VIII. Liberty and Catholics   *185*

EPILOGUE: Continental Congress, 1774   *197*

NOTES   *201*

LIST OF ILLUSTRATIONS *with Curatorial Acknowledgments
    and Notes*   *209*

BIBLIOGRAPHY *with Historian's Acknowledgments*   *222*

INDEX   *235*

"But what do we mean by the American Revolution?
Do we mean the American war? The Revolution was in
the minds and hearts of the people; a change in their religious
sentiments, of their duties and obligations . . . . *This
radical change in the principles, opinions, sentiments, and
affections of the people was the real American Revolution.*"

JOHN ADAMS to HEZEKIAH NILES, 1818

FOREWORD

In the Minds and Hearts of the People is the story of how and why the American colonies moved within a period of a little more than a decade from the bosom of the mother country to the threshold of independence.

The stage is set with the ascension to the British throne of a young king, intellectually and psychologically ill-prepared to govern an empire but inflexible in the certainty of his right to do so as he saw fit. Advised by ministers whom he chose either out of personal friendship or because they were not tainted by having served at his grandfather's court (which he detested), George III deprived himself of the one great ministerial genius, William Pitt the Elder, whose wise counsel might have diverted British policy from its collision course with the American colonies.

In explaining the ideas and recounting the events which form the structure of this narrative, our special focus, as is uniquely appropriate to the National Portrait Gallery, is biographical. Here the thoughts and actions, as well as something of the personal aspirations and idiosyncracies, of more than a hundred key figures—men and women, Americans and Englishmen, Frenchmen and Indians, soldiers and mariners, artists and pamphleteers, clergymen and doctors, merchants and customs agents, farmers and lawyers, peers and commoners, revolutionaries and loyalists—are woven into the fabric of our chronicle to reveal the rich and intricate pattern of a turbulent and decisive era.

The portraits reproduced in these pages are intended not merely to illustrate the text but to stand as historic documents in themselves. The portrait, because it is a visual record of a person and an era, bears honest witness to each sitter's true role in the American experience; and it deserves to be studied as a critical piece of evidence in its own right. The National Portrait Gallery seeks to illumine and enliven American history by bringing to it this extra dimension of personal reality as conveyed by the portrait and by the biographical approach (as opposed to the usual textbook treatment of history which tends to become more abstract as it neglects the human elements involved). Moreover, as Carlyle observed, "Often I have found a Portrait superior in real instruction to a half-a-dozen written Biographies . . . or rather . . . I have found that the Portrait was as a small lighted candle by which the Biographies could for the first time be read, and some human interpretation be made of them. . . ."

This book is the first of three National Portrait Gallery publications which will accompany exhibitions organized to commemorate the Bicentennial of the American Revolution. Each of these presentations is designed to deal with the Revolutionary period itself or with some aspect of American life spanning the first two centuries of the nation's history.

As our first volume takes pains to point out, there were problems confronting the Crown in its relations with the thirteen colonies beginning in the early 1760s which were not by any means merely the result of irrational impulse or unreason in London. Chief among these problems was the military expense of making the colonies secure in the face of French imperial interests in North America. It was not illogical to assume that British Americans should help to foot this bill, and furthermore that they should desist from compounding the problem by trading with the French. Unfortunately, however, profits from such trade enabled many a merchant to pay the taxes levied by colonial legislatures to support the British war effort. This problem, then, was both real and complicated.

The solution the Crown chose—writs of assistance—in an attempt to inhibit the smuggling necessary to carry on trade with the French was the first of several disastrous measures instituted to collect colonial revenues which were to have repercussions far beyond the pocketbooks of Americans. Writs of assistance were general search warrants that did not require a sus-pected smuggler to be named nor his contraband to be located before they were issued, and since they were transferable, anyone could be deputized to use them. In denouncing the writs, James Otis, Jr., not only condemned what he believed to be their illegality as "the worst instrument of arbitrary power, the most destructive to English Liberty, and the fundamental principles of the constitution," but in so doing he argued that every man had a "right to his life, his liberty . . . his property." Furthermore, he defined these rights as "written on [man's] heart, and revealed to him by his maker." They were, Otis maintained, "inherent, inalienable, and indefensible by any laws, pacts, contracts, covenants, or stipulations, which man could devise. . . ."

Spoken in 1761, the idea that these words express was to become so deeply ingrained in the minds and hearts of Americans in all parts of the colonies that it would animate the explosive chain of events recounted in this narrative, and two years later find fuller and finer utterance in the Declaration of Independence.

Marvin Sadik, Director
National Portrait Gallery
Smithsonian Institution

In the Minds
and Hearts of the People

Prologue to the
American Revolution:
1760-1774

INTRODUCTION:

The Spark that Fired

On July 4, 1754, Colonel George Washington of the Virginia militia surrendered the British garrison, Fort Necessity, to a combined force of French and Indians under the command of Coulon de Villiers. The drummers beat a military march and a flag flew high to fulfill "the honors of war." But, ironically, no war had yet been declared between the British and the French, and Washington's capitulation at Great Meadows merely marked his defeat in a fight over ownership of land whose jurisdiction had not yet been determined. However, the "little skirmish," in Voltaire's words, fired "the signal that set Europe in a blaze." Inadvertently, Washington was responsible for shedding the first blood in the French and Indian War, known as the Seven Years' War in Europe, which grew into a conflict that cost the lives of about 853,000 soldiers and hundreds of thousands of civilians, and provided a root cause for the American Revolution.

Washington's presence at Great Meadows resulted from the competition between the British and the French for the American West. Land, with all that it promised in the way of wealth and power, was the magnet that drew the armies of the two nations to the American forests and young Washington to the fork of the Ohio River as a British emissary with orders to drive the French out—"by force of arms" if necessary. Washington's brother, Lawrence, was president of the Ohio Company, the membership of which represented the wealth, aristocracy, and power of Virginia. Through an award by the British Crown, the company laid claim to half a million acres of the land that drained into the Ohio River. It planned to build a fort and trading post and establish two hundred families in the area, but in 1753, British King George II, upon hearing that the French were penetrating the wilderness south of their fort at Niagara, decided to establish Britain's claim to the rich lands once and for all by establishing a garrison at the confluence of the Allegheny and Monongahela rivers—exactly where the Ohio Company had planned to build its fort. George Washington, who was connected through his brother with the Ohio Company's enterprise and who held a commission as adjutant from his district, was chosen by Virginia's Lieutenant Governor Robert Dinwiddie to head the Crown's expedition into the wilderness to build the desired fort.

George Washington was an impressive young man at nineteen. Extremely energetic and strong from years spent riding, surveying, and overseeing on a Virginia plantation and in the Virginia frontier, he was over six feet tall and weighed almost two hundred pounds. The young Washington moved with the grace of a trained athlete, while his steady blue eyes and proudly held head of chestnut hair struck confidence among those he was given to lead, and camouflaged to some extent his youth and naiveté. Washington did not really understand the politics and diplomacy involved in his mission. "It was," he recalled years later, "deemed by some an extraordinary circumstance that so young and inexperienced a person should have been employed on a negotiation with which subjects of the greatest importance were involved." [1]

Accompanied by Indian chiefs and a Dutchman who claimed to know French, Washington rode into the wilderness to the site of the proposed fort where the French were encamped and handed the French a warning to retire from the British-claimed lands. When the French military force refused to accept the "pretensions of the King of Great Britain," he left a small garrison behind to build the fort and returned to the capital to recruit a regiment and to procure military and food supplies for its fortification. By the time he returned, however, the French had captured the newly built fort, leaving a ragged force of thirty-three British regulars shelterless.

Accepting the offer of an Indian alliance, Washington decided to fortify a storehouse near the fork in the rivers, but some twenty miles from his objective, he was stopped by a flooding river. In a wild field on the stony side of Laurel Ridge called the Great Meadows, he found "two natural entrenchments" so close together that the sides could be closed in with wagons to form a hollow square—"a charming field for an encounter," he wrote to the authorities at home. Eager to engage the French, Washington rode out into the forest, discovered a small French encampment almost by accident, and ordered his men to fire. Through the exchange of fire, his exposed company stood fast. Later, Washington wrote to his brother that he "heard the bullets whistle, and, believe me, there is something charming in the sound." (To which George II is said to have commented that Washington would not have thought the sound of bullets so charming "if he had been used to hear many.")[2]

In fifteen minutes, the little skirmish was over; the French surrendered and Washington found himself with twenty-two prisoners, ten Frenchmen, including the commander, having been killed. The French were carrying diplomatic credentials and claimed that they were "ambassadors" who had come to present Wash-

William Shirley by Thomas Hudson, 1750.

ington with messages offering peace and a warning to remove himself from French territory.

The English later placed responsibility for the battle on the Indians; but they could not use that explanation a few weeks later when Washington again met the French at his Fort Necessity, a quickly erected palisaded fort that the Indians scornfully called "that little thing in the Meadow." The Indians had decamped, abandoning Washington because they believed he was treating them "as slaves," and, even more important, because they had no faith in his strategy of fighting "in open field." Accustomed to ambush tactics, they could not accept the risks of an open battle where men were expendable and defeat, they believed, sure.

Lack of food, a surplus of rum, an exposed position, and a tremendous rain that rendered ammunition and powder useless weakened Washington's army and made his position untenable. Under constant fire from the French, one-third of his men were killed or seriously wounded. Without horses, wagons, or food, they were ready to accept the generous surrender terms offered by the enemy.

Washington's defeat at Great Meadows had great consequences for Indian relations, for it confirmed the Indians' belief both in Washington's incompetence and in the superiority of the French over the English. As Indian agent Daniel Claus summed it up, "There was never the like seen how quick the nations turned after Colonel Washington's defeat." Even more significant, however, his failure to stop French penetration of the western wilderness, together with Major-General Edward Braddock's defeat by a combined force of French and Indians at the Monongahela River a year later, signaled a full-scale eruption of hostilities between France and England in the New World. This was to be England's last, and most successful, conflict with another European power on American soil.

From 1702 on, Great Britain had engaged in successive wars with Spain and France, on the continent and on the high seas, each of which had spilled over to the North American continent. War did not hinder colonial growth, however. From a population in 1670 numbering 85,000, the Americans had multiplied to a total of 1,500,000 in 1754, a sum that included 300,000 Negroes, mostly slaves, and many non-English peoples. The area of settlement had tripled as settlers pressed into the hilly interior of New England and moved into the lands west of the lower Hudson River and central Pennsylvania. In the South, emigrants traveled into the piedmont area between the fall line of the rivers up to the Blue Ridge and Smoky mountains.

In the course of these wars, the European settlers became so rooted in the American environment that by the 1740s colonial troops stopped calling themselves "provincials" and insisted upon being called "Americans." American stakes in the fighting were quite different from British goals. England's immediate concern was ownership of the sugar islands in the Caribbean. In the South, Carolinians and Virginians sought to clear their borders of hostile Indians or the menacing Spanish, while expanding into Indian hunting grounds. The same factors, Indian harassment and land hunger, also played a large role in determining the participation of New Yorkers, New Hampshire farmers, and Pennsylvania Germans in British-led armies on American soil. New Englanders sought to extinguish popery in the North and to acquire important fishing rights in the North Atlantic. New Englanders and New Yorkers were also concerned with destroying French power on their northern and

eastern boundaries. In fact, it was with such ends in mind that Governor William Shirley of Massachusetts and William Pepperrell, merchant of Kittery, Maine, outfitted and led a successful New England expedition against Louisbourg in 1744. When, however, much to their dismay, Louisbourg was returned to the French at the Treaty of Aix-la-Chapelle in 1748, New Englanders became convinced that the British cared little for their interests. The other colonists soon arrived at the same conclusion. Distrust of British policy among independent and hardy settlers whose aims were practical rather than political smoldered even while peace descended temporarily on the New World.

Further events occurring during the uneasy peace that prevailed during the 1750s continued to set

William Pepperrell by John Smibert, 1747.
In the background the artist has depicted the
siege of Louisbourg.

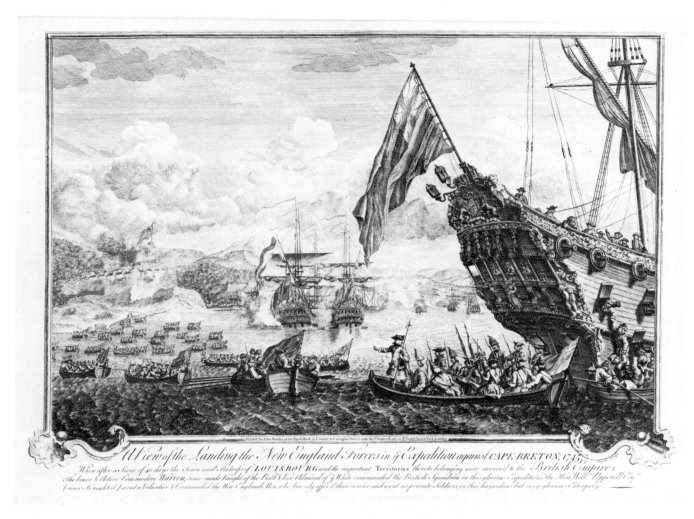

A View of the Landing the New England Forces in ye Expedition against CAPE BRETON, 1745.

The landing of William Pepperrell's New England troops at the siege of Louisbourg, 1745, shown in an engraving published in London sometime after 1746.

Americans apart from their British cousins. When Major-General Braddock suffered defeat at the hands of a combined force of French and Indians in 1755, the colonists attributed his failure to the "dastardly behavior"—in George Washington's words—of the British regulars, ". . . [which] exposed all those who were inclined to do their duty to almost certain death."[3] Americans, on the other hand, gloried in Washington's brave attempt to halt the British panic during the battle. Despite illness and the loss of two horses which had been shot from under him during the course of the battle, he had urged on the force of Regulars and Americans with "courage and resolution"; but the British, Americans believed, had betrayed colonial trust. The fact that the English high command blamed Braddock's defeat on colonial officers who had filled the Regulars with fear that if they "engaged the

Indians in the European manner of fighting, they would be beat," merely widened the chasm between the British military leadership and the American farmers they were sent to lead.[4]

In August 1756, when England's ally Frederick of Prussia marched across the Saxon border, war was formally declared between England and France. To secure North America for England and her colonies, the British planned to cut off the supply line from French Canada to France's western forts, hoping to starve these fortifications out of existence. To effect this, General William Johnson, fur trader and adopted chief of the Mohawks, was sent to Lake Champlain to build a fort at Ticonderoga that would block the activities of the French fort at Crown Point, and Governor William Shirley of Massachusetts was given charge of an expedition to Fort Niagara that would similarly cut off supplies from Fort Duquesne at the juncture of the Monongahela, Ohio, and Allegheny rivers.

British plans were only partially successful. William Johnson, unable to capture the strongly fortified garrison at Crown Point, attempted to build Fort William Henry on the lake's northern tip, while the ineptness of the British commander in chief in America, the Earl of Loudon—whom Shirley called "a pen and ink man whose greatest energies were put forth in getting ready to begin"—prevented Governor Shirley's expedition from getting off at all.[5]

James Wolfe by George Townshend, 1759.

An early engraved view of Braddock's death in 1775.

George Washington's concerns remained with Virginia's Shenandoah Valley, which on August 14, 1755, he was commissioned to defend. "Colonel of the Virginia Regiment and Commander in Chief of all forces now raised in the defense of His Majesty's Colony," at the age of twenty-three, Washington had to cope with a badly organized army given to mutiny and desertion. He had to provide supplies over bad trails and from long distances. He had to handle recalcitrant settlers who would not sacrifice their personal convenience for the success of his larger mission, and he had to contend with the jealousy of other colonies, each of which pursued its own interests. Washington's zeal for carrying on his thankless task was strengthened when he began to view the war as involving the safety of his native colony of Virginia, rather than being one of "the usual contests of empire and ambition." This change of perspective came about only after he had experienced frustrations attempting to advise and participate in decisions of the British high command under the leadership of the Earl of Loudon. The Earl did not hide his suspicions of Washington's loyalty, nor did he conceal his supercilious attitude toward Americans. He would not incorporate Washington's militia regiment into the regular British military establishment, and he would not consider recommending Washington for a British commission.

One Corporal & 4 light Horse to march tomorrow morning with ye detachment under Col. Gage's Comd. and to remain with him.

The Detachmt. of seamen, and Captn. Stuart with 1 Suballtern & 10 light Horse to march on Thursday morning

No woman to be victualled upon the Detach that marches tomorrow and Thursday

After Orders

Each of the two Regt. as also Captn. Gates's Independant Company to ~~send~~ send a sufficient numbr. of Tents ~~under ye comd.~~ for ye respective Detachmt. that march tomorrow under ye comd. of Lt. Col. Gage

After Orders

This Excellency has been pleasd to appoint Lt. Buchannan of ye Artillery to march with ye two Guns tomorrow Morng. & Captn. Lt. Smith and Lt. McLeoud of ye Artillery to march with ye Detachmt. on Thursday Morng. The men that march tomorrow & on Thursday Mg. to be compleated to be compleated to 24 Rounds of Ammunition

The last page, for June 17, 1755, in a surviving fragment of Edward Braddock's Orderly Book. Braddock was killed less than one month later on July 13.

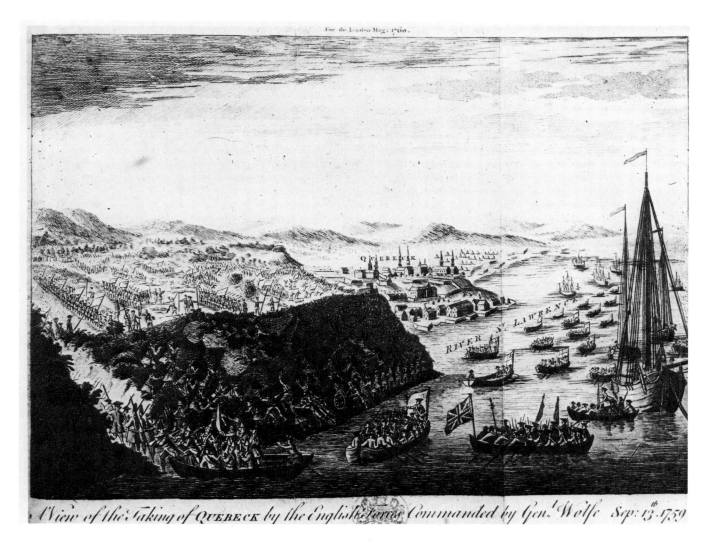

A View of the Taking of QUEBECK by the English Forces Commanded by Gen.l Wolfe Sep: 13.th 1759

The storming of the Plains of Abraham above Quebec in 1759,
as seen in an English engraving of 1760.

Rebuffed and discontented, Washington wrote angrily to Lieutenant Governor Dinwiddie what was to become a common American complaint: "We can't conceive that being American should deprive us of the benefits of British subjects." Now Washington began to relinquish his dreams of glory for the mother country; imperceptibly but surely, his thoughts turned toward achieving "the friendly regard of my acquaintances" and the welfare of "my country." [6]

When Brigadier General John Forbes was sent to America to command the Ohio Valley attack against French-held Fort Duquesne, Washington's Virginia regiment was incorporated finally into the British Regulars, but Washington was placed in a subordinate position to the fifty-year-old Scot whose expertise lay in military organization. Washington's participation in

Forbes's campaign provided more frustrations. General Forbes insisted upon building a road to Duquesne and the Ohio Valley through Pennsylvania, whereas Braddock's road, cutting through Virginia, had promised to that colony, once the war ended, a route by which the commerce of the Ohio Valley would reach Virginia ports and enrich Virginia merchants. Colonial rivalry as well as military expediency dictated Washington's involvement in the fight over the road's route. Arguments over battle strategy, too, offended the young Colonel, and the success of the Swiss-born mercenary Colonel Bouquet in capturing Fort Duquesne for the British aroused more jealousy than happiness at a goal secured.

In 1759, Washington resigned his commission and returned to civilian life. He was bitter at the injustice he believed had been rendered him by a British commander and troubled by a lingering feeling that his efforts had failed while the British had been successful. His participation in the French and Indian War, however, remained an important part of his life, as testified by the fact that he chose to have Charles Willson Peale portray him in 1772 in his colonel's uniform, with the gorget of an officer dangling from his neck.

Just as the French and Indian War was important for Washington's later development as a man and military leader, so it was for the colonies'. The colonies learned that Great Britain could ignore them or use them as it was expedient. From this they concluded that Great Britain was fighting the war for her own imperial reasons and not for their protection or prosperity. Later, when British ministers sought to have Americans pay for that war, Americans were quick to respond that it was not their responsibility since the war had not been fought for them.

British arrogance and misunderstanding of the American temperament and capacities also taught Americans a lesson during the course of warfare. The British were cold brothers indeed; and their display of superiority heightened and reinforced the sense of separate identity that a long period of "salutary neglect" had begun to create. Forced to fall back on local loyalties when denied the opportunity to partici-

View of Quebec. Engraving by Thomas Johnston, 1759.

Celebration of Britain's heroes, King George III, William Pitt,
and General Wolfe. Engraving by Nathaniel Hurd, 1762.

pate fully in British institutions such as the army, Americans soon transformed such loyalties into national virtues worth fighting to preserve.

The removal of the French from the New World by 1760 with the decisive defeat of Montcalm by General Wolfe on the Plains of Abraham presented the British with problems of imperial organization of size and importance never before experienced. How to utilize the enormous acreage wrested from the French became the most crucial question, involving Indian policy, military defense, and revenue raising. Changes in colonial policy were necessary. But the colonists could not accept lightly changes that were antagonistic to colonial traditions. They viewed the new policies as encroachments upon their constitutional rights as

Englishmen, and upon the social, political, and religious institutions which they believed embodied these rights. The new policies involved British intervention in their affairs such as they had never before experienced. Chafing under this interference, the colonists began to look back longingly to the period before the peace, when life seemed simpler and England kept out of colonial affairs.

The American Revolution was born, as John Adams said, in the minds and hearts of Americans once they realized their separate identity under the pressure of policies and events that goaded them to violent resistance. These events took place between 1760 and 1774. After that, the process became inexorable. There was no turning back.

The King and His Men

The Coronation of a King

The coronation ceremonies for King George III proceeded without incident on Tuesday, September 22, 1761. For almost a year, officials had been engaged in preparations for the event, exciting the public to "a greater degree than ever had been known on the like occasion." As platforms along the processional route from Westminster Hall to the west door of Westminster Abbey were erected, prices for choice seats skyrocketed. For a seat in the "coronation theatres"—large booths that contained from twelve to fifteen hundred people—the prices "were beyond all precedent." [1]

The crush of people necessitated special regulations for fireworks, artillery salutes, traffic flow, even the amount of money hackney coachmen and chairmen could charge. Hospitals readied for "the reception and speedy relief of the unfortunate." Light-horsemen stood by to aid magistrates in the event of "tumults, riots, or other disorders." As a result, "No accident of any kind did happen on that day, which human wisdom could have prevented," reported *The Gentleman's Magazine*. A horse rode over a bystander and the great diamond in His Majesty's crown fell out of its setting on the return to Westminster Hall but was immediately found and restored—minor mishaps in a perfectly planned ceremony of symbolic significance for the entire British Empire. [2]

What manner of man was George III, whose long reign was to embrace so much of crucial importance in the history of Great Britain and the United States, whose name was to be identified with vile tyranny, and who was to go down in history as a stupid and mad king ready to sacrifice an empire to his obstinacy?

GEORGE III

So slow-witted that he frequently was considered "stupid," with a tendency toward corpulency and sluggishness, George's personality was marked by a stubborn and dogmatic obstinacy. Lord Waldegrave, who had been governor to George when he was Prince of Wales, noted the youth's "strong prejudices," his "indolence in all affairs," his sullenness and melancholy, and his tendency to shift blame on to others in order to relieve the bitter consciousness of his own failures. Throughout his reign, the King's character remained remarkably unchanged, despite the demanding pressure of events that required flexibility and despite the hereditary disease—called *porphyria* by twentieth-century medical researchers—that rendered

St. Edward's Crown, worn by George III at his coronation.

him "mad" or mentally incompetent for increasingly longer periods of time.

While a child, George had been subjected to disparaging comparisons between himself and his younger brother, the Duke of York, which contributed to his sense of inadequacy. Because his mother was "averse to the young people, from the excessive bad education they had, and from the bad examples they gave," the boy grew up in near isolation. British historian Lewis Namier called his "well-regulated nursery" the "nearest approach to a concentration camp. Lonely, but never alone, constantly watched and discussed, never safe from the wisdom and goodness of the grownups, never with anyone on terms of equality, exalted yet oppressed by deferential adults," it was natural, Namier concludes, that George should develop a silent, sullen anger. Since he was always with adults, he never had the opportunity to develop self-reliance: "at nineteen he dreamt of reforming the nation," writes Namier, "but his idea of acting the man was to repeat without blushing or fear what he had to say." [3]

The Prince's education had been permeated by eighteenth-century ideas that emphasized the king's leadership in reviving the national spirit and regenerating the country's political life. The patriot king was to raise England to its former glories, not by despotic acts or at the dictation of a faction, but in accordance with the popular will. In doing so, he would find his satisfactions in the execution of the wishes of his subjects.

George III's familial experiences encouraged him to look outside the family to the people for the affection and trust he sought. Great antagonisms existed between royal parents and their heirs. George III's grandmother, Queen Caroline, found the thought of her son Frederick—George's father and leader of the opposition—almost unbearable. "If I was to see him in hell," she wrote, "I should feel no more for him than I should for any other rogue that ever went there." Her husband, George II, regarded his renegade son as "a monster and the greatest villain that was ever born." [4]

The Court's environment—marked as J. H. Plumb puts it, by "the politics of hatred and the politics of

Edward Augustus, Duke of York, with his older brother, the future George III, by Richard Wilson, circa 1751.

betrayal"—accentuated George's sense of personal inadequacy and strengthened his tendency to neurosis. Combined with his sense of the immensity of his role as king was his awareness of his youthfulness—he was, after all, just twenty-two. Dedicated in purpose, nevertheless, and believing in the necessity for strong and efficient government, George III vowed to throw off his constitutional lethargy and, as he promised his beloved adviser Lord Bute, correct his "various faults . . . that I might repent of them." [5]

George III was rigorously trained in eighteenth-century constitutional theory which emphasized the idea of a balanced government. The British King was expected to choose his ministers from the parliamentary leadership; frequently forced to choose between political rivals each of whom had a strong party following, the King's choice of ministers influenced governmental policy. George III, however, disliked the idea of parliamentary cliques, believing that they disrupted the nation's harmony. Rather than powerful party leaders, he appointed men whom he liked and trusted.

Although he regarded himself as a constitutional monarch, George III never contemplated democracy. A king, he believed, was the steward of the people, bound only by the obligation to protect "the Liberties, Rights, and Privileges of all His Subjects." [6] As a result, the "personal government" he practiced during the first years of his reign and the period of the American Revolution often conflicted with the popular political mood. Plagued by the dilemma of finding a ministry that would accept his guidance and fulfill his aims while receiving popular support, he alternated between trustworthy servants such as Lord Bute and popular leaders such as William Pitt, neither of whom could satisfy both his aims.

The King's Men

WILLIAM PITT, LORD CHATHAM
(1708–1778);
JOHN STUART, LORD BUTE (1713–1792)

In 1735, William Pitt took his brother's place in the House of Commons, beginning the political career that would earn him the sobriquet, "the Great Com-

Transfer-printed Liverpoolware mug bearing the likeness of William Pitt, after 1756.

moner." Arrogant, aloof, egotistical, he was also highly original and brilliant, capable of spellbinding eloquence that could inspire, if it did not excite, fear. "No one ever left Pitt's closet," wrote C. W. Colby, "without feeling himself a braver man." [7] Much of Pitt's inspiration derived from his vision of empire that extended beyond the boundaries of his little island. He believed that the state ought to be run for the benefit of all and that the national will expressed itself through popular approval. He saw his mandate as emanating from the people, and by that mandate he sought power.

From 1736 to 1742, Pitt developed his oratorical powers at the expense of George II's minister, Robert Walpole, opposing on nationalistic grounds the subsidization of the King's Hanoverian possessions. His eloquent speeches—filled, according to Horace Walpole, son of the minister, with "humor, wit, vivacity . . . boldness"—reached beyond the halls of Parliament into the hearts of the British people. Although he incurred George II's hatred, Pitt continued to rise in public favor. In 1746, much against his will, George II was forced to yield to Pitt's appointment to the cabinet; soon afterwards, he became a member of the

Privy Council, meanwhile continuing to ingratiate himself with the people.

The Seven Years' War presented Pitt with his greatest opportunity for statesmanship. At "popular demand," he formed a ministry in 1756 and devised a strategy which by 1763 would win an empire for Britain with the signing of the Treaty of Paris. His most glorious years were those from 1757 to 1761, when, because of his inspired leadership, the tide was turned for the British in North America and the East Indies. So numerous were British military triumphs during his leadership that Horace Walpole sardonically commented, "We are forced to ask every morning what victory there has been for fear of missing one." [8]

With George III's accession, however, Pitt's fortunes changed. Before he could complete his mission of creating an empire for "liberty and independence," Pitt was rendered politically helpless by George's trusted friend and adviser Lord Bute. Since Pitt had been counselor to George II, he was in George's grandson's view "the blackest of hearts," a "true snake in the grass." [9] As a member of an old gang of corrupt politicians, he deserved to be swept from office. Pitt's conduct of the war also disturbed the thrifty King, who was appalled at the huge sums spent to support Frederick of Prussia's efforts in central Europe. Lord Bute urged immediate peace, but Pitt advocated delay until he was certain that France would surrender Canada and the Newfoundland fisheries. The minister's terms, however, were rejected by France, now strengthened by an alliance with Spain. The cabinet refused to declare war against Spain as Pitt demanded, and in 1761, the "Great Commoner" resigned "since my advice is not taken."

Pitt's resignation was not unsought. The King had long wanted to have his close friend Lord Bute near at hand; and in October 1761, Bute became First Lord of the Treasury and leader of the new ministry.

Lord Bute had entered George's world in 1747 when he accidentally met George's father, Prince Frederick, at the Egham races. Bute had just come out of a self-imposed exile on his estate in Scotland, where he had retired after losing his seat in Parliament because of his anti-war policy. Exclusion from public activities had left him, as Lord Shelburne described him,

proud, aristocratical, pompous, imposing, with a great deal of superficial knowledge . . . chiefly upon matters of

natural philosophy, mines, fossils, a smattering of mechanics, a little metaphysics, and a very false taste in everything . . . he had a gloomy sort of madness which made him affect living alone . . . in the Isle of Bute, with as much pomp and as much uncomfortableness in his little domestick circle, as if he had been king of the island, Lady Bute a forlorn queen, and her children slaves of a despotick tyrant. [10]

Bute's exile had left him in poor financial condition. Resolving to try his fortune again in England, he rented a house at the fashionable resort of Twickenham and joined the royal entourage, becoming Frederick's Lord of the Bedchamber. After Frederick died, Bute remained at the Princess Dowager's house, almost unnoticed by court circles but exercising considerable influence within her family. Handsome and well-built, possessing a taste for literature and the fine arts, he could be a fascinating companion if he chose; and "the grave, lean, demure, elderly woman," as Thackeray called her, must have welcomed his sympathy. Although there is no proof that he and Frederick's widow were lovers, their intimacy became a subject of gossip and scandalous rumors. Acting as a father substitute, Bute instilled in young George serious thoughts about the responsibilities of the

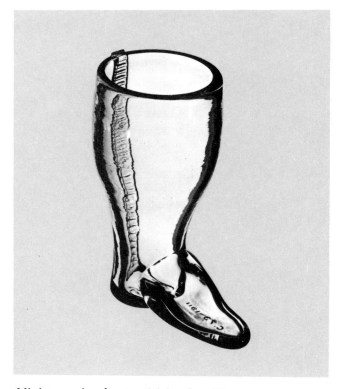

Miniature glass boot satirizing Lord Bute.

kingship. He especially inculcated in the Prince a strong distrust of politicians who with their "interested views, riches, ambitions, honours, will contaminate every advice they give." [11]

With George III's accession to the throne, it was inevitable that Bute and Pitt would clash and that Bute would win. Even before he formally headed the ministry, he was considered the King's spokesman, and it was only a matter of time before he would persuade the King and his cabinet to his policies.

Bute's goals were to conclude a peace with France, break the connection between English and German politics, which he believed embroiled England constantly in continental controversies, destroy the Whig opposition, and make the King supreme over Parliament. To Pitt, supremacy of the King over the people's legislature spelled tyranny; making peace with France at that time, folly. In the cabinet, Bute prevailed over Pitt, but not with the people. Disliked by most Englishmen, who still associated Scotland with the Stuarts and Catholicism (although Bute's family had been loyal to the Protestant Succession), the Scottish Lord became one of England's most unpopular ministers. When he dared to go out unattended, he was unsafe, and the old rumors of a liaison with the Princess Dowager added charges of adultery to an already blackened reputation. Emblems of the two—the jackboot and the petticoat—were

John Bull's House sett in Flames. *Engraving, 1762.*

The Times. William Hogarth's cartoon defense of Bute's policy, published in response to John Bull's House sett in Flames, *1762.*

burned by street mobs in protest against his influence and policies.

Meanwhile, events proved Pitt correct that England ought to declare war against Spain, before Spain could come to France's aid. When that alliance took place, the English had no alternative but war; on January 4, 1762, Bute so informed Parliament. A month later, he found it necessary to follow Pitt's recommendation not to withdraw English troops from Germany. If France and Spain were engaged on the continent, they could not throw their whole weight against the British armies in North America.

Although the facts of war militated against Bute's plans for "a speedy, honourable and permanent peace," he continued to work secretly for an accommodation. Through bribery and intimidation, he managed to have the preliminary peace treaty approved by both houses of Parliament in December 1762. On February 10, 1763, the definitive treaty was signed at Paris, on terms much less advantageous to Great Britain than those advocated by Pitt. When the contents of the treaty became known, Bute became even more unpopular. The people were convinced that Bute had "got money by the peace of Paris." By April 1763, Bute could no longer maintain his burdensome and unpopular position. Close to a nervous breakdown, he persuaded the King to accept his resignation and form a new ministry.

Colonial Stirrings

While British politicians played the game of politics and engaged in empire building, their decisions affected American life enormously. It was easy enough for British statesmen to vote measures into effect in the halls of Parliament and dismiss them from their mind while they pursued the pleasures and interests of their privileged lives. But in the towns and cities of North America, their decisions created consternation, anger, and fear. And in the American forests, their decisions led to mortal combat and terrorism that contrasted strangely with the drawing-room quality of the British political scene.

Writs of Assistance (1761)

The colonists' lucrative but illegal trade with the French became one of the first issues to arouse American resentment of British policy. The Molasses Act of 1733 had imposed duties of six-pence per gallon on rum, molasses, and sugar imported from foreign sugar islands to America. During periods of war, trade with the enemy was outlawed altogether. Since this trade constituted an important part of colonial commerce, however, American merchants universally violated the law, even though by doing so they aided the enemy. In 1755, for instance, at least forty ships, mainly from New York, Rhode Island, and Boston, were seen in the harbor of Louisbourg with provisions sufficient to meet French needs for the spring campaign. A few years later, American ships so thoroughly provisioned the fleet of French Admiral de Beaufremont in the West Indies that it was able to sail quickly to the defense of Cape Breton and prevent Britain's Lord Loudon from capturing the island.

Illicit trade provided the colonists with money to pay taxes levied by colonial legislatures to meet war expenses. Without such smuggling enterprises, the colonists argued, they would be unable to meet British requests for help in the field. Smuggling, moreover, was not regarded as a heinous crime. In England, for example, 40,000 smugglers were estimated to be busily at work in 1773. Most merchants regarded it as an aspect of business. The power of the illicit traders was so great and their activities so well approved by Americans that when, in 1760, a smuggler, George Spencer, attempted to confess his activities in a local New York paper, he was set upon ferociously. The printer refused to publish his confession, and a mob pelted him with filth and threw him into jail on a trumped-up charge. Nobody wanted such practices publicized because of fear, as Spencer wrote, they would bring on regulations that would "Effectually prevent any Illicit Contraband Commerce for the

Future and Especially Stores or Ammunition, either directly or indirectly to the Enemy. . . ."[1]

To crack down on smuggling, the customs commissioners believed it was necessary to obtain writs of assistance—general search warrants. Since such warrants did not require that suspected smugglers be specified by name or that the contraband's storage places be specifically located, authorities could more easily surprise a suspect. Moreover, the writs were transferable, which meant that anyone could be deputized to use them. Such writs were commonplace in England, but their arbitrary use was checked by the custom which made the officers responsible at their own "peril" for proving that the seized goods were imported illegally. That custom had not developed in America, where there was still some question as to the legality of writs of assistance and considerable fear of their indiscriminate use.

On May 16, 1760, twenty-six hogsheads of rum, illegally imported into Massachusetts, were seized and condemned. A week later, a quantity of smuggled tea was condemned, and soon after, a number of barrels of sugar. From that time on, almost every month witnessed a seizure of cargo and its condemnation. Some of these were carried out with the aid of writs of assistance issued by the Superior Court, general in form and without limitation in time.

In December 1760, news of the death of King George II was received in Massachusetts Bay, rendering all writs issued in his name void after six months. Anticipating that the customs officials would have to petition for new writs, in February 1761, sixty-three Bay merchants, lead by Boston lawyers Oxenbridge Thacher and James Otis, asked to be heard in Superior Court to test the writs' constitutionality.

FRANCIS BERNARD (1712–1779)

The British official who found himself in 1761 in the midst of controversy was Francis Bernard, former governor of New Jersey and governor of Massachusetts Bay from 1760 to 1769.

Son of a country rector of an old and well-connected British family, Bernard had settled in Lincolnshire as a provincial counsel and remained there for twenty years, during which time he married a lady of higher rank and fortune than his own, sired eight children, and enjoyed the pursuit of music, poetry, and

Sir Francis Bernard by John Singleton Copley, 1767.

architecture. With a growing family, however, he found that the costs of maintaining his aristocratic tastes far exceeded his income. He also nourished ambitions to be active beyond "a restricted compass"; and when the office of colonial governor in America was made available, the idea "seized upon his imagination." In 1758, then, through the assistance of an influential relative, Bernard was appointed governor of New Jersey. After two successful years there, marked by the birth of two more children, he was promoted governor of Massachusetts at the intervention of his "old friend and neighbor," John Pownall of the Board of Trade.[2]

It was not easy for an Englishman to take office in America, even if it was a sinecure. Although Bernard's salary was attractive at £800, he had to pay £400 for his commission and £1,200 to move his family and furnishings across the ocean. When he was transferred to Massachusetts, his salary increased by £300; but again he had to pay the costs of moving and another £400 for his new commission. At the death of George II, Bernard had to renew his commission for an additional £400.

With such expenses, one wonders why individuals

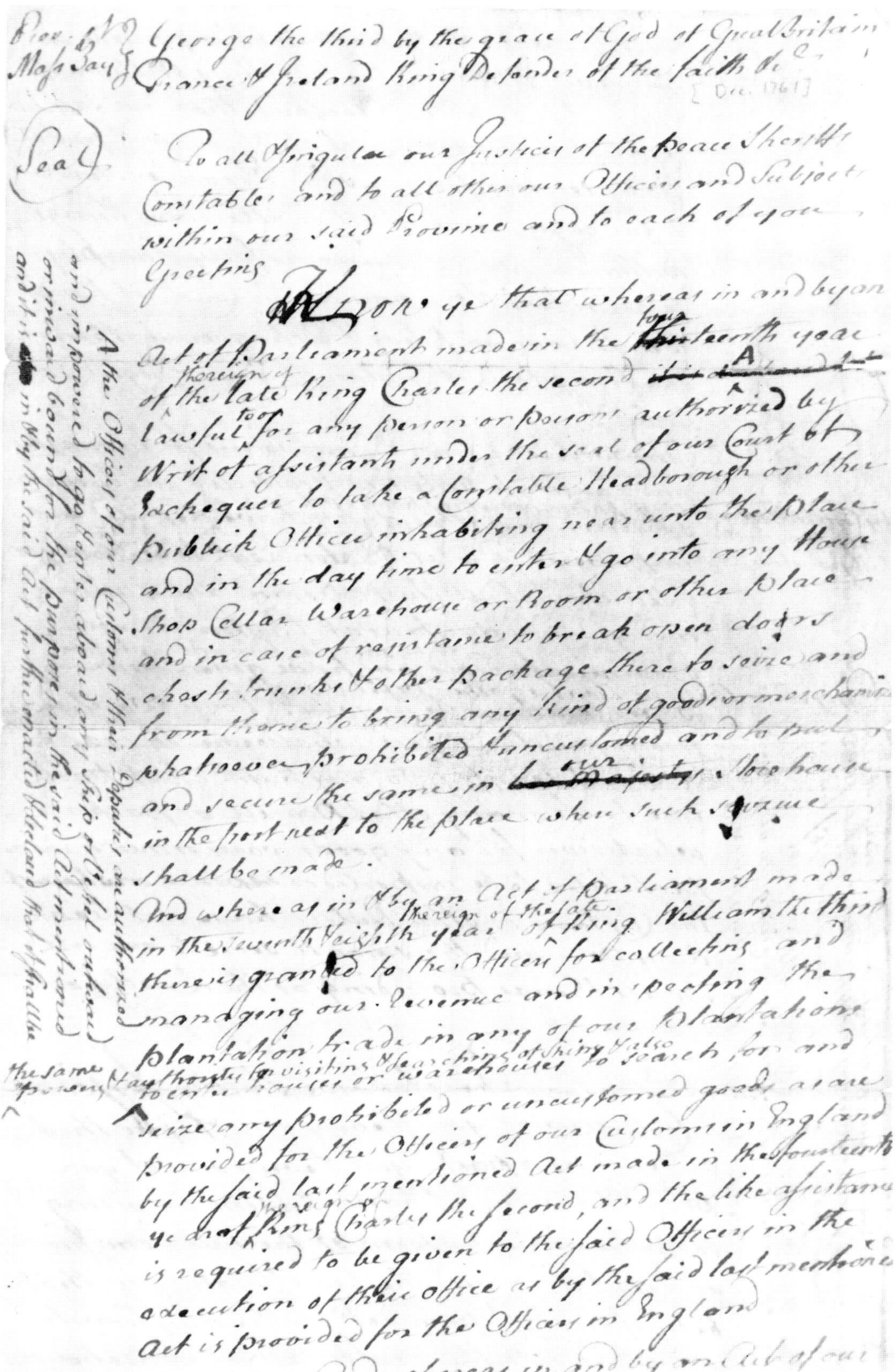

Prov. of Mass Bay — George the third by the grace of God of Great Britain France & Ireland King Defender of the faith &c. [Dec. 1761]

(Seal)

To all & singular our Justices of the Peace Sheriffs Constables and to all other our Officers and Subjects within our said Province and to each of you Greeting

Know ye that whereas in and by an Act of Parliament made in the ~~thirteenth~~ fourteenth year of the reign of the late King Charles the second ~~it is declared~~ A lawful too for any person or persons authorized by Writ of assistants under the seal of our Court of Exchequer to take a Constable Headborough or other publick Officer inhabiting near unto the place and in the day time to enter & go into any House Shop Cellar Warehouse or Room or other place and in case of resistance to break open doors chests trunks & other package there to seize and from thence to bring any kind of goods or merchandize whatsoever prohibited & uncustomed and to put and secure the same in ~~his Majesty's~~ our Storehouse in the port next to the place where such seizure shall be made.

And whereas in & by an Act of Parliament made in the seventh & eighth year of the reign of the late King William the third there is granted to the Officers for collecting and managing our Revenue and inspecting the plantation trade in any of our plantations the same powers & authority for visiting & searching of ships & also to enter houses or warehouses to search for and seize any prohibited or uncustomed goods as are provided for the Officers of our Customs in England by the said last mentioned Act made in the fourteenth year of the reign of King Charles the second, and the like assistance is required to be given to the said Officers in the execution of their office as by the said last mentioned Act is provided for the Officers in England

And whereas in and by an Act of our

A the Officers of our Customs & their Deputies are authorized and impowered to go & enter aboard any ship or vessel outward or inward bound for the purposes in the said Act mentioned and it is in & by the said Act further enacted & declared that all the [illegible]

Recto of a manuscript draft of a writ of assistance in the hand of Thomas Hutchinson, 1761.

said Province of Massachusets bay made in the reign of the eleventh year of the late King William the third it is enacted & declared that our Superior Court of Judicature Court of Assize and General Goal delivery for our said Province shall have cognizance of all matters and things within our said Province as fully & amply to all intents & purposes as our Courts of King's Bench Common Pleas & Exchequer within our kingdom of England have or ought to have.

And whereas our Commissioners for managing and causing to be levied & collected our customs *by Commission or Deputation under their hands & seal dated at London the 2nd day of May in the subsidies and other duties have deputed and first year of our Reign* impowered Charles Paxton Esqr. to be Surveyor & Searcher of all the rates and duties arising and growing due to us at Boston in our Province aforesaid *in & by said Comission or Deputation* and have given him *any ship Bottom Boat or other Vessel & alighting* power to enter into any Shop House Warehouse Hostery or other place whatsoever to make diligent search into any trunk chest pack case trust or any other parcell or package whatsoever for any goods, wares or merchandize prohibited to be imported or exported or whereof the Customs or other Duties have not been duly paid and the same to seize to our use, In all things proceeding as the Law directs

Therefore we strictly Enjoin & Command you & every one of you that, all excuses apart, you & every one of you permit the said Charles Paxton according to the true intent & form of the said comission or deputation and the laws & statutes in that behalf made. & provided in the day time to enter & go into the vaults cellars warehouses

Shops

such as Bernard were so eager for American offices and promotion. Perhaps he was motivated by political ambition, but it is more likely that Bernard expected that the benefits of his office—the grants of land, fees, and "gratuitys"—would more than adequately compensate for the high costs he had incurred.

Bernard obviously worried about money greatly. Soon after his arrival, in 1761, Samuel Allyne Otis wrote to his brother that Bernard ought to admit that "he is poor and wants to make what money he can of us." Yet, went on Otis rhetorically, should he "oppress the industrious merchant to fill his own pockets and gild his own Chariot with anothers gold: or aggrandize his famili with the neighbours property?" Bernard was also worried about social status. Not of a high social rank despite his connections, he was always sensitive about being treated deferentially and having his authority recognized.[3]

Concerned with money and law enforcement, and suffering from a sense of inferiority, Bernard found it difficult to maintain cool judgment and an impersonal position in the midst of political turmoil. His troubles began almost from the first day he arrived in Boston to take over the gubernatorial office. The city was still recovering from a devastating fire that had swept through the town on the morning of March 20, 1760, destroying 174 houses and 175 shops and leaving 220 families without homes. A month later, another fire gutted Faneuil Hall and its market stalls. The necessity to reduce taxes to help individuals and business concerns left the town without resources. Although private contributors throughout the colonies and legislatures as far south as Maryland and as far north as New Hampshire—even London merchants—sent contributions for the relief of the sufferers, bankruptcies and economic stringency still resulted. In the minds of the people, the fire became a catastrophe with political overtones. "Consequently," writes historian G. B. Warden,

every act after 1760 echoed the old issues and bitterness of former conflicts in Boston's history and, like the wind and waves which rocked every boat in the harbor, eventually affected all political groups in the town and spread . . . to sympathetic groups elsewhere in America.[4]

Bostonians were highly sensitive politically; they were "not easy to govern." Since the first revocation of their charter in 1686 by King James II, the independent Bostonians had been engaged in political warfare to maintain control over their provincial

legislature and town government. During this period, the people had found themselves heatedly discussing representation and taxation, and the proper relations that ought to exist between the two. They had learned to draw up instructions to their representatives which they expected to be obeyed. They knew how to get around decisions of a conservative legislature and how to handle a recalcitrant governor. In 1689 they had got rid of Governor Andros, "a tyrant, as any New England schoolboy will tell you." Governor Dudley, "a cunning politician," was brought low in the same way. Governor Shute had been "frightened" out of the province, while the "learned" Governor Burnet had been "tormented into a mortal fever." Bernard's predecessor, Thomas Pownall, recognizing the temper of the people, had not attempted to thwart them, but Governor Bernard, lulled by his success in New Jersey, was slower to make such discoveries.[5]

Bernard's arrival in the colony was not viewed with great enthusiasm by those townspeople who remained loyal to the old charter which had granted them control over their own political, religious, and social life. They watched carefully when Bernard was put to the test early in his administration by the necessity to appoint a new chief justice to replace Stephen Sewall who died soon after scheduling a hearing on writs of assistance for February 1761. Sewall, "a zealous Friend of Liberty" according to John Adams, had expressed "some doubts of the Legality and Constitutionality of the Writ, and of the Power of the Court to sign it."[6] Whether the new chief justice would agree with Sewall was a matter of crucial importance to the merchants whose hopes rode high on the unconstitutionality of writs. As anxious to please the British government as to participate in the fees collected from the confiscation of smuggled goods, Bernard determined to enforce the trade laws. A cooperative chief justice was necessary to fulfill his intent. Thomas Hutchinson was his man.

THOMAS HUTCHINSON (1711–1780); JAMES OTIS, JR. (1725–1783); OXENBRIDGE THACHER (1719–1765); JEREMIAH GRIDLEY (1701/2–1767)

Thomas Hutchinson was reluctant to accept the honor of being appointed chief justice on the Superior Court

G.3;   R.

By His EXCELLENCY

FRANCIS BERNARD, Esq;

Captain-General and Governor in Chief. in and over His Majesty's Province of
the MASSACHUSETTS-BAY in NEW-ENGLAND, and Vice-Admiral of the same.

A PROCLAMATION.

HEREAS the General Court, in Obedience to His Majesty's Commands, signified by
His Secretary of State, in order to provide for the Security of His Majesty's Dominions
in NORTH-AMERICA, and particularly of the Possession of His Majesty's Conquests there,
during the Absence of such Part of the Regular Forces as shall be employed in an
Enterprize against the Enemy, hath made Provision for raising Three Thousand Men,
to be formed into three Regiments, under the Command of Gentlemen of this Province
to be commissioned for that Purpose, and to be put under the supreme command of
General AMHERST his Majesty's Commander in Chief in *North-America* : I have
thought fit to issue this Proclamation, as well to invite his Majesty's good Subjects to inlist in such Service,
as to make publick the Terms of the Enlistment.

THE Men are to be inlisted to serve till the first Day of *July* 1762, but will probably be dismissed
much sooner either upon the Return of the regular Forces, or by the Intervention of a Peace ; in which last
Case they will be discharged as soon after as the Security of his Majesty's Dominions and Conquests in *North-
America* shall be effected ;   And they will not be employed or sent to the South-westward of the River
Delaware.

THEY are to receive the Bounty of *Nine Pounds* each, *three Pounds fourteen Shillings and eight Pence* of
which will be paid in a handsome Suit of Cloaths, *&c.* the remaining *five Pounds five Shillings and four
Pence* in Money : And that they may be assured that the Suit of Cloaths is of the full Value of what it is
charged at, a Suit will be put into the Hands of every Captain to be viewed as a Pattern.

THEY will have the same Pay, and be provided with Victuals, Tents, Camp-Equipage and all other
Accommodations in the same manner as last Year :   And as All the Officers are appointed before they
receive Beating-Orders, they may in general depend upon serving under the Officers with whom they inlist.

Given under my Hand at Boston, *the* Twenty-first *Day of* April, *in the Year of our Lord* 1761.
and in the First *Year of His Majesty's Reign.*

By His *Excellenty's Command,*
THO. GOLDTHWAIT, *Secr'y at War.*

Fra. Bernard.

GOD Save the KING.

BOSTON : Printed by *John Draper*, Printer to His Excellency the Governor and the Honorable
His Majesty's Council, 1761.

of Massachusetts Bay. Aware that his appointment would cause dissension and protest among certain elements in Boston, he warned the Governor that, in particular, the Otis family of Barnstable would not look with favor upon the appointment.

Hutchinson's was an old colonial family, established in the New World in 1634 when the first of the tribe—William, his wife Anne, and their fourteen children—crossed the Atlantic to settle in the religious utopia of Massachusetts Bay. Immediately, Anne had become involved in a religious controversy with the Puritan divines and was punished with exile from the tightly knit colony. A branch of the family, however, remained in Boston to become prosperous merchants and powerful politicians. At the death of his father in 1739, Thomas Hutchinson, II, came into possession of one of Boston's largest fortunes.

Thomas Hutchinson's rise was as prodigious as his family's. He was enrolled at Harvard when twelve years old; by the age of twenty-one, he had already engaged in a successful mercantile venture. At twenty-five, he allied himself through marriage to the powerful Olivers and Belchers. The following year, he was elected to the House of Representatives of the Massachusetts Assembly and became Speaker of the House.

Hutchinson, like other gentlemen of "good estates," opposed radical economic measures, such as the Land Bank of 1740 and the issuance of paper money or bills of credit, which too easily inflated beyond their initial value. In his *A Letter to a Member of the Honorable House of Representatives, on the Present State of the Bills of Credit,* Hutchinson defended currency reform and proposed that the hard cash sent over by the British government to reimburse Massachusetts for expenses incurred in the earlier Louisbourg campaign be used to retire outstanding bills of credit. Ousted from his seat in the House by Boston voters who lost heavily by such reforms, Hutchinson was appointed immediately to the Governor's Council where he was able to combine forces with other advocates of "hard money" to gain his point.

With a town house in Boston and a country house in Milton, Hutchinson lived a lordly life—gardening, riding, collecting books and art objects for his palatial homes. In 1752, he was appointed judge of the Probate Court and associate justice of the Suffolk Common Pleas Court. He retained his post, and influence, on the Council and frequently was called upon to serve in positions of distinction and power, such as represent-

Thomas Hutchinson as a young man, by Edward Truman, 1741.

ing Massachusetts at the Albany Council. Later, he was appointed lieutenant governor of the province, and by 1759 anticipated an appointment as governor. But Thomas Hutchinson's was not the kind of personality that aroused popular enthusiasm. His many offices, combined with his dignified and aristocratic demeanor, set him only further apart from the popular Boston factions. John Adams found his multiple office-holding "Foundation sufficient on which to erect a tyranny." "His thin, handsome face," wrote Edmund S. Morgan,

handsome in spite of its long nose, and his tall spare frame held precisely erect, combined to give an impression of remote dignity—a cool man this, who could swallow half the offices in the province and look as though they belonged to him by divine right.[7]

Although Hutchinson was a man of high moral principles, he never saw the possible conflict of interests inherent in his multiple office-holding, which included legislative, executive, and judicial powers. His short-sightedness in this respect was as much a result of his aristocratic heritage, which accepted all things coming to him as his rightful due, as it was of an obstinacy of mind that was as inflexible in its honesty as it was in its philosophical commitments. In the writs of assistance case, Hutchinson chose to defend the principle of parliamentary authority rather than his own colonial mercantile interests.

James Otis, Jr., deputy advocate-general of the Vice-Admiralty Court when the writs of assistance emerged as an issue, was considered "the most able, manly, and commanding character of his age at the bar." [8] But Jemmy Otis, as he was called, also had an eccentric streak. Occasionally, he would lash out at judges and contending lawyers with a savagery that the occasion did not warrant. Such erratic behavior could result in his attack on the members of the House of Lords as "venal . . . corrupt, and debauch'd in their Principles" who knew nothing but "Whoring, Smoaking, and Drinking," and the House of Commons as "a parcel of Button-makers, Pin-makers, Horse Jockeys, Gamesters, Pensioners, Pimps and Whore Masters." But he was no kinder to the selectmen of Boston, whom he charged with "timidity, haughtiness, arbitrary dispositions, and insolence of office." [9]

Vacillating between a radical posture and a highly conservative position, he could talk, on the one hand, about the foolishness of submitting to restrictions on trade laid upon merchants by the British Parliament, and on the other, about Parliament's "right to tax the colonies."

A strange, willful, unstable man, James Otis, Jr., linked his reputation to the American Revolution by delivering a speech in 1761 whose political creed would become the basis of revolutionary ideology. As a member of a mercantile family and longtime friend of the merchant community, Otis did not favor rigid enforcement of the laws of trade and seizure. He had come to believe that the issuance of writs of assistance was not only illegal but constituted a fraud against the Commonwealth. The forfeiture law of George II had called for a three-way division of the goods seized in illegal trading, one-third going to the province, one-third to the governor, and one-third to the customs official responsible for the information leading to the seizure. In Massachusetts, the court used the province's share to pay the costs of the informer, a procedure not warranted by law but one that assured greater profits to the governor and the informer.

On December 17, 1760, Otis presented a petition of his merchant friends to the General Court, noting the irregularity in the admiralty court's procedure and asking that the province, through its treasurer, sue the customs for its proper share of seizure profits. Furious at legislative interference in a matter he deemed to be the concern of the executive alone, Governor Bernard refused to sign the legislative act agreeing to the petition, claiming that only the attorney general could institute such suits. Bernard was wrong, but his real reason, as Hutchinson later admitted, was "to prevent Mr. Otis from carrying on the suit." Although Otis did not succeed, his brilliant handling of the matter presaged his opposition to the writs of assistance. By bringing the issue of enforcement into the General Court, he gave it political significance. In the future, the admiralty court was forced to follow the law and deduct the costs of gaining information equally from the governor's and customs' shares, thus reducing the profits to be derived from strict trade enforcement.

The writs of assistance case followed soon after. Here, however, Otis was not the cool and logical lawyer of his previous appearance. Family honor and position were at stake, for the newly appointed Judge Hutchinson who heard his arguments was, he believed, an enemy to the family and a usurper of a position that should rightfully have gone to his father, Colonel James Otis, Sr. Angry at Governor Bernard for depriving his father of a promised seat on the Superior Court of Massachusetts, James, Jr., had vowed to "set the Province afire."

Otis's speech in the Council Chamber of the Boston Town House in February 1761, was one of his most eloquent. "All the barristers at law of Boston and of the neighbouring county of Middlesex," according to John Adams, crowded into the chamber. Following the learned Jeremiah Gridley, who argued for the customs house officers, and the erudite Oxenbridge Thacher, who quietly rebutted Gridley in terms of precedents, Otis began his address quietly. Then, for between four and five hours, he transfixed his audience with his oratory. [10]

Speaking in behalf of the "inhabitants of Boston," Otis disclaimed any interest in the case beyond the principle of "British Liberty." The writ that was sought was "the worst instrument of arbitrary power, the most destructive to English liberty, and the fundamental principles of the constitution." To allow arbitrary searching of a man's home, which rightly and constitutionally ought to be considered his private domain, was contrary to "the fundamental principles of law." To Otis, contemporary American practice, which avoided the use of general writs, took precedence over earlier parliamentary statutes allowing those writs which were issued when kings, such as the "tyrant" Charles Stuart, were "in the zenith of arbitrary power." [11]

Every man, argued Otis, has a "right to his life, his liberty . . . his property." These rights were "written on [man's] heart, and revealed to him by his maker." They were "inherent, inalienable, and indefeasible by any laws, pacts, contracts, covenants, or stipulations, which man could devise, and were wrought into the English Constitution as fundamental laws." The Navigation Acts passed in the reign of a rigorous king— Charles II—and the writs of assistance which were designed to aid in the execution of such "rigorous statutes" were "instruments of slavery on the one hand or villainy on the other." To his "dying day," Otis declared, he would oppose them, as "opposition to a kind of power . . . which in former periods of English history cost one King of England his head and another his throne." "An act against the Constitution," declared Otis, "is void," and it was "the business of this court to demolish this monster of oppression, & tear into shreds this remnant of Starchamber Tyranny." [12]

"Otis was a flame of fire," reported John Adams; "with . . . a rapid torrent of impetuous eloquence, he hurried away all before him. . . . Every man of an immense crouded [sic] audience appeared to me to go away, as I did, ready to take arms against Writs of Assistance." [13]

The judges were not so easily persuaded. At the behest of Chief Justice Hutchinson, they delayed their decision until it could be ascertained whether or not such writs were still being employed in England—an important consideration, since only acts operative in the mother country could be extended to the colonies. Months later, word came that this type of writ was legally in use in England, and the Superior Court had no choice but to grant customs officials the right to use such documents.

Otis lost his case, but his spirited defense was not without effect. British officials found the writs difficult to enforce in a balky community, and in March 1762, the General Court of Massachusetts passed a bill making it necessary to indicate "the Names of the Person Informing & ye Place informed against" on all applications for writs of assistance. Governor Bernard vetoed the bill angrily, but, faced with the solid opposition of the mercantile community, neither he nor the customs officers dared invoke the writs. Moreover, British officials, investigating complaints against Bernard's trade enforcement policies, reprimanded the Governor for the exorbitant fees imposed in seizure cases. By the spring of 1762, undoubtedly in response to Otis's protest, there was a marked relaxation of enforcement procedures.

Thomas Hutchinson gained nothing from his decision favoring parliamentary legislation over the custom of the community, or what came to be called "natural" law. His loyalty to Parliament placed him politically just where Otis had tried to put him—in opposition to the town's mercantile interests and alienated from the society he hoped to dominate. Hutchinson paid dearly for his allegiance. His home was vandalized and gutted by an angry Stamp Act mob, and in 1774 he left Massachusetts, an exile from his native land.

Otis, on the other hand, rose to power and prominence. Seeking at the beginning of his political involvement the rewards of position and wealth through appointment to public office, he became, as a result of his radical rhetoric, a leader against the patronage system that underlay eighteenth-century political and social life. The more he sought support for his position, the more "wild and explosive" and unpredictable became his conduct, so that his conservative family, who had benefited from his rise to power by finally receiving political appointments from the frightened Governor Bernard, now began to fear his "wild democracy."

His last years were tragic. The wildness noted in his early behavior turned to violence. In September 1769, he became involved in a tavern brawl with the "gentle and reasonable" customs officer John Robinson. Believing that Robinson had called him a traitor, he accosted the officer, called him a "superlative blockhead," and declared that he had "a natural right . . . to break his head." The customs officer, fearing an attack, struck him with his cane. For about a minute the two men engaged in battle and then were separated. Eventually they reconciled their differences and John Adams remarked that Otis seemed much better mentally than he had been for a long time.

But Sam Adams and his radical friends exaggerated the incident and turned Otis into a martyr—"the God-like Otis." Later biographers blamed the clubbing for his madness. Otis's incidents of eccentricity had occurred, however, long before the "braining." Unfortunately, he got worse, and occasionally had to be sent to the country for recuperation. In later years, he was tormented by the belief that he had "ruined his country," especially after Independence. "Zounds!

THE

SENTIMENTS

OF A

Britiſh American.

O. Thacher Esquire

Aſellum in prato timidus paſcebat ſenex.
Is, hoſtium clamore ſubito territus,
Suadebat aſino fugere, ne poſſent capi.
At ille lentus : quæſo num binas mihi
Clitellas impoſiturum victorem putas ?
Senex negavit. Ergo quid refert mea
Cui ſerviam ? clitellas dum portem meas.

PHÆDRUS.

B O S T O N:

Printed and Sold by EDES & GILL, next to the
Priſon in Queen-Street. 1764.

[Price Six Pence.]

Title page of Oxenbridge Thacher's pamphlet,
The Sentiments of a British American, *1764.*

What have we here?" he is reported to have exclaimed at a newly elected legislature. "The world butt end foremost." At other times, he had great hopes for the new country, especially if it continued to "set new precedents based on reason and common sense, as befitted . . . an emancipated nation." [14]

Oxenbridge Thacher was more consistent in his concern for maintaining the liberties of the people, and suffered no afterthoughts about his participation in "Fair Freedom's Cause." He had always been sensitive to injustice: his emotions were, John Adams noted in his diary, "easily touched, his shame, his compassion, his fear, his anger, etc." Thacher brought to the practice of the law and the study of constitutional theory all the zeal of his Calvinist upbringing that had almost taken him into the ministry and the warmth of a "queer and affected . . . not easy" personality. [15]

The grandson of a Boston minister, Thacher was educated at Harvard for the clergy, but abandoned it for the law only because of the frail state of his health. But he always remained committed to theology. According to John Adams, he was willing to spend entire evenings discussing "original sin, origin of evil, the plan of the universe. . . ." [16]

Despite his frailty, Thacher held various elected offices and labored for years on committees established by the Boston town meeting. Two issues in particular drove him to take a strong position: multiple office-holding, especially as it was demonstrated in Thomas Hutchinson's public life, and the currency question. Thacher saw Hutchinson as a "summa Potestatis," a man so gluttonous for high office that he was willing to enter into "a deep and treasonable conspiracy to betray the liberties of [his] country, for [his] own private, personal and family aggrandizements." In his pamphlet, *Consideration on the Election of Councellors . . .* (1761), he concluded that the combination of legislative, executive, and legal powers in one person constituted a threat to liberty. As for the currency question, Thacher associated hard money with the attempt of the

King, ministry, Parliament, and the nation of Great Britain . . . to re-model the colonies from the foundation, to annul all their charters, to constitute them all royal governments, to raise a revenue in America by Parliamentary taxation, to apply that revenue to pay the salaries of governors, judges, and all other crown officers . . . and further, to establish bishops and the whole system of the Church of England, tithes and all, throughout all British America. [17]

Such a system, Thacher reportedly claimed, "would extinguish the flame of liberty all over the world."

Presenting his argument in the writs case "with . . . the ingenuity and cool reasoning, which were remarkable in his amiable character," Thacher held that the Superior Court of Massachusetts did not possess the same power held by the Exchequer Court of England, which traditionally issued such writs. In England, he asserted, the writs were limited because they were returnable—that is, they had to be proved necessary. In Massachusetts this was not the case.[18]

Thacher and Otis lost their case, but the storm they raised was sufficiently threatening to cause Governor Bernard to compromise the differences between the colonial factions in order to establish a coalition government. Bernard's peacemaking filled Thacher with even more anxiety. Writing to a friend in 1762, he expressed his foreboding:

We seem to be in that deep sleep or stupor that Cicero describes his country to be in a year or two before the civil wars broke out . . . whether this profound quiet be the forerunner of a storm I leave to your judgment.[19]

The storm did indeed come, but several years later. Thacher did not live to see it. In the midst of the Stamp Act controversy, he died from complications following a smallpox inoculation.

Jeremiah (or Jeremy, as he frequently signed himself) Gridley, a Boston-born lawyer, was not as stirred as Thacher was by the implications of the writs of assistance. Not involved with mercantile interests, he could remain unruffled by a storm that did not immediately affect him.

In 1761, it was Gridley's job to present the petitions for writs of assistance to Judge Hutchinson and defend their legality. He did so on the assumption that in certain cases, individual rights had to be sacrificed for the good of the state. The state, he argued, could not protect itself from the "invasion of her foes, nor the tumults of her own subjects" if it did not possess revenues. General search warrants, authorized by Parliament in the time of Charles II and extended to the colonies during the reign of William III, were essential to the collection of such revenues, and the "*Necessity* of having public Taxes effectually and speedily collected" was of "infinitely greater moment to the whole than the liberty of any individual." There was no higher law, Gridley insisted, than the survival of the state.[20]

Gridley's argument was answered by Otis's more revolutionary contention that a higher law than the state did exist—the unalterable law of nature. It was not to be expected that the Court would accept such a radical position, however, and Gridley's argument carried the day.

Gridley's conservative position in the matter of the writs was paralleled by his support of a "sound" currency. His was the conservatism of a self-made man, for Gridley had been born poor, the son of a currier who died when his son was only thirteen. Early in life, he was made to realize that any social or professional prominence he achieved would have to be earned, not inherited. Two Harvard degrees and a successful law practice did not completely convince him, for he continued to seek social acceptance and opportunities for leadership in numerous social and professional clubs and to frequent taverns and coffeehouses with associates such as James Otis. For all his congeniality, however, and his many acts of kindness, he impressed many as aloof. Charles Chauncy, the Boston minister, described "his air, and whole manner of behavior" as being "so haughty and forbidding and insolent, that but few cared to have to do with him." [21]

Although Gridley seemed to favor British interests over American in the writs of assistance case, earlier in 1757 he had advised Lord Loudon not to irritate the colonists by extending Britain's Quartering Act to America; instead, he suggested that Loudon house his troops at the Castle in Boston Harbor.

Gridley's seeming inconsistencies were shared by many other Americans of his class and station. Nobody in Massachusetts or in any of the other colonies wanted independence from Great Britain in the 1760s. They were concerned only with the question of how far British power could extend in the colonies. Gridley, an owner of lands in New Hampshire and an investor in an iron foundry in Marlboro, naturally defended the British sound money policy as protection for property interests; and he favored the use of writs of assistance since there was no doubt as to their legality. If he saw the value to the State of the writs, however, he also saw the need of functioning courts. So, in 1765, at the time of the Stamp Act crisis, he joined James Otis and John Adams to petition Governor Bernard to open the courts and allow them to operate without stamped paper—not because he agreed with them about the illegality of such taxes, but because of the expediency of having functioning courts. Like so many of his contemporaries, Gridley was not committed to ideology. As pragmatists, they responded to each situation individually. But as British policy began to present more difficult choices, these men found themselves increasingly in opposition to Great Britain's power. Before many of them realized it, they were engaged in revolution.

The furor aroused by the writs of assistance quieted soon after 1761, but the political factions polarized by the issue continued to develop in Massachusetts. In

Virginia, also, events occurred that placed Virginians in opposition to the mother country. The most revealing was the Parsons' Cause or the Two-Penny Act of 1758.

Pennies and Parsons

In 1755, the Reverend James Maury of Virginia wrote with melancholy resignation of the "national or private calamities" that were affecting the British plantations in North America. "Our frontiers are daily ravaged by savages," he reported,

and worse than savages, papists, who in conjunction with them, captivate and butcher our out-settlers, and have drove great numbers of them into the thicker inhabited parts, who, as they have left their farms and stocks, must be supported by us, who shall be scarcely able to support our own families.[22]

What compounded the settlers' difficulties was a crop failure; the settlers' "wheat, barley, oats and rye have been ruined by an early drought," complained Maury. "Our Indian corn, the main support of man and beast in this part of the world, has been so much hurt by a later drought, that I fear scarce enough will be made for the sustenance of our people. . . ." In such a state of affairs, both taxes and debts multiplied—taxes for the support of regiments to pursue the war, debts that resulted from the failure of the tobacco crop.[23]

Virginia's financial health was inextricably linked to tobacco. Since the colony was almost always short of money, Virginians frequently used tobacco instead of cash to pay debts and taxes, to purchase manufactured goods, or to pay salaries. But in 1755, with tobacco plants drying in parched fields, growers found themselves in a predicament. A short crop meant that whatever tobacco they saved and brought to market would bring a higher price than usual. If they paid their debts and taxes in tobacco at the rate set by law, they would lose the benefits of the price rise, while the creditors would gain. To meet this contingency, the Virginia Assembly in 1755 passed the Two-Penny Act, allowing two-pence per pound of tobacco for the payment of debts and taxes. Since the situation was an emergency, the Assembly did not allow for suspension of the Act until it received the approval of the Board of Trade and the King's Council. To wait would be to lose the Act's immediate benefits. Since it was a temporary measure, the Governor signed it despite the fact that it did not carry the necessary suspension clause.

The substitution of pence for tobacco hit Virginia's Anglican clergymen hard. Since they received their salary—approximately 16,000 pounds of tobacco yearly—from taxes levied by the Assembly, the use of tobacco as currency meant that the clergy's income rose and fell with the fluctuations of the one-crop economy. In 1755, they stood to gain, until the Two-Penny Act wiped out their profits. While most ministers were willing "to share in the misfortunes of the community," a few malcontents, such as the Reverend John Camm, believed that the Two-Penny Act unfairly singled out the clergy to bear the brunt of the economic calamity. In 1758, the clergy confronted a second Two-Penny Act.

During the intervening three years, the Anglican clergy had been facing increasing dissent from Quakers, Baptists, Presbyterians, and Methodists, who had settled in the colony's western regions. These sects revived religious enthusiasm among the settlers, alleviating lives that were otherwise harsh and barren. Soon the settlers began to question the formalized Anglican doctrines and services that seemed so cold compared to the warmth of religious revivalism. They frowned on the relaxed life enjoyed by the Anglican clergy, questioned their morals, and challenged the idea of an Established Church and its right to governmental support.

In turn, the Anglican clergy felt humiliated by the lack of respect shown them by the community. They were leading "the Life of Post-Boys," they complained, forced to ride long distances between widely separated parishes without being accorded those "rights and Privileges" all civilized societies bestow on their spiritual leaders. Within their churches, vestries were asserting their right to hire and fire them at will. The absence of a resident bishop in Virginia had given vestries undue power over their ministers, which some clergymen bitterly resented. The ministers also saw anticlericalism manifested in the growing secularization of education. The Two-Penny Act, they believed, was the final step in a maliciously conceived program aimed at reducing their status and authority in the colony.

With Church and State so intimately related in Virginia, the stakes of power within the parish churches were high. Churches not only looked after

Tobacco merchants on an American wharf. Vignette of a map published in London in 1751.

the community's morals and provided for the poor, the orphaned, and other wards of society, but also laid parish taxes and saw to the division of parish lands. When controversy arose between the governor and local vestries on the question of church patronage, or the right to appoint clergymen to vacancies, the controversy usually opened up the larger question of the right of localities to govern themselves and to control their own appointments. In the Parsons' Cause, the struggle for power encompassed questions of the royal veto, control of colonial institutions from London, the necessity or dangers of a colonial episcopate, the relation of Church to State, and the general problems faced by planters who had been suffering for decades from the intervention of London merchants in their affairs.

JOHN CAMM (1718–1788); RICHARD BLAND (1710–1776)

Of all the ministers troubled by the changing status of the Anglican clergy, none was more articulate than the Reverend John Camm. Described by Governor Francis Fauquier as "a man of abilities but a turbulent man who delights to live in a flame," Camm came to Virginia in 1741–42, soon after receiving his bachelor degree at Trinity College, Cambridge.[24] Intent upon maintaining the prestige and honor of the Crown and the Church, he was appalled at the independence enjoyed by vestries in the selection and dismissal of their ministers. Throughout his life in Virginia, Camm sent many longing glances back to England, always hoping, as he wrote, "for a Living of one hundred nett" that would enable him to return. At one point, he was willing to pay "a bribe" to some Virginia friends vacationing in Bath for their assistance: "the larger the Living or the Post . . . the better for both," he reminded them.[25]

From the time Camm set foot on Virginia soil, he engaged in controversy, especially as it involved the rights of the clergy. He was even accused of indulging in "notorious falsehoods to inveigh as many [clergymen] as possible" into cabals. Indoctrinated in Tory principles, Camm was unsympathetic with the rising republicanism within the colony that was moving Virginia toward disestablishment—separation of Church and State—and control by vestries over their ministers. Although he sometimes utilized a liberal rhetoric, religious liberty in his definition was a right to be enjoyed by a special group, not by dissenters who sought to cut the cords that bound Church to State.

Camm played a crucial role in the crisis prompted by the Two-Penny Act. Believing that it constituted a "breaking in upon our Establishment," with his usual impetuosity, he immediately attempted to organize the clergy in opposition. Successful only in arousing a small number of ministers, Camm's efforts failed. Governor Fauquier refused to veto the Act, and Camm, not realizing the resentment that would be aroused by his going over the Governor's and Assembly's heads, attempted to obtain the intercession of the King. As a result, he was removed from his post on the faculty of William and Mary College on trumped-up, but effective charges. It was only after a lengthy appeal to the Privy Council that he was reinstated.

Camm had not learned his lesson, however. In 1758, when the Assembly passed the second Two-Penny Act, he became even more determined to protest what he believed was an act of contempt for Anglican ministers. Under his guidance, some members of the clergy met in Williamsburg to draw up a list of grievances for Camm to lay before the King and a petition asking the King to declare the Two-Penny Act "null and void" from the beginning.

Armed with the clergy's "Representation of the Clergy of the Church of England," Camm undertook the long journey to England. Through the aid of the Bishop of London, he succeeded in having the Acts of

The 1697 Wren Building of the College of William and Mary.

1755 and 1758 disallowed by the King, but, overconfident, he lingered in London for ten months before returning to the New World. In the meantime, news of his victory trickled back to the colonies. When he finally returned, triumphantly bearing the official documents detailing the King's veto, he found himself in the center of a heated debate. The people now openly questioned if "any other will than that of the Assembly should prevail" in what was, they believed, purely a local matter.

Camm and other clergymen sued for their back pay, arguing that the 1758 act was invalid from the beginning because of the absence of a suspension clause. Their contention was never directly answered. Camm's trial, which dragged on until April 1764, ended unsuccessfully. When his appeals also failed, he resorted to pamphlets to argue his cause. He was answered by Richard Bland, one of the colony's ablest pamphleteers and legalists.

Richard Bland was raised and educated by his uncles William and Richard Randolph, members of one of Virginia's leading families. John Adams described him as "a learned, bookish man." Although a member of the upper class of a highly stratified society, he held liberal social views, especially on the question of the rights and privileges of the colony. Public office was his as a matter of birth, as well as a "reward of ability," and he used it to protect "Liberty and Property." Attempts to "break these down," he wrote, "must be opposed in every legal way." Although Bland was thinking of freedom in relation to himself and other members of the planter aristocracy, nevertheless in his constant questioning of the authority of governor, council, Parliament, and Crown, he used arguments and rhetoric that would eventually serve more democratic purposes.

As a "committee of one," Bland was largely responsible for writing the Two-Penny Act of 1758 and forwarding its passage. When members of the clergy attacked the Act in public print, he became its chief defender. An Anglican, Bland's opposition to the clergy's demands was politically, not religiously, motivated. "I profess myself a sincere Son of the Established Church," he wrote to John Adams, "but I can embrace her Doctrines without approving of her Hierarchy, which I know to be a Relick of the Papal Incroachments upon the Common Law." [26] In his *Letter to the Clergy of Virginia* (1760) he denounced the Bishop of London for his accusations that Virginia

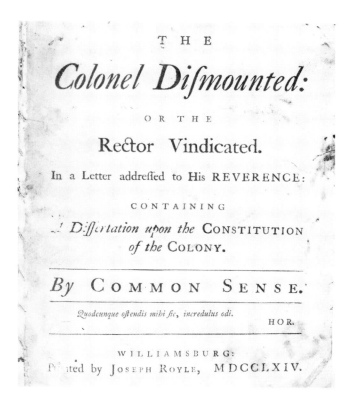

Title page of Richard Bland's pamphlet, The Colonel Dismounted: or the Rector Vindicated, *1764.*

was led by "a set of artful designing men" intent upon undermining the Church and lessening the prerogative of the Crown. Bland found it "opprobrious and outrageous" for the Bishop to infer that the colony was "swarming with dissenters"; if clergymen were treated disrespectfully, it was usually because they were "a disgrace to the ministry." Bland opposed the establishment of an American bishopric and defended the constitutionality of the Two-Penny Act on the basis of "the most pressing necessity" and the public welfare.

A blizzard of pamphlets followed. Camm's *A Single and Distinct View of the Act . . .* (1763) was so vituperative that no printer in Virginia would undertake its publication and it finally had to be published in Maryland. A second pamphlet was published in April 1764. That August, Bland responded to Camm's two pamphlets in his *The Colonel Dismounted; or the Rector Vindicated,* which so summed up the constitutional issue at the heart of the Anglo-American struggle that it has remained one of the most significant documents of the revolutionary era.

After twenty pages of poking fun at the Reverend Camm—a "wonderful genius! who with infinite wit and humor can transform . . . the most arrant *trash* into delicious fruit"—Bland turned his more serious efforts to an explanation of the constitutional relationship between Great Britain and the colonies. Asserting that all Englishmen—including British Americans—are "born free" and as such "are only subject to laws made with their own consent," Bland attempted to distinguish between areas of colonial and imperial authority. Matters of *internal* importance, involving domestic affairs, were, he claimed, the exclusive concern of the Virginia legislature; matters of *external* government came under the authority of the British Parliament.[27]

As a moderate, Bland was forced to admit certain areas of British control. If consent of the governed was the single issue, then the only connection with England was through the Crown, a tenuous connection which very few Americans in the 1760s were willing to admit. Like many other colonists at the time, Bland could not face the logical consequences of his reasoning. "[Bland] would set out on sound principles," wrote Jefferson,

pursue them logically, till he found them leading to the precipice which he had to leap, start back alarmed, then resume his ground, go over it in another direction, be led again by the correctness of his reasoning to the same place, and again back about . . . [until he] finally left his reader and himself bewildered between the steady index of the compass in their hand, and the phantasm to which it seemed to point.[28]

The necessity to justify legislative action in the Parsons' Cause, however, led Bland on a course which, though marked by retreats, resulted in pamphlets arguing against the Stamp Act, in resolutions against the Townshend Acts, and in the calling of five Virginia conventions (1774–1776) and two Continental Congresses (1774 and 1775). Expounding ideas that were in every thinking colonist's mind, he was among the first Americans to state clearly that "Any Tax respecting our INTERNAL Policy . . . imposed on us by Act of Parliament, is arbitrary, as depriving us of our Rights, and may be opposed."[29] His bold statements were lost amid the ringing phrases of more dramatic revolutionary heroes (just as his portrait was later lost, first when it was slashed by British soldiers in 1781, and then, when it was carried away, possibly by one of Ben Butler's boys in 1864). Yet Bland's arguments laid the foundation for the Declaration of Independence.

JAMES MAURY (1718 o.s.–1769); PETER LYONS (1734–1809); PATRICK HENRY (1736–1799)

That James Maury, described as "the fountainhead of Whiggish principles," should have opposed the Virginia Assembly and been denounced as an enemy of the community was ironic, for Maury was a liberal minister of the Anglican persuasion who preached toleration of "any one honest and well disposed person of whatever persuasion."[30]

Born in Dublin, Maury had been brought to Virginia as a baby by Huguenot parents seeking religious ease in the New World. Growing up in a devout and cultivated family, he seemed destined for the ministry. After graduating from William and Mary College, he traveled to England for ordination and within eight years had become rector of Fredericksville Parish in Albemarle County, "the most extensive and inconvenient parish in the colony," as he humorously remarked. Having married at a young age, Maury soon found himself supporting a large and growing family. Its demands made it necessary for him to supplement his income by teaching. Possessing one of the largest libraries in the colony, especially proficient in the classics and physical sciences, Maury played an influential part in the intellectual life of Virginia as tutor to the children of some of the colony's leading families. Thomas Jefferson's scientific interests were certainly encouraged during the two years that Jefferson studied in the clergyman's log schoolhouse.

In 1756, although he stood to lose "a considerable sum," Maury did not protest the first of the Two-Penny Acts. "Each individual," he wrote, "must expect to share in the misfortunes of the community to which he belongs."[31] In 1758, however, when the second Two-Penny Act was passed, Maury, alarmed by the increase in religious dissent, had changed his mind, and decided to initiate a suit against the collectors of the parish levies to obtain his salary in tobacco. In November 1763, the court declared that, with the Crown's veto, the Two-Penny Act was void, and that at the next court a jury should determine damages. The lawyer for the parish, believing that little else remained to be argued, retired from the case. In his place, Patrick Henry, a young and not well-known lawyer, was engaged.

On December 1, 1763, a great crowd filled the

small courthouse in Hanover County where the case was to be heard. Judge John Henry, father of the defending lawyer, presided. When several planters refused to serve on the jury, the sheriff filled their places with small-farm owners, several of whom were dissenters. As Maury later reported, the sheriff made only feeble attempts "to summon gentlemen." Instead, he went "among the vulgar herd. . . ."

Peter Lyons, King's attorney for Hanover County, presented Maury's case in simple legal terms. Since the Two-Penny Act had been declared null and void by the King in Council, it did not carry the force of law, Lyons argued, and Maury deserved to be paid in tobacco as set forth in the law of 1748. But Lyons did not realize the strength of popular feeling in a cause that carried revolutionary portent, and he lacked the imagination that would have enabled him to perceive the underlying conflict in what seemed an open-and-shut case.

Patrick Henry, however, did. Young and relatively untried as a lawyer, despite the fact that he had managed 1,185 cases during his three-year career, he was facing his first major trial. He had come to the law after an unsuccessful academic life, two unsuccessful attempts at storekeeping, and a disastrous two years as a farmer. In 1760, after "reading" law for not quite eight months, he received his license to practice. With the law, Henry came into his own. In addition to a thorough familiarity with the classics and religious sermons, he had mastered the rhetoric of the law under the tutelage of his father, who was a justice of the peace, and ministerial rhythms of speech from his uncle, the Reverend Patrick Henry.

Yet he was still a fledgling in the courtroom when he rose before his father, a jury, a bench filled with twenty clergymen, and an overflowing courthouse to argue the case of the vestry against the demands of the Reverend James Maury. With his thin angular body loosely clothed in homespun and slightly stooped, his long nose, beetleng eyebrows small and deeply set blue eyes, he made an unprepossessing appearance, which was not at all helped by a faltering beginning.

Contending that a contract existed between the King and the people, Henry accused the King of breaking his part of the contract—his promise to protect the people—when he vetoed an act that was essentially for the people's benefit. "By disallowing acts of this salutary nature, from being the father of his people, [the King]," Henry is said to have declaimed, "degenerated into a Tyrant, and forfeits all right to his subjects' obedience." Undeterred by cries of "Treason!" Henry boldly turned to the ministers in the audience and denounced them for trying to improve their condition at the expense of the people. "The only use of an Established Church and Clergy," he declared, "is to enforce obedience to civil sanctions." When a minister failed to perform this duty, then he could justly be dismissed. "The Clergy of Virginia, in . . . refusing to acquiesce in the law in question," had, he insisted, ceased being "useful members of the state" and "ought to be considered as enemies of the community."

Do they manifest their zeal in the cause of religion and humanity by practicing the mild and benevolent precepts of the Gospel of Jesus? Oh, no! Gentlemen. Instead . . . these rapacious harpies would . . . snatch from the hearth of their honest parishioner his last hoe-cake, from the widow and her orphaned child their last milch-cow.[32]

Heedless that the ministers in the courtroom had left in indignation, Henry went on to warn the jury against riveting "the chains of bondage on their own necks." An example ought to be made of the Reverend

Peter Lyons by Thomas Sully, 1806.

47

Maury, he suggested, as a warning to clergymen that they must accept laws passed by the Assembly and approved by "a kind and benevolent and patriot Governor."

Henry's "harangue" made some of his listeners wince, but most responded enthusiastically. The community was troubled by deep hatreds directed primarily against the Established Church. When Henry portrayed the royally supported clergy as threats to self-government, he turned the people's resentment also against the power of the Crown that had frustrated their desires through the exercise of the royal veto. The jury, returning with a verdict of one-penny damages for the Reverend Maury, demonstrated this bitterness.

Gadsden and the Governor

In South Carolina, conservative planters and merchants turned into fiery revolutionists as a result of the overzealous interference of the British-appointed governor Thomas Boone in matters which traditionally were assumed to be the responsibility of the Commons House. Young Carolinian politicians stubbornly opposed the Governor while clarifying their own ideas about the basis and purpose of representation in a colonial assembly. Their conclusion—that liberty in South Carolina rested upon the existence of "a *free* assembly, *freely* representing a *free* people"—provided them with a defined ideology for the approaching revolutionary movement.

The question was clear-cut: could a royally appointed governor challenge the right of the Commons House of South Carolina to determine the validity of the election of its own members? Lower houses of colonial legislatures had exercised that right freely since their inceptions. In South Carolina, the power had been assumed as early as 1692, when the Commons House appointed a special committee to review disputed elections. In 1725, when Governor Nicholson had refused to administer an oath to an elected representative who was being indicted for a felony, the Commons protested immediately. "We are," it declared, "the Sole judges of our own privileges & of the Qualifications of our own Members." [33] After such a strong assertion, the Governor retreated, and no further executive intrusion upon the Commons' power occurred until 1762.

THOMAS BOONE (1730–1812); CHRISTOPHER GADSDEN (1724–1805)

That year, Governor Thomas Boone, only a month in residence, attempted to challenge the election practices of the colony in order to limit what he believed were the too extensive powers of the Commons House. Boone was undoubtedly confident of his capacity to handle the situation because of his successful stint as governor of New Jersey. Moreover, as a descendant of an old Carolina family, nephew of one of the colony's leading political figures, and husband of a Charlestonian, he had been happily received by the citizens of Charleston. "Expressions of joy" had greeted him and toasts drunk to a cordial and harmonious future. There was no gentleman in South Carolina, members of the Council and the Commons had declared, whom they would have preferred as governor to Thomas Boone.

Boone's honeymoon with the people of Charleston did not last long. As early as January 1762, he was writing to a friend that the lower house of the South Carolina Assembly, the Commons House, had assumed powers beyond its authority and that he expected to become involved in disputes with its members. Boone soon made good his word. First, he attempted to reduce the authority of the Commons House by controlling the times when it would meet and adjourn, contrary to custom which permitted the House to decide these dates itself. He also refused to allow a committee of the House to assist in the distribution of presents to the Indians as was the custom. To both these challenges, the Commons House acquiesced silently. But when Boone proposed a new election law to replace the law in effect since 1721, members of the Commons resisted. Politely indicating that they saw no reason to change a law that had operated comfortably all these years, they refused to accept his recommendation. Offended, Boone decided to demonstrate the flaws in the act as soon as possible.

His opportunity came in September 1762, when Christopher Gadsden, a successful merchant-planter of Charleston, appeared to take his seat for the parish of St. Paul. Gadsden was a native Carolinian, who had received a classical education in England before training for the mercantile life in a Philadelphia counting house. Returning to Charleston, he relentlessly pursued wealth, lending money at interest, handling

48

plantation affairs, speculating in land, importing and exporting goods and selling them at both wholesale and retail.

As a result of a special election called by the Governor to fill a vacancy for his parish, Gadsden was elected to the Commons House. Unfortunately, the church wardens of the parish, whose job it was, under the Act of 1721, to execute election writs, had neglected to take the required oath before a justice of the peace for the faithful execution of the writs. The Commons realized this omission, but since no other irregularity in the election had taken place and since Gadsden had received nearly eighty percent of the votes in a three-way contest, it determined to declare Gadsden the people's choice. Acting on the assumption that the spirit of the law was more important than its actual letter, the Commons administered the oath to Gadsden, and two members were appointed to accompany him to the executive chamber to witness his taking of the state oath before the Governor.

The Governor had no intention, however, of adding to "an undeniable . . . infraction of the election act." He refused to administer the oath to Gadsden, immediately dissolved the Commons, and issued writs for the election of a new house. When thirty-seven of the forty-eight members of the previous house were returned—including Gadsden—Boone prorogued the session for a month in order to emphasize his point.

When finally permitted to meet, instead of taking up the business recommended by the Governor, the Commons appointed a committee to investigate the Gadsden election case to determine whether the Election Act had been violated; the committee was also charged to define "the Liberties and Privileges of this House, with regard to the right of determining their own Elections" and the "governor's speech at Dissolving the last General Assembly." [34]

The committee's report asserted that "it is the undeniable fundamental and inherent Right & Privilege of the Commons House of Assembly . . . solely to examine and finally determine the Election of their own Members." The church wardens were not required to take special oaths for each election, it argued, since they took a sworn oath upon entering office. Basing their claims for representation on their rights as British subjects as confirmed by charter, it declared that the right to determine validity of elections belonged solely and absolutely to the representatives of the people. Boone's refusal to administer the oath to Gadsden was "a breach of . . . Privileges" and "the abrupt and Sudden dissolution of the last Assembly . . . was a most precipatate [sic], unadvised, unprecedented Procedure." By this violation of freedom of elections, the Governor was reducing them to slavery.[35]

Boone refused to acknowledge the Commons' contentions and insisted that he had acted wisely in "having checked Constitutionally so dangerous an Usurpation" of power by the Commons. If the Commons believed it was oppressed, he recommended that it take the matter "to the Royal Ear."

As Boone continued to deny satisfaction to the Commons, the Assembly voted to end all business until he had apologized for violating its rights and privileges. Public opinion crystallized; the press kept tempers boiling. For nearly two years the stalemate continued. The Commons met but once to appoint a committee to prepare an address to the King, denouncing Boone and reasserting the right of the members to judge their own elections, upon which rested their future as "either Freemen or Slaves." In June 1764, Boone decided to return to England. Departing without ceremony, he arrived in London nearly three weeks after the Earl of Halifax had officially ordered him home to give an account of the controversy. The Board of Trade ruled that the Governor had acted with "more Zeal than prudence . . . inconsistent with good Policy and unsuitable to the dignity of his Situation." But it also criticized the conduct of the Commons in neglecting its business.[36]

Although the Gadsden election controversy did not provide cause for revolution in South Carolina since the Commons House had emerged victorious in the struggle, it did provide a nursery for the development of revolutionary ideas and methods. The men who figured in the controversy—Gadsden, John Rutledge, Rawlins Lowndes, among others—would guide the colony through war and into independent statehood.

III

Indians, Land, and the Proclamation of 1763

The French and Indian War originated in the interior of North America and it ended with the cession of wilderness territory. Throughout the years of conflict, two questions loomed large for colonists and British administrators: how to deal with the Indians and how to utilize the enormous acreage that fell to the British as victors in the seven-years' battle. Since the two problems were closely related, their solutions had to be sought simultaneously. Unfortunately, British ministers, making their decisions in the safety of Whitehall, could not identify with colonial interests with respect to this large domain. The British sought to preserve the land for the fur trade and future English use. To accomplish this, it was necessary to appease the Indians. American settlers, on the other hand, saw the land as an invitation to expand and prosper. They cared little for the Indian tribes and even less for the preservation of their hunting grounds. In their differences of interpretation and prescription, the two interests—colonial and imperial—clashed.

British policy with respect to the West and the Indians was dictated by the response of successive administrators to specific problems as they arose. The ministry's first inkling of what would be required if Britain were to win the confidence of the Indian tribes and maintain control over the West came with the outbreak of the Cherokee wars of 1759–1761. These proved what past experience had already demonstrated—that the colonists could not unite to meet a common danger. "Fire and water," reported the English traveler Andrew Burnaby, ". . . are not more heterogeneous than the different colonies in North America." The colonists, George Grenville believed, displayed a "peevish reluctance to associate and unite" even though the Indians were pounding on their frontier. This being the case, it was necessary for the British to promulgate a policy for America that would protect their mutual interests.[1]

The Cherokees at Bay: (1759-1761)

"Cool, sequestered, rocky vales" provided home for the Cherokees, a large group of energetic and independent eastern Indians who occupied a hundred towns in three mountain valleys overlooking the borders of Georgia. Generations before the English and French arrived in the area, five thousand warriors and their families had created a unique civilization. In 1721, the Cherokees had begun bringing their deerskins to British posts in Virginia and South Carolina to trade for weapons and ammunition. The Cherokee-British alliance was officially cemented in 1730, when a group of Cherokee chiefs sailed to London to sign the Articles of Friendship and Commerce between the two nations, inaugurating a series of similar treaties designed to strengthen trade relations and procure land for the British.

ATTAKULLACULLA (LITTLE CARPENTER) (c. 1700–c. 1780); OCONOSTOTA [CUNNE SHOTE] (GREAT WARRIOR) (?–1783)

Among the Cherokee visitors to London was the young Attakullaculla, a chief's son destined to become "Second Man of the Nation." Attakullaculla was hugely impressed by puppet shows, parades of the Horse Guards, receptions in churches, and a colorful and pompous ceremony in George II's court. In particular, the architecture, busy shops and crowded streets, and the artillery dragged out to honor his comrades conveyed to Attakullaculla the strength and power of the English nation.

Returning home laden with presents and honors, Attakullaculla also carried with him memories of George II· and his court—the man he called "our King, our head, our father." Although he later came to question English justice and honesty, he never doubted that the British would prevail in America. His years spent as a captive of the Ottawas in Canada only reinforced his bias in favor of the English. Although he met French soldiers, traders, and priests—even the French governor of Canada at Quebec—he never seriously considered breaking the British alliance.

Attakullaculla was primarily a Cherokee nationalist who related Cherokee safety and prosperity to British protection. Wherever he could play off the French against the English, or one colony against another, to improve the Cherokee trading position, he did. In 1754, for example, he pitted Virginia against South Carolina to break the Carolina trade monopoly which limited the prices offered for Cherokee skins. He also used the alliance to force trade concessions. But he was most successful when he obtained from the Carolinians a promise to build a fort to protect Cherokee towns from hostile Indian tribes and the French. In turn, he promised to send war parties against the enemies of King George.

By the outbreak of the French and Indian War in 1756, Attakullaculla had earned the respect of the British. "He is a very great man in this nation," wrote Governor Lyttelton, "and what he says is law." [2] A dignified chief, he would accept no humiliating treatment of himself or his people. "I am not a boy," he bitterly reprimanded the Carolinian commander who accused him of duplicity in 1757, "but the headman of this nation. . . . My mind has always been straight." [3] Described by the naturalist William Bartram as "a man of remarkably small stature, slender, and of a delicate frame," Attakullaculla made up for his size by his "superior abilities." But his task was a difficult one, and in the long run doomed to failure.

In 1758, the English came to Attakullaculla seeking help for General Forbes's expedition against Fort Duquesne. As a result, over four hundred warriors joined the Virginia troops at Winchester, but so many Indians together boded trouble for the white soldiers and settlers. A few weeks after they had assembled,

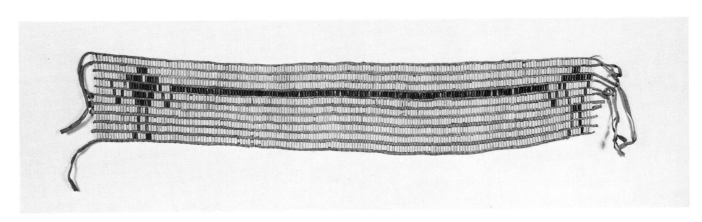

Wampum belt sent by Governor Denny to the Indians of the Ohio Valley in 1756 inviting them to a council in Philadelphia.

OK OUKAH ULAH. 2.K.SKALILOSKEN KETAGUSTAH 3.T TATHTOWE. 4 C CLOGOITTAH. 5. K KOLLANNAH. 6. U UKWANEEQUA. 7. O OV

Attakullaculla (at far left) in an engraving by Isaac Basire,
published during the Cherokee visit in 1730.

some Cherokees, disgruntled with English treatment and unhappy about their participating in the English war, began to leave. One discontented group looted the homes of settlers at Otter Creek in southwestern Virginia. Frightening the settlers with their grim appearance, the Indians alarmed them even more when they ripped up featherbeds, and carried off clothing and household utensils on stolen horses. Some settlers pursued the warriors, only to come upon them—"painted . . . some black, some red, but mostly black"—sharpening their tomahawks around a campfire. Asking for their goods and horses presumably in "brotherly fashion," the settlers were answered by "a

kind of grunt" and a challenge to fight. "The Indians," according to the official report,

threw tomahawks . . . and pursuing [the whites] and they retreating . . . they were nearly pushed to the river bank . . . a gun was fired upon which the engagement ensued . . . in which [one of the whites] fell . . . mortally wounded . . . three Indians fell.[4]

A week later, a party of thirty-five Virginians encountered a large party of Cherokees also returning from Winchester. When approached by the Virginians, who expressed a desire "to be in friendship with them," the Cherokees pretended to be hostile Shaw-

53

nee Indians and forthwith set upon the Virginians "and stripped and beat them." The incident became a matter of great concern to the British. Demanding that the Indians be handed over to them for judgment, the British entered into a course of action that could only provoke the Cherokees into war.

The Indians were not entirely to blame. The Scotch-Irish who lived in the outposts of civilization—the English whom the Cherokees believed they had come to help—frequently met the Cherokees who were returning exhausted from battle with insults and violence. They had also stolen the Cherokees' horses and denied them food and water.

Attakullaculla recognized that many of his people misbehaved, but he also saw that the English were not blameless. Sensibly, he suggested to the British authorities that they overlook the incident since both parties had been injured. But the British were not to be placated.

Attakullaculla faced a dilemma. The Indians responsible for the attack on the Virginians were merely obeying their custom of avenging the killing of their brothers by white settlers. But how to persuade the British of this? When he approached General Forbes, still tediously building a road into the Pennsylvania wilderness, Forbes treated him "with the greatest signs of indifference and disdain." Forbes's insult to the Little Carpenter fed the anger of Indian nationalists intent upon seeking vengeance and hampered Attakullaculla's peace efforts. Into this situation stepped the Great Warrior, Oconostota of Tanase.

In the vigor of his manhood in 1759, Oconostota viewed the settlers hungrily eyeing his people's land with greater hostility and bitterness than did the older chief. He particularly felt injured by the insulting behavior of the English toward his people. Indians and Englishmen continued to engage in murderous attacks and insulting encounters; and as the French continued to infiltrate the Indian villages stirring up hostility, Oconostota's sense of grievance increased. When the British stopped the sale of ammunition to the Cherokees, it was with difficulty that Oconostota restrained his tribe from taking up the hatchet. Appearing before the English officer Captain Raymond Demere, commander of Fort Loudon, Oconostota boldly declared that future trouble could only be avoided by lifting the ban.

In November 1759, Oconostota, still striving for peace, led a delegation of Cherokees to Governor Lyttelton in Charleston. To take such a trip into the

William Lyttelton by Sir Joshua Reynolds.

heart of English territory involved a risk, but the Indians were willing to take it in order to maintain the English alliance. Unfortunately, Governor Lyttelton, influenced by reports from his captains in the wilderness, distrusted the peace mission and was already organizing an expedition against the Cherokees. Balked by the Commons House of South Carolina, who limited his funds for an expedition to a period of three months—much too short a time to be effective—Lyttelton clung to his decision to bring the Cherokees under control despite reports that Oconostota's peace mission was on its way. He determined to hold Oconostota and his companions as hostages while he moved into Indian territory at the head of an army. Oconostota, who had been reassured by Indian agent John Stuart and Captain Corymore of safe conduct, walked into Lyttelton's trap; later, he could only conclude that the trap was baited with English double talk.

When the Cherokees were admitted into the council chamber, Lyttelton did not offer to shake hands, nor would he offer the expected speech of

54

conciliation. Even more shocking to Oconostota was Lyttelton's refusal to accept the deerskin which he had placed at the Governor's feet as a pledge of his desire for peace. Lyttelton, instead, insisted that the delegates accompany him and his army as hostages into Cherokee territory. "Stung to the heart by such base treatment," Oconostota had to agree.[5]

Delays and misunderstandings continued to embitter the Great Warrior. A month later at Fort Prince George, Oconostota and the captive headmen, faced with an army of over a thousand men, promised Lyttelton that they would deliver "every man in the nation who had committed a murder or an intrigue." The Governor was still not satisfied. Releasing fifty members of the delegation, he retained twenty-eight at the fort until the Indian promise was fulfilled.[6]

Meanwhile, Little Carpenter continued his attempts to prevent the Cherokees from plunging into an English war. He had wept when he heard of Lyttelton's demands for surrender of the Indian culprits because he knew that these men had acted according to the basic law of family and clan and that now he must deliver them to what could be their death, in order to bring peace. Facing accusations from within his tribe of being a traitor to his people, he was unable to convince the Indian council to authorize him to confer with the English. At a meeting late in December, Little Carpenter was able to arrange for the release of six hostages—including Oconostota—whom he believed would help him in his desire to maintain peace. But twenty-two Indians were still being held, and more significantly, Attakullaculla had negotiated a treaty that was not acceptable to his people.

As smallpox and measles spread within Fort Prince George, Lyttelton and his army were forced to ride back to Charleston, leaving behind at the fort twenty-two important hostages waiting to be exchanged for the Indians the Cherokees were unwilling to surrender, and a large supply of ammunition which the Cherokees could only regard anxiously.

Two months later, Oconostota determined upon war. Through trickery, he lured the commander of the fort outside and had him killed. Unsuccessful in razing the garrison, the Indians had to retire, but during the fighting, the British soldiers put the hostages to death "one by one, in a manner too horrible to relate."

Now the whole Cherokee nation took up the tomahawk and began slaughtering entire families along the frontier of Carolina. In a successful siege of Fort Loudon, Oconostota and his Indian warriors forced the fort to surrender with the promise that the surviving soldiers could leave in peace. Then, craftily ambushing the departing English force, his warriors killed all except the agent John Stuart, whose life had been purchased by Attakullaculla "at a considerable price." Their thirst for revenge slaked, the Cherokee braves prepared to make peace. On September 26, 1760, Oconostota helped raise the English flag at Nucassee town and sent out a peace delegation to Lieutenant Governor William Bull of South Carolina, who had replaced the truculent Lyttelton.

Lieutenant Governor Bull, however, continued Lyttelton's policy of making the Indians pay heavily for the infringement of white man's law. His experiences managing the family plantation and serving as a captain in a South Carolina militia company should have accustomed him to Indian ways, but Bull shared the Englishman's general ignorance of Indian culture and customs and the belief that Indians were cruel barbarians who could only be controlled by force. Thus Bull sent for more troops instead of making peace.

In 1761, the British General James Grant arrived from the North to carry out a scorched-earth policy. Refusing to accept Little Carpenter's peace proposals until all the white captives were released and all of the Cherokees had laid down their weapons, Grant marched into Indian territory, destroying sixteen Cherokee towns and laying waste to crops in "the rich and beautiful little Tennessee and Tuckaseegee valleys." Not until he had driven the Indians into the high mountains "to starve," was he willing to listen to peace talks.

By this time, Attakullaculla was no longer the spokesman of his people. During the years of conflict, his friendship with the British had cost him his leadership of the Cherokees, and Oconostota had assumed power within the nation. But in his speech before the treaty-making assembly, Attakullaculla remained the ever-resourceful diplomat. With his intense eyes fixed on his audience, he reminded his listeners of George II's treaty with the Cherokee headmen in 1730 and of his own determination to maintain it. With ceremonial feathers he cleaned the path as a token of wiping away the blood spilled during the conflict. Handing the tail of an eagle to the commissioners together with a string of wampum, he added: "And I will leave these feathers with the Governor as a sure token that no more [blood] will be spilt by us. . . ."[7]

Uprising in the West, 1763

PONTIAC (c. 1720–1769)

Hardly had the eastern frontier recovered from the Cherokee rebellion when chiefs and warriors of the western Indian nations—Shawnee, Delaware, Seneca, and Ottawa—assembled at the Ecorse River, eight miles south of Detroit, to participate in a war council. "We must exterminate from our land this nation [the English] whose only object is our death," read the colorful wampum belts summoning them to the meeting in April 1763; ". . . we must destroy them without delay. Are we not men? . . . What do you fear? . . . There is no longer any time to lose." [8]

The complaints of the western Indians against the English were many. British regulars and officers were treating them contemptuously. "When I go to see the English Commander," complained Pontiac, a chief of the Ottawas, "and say to him that some of our comrades are dead, instead of bewailing their death as our French brothers do, he laughs at me and at you." [9] Pontiac feared, in particular, a British trade monopoly that would virtually make the Indians slaves to one great power. Before the British could strengthen their hold on the West, his people must drive them from their land and strike the chains that held them in unmanly bondage.

A "remarkably well-looking man; nice in his person, and full of taste in his dress, and in the arrangement of his exterior ornaments," Pontiac was a powerful figure among the Indian tribes that clustered around Lake Michigan and the Detroit River. In 1763, he appeared as their potential liberator from English control.

The Ottawas had allied themselves with the French during the Anglo-French conflict in North America. As late as 1763, when General Amherst's messengers called upon him to submit to "his Britannic Majesty," Pontiac is reported to have reasserted the tribe's fealty to the French king, "The Great Onontio." "Answer me, Englishmen," the legend has him saying, "can a child have more than one father? . . . How pretendest thou that we now have another?" [10]

But Pontiac was a realist. Toward the end of the French and Indian War, when it became evident that the French were losing, he gradually came to terms with the British. For the last year of the war, his tribe remained neutral, and shortly after the British army occupied Fort Detroit in 1761, an Ottawa spokesman welcomed the conciliatory English agent Sir William Johnson, and optimistically spoke of a "covenant of friendship" with the British. When Sir William's promises, however, were not fulfilled by the British, Pontiac soon ceased trusting both the friendly agent and the nation he represented.

Pontiac's revolt was not the work of Pontiac alone, nor was it a conspiracy of a single tribe of Indians. It was primarily the result of the short-sightedness of British Indian policy and lack of understanding of Indian customs and needs. What Pontiac hoped to obtain through the uprising is not clear. Probably he hoped that Indian efforts to oust the British from the Indian hunting grounds would stimulate the French to return to battle and restore the old balance between competing whites that had worked out so favorably for them in the past. Once the English were defeated, Pontiac believed "we shall see what there is left to do, and we shall stop up the way hither so that they may never come again upon our lands." [11]

Pontiac's plan followed previous patterns of Indian attack. Assaults on British forts and settlements were to take place simultaneously. Pontiac himself led a surprise attack on Fort Detroit at the head of a band of sixty selected warriors; but his ruse was discovered by the commander and he was forced to besiege the stronghold. Detroit withstood Pontiac's assault, but other forts fell in rapid succession to determined bands of Indians, who followed up their victories with pillaging and killing that terrorized the farmers and traders of the western regions. By June, only Detroit and Fort Pitt remained in British hands.

Pontiac and his Indian allies, however, lacked the force and unity to bring their uprising to a successful conclusion. Moreover, when British goods were no longer available to them, they felt the pinching effect of going without the cloths, blankets, and utensils they depended on. Pontiac lifted his siege of Fort Detroit when his force had dwindled to insignificance. Promising that he would "think nothing but good," for two more years he continued to plot along with a few other diehards against the English. The rebellion, however, was over.

In 1766, Pontiac met with Sir William Johnson at Fort Ontario and promised that he and "all the nations over whom I have any influence" would "preserve the public tranquillity from being disturbed." This was Pontiac's finest moment. He returned home to meet the criticism of those chiefs who still wanted to keep the hatchet "bright till spring, when it should be used with more vigor than ever." His influence waned, even among his own people. Left with a small following, he was assassinated in the French settlement of Cahokia by a hostile Peoria warrior.[12]

JEFFERY AMHERST (1717–1797)

The uprising of Pontiac was to a great extent the responsibility of General Jeffery Amherst. As commander in chief of the British forces in North America, he had decided that the custom of giving presents to the Indians was an extravagance no longer required. To the Indians, however, gift-giving indicated friendship and hospitality; its cessation spelled stinginess and hostility, which they found difficult to understand.

More serious was Amherst's order stopping the sale of ammunition and guns to Indians. As hunters and warriors, western Indians had become dependent on European firearms for food and protection. To be deprived of such essential items was a serious blow indeed.

Adding injury to insult, General Amherst had broken his promise to the Indians and was now establishing military garrisons hundreds of miles beyond the line of white settlement. In addition, he was giving away Indian lands to his officers as bonuses after promising the tribes that whites would not be allowed in their hunting grounds. The resentful Senecas believed that he was "giving away their

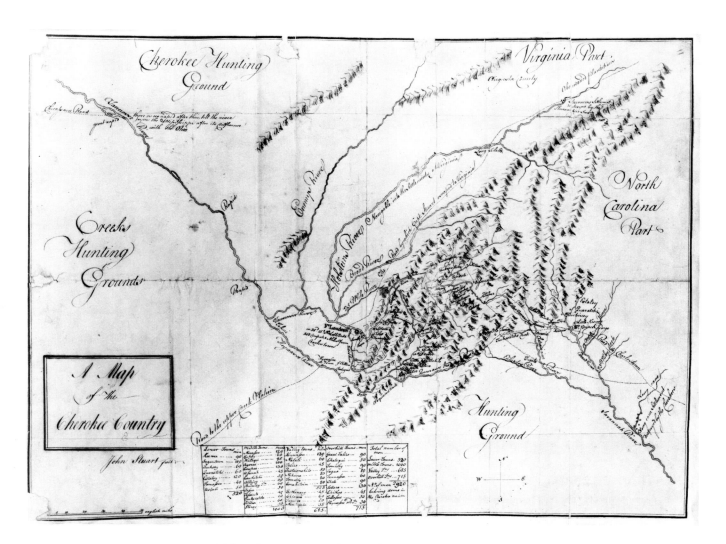

John Stuart's handdrawn map of Cherokee country, circa 1760.

The English camp at Crown Point after the fall of the French fort in 1759.

country to be settled, which the King of England long ago Promised to secure for their use." Obviously, the English were determined "to cut them off the face of the Earth." [13]

Amherst had never respected the Indians, even when as auxiliaries in his army, they had fulfilled bravely many difficult assignments. To Amherst, the Indians were "more nearly allied to the Brute than to the Human Creation." Once having made use of them, he saw no further need for conciliation. They were, he wrote, "an execrable race," and he was fully resolved, "whenever they give me an occasion, to extirpate them root and branch." [14]

Amherst had entered the British army as an ensign in the Guards at the age of fourteen, and his personality and character were molded by his military experiences. Even his physical appearance reflected a military regimen. Tall and extremely thin, with "a large Roman nose and full blue-grey eyes," his weather-beaten complexion suggested a man accustomed to being in the field. Of plain and neat dress, when foppery was quite common among men of his

class, he indulged no special tastes for food or drink. In the face of danger, he was reported to be "always steady, cheerful, and alert."

A brilliant tactician and a young man of obvious ability, the cool and efficient Amherst had been singled out by William Pitt to assume the responsibility of implementing Pitt's strategy in the French and Indian War. In July 1758, he captured the French stronghold of Louisbourg on Cape Breton Island. In November he took Fort Duquesne. In July 1759, Fort Ticonderoga on Lake Champlain fell, and in August, Crown Point. In 1760, after Wolfe's great victory at Quebec, he participated in the surrender of Montreal. In recognition of his services, he was made governor general of British North America and knighted—an honor he rejected in pique, for he had hoped for a peerage.

With the war's end, Amherst anxiously awaited orders to return home. Pontiac's uprising came as a surprise. Amherst had not believed that any post "commanded by [British] officers could be in danger from such a wretched enemy as the Indians are." [15]

Thus he had not prepared the western forts against an Indian attack, nor was he ready with aid when the attack came. Amherst's contempt for the Indians prompted his proposal that smallpox be disseminated among them by means of infected blankets, and that bloodhounds be used to track down lurking warriors. Before his advice could be acted upon, the orders he was awaiting arrived. He returned to a hero's welcome in England in November 1763.

SIR WILLIAM JOHNSON (1715–1774)

The Indians' greatest friend among the English was an Anglo-Irish tenant farmer's son who did not arrive in America until his twenty-third year. Democratic in his sympathies, gregarious, generous, and honest, William Johnson was the most popular and widely known trader among the Six Nations of western New York. From the moment he set himself up as a fur trader,

Sir William Johnson by an unidentified artist.

Johnson achieved success in a business that was as precarious as it was profitable. Although he had come to the Mohawk Valley to manage his uncle's thirteen-thousand-acre estate, he soon bought land for himself across the Mohawk River, built a baronial manor, Mount Johnson, and took an Indian wife, the sister of the Mohawk chief Joseph Brant. In pledge of their friendship, the Mohawk Indians gave him almost one hundred thousand acres of land, trusting that his proprietorship would safeguard their adjacent hunting grounds against further encroachment of white settlers. By the 1760s, Mount Johnson had become the regular meeting place of the Six Nations of western New York.

"Warrayghijagey" (he-who-does-much), as Johnson was affectionately called by the Iroquois, was the perfect intermediary between Indians and whites. Dressed in the deerskins of a war chief, his painted face and plumed headdress contrasting strangely with his sharp blue eyes and stocky figure, he became to all purposes the delegate chief of the Mohawks, who looked to him to represent their interests before colonial assemblies and British administrators. Johnson could sympathize with the Indians' fears for the land and with the European settlers' desire for it. Concluding that the Indians must have time to come to terms in their own way with the presence of the white man, he advocated a policy of gradual settlement. The adjustment of the Indians to the alien whites had to "flow" in large degree from themselves, he believed; it could not be imposed.

During the 1740s and '50s, Johnson's intimate relationship with the Six Nations proved of great advantage to the British. Under the trader's guidance, the Mohawk Valley tribes rallied against the French in 1746. During the French and Indian War, as a result of Johnson's intervention, the tribes of the Six Nations joined the British, and from that time on remained closely allied to British interests in the New World.

If Johnson had had his way, the uprising of the Indians on the western frontier would never have occurred. Indeed, it was through his exertions that five of the six nations—all except the Senecas—remained out of the rebellion. Understanding that free ammunition and provisions had played a large part in ingratiating the western tribes to the French, Johnson urged Amherst—in vain—to emulate French generosity. Although ailing from an old wound, the elderly trader traveled to Detroit in 1761 at the request of General Thomas Gage, Amherst's successor, to meet with the

Obverse and reverse of a 1766 silver medal of George III of the type given to friendly Indians.

Ottawas and their Indian neighbors in order to persuade them to make peace. Promising them "free and open trade," he was able to influence the Senecas to withdraw, but it took more years of conflict before the other tribes were reconciled to British control.

In 1764, wrapped in his red blanket with its gold fringe, the adopted chief of the Mohawks met again with Pontiac and the rebellious Indians at a great peace council at Niagara. Here he exhorted the Indian deputations to lay down their hatchets and negotiate a settlement. Again, he succeeded, although Pontiac's promise of peace was only tentative and two more years of frontier fighting passed before it was fully realized.

Finally, in 1766, Johnson met Pontiac at Oswego and accepted the proud chief's promise of peace, in a meeting that marked the end of formal resistance to British control over the western territory. For the rest of his life, he struggled to protect his Indians from the consequences of the peace. For once the Indians had put down their hatchets, white settlers and land speculators swarmed into the Indian territory like locusts. "I have daily to combat with thousands, who, by their avarice, cruelty, or indiscretion, are constantly counteracting all judicious measures with the Indians," wrote Sir William Johnson, a month before his death.[16] But neither the Proclamation of 1763 nor the Treaty of Fort Stanwix (1768), which he was instrumental in arranging, could hold back the horde of trappers, traders, and speculators from the rich lands that constituted the Indian hunting grounds.

ROBERT ROGERS (1731–1795)

Frontier soldier-of-fortune Robert Rogers lived a life marked by adventure. As a captain on William Johnson's expedition against Crown Point, he proved indispensable as a scout and leader of a ranger party engaged in irregular warfare against French forts and villages. Impressed with Rogers's "bravery and veracity," Johnson was convinced that the scout "was superior to most, inferior to none, of his rank." [17] With nine scouting companies called Rogers's Rangers, Rogers accompanied Lord Loudon in his attack on Halifax in 1757, Lord Abercromby in his unsuccessful siege of Fort Ticonderoga in 1758, Amherst in his daring attack on Crown Point in 1759, and again, in 1760, against Montreal. Later in 1760, Rogers was sent to Detroit and Shawneetown to receive the surrender of all French posts in the West.

Rogers's last efforts in North America were made in defense of Detroit against Pontiac and his warriors. When news reached New York that a concerted uprising of the Indians was endangering the western posts, Rogers was ordered to lead a party of two hundred seasoned veterans of forest warfare against the Ottawas. Traveling in oppressive heat through forests, underbrush, and villages burned and destroyed by marauding Indians, they made their way to the Detroit River. Under cover of night they ascended the stream and by sunrise gained the protection of the fort's guns. The second day after their arrival, Rogers's force helped defend the post against an Indian ambush in what came to be known as the Battle of Bloody Run. Rogers remained at Fort Detroit until the Indians departed for their winter hunts. Without much to do, however, except engage in illicit trading with the Indians, he incurred the criticism of Sir William Johnson, and in disfavor, fled to Connecticut where he surrendered his commission. Deeply in debt, his one hope lay in England where he attempted to promote his interests among the upper classes of London society who sought excitement in novelty.

The rest of Rogers's life appears to have been downhill. Without loyalties or honesty, he was arrested and acquitted of charges of treasonable dealings with the French. Later, he was thrown into debtor's prison in England, and on returning home, in 1776, he was imprisoned by Washington as a spy. In 1780, he again fled to England, where he died fifteen years later in a cheap London lodging-house.

COLONEL HENRY BOUQUET (1719–1765)

In December 1764, Major General Gage reported to the Earl of Halifax, one of the secretaries of state, that the western country in North America was "restored to its former tranquillity." He attributed the peace to the exertions of Colonel Bouquet, whose "firm and steady conduct . . . in all his transactions with those treacherous savages" was responsible for forcing them to put down their arms against His Majesty.[18]

Colonel Bouquet was bound to be successful in frontier fighting: as a professional soldier, he had

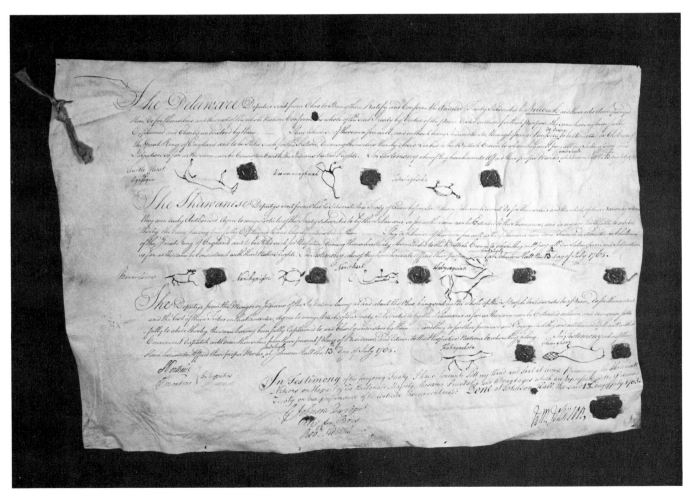

Treaty between Sir William Johnson and representatives of the Delaware, Shawnee, and Mingo nations, dated at Johnson Hall, July 13, 1765.

Testimonial certificate for distribution to friendly Indians, engraved by Henry Dawkins, 1770.

devoted careful study to the exigencies of forest conflict, and he had tried to adapt his experiences in America to his already thorough knowledge of military science and procedure.

A Swiss mercenary, who in 1736 had entered the service of the States-General of Holland, Bouquet served the King of Sardinia and the Duke of Orange in the War of the Austrian Succession before accepting a lieutenant-colonelcy in the newly formed Royal American Regiment in 1755.

Promoted to colonel in January 1758, Bouquet served under General Forbes in his expedition against Fort Duquesne, and with patience and tact managed to organize the difficult colonial troops and uncertain transportation facilities to help bring victory to the British. Under his command, despite George Washington's opposition, "Forbes Road" was cut through the mountains and forests of western Pennsylvania, a

feat that contributed to the French surrender of Fort Duquesne.

Bouquet's services in helping to quell Pontiac's uprising constituted his greatest military achievement in North America. Sent by Amherst into the upper Ohio area and via Lake Erie to Detroit to put down the rebellious tribes, he faced enormous problems involving insufficient personnel, inadequate means of transportation, and lack of cooperation from the Quaker majority in the Pennsylvania Assembly.

Bouquet was outraged at the sight of settlers fleeing from their ravaged frontier homes. "The list of people known to be killed increases every hour," he wrote to Amherst. "The desolation of so many families, reduced to the last extremity of want and misery; the despair of those who have lost their parents, relations, and friends, with the cries of distracted women and children, who fill the streets—form a scene painful to humanity and impossible to describe."[19] So distressed was Bouquet by the suffering he witnessed that he was ready to agree to Amherst's suggestion to spread smallpox among the tribes. There is no evidence, however, that he actually did so, even though a smallpox epidemic raged among the Ohio Indians before the year's end.

Bouquet's was a small force of less than five hundred men, composed of Royal Americans and Highlanders. Toiling over the main range of the Alleghenies, he approached the spot where Braddock, less than ten years previously, had been cut off in a surprise attack by Indians hiding among the trees. Here at Bushy Run, the Indians engaged Bouquet in two days of almost face-to-face fighting. But when Bouquet formed his troops into a circle on the second day and lured the Indians into it by a feigned retreat of one

Henry Bouquet by John Wollaston, circa 1760.

Imaginary likeness of Robert Rogers, engraved in mezzotint by Johann Martin Will, London, 1776.

section, he changed the direction of the day's fighting and brought the Indian war to a speedier conclusion. For the first time at Bushy Run, the Indians were beaten in a place and at a time of their own choosing. When Bouquet next marched into the wilderness, they were not so eager to encounter him.

Bouquet still faced large problems. Indian devastation of the frontier was continuing with even greater savagery and his American regiment was being decimated by desertions. When finally provincial authorities were able to round up recruits, it was too late in the season to use river transportation, and Bouquet had to resort to the more difficult overland march through the forests. Not until October did he advance into Indian territory, but now he had with him a larger and more disciplined army that consisted also of several hundred frontiersmen skilled in frontier fighting. Aiming at the principal towns and storehouses of the Shawnee, Delaware, and Mingo tribes, Bouquet maintained a relentless advance that convinced the watchful Indians of the wisdom of making peace. He returned to Pittsburgh without having fought a battle but having won a victory of significant dimensions.

The Proclamation of 1763

While Pontiac and his Indian allies were raiding western settlements and destroying English forts, administrators in Whitehall were devising a policy to meet the crisis posed by the rebellion. Aiming at the establishment of a secure and cohesive empire in North America, George Grenville's two ministers in charge of western policy, Lord Egremont and Lord Shelburne, had come to believe that firm control over the new western territories was a necessity. No longer could they permit the colonies to have a free hand in developing settlements beyond the Alleghenies. Colonial settlement, Grenville's ministry decided, must be restricted to the eastern seaboard if the Indians were not to be alienated and if the Americans were to remain dependent on English manufactures. Once far from the seaboard, English planners believed, the colonists would be tempted to manufacture their own

necessities simply because of the expense of transporting imported articles from seaport wharves into the interior.

To keep the Indians peaceful, the Indian commissioners John Stuart and William Johnson had been charged with keeping new settlers away from their hunting grounds. To do so, however, was to thwart nature itself, for Stuart, Johnson, and the ministers at Whitehall soon found themselves confronting hordes of immigrants who, like George Washington, regarded the restrictions merely "as a temporary expedient to quiet the minds of the Indians. Any person," wrote Washington, "who neglects the present opportunity of hunting out good lands and . . . marking . . . them for their own . . . will never regain it."[20]

CHARLES WYNDHAM, LORD EGREMONT (1710–1763); WILLIAM PETTY, LORD SHELBURNE (1737–1805)

The two politicians responsible for the execution of Great Britain's western policies were as strained in their relations as they were years apart in age and experience. Charles Wyndham, Lord Egremont, was in middle age and poor health when in 1761 he took on the position of Secretary of State for the Southern Department; William Petty, Lord Shelburne, half his age, was vigorous and ambitious when two years later he joined the ministry as president of the Board of Trade.

Since Egremont and Shelburne shared the responsibility for formulating policy for the new territory obtained from France in North America, it was to be expected that the two would clash. Egremont, described by Horace Walpole as being "a composite of pride, ill-nature, avarice, and strict good-breeding," was irritated at Shelburne's interference in matters to which he had given intense study and which he felt capable of handling. He also was "uneasy" about Shelburne's close relationship with Lord Bute. In turn, Shelburne resented Egremont's power; he was unhappy about the minor role to which he was assigned, and he could not be satisfied with the explanation that he was doing quite well for a young man of twenty-six.

Both Egremont and Shelburne were men of great

Bouquet meeting with Indians. Engraving by Charles Grignon after a drawing by Benjamin West.

George Washington by Charles Willson Peale, 1772.

*George III
by Allan Ramsay,
1761.*

*John Stuart
by Sir Joshua
Reynolds,
date unknown.*

68

OPPOSITE PAGE:
William Pitt by William Hoare, 1745.

ABOVE LEFT:
James Otis by Joseph Blackburn, 1755.

ABOVE RIGHT:
Christopher Gadsden by Jeremiah Theus, date unknown.

LEFT:
Patrick Henry by Lawrence Sully, 1795.

Benjamin Franklin by Mason Chamberlin, 1762.

Cunne Shote, also known as Oconostota, by Francis Parsons, 1762.

Sir Jeffery Amherst by Sir Joshua Reynolds, 1765.

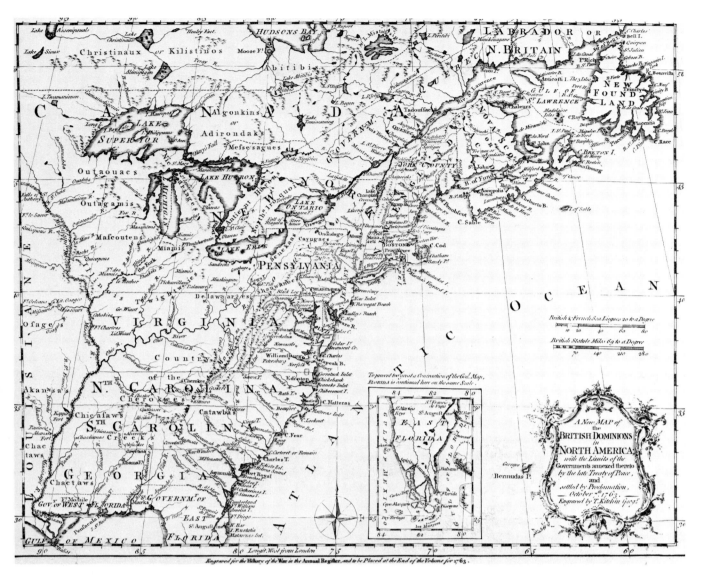

Map of North America published after the Proclamation of 1763.

capacity. Egremont came from an old Tory family in Somerset, but after losing his seat in Parliament in 1741, he changed his politics and allied himself with prominent Whigs. He returned to Parliament in 1747 as a Whig, and remained there until 1761, when he became a member of the Privy Council. With the resignation of Pitt later that year, he took over the position of Secretary of State for the Southern Department. In that capacity, he supported court policies, but like his brother-in-law, George Grenville, never thoroughly identified himself with the "king's friends." He opposed Bute's desire to remain at peace with Spain and enthusiastically wrote the masterly state paper that put the onus for hostilities on the Spanish. Successful

in persuading the Cabinet to accept his proposals over Bute's peace-at-any-price views, he continued to exert influence on policy as a member of an informal triumvirate that included Grenville and Lord Halifax. The three men attempted to carry out the King's wishes while resisting the secret influence of Lord Bute.

Lord Shelburne, as a protégé of Bute's, had frequently acted as Bute's "lieutenant" to other parliamentary leaders. As a reward for his services, he gained an important post in the Grenville ministry that brought him into conflict with Egremont, and he learned some important political lessons.

Although Shelburne allowed himself to be used—

even by the King, who later confessed that he had shown favor to Shelburne "in order to play [Egremont and Shelburne] one against the other, and by that means to keep the power in his own hands"—he was neither stupid nor naive. Born in 1737 in Dublin, he was deprived of the good education that should have been his lot considering his high birth. His youth was a lonely one spent under a tyrannical grandfather and an affectionate aunt. At Christ Church, Oxford, he had "the misfortune to fall under a narrow-minded tutor" who increased his sense of inadequacy. Quick to be offended and to feel slighted, he also was prompted to work harder and think more deeply. He immersed himself in his studies, emerging as perhaps one of the better-informed public figures of the time—but also ambitious, austere, and autocratic. Many years later, Disraeli called Shelburne "the ablest and most accomplished minister of the eighteenth century." [21]

In 1757, Shelburne joined the twentieth regiment of foot. He served in America under General Wolfe and was rewarded for his courage with the rank of colonel and an appointment as aide-de-camp to the King. In

Charles Wyndham, Earl of Egremont, by William Hoare, date unknown.

1761, he inherited his father's name, fortune, and position in the House of Lords; and in 1763 joined Grenville's ministry as president of the Board of Trade.

Cat-and-mouse politics characterized Shelburne's and Egremont's relationships in formulating a western program. Egremont had on his side Henry Ellis, the former governor of Georgia; Shelburne, John Pownall, former governor of Massachusetts Bay. While each man was urged on by his advisers to thwart the purposes of the other, the problems of a vast land went unsolved.

Before his death, Egremont had drawn up a plan with Ellis's help that defined important principles for imperial organization. Two major and related questions confronted him: how to obtain the best commercial advantages from the new territory and how to provide security for those advantages. What kinds of government could best accomplish this, what military protection was called for, how could the Indians be conciliated and kept peaceful, and, above all, what should be the colonists' economic and military role in the whole arrangement—these were all contingent questions.

Henry Ellis's hand in Egremont's plan may be inferred from the recommendation that the governments, with the exception of Canada and the new provinces, be formed on the model of Georgia or Nova Scotia—"the freest from a republican mixture." Georgia was a royal government, consisting of a governor with large powers over the legislature, appointments, and courts; a council which also composed the second house of the Assembly; and a court system. For Canada, since its foreign population was unaccustomed to representative government, a governor and council only were provided. A line of demarcation was set beyond which settlement could not go, with the lands beyond the line reserved for the Indians. Egremont also emphasized the principle of fair purchase of Indian lands.

Shelburne acted upon Egremont's outline when he came to fill in the details and write his report on Britain's newly acquired lands. Shelburne's report eventually became the basis for the Proclamation of 1763 issued by Lord Halifax, Shelburne's successor. The Proclamation defined the territory of the new colonies and their immediate and future forms of government. It opened them for settlement, ordered courts of justice to be erected to operate as closely as possible to the laws of England, specified a temporary

William Petty, Earl of Shelburne,
by Jean Laurent Mosnier, 1791.

Indian reservation and forbade grants of land in that area without express permission from the Crown, opened the territory to licensed trade, and arranged for the seizure of escaped criminals.

Partly out of ignorance of the size and population of the old French settlements in Illinois, the ministers failed to provide government for these older settled areas in the Mississippi Valley; and also out of ignorance of the special nature of the already existing French legal system in Canada, they imposed on the Canadians an English system of law that could only confuse and bewilder the inhabitants and which had to be changed later in the Quebec Act. Their major error in the Proclamation as far as colonial relations were concerned, however, was the limits imposed on the American urge to expand. No imaginary line could possibly confine land-hungry Americans to the already settled eastern portions of the country. And the belief that Americans would pay willingly for a military establishment which would keep them pent in behind that line was a piece of folly. As for the Indians, Americans eager to move into the fertile territory of the trans-Appalachian West were ready to meet their

challenge: the Indians would either have to retreat into the interior or face their muskets and powder. Only a few Americans in 1763 could sympathize with the concern of the British ministers for a policy of conciliation and peace with the Indians. Certainly not the Paxton boys, who in 1764 were to put the policy of conciliation to the test and, in doing so, provide a harbinger of events to come.

The Paxton Riots, 1764

Paxton, Pennsylvania, experienced hard times during the winter of 1763. Indian raids, which Pontiac's uprising had sparked, ravaged the town leaving behind family tragedies and bitter suffering. Obviously, there was need for armed intervention by colonial authorities, but the Quaker-dominated legislature of Pennsylvania, deadlocked as a result of a constitutional controversy with the proprietary—the descendants of William Penn—had been either unwilling or unable to provide for frontier defense. Convinced that they lacked an effective voice in government as a result of an apportionment system that permitted the eastern counties and the city of Philadelphia greater representation, feeling alienated from eastern interests as a result of their Scotch-Irish Presbyterianism, far more militant than the controlling aristocracy, and more impoverished and always troubled by debt, the highly individualistic men of Paxton could not wait patiently for redress of grievances. Their understanding of their situation was simple. When faced with the horrors of Indian raids, "the Men in Power refused to relieve the Sufferings of their fellow Subjects." Therefore, they believed, they had two enemies, the native tribes and the Quakers who preferred to protect "His Majesty's Perfidious Enemies" while ignoring "our suffering Brethren on the Frontiers [who] are almost destitute of the Necessaries of Life and are neglected by the Public." Bearing little love for Indians, because they murdered and destroyed "defenceless People," the settlers believed that they should either be removed from white settlements completely or destroyed.[22]

In December 1763, Lazarus Stewart, Matthew Smith, and James Gibson, desperate young men from Lancaster County, led a group of their neighbors in an attack upon a village of huts belonging to the Conestoga Indians, who lived by begging and by selling baskets and brooms. It had been rumored in Paxton that these Indians offered shelter to war parties while pretending to be peace-loving and friendly. With the fury of a lynching party, Smith led the armed and mounted men into the village where they murdered three men, two women, and a child. Fourteen other Indians, who had been away from the huts during the raid, were taken into protective custody by the sheriff of Lancaster County and locked in the workhouse. The Paxton boys, infuriated that their victims had escaped and convinced that one of the surviving Indians was a murderer, two weeks later galloped into Lancaster, smashed open the workhouse door, and killed the fourteen prisoners.

News of the massacre shocked government officials and Quakers in Philadelphia. Lieutenant Governor John Penn issued a proclamation denouncing the murderers for their "outrageous" act, while the legislature voted to take measures to protect the 140 Indians who had been converted to Christianity by the Moravians and were being sheltered in Philadelphia.

The government's action further infuriated the Paxton boys. They found it intolerable that the government should support Indians while refusing to protect the frontier. In early February 1764, more than five hundred frontiersmen marched toward Philadelphia, angrily determined to force their demands on the Assembly and kill the Indians under its protection.

The Philadelphians acted with unaccustomed speed. The Assembly quickly passed a bill for public defense, threw up a barricade around the Indian barracks, and many townspeople, even pacifist Quakers, began to arm themselves. No battle took place, however. A delegation from the Council and the Assembly, including Benjamin Franklin, Benjamin Chew, Mayor Thomas Willing, and Joseph Galloway, met the frontiersmen outside of Philadelphia at Germantown and worked out an agreement allowing the rioters to present a petition of grievances to the Governor and the legislature. Once the crisis had passed, the Assembly did little more than debate their declaration of grievances. Not until two years later, in March 1766, were the problems of the frontier settlers met, and equal representation in the Pennsylvania Assembly voted into effect.

The Paxton riots pointed up the differing views held by social groups in America as to the proper function of government. They accentuated the social tensions created by the presence in the New World of a heterogeneous people, professing different religious

John Penn by Richard Brompton, 1773.

faiths and of varying economic situations. The men in power in Philadelphia were forced to recognize the existence of discontented settlers in the West who were able to draw upon the sympathies of the discontented in the East. The Paxton rioters were not radicals, nor did they seek political or economic upheaval; but they did feel the injustice of their situation and sought through direct action to remedy their felt wrongs. The Assembly, on the other hand, looked beyond the immediate issue to the question of power and principle. They saw in the proprietary's use of the riots "a Tyrannical disposition . . . to enslave the good people of this flourishing and oppulent [*sic*] Country." [23]

BENJAMIN FRANKLIN (1706–1790)

The murder of the Conestoga Indians went unpunished, because, as Benjamin Franklin reported to an English correspondent, "the Action was almost universally approved of by the common People." The perpetrators were excused as men maddened by the murder of their relatives and neighbors; and, in fact, their direct solution to the problem of Indian terrorism encouraged more settlers to resort to violence for redress of their grievances. "The Spirit of killing all Indians, Friends & Foes," reported Franklin, "spread amazingly thro' the whole Country." Governor Penn's proclamations offering a reward for the capture, or for information leading to the capture, of any three "Ring leaders" produced no results; the people of the frontier continued to applaud the killings as fulfilling the purpose of a wrathful God who would not see his children exterminated by a heathen race.[24]

Benjamin Franklin, the colony's best-known citizen, was ashamed that Pennsylvania should condone such a foul act. "This is done," he pointed out, "by no civilized Nation in *Europe*. Do we come to *America* to learn and practise the Manners of *Barbarians?*" Anx-ious to stimulate Philadelphians to take up arms to protect the Moravian and Quaker Indians, who were "trembling for their Lives," Franklin, in an emotional pamphlet, urged "all good men [to] join heartily and unanimously in Support of the Laws, and in strengthening the Hands of Government; that JUSTICE may be done, the Wicked punished, and the Innocent protected."[25]

Franklin's pamphlet succeeded in its mission. According to his own report, "a sudden and very remarkable Change" occurred in the attitude of the citizens of the City of Brotherly Love. Over one thousand Philadelphians took up arms to confront the rioters who were marching on the city with rifles and tomahawks. "The Fighting Face we put on," explained Franklin, "made [the rioters] more willing to hear Reason, and the Gentlemen sent out by the

Satire of Benjamin Franklin and Israel Pemberton's efforts to aid the Indians, published in Philadelphia, 1764.

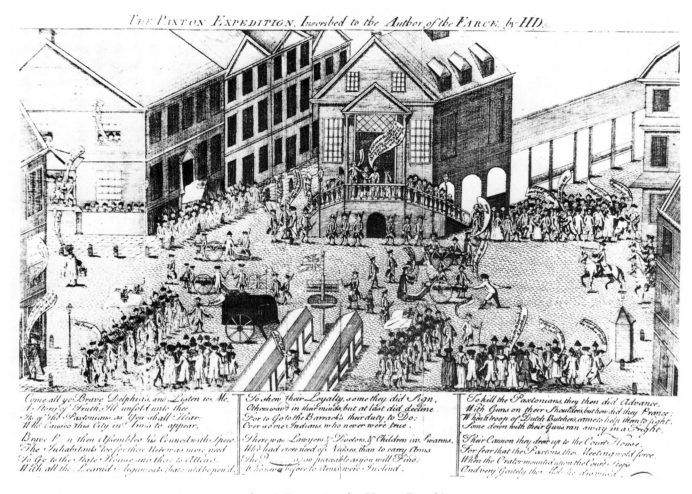

Come all ye Brave Delphia's, and Listen to Me. | To show their Loyalty, some they did Sign, | To kill the Paxtonians, they then did Advance,
A Story of Truth, I'll unfold unto thee | Others wavd in their minds, but at last did decline | With Guns on their Shoulders, but how did they Prance;
Tis of the Paxtonians, as You shall Hear | For to Go to the Barrack's their duty to Do: | When a troop of Dutch Butchers, came to help them to fight,
Who Caused this City in Arms to appear. | Over some Indians who never were true. | Some down with their Guns ran away in a Fright.

Brave Pen then Assembles his Council with Speed, | There was Lawyers & Doctors, & Children in Swarms, | Their Cannon they drew up to the Court House,
The Inhabitants too for there Heroes was more need | Who had more need of Nurses, than to carry Arms | For fear that the Paxtons, the Meeting would force,
To Go to the State House, and there to Illine, | And so peaceable as you will Find, | When the Orator mounted upon the Court steps,
With all the Learnd Arguments that could be pen'd. | It never before to Arms were Inclind. | And very Gentely the Mob he dismisd.

Philadelphia prepares to repel the Paxton band. Engraving by Henry Dawkins, 1764.

Governor and Council to discourse with them, found it no very difficult Matter to persuade them to disperse and go home quietly." [26]

Printer, author, philanthropist, inventor, scientist, statesman, and diplomat, Franklin had identified himself with the interests of his adopted city and colony almost from the day he had established his printer's shop in Philadelphia in 1728. He had arrived in that city at the age of seventeen, intent upon making his fortune after spending two disagreeable years in his father's tallow and soap business and five years apprenticed to his half-brother, a printer. He soon made Philadelphia acknowledge his talents and usefulness. From 1730 to 1748, he prospered in his printing shop and as publisher of *The Pennsylvania Gazette* by practicing the industry and thrift he advocated in *Poor Richard's Almanack* (1732–1757). His passion for improvement led him to help in the establishment of a city police, the paving of sidewalks, the founding of a circulating library, a city hospital, an Academy for the Education of Youth, and the American Philosophical Society. He invented the "Pennsylvania fireplace," Ferguson's clock, and a lightning rod. In 1748, he retired from business, intending to follow "philosophical studies and amusements," but six years later he was unable to resist the call of public affairs, and from that time through the rest of his life, he was chiefly engaged in politics and diplomacy.

Franklin was particularly active in the dispute between the Pennsylvania Assembly, a unicameral legislature, and the proprietary descendants of William Penn who lived in England and who, according to the charter of the colony, were responsible for appointing and instructing the governors of Pennsylvania. The proprietors forbade the Governor to allow money bills for defense to pass the Assembly unless the vast proprietary estates were exempt from taxation. As a result, the defense of the frontier suffered while the Assembly refused to take the necessary fiscal measures for the benefit of the colony.

In 1757, Franklin was sent to England to present the case of the Pennsylvania Assembly to the King and his Council. Three years later, the King was finally persuaded to allow an Assembly bill taxing the proprietary lands. Franklin returned to Philadelphia in 1762, in time to witness the Paxton affair. In Franklin's total career, the Paxton affair occupies small space, but at the time, the riots were of importance as Franklin himself well understood, for they became caught up with the problems faced by the Pennsylvania Assembly in its relationship with the proprietors. They fostered an antagonism between Franklin and Governor Penn which was never to be mitigated.

Using the riots as an excuse, Governor Penn forced the Assembly to pass a militia law and a money bill to put down the "Armed Mob." Franklin had hoped that the bills would not be passed: "the Jealousy of an Addition of Power to the Proprietary Government which is universally dislik'd here, will prevail with the House," he hopefully wrote.[27] But the Assembly, according to Assemblyman Samuel Foulke, because of their "Ill-Judged fear of going out of the beaten track to try a new Method of making Money, which probably would have exempted them & their Constituents from ye necessity of wearing that Servile puiece [sic] of furniture call'd a Neck-Yoke, & of putting their necks under the Tyrant's foot," voted a money bill in favor of the proprietary.[28] The Assembly balked, however, at passing a second militia bill that would allow the Governor to appoint all militia officers and also inflict punishment on those who might be "unfortunate enough to incur their displeasure &c." This was contrary to all notions of civil liberty entertained in the colonies at the time, and, according to Assemblyman Foulke, the proprietary, "that Monster of arbitrary power [would have] swell'd to an enormous size" at the expense of the lives and fortunes of those whom "by ye Laws of God & Nature" the Proprietors were "bound to cherish & protect."[29]

Franklin and John Dickinson actively debated these bills in the Assembly, Franklin "as a politician," and Dickinson "as an Orator." In their speeches, neither man was gentle, but Franklin, in particular, antagonized the Governor. "There will never be any prospect of Ease and happiness," Penn wrote to his uncle in England, "while that villain [Franklin] has the liberty of spreading about the poison of that inveterate malice and ill nature which is deeply implanted in his own black heart."[30]

Turning to the Presbyterians in the city and outlying counties for support, Governor Penn managed to revive the Proprietary party in Pennsylvania. Franklin charged that the Governor's failure to bring the Paxton boys to court and his wooing of the Presbyterians were indicative of his "private understanding with those Murderers, and that Impunity for their past Crimes is to be the Reward for their future *political* Services." But Governor Penn's efforts against Franklin were successful. During the election weeks of 1764, the Proprietary party accused Franklin of all kinds of public villainy, raking up the private scandal of his son's illegitimate birth, reminding the Germans that Franklin had called them "Palatine boors," and telling the Scotch-Irish that he had termed them "Christian white savages." On election day, Franklin was beaten by twenty-five votes, and one observer reported that "Mr. Franklin died like a philosopher."[31]

Well might he, for Franklin was always sure that industry and honesty would prevail. Although he lost his place in the Assembly, his party still held a majority of votes, and in the next session, the Assembly dispatched Franklin to England to present its petition for a royal government to the King. George III, asserted Franklin, "who has no views but for the good of his people, will thenceforth appoint the governor, who, unshackled by proprietary instructions, will be at liberty to join with the Assembly in enacting wholesome laws."[32]

But the proprietary issue was to be lost amid the greater issues that confronted the American colonies between 1764 and 1774—and with all of these Franklin was to be concerned, not only as agent for Pennsylvania, but also for Georgia, New Jersey, and Massachusetts. Not until May 1775, did he again set foot on American soil, only to be immediately swept into the activities of the Second Continental Congress and the drafting of the Declaration of Independence.

The Cost of Empire and the Sons of Liberty

While the recent victories in North America and the new lands acquired from the French fortified Britain's national ego, the harsh financial realities resulting from the Seven Years' War posed formidable problems to her policy-makers. Between 1755 and 1763 the national debt had risen from £72,289,673 to £122,603,336. Peace did not end military expenditures or mounting indebtedness. To maintain security against hostile French traders and Indians required more outlays. Pontiac's Rebellion demonstrated the need for a standing army in America of 10,000 men, at a cost of £200,000. But English taxpayers, having accepted higher taxes during the war, were antagonistic to the prospect of additional levies. So began the government's search for new sources of revenue—a formidable task, the responsibility for which fell to George Grenville.

GEORGE GRENVILLE (1712–1770); WILLIAM KNOX (1732–1810)

George Grenville arrived at his position of leadership as the result of careful study of parliamentary functions, diligent application to his assigned offices, and a capacity to shift with changes in the political wind. Entering the House of Commons in 1741, he joined the Whig group centering around William Pitt. But Grenville shared Pitt's ambition for advancement, and when Lord Bute's star began to rise, he abandoned Pitt and joined the political circle of the King's favorite. In 1762, upon Bute's resignation, he was appointed Secretary of State for the Northern Department, causing Horace Walpole to remark that "Lord Bute was in want of tools; and it was a double prize to acquire them from his rival's shop." Completely "ignorant of foreign affairs," according to Walpole, and possessing "no address, no manner, no insinuation, and . . . least of all, the faculty of listening," Grenville took office, as he said, "to preserve the constitution of my country, and to prevent any undue and unwarrantable force being put on the Crown." [1]

Despite his loyalty to George III, Grenville was not well liked by the easily bored King, who at one point declared that he "would rather see the devil in my closet than Mr. Grenville." [2] Undeterred by Bute's attempts to dominate him and by the King's coldness, Grenville went ahead to design a colonial policy that would place Great Britain's finances on a sound basis. Grenville's economic policies involved, primarily, retrenchment at home and a shifting of the financial burden of the Seven Years' War to the colonies where he believed it belonged. Grenville was also concerned with the commercial activities of the colonists which he viewed as competing with English trade and military interests.

Soon after his appointment as Chancellor of the

The Deplorable State of America. *The first anti-Stamp Act cartoon published in England, possibly on March 22, 1765, the day that the Act received the royal assent.*

Exchequer in 1763, Grenville moved to enforce the revenue-producing acts of trade which for years had been circumvented by the colonists as a result of lax administration by customs collectors performing their duties from their comfortable English residences. He ordered these officials to move to America or resign; at the same time, he ordered the navy to patrol American ports and inspect all ships for customs violations.

In March 1764, Grenville appeared before Parliament, budget in hand. For two hours and forty minutes, he tediously argued for his new economic policy based on his conviction that the colonies ought to be subordinated to the British Parliament. The Sugar Act defined this conviction more specifically, since accompanying the revisions in customs duties was a provision that gave exclusive jurisdiction in all customs cases to royally appointed admiralty courts. These, he hoped, would prove less susceptible to merchant pressures than the local civil courts. Grenville also proposed that customs officials be allowed to take their cases to Halifax where a newly established admiralty court could examine the charges free of local pressure.

A sympathetic Parliament passed Grenville's proposals without resistance, including the rather vague resolution that "it may be proper to charge certain stamp duties in the said colonies and plantation." [3]

Grenville became quite taken with the idea of a stamp tax, and he and his lieutenant, Thomas Whately, Secretary of the Treasury, set to work to spell out its specifications. In February 1765, Whately presented Parliament with his final version of the proposed act. Imposing an excise fee, in some cases ranging as high as £10, on such items as colonial land deeds and other legal documents, ship clearances, college diplomas, dice, pamphlets, newspapers and newspaper advertisements, the fifty-five resolutions that Parliament passed and which collectively came to be known as the Stamp Act, promised lucrative returns for the British treasury. One of these resolutions—as in the Sugar Act of 1764—provided for trying violators in the admiralty courts.

William Knox, the agent for Georgia in London, became one of the Stamp Act's strongest defenders, despite the fact that as a colonial agent it was his duty to present to English authorities the hostility of his colonial constituents to the Act. But Knox had always been more loyal to the Crown than to his fellow colonists. During his five-year residence in Georgia, his political and economic fortunes owed much to the colony's royal officials, especially to the royally appointed governor, Henry Ellis, through whose intervention he had received a substantial plantation and appointment to the Georgia Council. Identifying himself with the fortunes of Georgia's royal establishment, Knox was convinced of the supremacy of British authority in colonial matters. Reinforcing this conviction was Knox's strong political ambition. After arriving in England in 1762 and being appointed Georgia's agent a year later, he was anxious to advance in British politics. Favor from the right people was

necessary, and the best way to gain this favor appeared to be the defense of Grenville's colonial policies.

Grenville's revenue policies fit hand-in-glove with proposals written by Knox in 1763 and submitted to the Bute ministry. In his *Hints Respecting the Settlement of Our American Provinces*, Knox stated that the colonies' *raison d'être* lay in augmenting Britain's "wealth" and "power." Therefore, American markets should be safeguarded for Britain's manufactured goods by restraining settlement in the trans-Allegheny West. Knox also urged that Parliament revoke the charters of Connecticut and Rhode Island, which gave their inhabitants almost virtual autonomy in electing their officials and regulating their internal affairs. Once these colonies were organized under the Crown, their royally appointed officials would be paid directly

The Deplorable State of America, *attributed to John Singleton Copley, published in Boston, November 1, 1765.*

by the Crown to avoid intimidation from popularly elected assemblies. Finally, he urged Bute to station "Regular Troops" in North America to guard against the thwarting of British interests by independent-minded colonists, and suggested that revenues could be raised in the colonies for their support.

While other agents voiced objections to Grenville's revenue policies, Knox took them up with enthusiasm. In the spring of 1765, he wrote a ringing defense of the Stamp Act, in which he praised Grenville for his equitable treatment of the colonies and pointed out that the stamp tax was actually rather generous; it would have been to Parliament's advantage, he wrote, to load the colonies with even heavier taxes in order to lighten the tax burden of English landowners.

While no doubt pleasing to Grenville, Knox's reasoning did not sit well with Georgians. In October 1765, the president of Georgia's Council wrote the agent that his defense of the Stamp Act "has given the greatest Umbrage, and I am afraid has not left you a single person, who will open their mouths for you in the Assembly." By the end of the year, the Assembly had notified Knox that it "no longer had occasion for his services." [4]

OPPONENTS IN ENGLAND:
JARED INGERSOLL (1722–1781);
ISAAC BARRÉ (1726–1802)

The proposed Stamp Act was not a well-kept secret. Throughout the fall and winter of 1764 and 1765, while it was still being drawn up, talk of its expected provisions kept politicians and concerned citizens busily engaged in coffee houses both in London and in the various colonial capitals. Positions hardened while voices grew shriller. At the heart of the controversy was whether or not the colonies ought to be, or could be, subordinated to the British Parliament—as Grenville steadfastly insisted—and under what terms.

Grenville and his supporters believed that the entire British Empire ought to be united through parliamentary taxation. To get around colonial charters that granted the colonists the right to be taxed only by their own representatives, he and his publicists developed the theory that the whole Empire was represented collectively, although not geographically, in Parliament. Whately argued that given Parliament's constant concern for the welfare of the whole Empire,

the colonists were "virtually," if not actually, represented in that "August Assembly" and therefore subject to all its laws.

But there were Englishmen who were not so certain of the validity of Grenville's and Whately's position. Some merchants and manufacturers wondered what the effect of such a stamp tax would be on colonial trade. Might they be influenced to bring pressure on Parliament to veto the proposed act or mitigate its terms? Jared Ingersoll, agent for Connecticut, thought so. Moderate in his demands—perhaps too moderate for many of his constituents across the seas—he did his best to alert the Grenville ministry to the hazards of its course and to present alternative measures that would be acceptable to both the colonists and the ministry.

Jared Ingersoll was well-suited to the role of intermediary. A native of Connecticut and a graduate of Yale, he had been commissioned by the Connecticut government in 1758 to act as its London agent. Successful in securing for the colony reimbursement of money spent by it during the French and Indian War, he was successful also in the friends he made, among whom was Thomas Whately. Whately frequently called upon Ingersoll for advice in colonial matters. His conservatism made his judgments acceptable, as did his association with Connecticut's conservative establishment.

Ingersoll had returned to Connecticut in 1761 where he involved himself in the timber industry. In 1764, he returned to England to secure a contract for ship masts, but soon after his arrival he was notified that the Connecticut government wished again to appoint him their London agent. Instructed to oppose the projected stamp-tax bill, he joined other colonial agents in London to persuade Grenville to desist from such a plan. Utilizing a pamphlet he and Governor Fitch had earlier composed—*Connecticut's Reasons Why the British Colonies in America, should not be Charged with Internal Taxes by Authority of Parliament*—he challenged Parliament's right to impose an internal tax.

Grenville was not to be dissuaded. Instead, the Prime Minister convinced Ingersoll that the tract did not prove its case and that Parliament's right to levy the stamp tax was "universally yielded." Ingersoll then decided to concentrate his efforts on warning the ministry of the hazards of such an act, while urging it to permit colonial assemblies to vote the necessary revenues themselves. "If the King should fix the proportion of our Duty," he warned, "we all say we

Jared Ingersoll by an unidentified artist, date unknown.

tion as an officer in General Wolfe's regiment during the French and Indian War. Lacking the proper family connections, however, he was overlooked when Pitt's ministry considered military promotions at the end of the war. Frustrated and bitter, Barré sought more promising outlets for his ambitions. In 1761, with the help of Lord Shelburne, whom he had met during General Wolfe's expedition to France in 1757, he succeeded to Shelburne's seat in the House of Commons.

Possessed of a fiery eloquence which frequently went beyond the bounds of decorum, and which was heightened by his swarthy appearance and the "savage glare" of his left eye (caused apparently by a bullet lodged in his cheek), he soon cut a formidable figure in Parliament.

His own fight for position against the snobberies of England's aristocratic circles, together with the friendships he had formed with many colonists while serving in the French and Indian War, had made Barré sympathetic to colonial interests. Moreover, he had witnessed colonial conditions at first hand and could face realistically the maturity and independent strength of the colonies. In 1765, therefore, he ardently opposed the Stamp Act. The climax to his opposition came when Charles Townshend defended Grenville's proposal:

And now will these Americans, children planted by our care, nourished by our indulgence untill they are grown to a Degree of Strength and Opulence, and protected by our Arms, will they grudge to Contribute their mite to relieve us from the heavy weight of that burden under which we lie?

Rising to his feet, Barré launched into a point-by-point refutation:

They planted by your care? No! Your Oppressions planted Em in America. They fled from your Tyranny to a then uncultivated and unhospitable Country. . . . They nourished by *your* indulgence? They grew by your neglect of Em: —as soon as you began to care about Em, that Care was exercised by sending persons . . . to spy out their Liberty, to misrepresent their Actions & prey on Em, men whose behaviour on many Occasions has caused the Blood of those Sons of Liberty to recoil within them. . . .[6]

Barré's allusion to the "Sons of Liberty" resounded throughout America. The catch phrase came to symbolize colonial rights in the face of British oppression.

Barré continued to mount abusive attacks on Parlia-

will do our parts in the Common Cause, but if the Parliament once interpose & Lay a Tax, tho' it may be a very moderate one . . . what Consequences may, or rather may not, follow?"[5]

When Grenville still appeared immovable, Ingersoll reconciled himself to the fact that the ministry was determined on having a Stamp Act and began the last phase of his lobbying efforts, seeking to remove from the list of those items subject to duty certain popular papers such as marriage licenses, commissions of justices of the peace, and notes of hand. On other items, he persuaded Whately to set lower rates than Grenville had intended. The bill in this revised form passed Parliament. Now Grenville began to look around for agents to administer the act in America, and Ingersoll became a likely candidate. In early August 1765, he returned to Connecticut as stamp master.

Colonel Isaac Barré was perhaps the most strenuous and most perceptive opponent of Grenville's colonial policies in Great Britain. Barré had begun his career in the British army, where he gained moderate distinc-

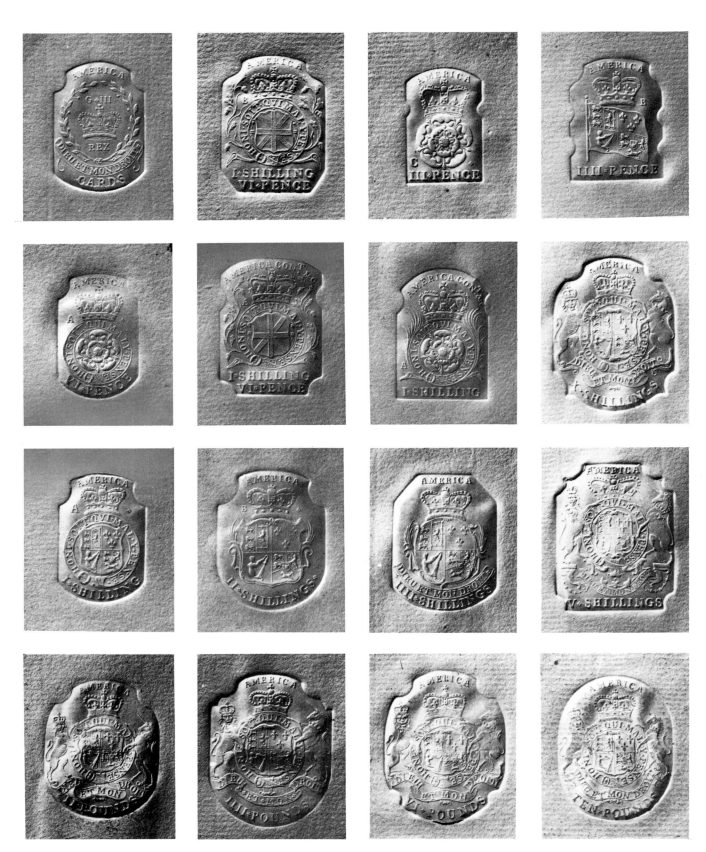

Test impressions of stamps issued in 1765 by
the British government for use in the American colonies.

ment's colonial measures until his words took on a prophetic quality. He foresaw an America matured into a "great Commonwealth," with territory "larger than Europe and perhaps on the whole, containing more inhabitants." How feasible would it be then to enforce Parliament's demands on a territory already feeling a national identity and destined to become so much larger and more populous? No accommodations, he believed, would ever satisfy the colonists so long as Parliament insisted on controlling their revenue:

If you do mean to lay internal taxes, act prudently and draw the sword. . . . All colonies have their date of independence. . . . If we act injudiciously, this point may be reached in the life of many of the members of the House.[7]

As Barré's speeches reached the colonies, he was toasted and eulogized from Georgia to Massachusetts. In 1769, members of the Connecticut Susquehanna Land Company memorialized his defense of colonial rights by naming their new town in Pennsylvania "Wilkes-Barré," which—as if to underline Barré's warnings—they were establishing against the will of British officialdom.

The Stamp Act in America

After listening to protests from colonial representatives and their British allies, Parliament passed Grenville's act by wide majority. But implementation was another matter. Writing to Benjamin Franklin in London in September 1765, the newly appointed stamp distributor for Pennsylvania, John Hughes, spoke ominously of his chances of carrying out his new duties successfully:

You are now from Letter to Letter to suppose each may be the last you receive from your old Friend, as the Spirit or Flame of Rebellion is got to such a high Pitch Amongst the North Americans; and it seems to me that a sort of Frenzy or Madness has got such hold of the People of all Ranks, that I fancy some Lives will be lost before this Fire is put out.[8]

Ironically, Jared Ingersoll was one of the first to feel the colonists' anger. He had accepted the position of stamp distributor for Connecticut—at the urging of Franklin—in the belief that he could administer the act more fairly "than a stranger." But mobs branded him a "Vile Miscreant" and burned his effigy in towns throughout the colony. Shortly before he was to assume his duties, Ingersoll succumbed practically at gunpoint to the cry for his resignation.

STEPHEN HOPKINS (1707–1785); MARTIN HOWARD (1730?–1782?)

Protest in the colonies was widespread, but in the vanguard were citizens of Rhode Island, led by the colony's governor, the merchant Stephen Hopkins.

Hopkins's constitutional position reflected his inter-

The Pennsylvania Journal and Weekly Advertiser, *October 31, 1765, announcing the closing of the paper due to the Stamp Act.*

ests as a shipowner and merchant heavily engaged in the busy molasses, rum, and slave trade that underwrote Rhode Island's economy. Grenville's Sugar Act, hampering the flow of molasses from the foreign West Indies, threatened to throw out of kilter the successful trading pattern that Rhode Island merchants had created.

From the time he was elected to the Assembly early in the 1730s, Hopkins was involved with Rhode Island politics. By 1755, he had begun to wield great influence, and for thirteen years thereafter he presided over the colony's political life, for almost all the period as governor. Rhode Islanders enjoyed the privilege of a royal charter that granted them almost complete autonomy in internal affairs, including the election of their governor. As one individual commented, Rhode Island was "a bodie corporate in ffact [*sic*] and name." As a product and leader of such an independent and democratic political structure, Hopkins was fierce in his maintenance of it. In 1765, then, when news of the impending Stamp Act reached the colony's shores and while the colony's citizens were still smarting under the provisions of the Sugar Act, Hopkins published a

Martin Howard by John Singleton Copley, 1767.

powerful tract, *The Rights of the Colonies Examined.* Here Hopkins temperately but firmly argued that neither the Sugar Act nor the Stamp Act fell within Parliament's right to regulate colonial affairs for the general welfare of the "whole" Empire. Taxes, he asserted, could only be determined by the colony's popularly elected representatives; to rule otherwise would be to deny to Americans rights that were theirs as Englishmen and that protected them from the "most abject slavery"—the rights to life, liberty, property.

Martin Howard, on the contrary, felt no sympathy for Rhode Island's independent and democratic traditions. An Anglican and a political conservative, Howard regarded the politics of his native province as expressions of venality and "licentiousness"—the "bane of industry and the curse of idleness." What the colony needed was a firm hand emanating from Great Britain so that it could learn "more Moderation & Civility, more Meekness and better Manners." [9]

Howard himself was devoid of meekness. As one of Newport's top-ranking lawyers, he was the leading spirit of the "Newport Junto"—a group described by the somewhat intemperate James Otis as a little "knot of thieves, beggars, and transports." Under Howard's guidance the cabal petitioned the King to revoke the colony's charter and make it a royal colony in order to save it from its wayward "democratic" ways. [10]

Particularly incensed at Hopkins's pamphleteering, Howard could not resist responding to the Governor's *Rights of the Colonies.* In his *Letter of a Gentleman at Halifax,* he argued Parliament's absolute authority over the colonies in all matters including taxation. There were many people in England, he claimed, who were unrepresented in Parliament. As with these, Parliament "may levy internal taxes as well as regulate trade" in America, regardless of representation or the possible local hardships such measures might cause.

Howard's *Letter* did not sit well with many of his Newport neighbors. In an Assembly session some representatives indignantly demanded that copies of the infamous *Letter* be publicly burned. Others urged that charges of libel be brought against the men who dared print it. By the end of August 1765, it was clear that Howard's days in Newport were numbered. Incessant newspaper attacks compared his views to such things as "a belch in the presence of company." After seeing his effigy dragged through the streets, strung up for all to view, and then burned, he fled to the safety of a British ship. Just as he was departing, a mob, armed with broadaxes, descended upon his house. Within hours the once commodious home was transformed into a shell-like frame.

LANDON CARTER (1710–1778); PATRICK HENRY (1736–1799)

The first Americans to assert "their Rights with *decent Firmness*," according to Oxenbridge Thacher of Massachusetts, were Virginians. In the summer of 1764, the Virginia Assembly's Committee of Correspondence instructed its agent in London to express the colony's objections to Grenville's proposal. Already feeling the burden of the Sugar Act in the price of imported silks and Madeira wine, the Committee determined to prevent a similar violation of a "most vital principle of the British Constitution"—that the colonists could not be taxed without their consent.

By October, Virginians were in a "flame." The General Assembly voted to address a protest to the King, a memorial to the House of Lords, and a remonstrance to the House of Commons. The Committee to draft these documents included Peyton Randolph, Richard Henry Lee, Benjamin Harrison, Edmund Pendleton, Archibald Cary, John Fleming, George Wythe, and Landon Carter, fourth son of Robert "King" Carter, one of Virginia's wealthiest landowners and one of the most commanding political figures of the colony's early years.

Landon Carter had long been recognized as a defender of the rights of Virginia Burgesses. For over sixteen years he served on some of the House's most powerful standing committees and helped prepare most of the important formal addresses submitted by the Burgesses to their agent in England and to English ministers. Along with Richard Bland, he stood constantly ready to defend the Burgesses in pamphlets and newspaper essays. After 1763, he adamantly opposed British encroachment upon American rights and was the first to raise the alarm in Virginia against the Stamp Act.

Carter combined a seventeenth-century skepticism and distrust of human nature with an eighteenth-century empiricism. Men, he believed, were basically corrupt and irrational, "intoxicated with either ambition, malice, avarice, or some of the other modes of corruption." "Corruption, once tasted," led directly to "barbarity, injustice, and Plunder." [11]

Despite his cynicism, Carter believed in the possibility of self-improvement, and his determination to improve himself became almost obsessive. Firmly committed to the eighteenth-century ideal of a virtuous and honorable life lived in service to the community, Carter believed he was obligated to serve the public by putting his learning and accumulated wisdom at the disposal of the people. His most conspicuous public service was in the political realm, and here Carter's pen did yeoman service.

Carter's arguments against the Stamp Act were included in Virginia's remonstrance to Parliament. The Stamp Act, Carter wrote, challenged Americans to preserve liberty, "to save [the] constitution from being overturned." Constitutionalism was the only bulwark men could throw up against the two enemies of freedom—corrupt and tyrannical ministers and complete subservience to popular will—both of which represented uncontrolled power. "Wherever there is a superiority in Power," he wrote in 1765, "Justice seldom prevails." By taxing the colonies, Parliament was attempting to achieve such a superiority and to wrest from Americans their "Privilege of being solely governed and taxed by Laws made with the Consent of the Majority of their own Representatives." Men must be exempt from "the force of *any* Law made without the consideration of their Representatives," he insisted, if they were to retain their natural rights. This went for stamp taxes, tea duties, or any other parliamentary intervention in affairs which properly ought to be exercised by colonial assemblies acting under charters that were "confirmation of the people's original Right [i.e., their right as Englishmen] of Government." [12]

The Stamp Act crisis produced in Carter a deep suspicion that corruption had taken hold in England, giving rise to a "sinister conspiracy . . . to reduce the subjects of Great Britain to slavery . . . beginning only by degrees with those in America." Although he still proclaimed that the "Colonies . . . glory in their connection with" Britain, he pointed out that the most valuable feature of that connection was Britain's preservation of "the Religion and Liberties of the people." When that went, so did all other connections. So fiercely did Carter believe in limiting power within government that he was ready to suffer "civil war" rather than establish "a precedent" against Liberty. [13]

In his diary Landon Carter wrote that he had never "courted Public applause; and if any endeavour assists my country, I care not who enjoys the merit of it." He was referring to Patrick Henry, credited by the Virginia Convention of July 1776, as being "the first who opened the breath of liberty to America." Actually, Henry's Resolutions to the House of Burgesses in May 1765, were based almost entirely on Carter's committee's remonstrances to Parliament the previous October.

Patrick Henry was "a rising sun" in Virginia politics. Having successfully argued against the Parson's Cause in December 1763, he was elected to the House of Burgesses. As Henry neared his twenty-ninth birthday, the major concern of the House was whether or not the Stamp Act ought to be obeyed. Richard Henry Lee, for example, believed that although the law was bad, it ought to be observed. For a time, indeed, he considered accepting the post of stamp distributor.

As one of the younger members of the House of Burgesses, Patrick Henry was impatient at the caution of the older members, who seemed inclined to postpone action until it was too late. Rising to his feet, he blazed out in a violent speech against the authority of Parliament and the King, denying altogether parliamentary intervention in colonial matters. It was his peroration, however, that endeared Henry to history. "Tarquin and Caesar," he warned, "each had his Brutus, Charles the First his Cromwell and George the Third . . ." "Treason!" shouted Speaker Robinson; "Treason!" echoed other members of the Assembly. But with enormous presence of mind, Henry finished, ". . . may profit by their example. If this be treason, make the most of it." [14]

Thus did Henry, in Jefferson's words, "baffle the charge vocifirated [sic]." And so successfully that the five "outrageous resolves" he moved were almost immediately passed, although one was erased after Henry's departure from the House. The remaining four were published in the *Virginia Gazette*, along with two others that had been laid before the committee but not reported to the House. The resolutions stated once again that "taxation of the people by themselves or by persons chosen by themselves to represent them" was the "distinguishing characteristic of British freedom . . . without which the ancient constitution cannot subsist." Virginia had "uninterruptedly" and with the knowledge of the King and people of Britain enjoyed self-government in the way of taxation and internal policy. The expunged resolution resolved that only the General Assembly of the colony could lay taxes and

that any effort to do so by others would result in the destruction of "British as well as American freedom." The two resolutions never voted upon, but published, were even more radical. They clearly indicated that the inhabitants of the colony were "not bound to yield obedience to any law or ordinance whatever, designed to impose any taxation whatsoever upon them, other than the laws or ordinances of the General Assembly," and that anybody who maintained otherwise "shall be deemed an enemy to his Majesty's colony." [15]

This was red-hot sedition, but it soon aroused like-thinking men in the other colonies. Oxenbridge Thacher of Massachusetts exclaimed of the Virginians, "Oh yes—they are men! they are noble spirits! It kills me to think of the lethargy and stupidity that prevails here." "It is inconceivable," remarked Governor Bernard, "how . . . [the Virginia resolutions] have roused up the Boston Politicians & have been the Occasion of a fresh inundation of factious & insolent pieces in the popular Newspapers." Governor Francis Fauquier of Virginia was equally aroused. Dissolving the Virginia Assembly for its "rash heat," he made it impossible for the colony to send delegates to the Stamp Act Congress in New York.[16]

Andrew Oliver by John Singleton Copley, circa 1758.

ANDREW OLIVER (1706-1774)

From New England to Georgia throughout 1765, popular and often violent outbreaks of hostility occurred. Stamp distributors could very well fear bodily harm or even death at the hands of angry mobs. In Maryland, distributor Zachariah Hood fled to New York after helplessly standing by while a mob tore down his Baltimore home. In Virginia, George Mercer, finding not "a single person" willing to support him in his new office, resigned as two thousand Williamsburg protesters cheered. New Hampshire merchants had warned distributor George Meserve what to expect before he left England. Prudently, he did not wait until he reached Portsmouth to respond, but resigned immediately upon his arrival in Boston.

In Boston, on the morning of August 14, 1765, stamp distributor Andrew Oliver awoke to find that sometime during the night a group of citizens had hung his effigy from what now was designated the Liberty Tree. Flanked by the devil and "Jack Boot," the symbol of Lord Bute, the stuffed "AO" bore the inscription:

> Fair Freedom's glorious Cause I meanly quitted,
> Betrayed by Country for the Sale of Pelf,
> But ah! at length the Devil hath me outwitted,
> Instead of Stamping others have hanged my self.[17]

Little did the people of the city care that Oliver too considered the Stamp Act a "public Misfortune" and that he had done "more to prevent this measure . . . than any other Man in this Province." Nor did they consider that for over a quarter of a century he had served Boston and Massachusetts Bay well—as town auditor, overseer of the poor, collector of taxes, member of the school inspection committee, assemblyman, member of the Provincial Council, and secretary of the colony. The fact remained that Andrew Oliver was now the individual specifically charged with carrying out the hated Stamp Act.

After leveling Oliver's newly built shops and offices and burning his effigy, the milling, yelling crowd went on to Oliver's house. While some concentrated on demolishing "his Looking Glasses, Tea Geer and Other China," others looked for the stamp distributor himself, "declaring that they would kill him." Oliver, however, after sending his family to safety, had taken refuge with a neighbor.

The next evening, the Boston protesters again besieged his house, this time threatening to level it entirely if he did not resign his new office. While hating the idea of giving in to a mob, Oliver finally succumbed to the fears of his family and agreed to "request the Liberty of being excused from his new office." His besiegers, after giving "three Cheers . . . took their Departure with Damage." [18]

Although Oliver said he would resign, he never officially surrendered his post, a technicality which by December assumed crucial importance for the protesters. The leaders of the mob, in particular, feared that the economic hardships caused by the stoppage of business might convince businessmen to accept the necessary stamps. Further concerted action was required. On the night of December 16th, a messenger delivered a letter to Oliver demanding that he make a "public Resignation" of his office. Added to the note was the warning: "Your non-Compliance, Sir, will incur the Displeasure of the Trueborn Sons of Liberty." Without choice in the matter, the once-venerated Oliver was forced to appear the next day at the Liberty Tree where four months earlier he had been hanged in effigy. Before a throng of more than two thousand spectators, he swore to take no steps "for enforcing the Stamp Act in America." [19]

SAMUEL ADAMS (1722-1803)

During the months following passage of the Stamp Act, Sam Adams kept himself carefully in the background. When asked at the Liberty Tree on August 14, 1765, who Oliver's effigy represented, he answered that "he [too] wanted to enquire." Many Bostonians, however, believed that Adams managed this first public demonstration. In the pillaging of Lieutenant Governor Thomas Hutchinson's home two weeks later, Adams's role as Boston's "Grand Incendiary" was more apparent. But Adams dismissed the riots as "the diversion of a few boys in the streets." The attack on Hutchinson, he wrote, had been perpetrated by "vagabond strangers." [20]

It was not difficult for Sam Adams to arouse his fellow citizens in Boston against the Stamp Act. Times were hard in Massachusetts in 1765 and the citizens were complaining that they were "miserably burthen'd and oppress'd with taxes." Many merchants were forced to close their doors, while other substantial mercantile houses declared bankruptcy. Even wealthy John Hancock felt that the town was experiencing "a most prodigious shock like an Earthquake."

On September 16, 1765, the *Boston Gazette* reported that it was a "time of more general distress and calamity" than any that had occurred since the founding of the colony.[21]

A hierarchy of leadership existed in Boston intent on fueling the discontent and turning it into a popular protest movement. At the lowest level was shoemaker Ebenezer McIntosh. To him fell the task of directing protesting wharfingers, artisans, and shipyard workers. It was he who led demonstrations that ended in the vandalizing of Oliver's and Hutchinson's homes.

Above him, and somewhat removed from direct contact with the unruly crowds, were the "Loyall Nine," which included the publisher of the *Boston Gazette*, Benjamin Edes; house painter Thomas Crafts; distillers Thomas Chase and John Avery; ship's captain Joseph Field; and jeweler George Trott, along with John Smith, Stephen Cleverly, and Henry Bass. They disseminated propaganda, distributed placards, and prepared effigies, but kept their identity secret in order to make mob violence appear as "spontaneous" outbreaks.

At the top of Boston's radical leadership were members of the "Caucus Club." Throughout the last half of 1765 and the beginning of 1766, this group of men, including James Otis, Jr., Dr. Joseph Warren, Josiah Quincy, Jr., and John Hancock, provided much of the fiery rhetoric against parliamentary usurpation of colonial rights. Foremost among the radicals was Sam Adams, Boston's chief agitator and spokesman for American grievances.

Politics came to Adams as naturally as breathing, and the writing of propaganda and manipulation of men called forth his best talents. He had shown no interest in business at all; by 1765, the brewing house he had inherited from his father had run down drastically and he owed the town of Boston over seven thousand dollars from defalcations in his account as tax collector. But steeped in a heritage of resistance to royal authority, Sam Adams knew by instinct how to move in the political world.

Two events had helped influence Sam Adams's political stance. The first was his father's involvement in 1741 in a Land Bank scheme, designed to meet a tight-money crisis by issuing paper currency backed by land. When Governor Belcher, horrified at the idea of paper money, learned that extreme supporters of the scheme stood ready to "raise a rebellion" to enforce the legality of Land Bank money, he prevailed upon Parliament to veto it. Many Bostonians, including Sam Adams's father, Deacon Adams, who had invested

Daniel Dulany, attributed to John Wollaston, circa 1755.

heavily in the Land Bank, suffered severely. Deacon Adams forfeited the greater part of his estate, and young Sam, a student at Harvard, found it necessary to wait on tables in order to finish his studies. By the time he came to deliver his Master's thesis, he had found an appropriate subject: "whether it be lawful to resist the Supreme Magistrate, if the Commonwealth cannot be otherwise preserved."

The second event that influenced Sam's career as a political radical was the Great Awakening of the 1740s, a religious revival led by George Whitefield that stressed the individual's independence of authority and called for a return to Protestant orthodoxy. The revival swept through Harvard College like a storm and departed as quickly as it came. But while blowing hot, it fired the students with religious zeal. On Sam Adams it left an enduring mark. He came to believe that the early Puritan morality, which had once kept New England free and alert to resist the tyranny of prelates and Kings, must be regained lest "our Morals, our Constitution, and our Liberties . . . degenerate." [22]

From 1748, when he founded the short-lived *Independent Advertiser*, until 1760, Adams's political activities were limited to attending meetings in taverns and attics and holding minor offices. After James Otis, Jr., assumed radical leadership in 1760, Adams became his lieutenant and chief propagandist. But Adams's real opportunity for political influence came in 1764 with the Sugar Act. Adams declared the Act a flagrant violation of Parliament's authority. "If our Trade may be taxed," he argued, "why not our Lands? Why not the Produce of our Lands & everything we possess or make use of? This we apprehend annihilates our Charter Right to govern & tax ourselves." [23]

In 1765, Sam Adams was elected to represent Boston in the General Court. Soon he managed to get elected to all the important committees, where as a result of his "pliableness and complaisance in . . . small matters"—so long as no vital principle was involved—he was quite successful and popular. Within these committees, he was able to get resolutions passed that contained attacks upon the royal government. Published in the *Boston Gazette*, they conditioned the public to Adams's revolutionary way of thinking. By the end of the stamp crisis, Adams was securely positioned as the colony's leading opponent to British authority.

DANIEL DULANY (1722–1797)

One of the most prominent legalists in Maryland was Daniel Dulany, province secretary, a man of a conservative cast of mind who yet assumed certain social obligations as the responsibility of his class. He expressed his distaste for the Stamp Act through resolutions and arguments in the belief that reason, not violence, would dissuade Parliament from continuing its present American policies.

A member of Maryland's social and political elite by birth as well as marriage, Dulany could not identify himself with popular protest movements and remained aloof from public disputes. Yet he was sensitive to the question of popular rights. His earlier struggles to allocate proprietary revenues for free education and frontier defense had prompted one property-minded official to write that Dulany was "fond of being thought a Patriot Councillor & rather inclined to serve the People than the Proprietary." [24] It was not out of character, then, that Dulany should sympathize with popular outcries against the Stamp Act or that he

should write his own polemic challenging its validity.

Considerations on the Propriety of Imposing Taxes in The British Colonies, For the Purpose of Raising a Revenue, by Act of Parliament centered around the question of America's representation in Parliament and disputed the ministry's contention that the colonies were "virtually" represented. "On the contrary," Dulany observed,

not a single elector in England might be immediately affected by a taxation in America. . . . Moreover, even acts oppressive and injurious to the colonies in an extreme degree, might become popular in England from the promise . . . that the very measures . . . would give ease to the inhabitants of Great Britain. [25]

In effect, argued Dulany, Americans were neither directly nor indirectly represented in Parliament. The Stamp Act, therefore, constituted an "indefensible" violation of Britain's time-honored principle of taxation by representatives of the people.

Yet, Dulany urged the people to submit to the Act, while carrying on "orderly and prudent" protest. He suggested a concerted colonial policy of "frugality" and the development of home manufactures to remind Parliament that it could not ride roughshod over colonial rights without jeopardizing Britain's own welfare.

Dulany's pamphlet was read widely. One doting Marylander exclaimed, ". . . as it abounds with so much good Sense, Sound Reason . . . the Spirit of Patriotism and Loyalty . . . I am in Love with the Author." [26] In London, many British politicians took it to heart. William Pitt's speech denouncing the Stamp Act, indeed, repeated many of Dulany's ideas.

THE CLERGY TAKES A STAND:
EZRA STILES (1747–1795);
JONATHAN MAYHEW (1720–1766)

To Ezra Stiles, Congregational minister from Newport, Rhode Island, the Stamp Act of 1765 represented God's punishment of His chosen people. What the colonies had done to deserve such punishment he was not sure, but there was little question that the colonists' enemies were God's "Instruments of Chastisement." "This is the Trial of our Faith," he warned his congregation; eventually, God would in His Time "work a Deliverance and protection." [27]

Stiles had reached this view of God's justice only after a long struggle with skepticism. The son of a minister, he had at first resisted a call to the ministry, finding the practice of religion incompatible with his doubts and the dictates of reason. His curiosity about the nature of the world influenced him to reject Scriptural revelation and to attempt to arrive at its ethical principles through the path of nature and reason. Reading extensively in the works of rationalistic and deistic eighteenth-century religious writers and studying the scientific principles of Newton and Bishop Berkeley, Stiles traveled the path from Calvinism to Deism and back again. From this intellectual voyage, he emerged, as Edmund M. Morgan has reported, "not only with a Puritan reverence for Scripture but with a profound conviction of the fallibility of human knowledge." [28]

In 1755, Stiles abandoned his plan for a career in the law and accepted a call to the ministry of the Second Congregational Church in Newport. Although he identified himself with orthodox Puritanism and preached old-fashioned but evangelical views such as the depravity of man and the omnipotence of God, he remained a child of the eighteenth-century Enlightenment, tempering his Puritanism with faith in human liberty and the efficacy of reason. "I inherit," he wrote to a friend on the eve of the Revolution, "from my Ancestors who came out of England . . . an ardent and inextinguishable Love of *Liberty, civil and religious*—which I pray God may overspread America, and be perpetuated into the millennial Ages." Liberty, for Stiles, meant freedom to propagate both truth and error; man's reason, which God guided, gave him the capacity to distinguish between the two, and "truth in its greatness," he was convinced, eventually "would prevail." [29]

Stiles feared that the Stamp Act would be the first step in bringing the Anglican Church to America, thereby destroying colonial religious freedom. Everywhere he looked he saw that the Anglicans were augmenting their power in the New World: in the southern colonies, they filled virtually all political offices; in the northern colonies, royal appointees had installed Anglican churches; in New Jersey Governor Josiah Hardy had tried, unsuccessfully, to pack the Board of Trustees of Presbyterian Princeton College with a majority of Anglicans. Stiles also suspected Anglican infiltration in the establishment of the society of Free Masons and even in Newport's own Redwood Library, which, founded by a Quaker and

intended to be nonsectarian, was now threatened by a majority of Anglicans who voted *en bloc*.

The Stamp Act also threatened Rhode Island's charter liberties, in Stiles's view. For simultaneously with its passage, a group of Newport Anglicans petitioned the King to revoke the colony's charter, which since 1663 virtually made the colony a self-governing republic. By replacing the charter with a royal government, the Anglicans hoped to introduce into the colony Anglican royal appointees.

Stiles's response was immediate: "The day that puts an End to our Charters," he wrote, "commences an Aera of Reproach to the Memory of the Minister or Judge of the Law who shall do us such a disagreeable service." If Parliament succeeded in imposing the proposed stamp tax, he feared that its income of "£4000 or £5000 per ann. [would be] appropriated for a half dozen Bishops on this Continent [who would] come in to throw the Ballance of Things in favor of Episcopacy." [30]

Beyond religion, Stiles saw that the results of taxation without the consent of those to be taxed struck

at the Root of american Liberty and Rights and effectually reduces us to Slavery. We are already equal to one quarter of England and may in Time surpass Britain in Numbers, and it will be hard to subject one half the Kings subjects to the Taxation of the other half. . . . Why should we be treated as a conquered Country? What more would France have taken from us than the powers of *Legislation, Taxation* and *Government?* Take these away from any Body of Men and what are they more than slaves? [31]

Stiles had built his life on a faith in reason, and thus even while he denounced the Stamp Act from the pulpit, he could only urge submission to it. He hoped that a change in the British ministry or some unforeseen intervention of God would bring about an end to its oppression, but he opposed violent measures to produce the desired end. When on the evening of August 27, 1765, a crowd erected a gallows near his house and hung from it effigies of Stamp Act defenders Augustus Johnson, Martin Howard, and Dr. Thomas Moffat, Stiles was shocked. However, as evidences of British tyranny increased, Stiles spoke to his congregation in increasingly radical tones. Soon he began to look forward to the day when "America shall have come to the Ages of Maturity" and be an "Independent State." [32]

*Jonathan Mayhew, attributed to
John Greenwood, circa 1750.*

Jonathan Mayhew, like Stiles, was regarded as one of the "Chief Instruments in promoting and spiriting up the people to that Pitch of Madness . . . which so generally prevailed . . . during Stamp Act Times." A clergyman of fiery eloquence, Mayhew had been a radical thinker since his youth. Harvard officials knew him as an "impudent" and "impertinent" scholar. He read widely "in the doctrines of civil liberty, as they were taught by such men as Plato, Demosthenes, Cicero, and other renowned persons among the ancients; and such as Sydney and Milton, Locke and Hoadley among the moderns." From Scriptures, Mayhew learned "that wise, brave, and virtuous men were always friends to liberty; that God gave the Israelites a king (or absolute monarch) in his anger, because they had not sense and virtue enough to like a free Commonwealth and to have himself for their King; that the son of God came down from heaven to make us 'free indeed,' and that 'where the spirit of the Lord is, there is liberty': this made me conclude that freedom was a great blessing." [33]

Having early developed a contempt for "Ministers who ought in Conscience to be very grave and Stupid," he believed that the hypocrisy of the clergy was hindering mankind in its religious progress. Before his ordination as minister of the wealthy West Church of Boston, Mayhew was deemed a heretic, unworthy of membership in the Association of Congregational Ministers. No Boston minister would attend his ordination ceremonies, but Mayhew continued on his liberal and rationalistic path, ignoring the mumbling criticisms of his peers.

To Mayhew's church were drawn liberal members of all the Boston congregations—James Otis, Samuel Adams, James Bowdoin, Robert Treat Paine, John Winthrop, Stephen Sewall, and Harrison Gray Otis. Paul Revere reportedly was whipped by his father for listening to Mayhew's heretical preaching. To Mayhew, politics served religious purposes, and civil and religious liberty were inseparable. "The purpose of the divine mission of Jesus Christ," he lectured, "is the happiness of man: but that happiness can only result from Virtue, and virtue is inseparable from Civil Liberty." [34] Although he opposed violence, such as he feared would accompany resistance to the Stamp Act, his fervent concern for liberty frequently led him into strong expressions from the pulpit—what Thomas Hutchinson had called "The D[octor's] venomous arrows."

Governor Bernard believed that Mayhew was a member of the "clubb of scandal" along with Sam Adams, James Otis, Jr., and John Hancock. Mayhew was, in fact, not involved with these radical leaders, nor did he share their hostilities. He certainly did not intend to excite a mob that Sunday, the 25th of August, when he lectured on the text "I would they were even cut off which trouble you for brethren ye have been called unto liberty." But the coincidence of this address with the sacking and destroying of Thomas Hutchinson's house brought on his head the blame for inciting the disorder. "God is my witness," wrote Mayhew to Hutchinson the next day, "that from the bottom of my heart I detest these proceedings; that I am sincerely grieved for them, and have a deep sympathy with you and your distressed family on this occasion." [35] If Mayhew did not mean to incite violence, his sermon did excite "some of his Auditors, who were of the Mob [and who] declared, whilst the Doctor was delivering it they could scarce contain themselves from going out of the Assembly and beginning their Work." [36] Mayhew continued to urge the defense of colonial liberties, but he also condemned "the riotous and felloneous proceedings of certain men of Belial, as they have been justly called, who had the effrontery to cloke their rapacious violences with the pretext of zeal for liberty." [37]

Mayhew's sermon on the repeal of the Stamp Act, *The Snare Broken*, which was reprinted both in America and in England, widely circulated the beliefs of Massachusetts Whigs that Great Britain had grown wealthy as a result of the colonies and that the taxation envisioned by the Stamp Act was unjustified. Such a tax, he declared, "threatened us and our posterity with perpetual bondage and slavery" since it took "the fruit of men's labors *lawfully* . . . from them without their consent." In this sermon, Mayhew articulated the mission of America: "if any miserable people on the continent—or isles of Europe, after being weakened by luxury, debauchery, venality, intestine quarrels, or other vices, should in rude collisions, or not uncertain revolutions of kingdoms, be driven in their extremity to seek a safe retreat from slavery, in some distant climate; let them find, O! let them find one in America. . . ." [38]

The Stamp Act Congress

Arriving in New York City five days before the opening of the Stamp Act Congress in October 1765, John Rutledge wrote to his mother, "This is my first trip to a foreign country." To a South Carolinian accustomed to the orderliness and atmosphere of Charleston, New York was indeed culturally and economically strange. Already on its way to becoming the greatest of American ports, it contained a cosmopolitan population—free blacks and slaves, sailors and streetwalkers, shopkeepers and mechanics, merchants and their elegant ladies—in a social amalgam that was neither democratic nor aristocratic, but partook a bit of both. It was a disorderly, noisy, active, dynamic town, and there was something suitable in the fact that the first intercolonial congress was scheduled to meet there. It was also appropriate that this first congress should have been called by Massachusetts radicals, led by James Otis, who saw the necessity of widening their protest against an arbitrary act of the English Parliament.

On October 8th, twenty-seven delegates to the congress gathered in City Hall. They represented nine provinces and all shades of opinion. Timothy Ruggles of Boston was elected president.

TIMOTHY RUGGLES (1711–1795)

Realizing that there was little he could do to prevent the meeting of the Stamp Act Congress, Governor Francis Bernard of Massachusetts saw to it that the Massachusetts delegation contained "prudent and discreet men such as I am assured will never consent to any undutiful or improper application to the Government of Great Britain." [39] One of these prudent men was Ruggles.

Why Sam Adams agreed to the appointment of a conservative to the delegation is hard to say. In 1765, lines between radical and conservative were not so clearly drawn as they would be ten years later. Ruggles, as the son of a Congregational minister, may have appealed to Adams's Puritan prejudices. Perhaps Adams believed that the presence of his radical ally James Otis would offset Ruggles's conservatism. Or perhaps he wished to establish the principle of colonial unity in the face of oppression and was therefore willing to chance Ruggles's conservative inclinations. However, Ruggles's instructions from Bernard would not have pleased Adams: the leader of the colony's delegation was so to influence the congress that it would recommend submission to the Stamp Act until Parliament could be persuaded to repeal it on the grounds that it imposed economic hardships on the colonies. No objections to the Stamp Act on constitutional grounds—which were, according to Bernard and Ruggles, at best questionable—were to appear in the resolutions emerging from the proceedings over which Ruggles presided. To achieve this end, Ruggles appointed men whom he believed were sympathetic to his conservative position to the important committees established by the congress, and through the aid of other conservative members he attempted to dominate discussion on the floor.

Ruggles was an eloquent and shrewd lawyer. From student days at Harvard he had revealed an independence of spirit and "disregard of custom and public opinion." "This Ruggles has an inflexible oddity about him," wrote John Adams, "which has gained him a character for courage and probity, but renders him a disagreeable companion in business." One unfriendly critic told him:

So mightily have you been revered as Chief Justice in the

96

County where you belong, that you could sit upon the Bench, and with your heavy lowering Brows and harsh thundering Voice, sway the whole Bench of Justices, Jurors, and all.[40]

But Ruggles could not exert the same power over the representatives assembled in New York. "They are of various characters and opinions," wrote General Gage, "but it's to be feared in general, that the Spirit of Democracy is strong amongst them." By "Democracy" Gage meant "Independence of the Provinces, and not subject to the Legislative Power of Great Britain." [41]

For twelve days, excluding Sunday, delegates argued, wrote, and rewrote, in order to produce declarations to the King that would represent the colonial point of view while persuading him to adjust their grievances with respect to Parliament. Their central concern involved defining the proper constitutional relationship that ought to exist between Parliament and the colonies, and it was on this definition that opinions strongly differed. The final resolution revealed a compromise. The delegates were ready to declare their "Allegiance to the Crown of *Great-Britain*," but only "due Subordination" to Parliament. The phrase "due Subordination" was taken from William Samuel Johnson's draft "Report of the Committee to whom was refer'd the Consideration of the Rights of the British Colonies," the phrases and vocabulary of which were used by the congress for its final resolutions.

WILLIAM SAMUEL JOHNSON (1727–1819)

William Samuel Johnson was a moderate delegate from Connecticut, whose abilities as a lawyer once led Noah Webster to dub him one of the "Mighties" in his profession. Son of Samuel Johnson, one of Connecticut's most distinguished Anglican ministers, Johnson shared the conservative political attitude of his father who never doubted Parliament's authority in colonial matters. At the same time, he appreciated the traditions of his colony, which next to Rhode Island enjoyed the greatest autonomy from British rule of all the colonies. As a member of Connecticut's Assembly since 1760, he understood, even though he did not completely agree with, the objections of his colleagues to the principle implied in the Stamp Act. Thus he could not agree with Ruggles that Parliament's power included internal taxation. The Stamp Act, he as-

serted, reduced the colonists to "absolute Slaves" and bound them in "Chains and Shackles." But as a prominent lawyer, accustomed to quote from Pope that "whatever is, is right," Johnson abhorred violence and was ready to accept the final authority of Parliament.

The Connecticut Assembly had met at a special session late in August to choose representatives to the Stamp Act Congress. A display of mob rule against stamp distributor Jared Ingersoll, just preceding the opening of the Assembly, had sobered members of the legislature who proceeded more cautiously than usual. The result was a fairly conservative delegation bound by the necessity to submit all decisions made by the congress to the Assembly for legislative approval.

Like most members of the congress, Johnson did not seek a rupture with the mother country; rather, like them, he hoped for redress of grievances. He would have liked the congress to be more explicit in its acknowledgment of parliamentary power, but his fellow members preferred the nebulous phrase "due Subordination." In the interests of unity, he finally acquiesced.

Robert Ogden and Timothy Ruggles did not acquiesce, however, and both refused to sign the proceedings of the congress because it omitted precise acknowledgment of Parliament's authority. Ruggles's refusal to go along with the majority, when he seemed to be in "accord" with their views, incensed Thomas McKean of Delaware, who forthwith challenged him to give his reasons for his refusal. When Ruggles after a pause remarked that "it was against his conscience," McKean

then rung the changes on the word "conscience" so loudly and so long that a challenge was given and accepted between himself and Ruggles in the presence of the congress, but Ruggles left the next morning at daybreak, so that the duel did not take place.[42]

THOMAS McKEAN (1734–1817)

During the Stamp Act Congress, Thomas McKean, a member of the Delaware Assembly, remained at the opposite pole from Ruggles. Hotheaded and proud, the young McKean had become one of the most influential members of the congress because of his membership on the committees that drew up the memorials to the Lords and Commons and that revised the congress's proceedings.

Thomas McKean, attributed to Charles Willson Peale, date unknown.

McKean did not doubt that British constitutional limits provided, as his committee wrote in its petition to the Commons, "the most perfect form of government." Such limits, however, extended to trial by jury and the right to grant "our own property for his majesty's service"—i.e., the right to tax themselves. Neither of these rights could be lawfully abrogated by the Stamp Act. Great Britain, therefore, should repeal the Act which was contrary to tradition, constitutionality, and practical economics.

McKean's insistence upon colonial autonomy derived from the experiences of the three counties on the Delaware he represented, which had become part of the new colony of Delaware only after years of conflict with Maryland and Pennsylvania. Accustomed to fight for their rights against proprietary claims, the people of Delaware had opposed Quaker pacifism during the French and Indian War and by their own efforts, had rid their harbors and cities of pirates and their frontiers of Indians. Having run their own affairs for so long, they were certainly not going to accept an English tax on their legal papers and court

proceedings. Certainly the fiery McKean, long a trustee of the loan office of New Castle County, did not welcome the necessity to affix stamps on every paper issuing from his office.

Their fourteen declarations defined, the members of the Stamp Act Congress traveled home to meet varying receptions. Timothy Ruggles was met by an Assembly ready, at Sam Adams's suggestion, officially to censor his conservative behavior. Several months later, the *Boston Evening-Post* listed him among those who "ought to be HUNG UP and exposed to Contempt."

Johnson, on the other hand, met the approbation of the Connecticut General Assembly, which voted to accept the declarations. The lower house of the Assembly, however, was far more radical in its leadership and rejected Johnson's phrase "due Subordination." Passing its own resolves, the lower house asserted that only members of the General Assembly could legally represent inhabitants of the colony of Connecticut in taxation as well as in all other matters.

McKean had carried out his colony's wishes exactly, and continued to act in the spirit of protest during the months following. Appointed sole notary of the lower counties of Delaware and judge of the court of common pleas in 1765, he ordered that all the court's proceedings be recorded on unstamped paper—the first court in the colonies to so act. By the 1770s, McKean had emerged as one of Delaware's leading critics of British policy.

Repeal

WILLIAM PITT; CHARLES WATSON-WENTWORTH, THE MARQUIS OF ROCKINGHAM (1730–1782); BARLOW TRECOTHICK (1719–1775)

Riots, memorials, pamphlets, outright violation of the Stamp Act, and non-importation agreements in New York and Philadelphia had their effect in London by the end of 1765. American violence and disobedience demonstrated the Stamp Act's unenforceability, while American petitions and pamphlets convinced members of Britain's ruling circles that the Act was unconstitutional. When George Grenville called for a parliamentary resolution urging the King to take all means necessary to enforce the revenue measure, one aging member of the Commons answered that "before he would embrue his hands in the blood of his countrymen who were contending for English liberty, he would if ordered, draw his sword, but would soon after sheathe it in his own body." To Grenville's inquiry as to when Americans had been "emancipated" from their obligation to obey Parliament, William Pitt retorted that he wished to know when "they were made slaves." [43]

Pitt's re-emergence into English politics came after he had already withdrawn into semi-retirement. In poor health, sitting huddled on his bench as the Elder Statesman, already showing signs of the eccentricity that marked his family as "odd," Pitt still had full command of his oratorical powers. But since 1763 he had ceased to lead, having come to believe that "true political moderation consists in not opposing the measures of Government except when great and national objects are at stake." [44] Pitt, however, retained his vision of public service. And the one overriding concept that had structured his earlier vision and brought about his success during the Seven Years' War was his vision of Empire in which the American colonies formed the strongest element. Thus when

Grenville's contemplated revenue policies involving taxation of America began to be described throughout the summer and fall of 1764, he was so disturbed that during the following January he traveled to London to "deliver his mind and heart on the state of America." [45]

Pitt's address to Parliament brought him once again into the forefront of power. Insisting all along that "the Parliament has a right to bind, to restrain America" in trade regulations and manufacturing, he asserted that under no circumstances did "this Kingdom [have the right] to lay a tax upon the colonies." When the opposition charged that he was encouraging sedition in America, he admonished his peers to "be to her faults a little blind/Be to her virtues very kind." Then he added, "Three millions of people so dead to all the feelings of liberty as voluntarily to submit to be slaves would have been fit instruments to make slaves of the rest." The Stamp Act, concluded Pitt, must be repealed "absolutely, totally and immediately." [46]

In the summer of 1765, Grenville's ministry collapsed, not because of the Stamp Act, of which the King approved, but because of Grenville's failure to include the Queen Mother's name in a bill providing for a regency in the event of the King's becoming incapaci-

*Obverse and reverse of a privately minted token saluting
William Pitt, 1766, and the rescinding of the Stamp Act.*

tated. This oversight so angered George III that he set about forming a new ministry. He first looked to Pitt, but the "Great Commoner," able to count on only a small following, declined. As second choice, the King turned to Charles Watson-Wentworth, the second Marquis of Rockingham.

Rockingham was in a weak position when called upon by the King to head a new cabinet. He was young, politically inexperienced, and not liked by the capricious King. A member of a distinguished Whig family, who had long defended constitutional government, Rockingham was sympathetic with American arguments against the Stamp Act. His problem was to reconcile the opposition's determination to assert parliamentary power over the colonies with his own sense that Parliament had gone too far. Turning to Britain's merchants for much-needed political support, he hoped that their loss of American business as a result of the closing of colonial ports and their fear of violence to their vessels by an angry mob would justify repeal of the act, while not calling into question the validity of a policy supported by the King.

In Barlow Trecothick, head of one of London's largest mercantile firms, Rockingham found a solid ally. Trecothick had been raised in Boston and had married a Boston girl, the daughter of the merchant Charles Apthorp. His personal friendships and family connections in America made him sympathetic to the colonial plight. Moreover, American resistance threatened his prosperous colonial trade. If this continued, he predicted, the economic "diseases" now plaguing the nation might become "incurable."

Under Trecothick's urging, merchants of some twenty-six towns petitioned Parliament to repeal the Stamp Act because of its debilitating consequences on their prosperity. As Trecothick forwarded the petitions to the Commons, British legislators were forced to realize that the country's economic welfare was threatened. Trecothick's well-orchestrated movement worked. As Pitt and Barré continued to challenge Parliament's right to tax the colonies, and as some legislators raised the specter of a costly armed confrontation with the colonies should Parliament insist on enforcing the Act, others began to talk of Britain's economic health. In March 1766, Parliament repealed the Stamp Act.

As a salve to the King and Grenville, Rockingham introduced an act asserting the inalienable right and power of Parliament "to bind the Americans in all cases whatsoever." This Declaratory Act was given teeth by the Mutiny Act, which required provincial assemblies to appropriate funds for the quartering and maintaining of British troops in the colonies. Pitt objected to the Declaratory Act and refused Rockingham's solicitations to join his ministry. The King, angered at the repeal of the Stamp Act, which he interpreted as weakening Britain's authority in America, looked around for a replacement for his unsatisfactory minister. Again, his eyes alighted on William Pitt, now considerably weakened physically as well as politically.

Broadside issued jointly by four Boston publishers of newspapers, celebrating the repeal of the Stamp Act in 1766.

This time Pitt heeded the call. He had come to believe that the source of England's difficulties lay in the existence of parties, "factions" that destroyed the "dignity" of the government both at home and abroad. His cabinet reflected the heterogeneous elements that made up British politics—"patriots and courtiers, King's friends and open enemies . . . a very curious show utterly unsafe to touch and unsure to stand on," in Edmund Burke's words.[47] Upon taking office, Pitt accepted a peerage and became Lord Chatham, hoping that the House of Lords would prove less strenuous than the Commons. But the public did not accept his explanation and instead, chose to believe that he was kowtowing to the King; their response was similar to that of the caricaturist who depicted a bandaged, majestic foot emerging from the door of an inn at the sign of "Popularity the blown bladder by W. P." Pitt was believed to have sacrificed his integrity for "a paltry annuity, a long-necked peeress, and a couple of Grenvilles." "The joke here," wrote Lord Chesterfield to his son, "is that he has had a fall upstairs, and has done himself so much hurt that he will never be able to stand upon his legs again."[48]

During the five months Pitt actively engaged in office, he ruled with his accustomed firm hand, and, indeed, with such decisiveness that it is reported Charles Townshend walked out of a cabinet meeting on one occasion muttering, "What inferior animals the rest of us appear."[49] But when Pitt was forced to retire to Bath from early 1767 to October 1768, to a world attended only by his wife and doctor, and the Duke of Grafton assumed the responsibilities of prime minister, the cabinet divided and Parliament became unruly. Chatham's policies were overturned by his colleagues, and on October 15, 1768, Pitt resigned.

Between 1770 and 1773, Pitt's health grew so poor that he rarely attended sessions of the House of Lords. Whatever energies he was able to muster were directed toward forcing the government to take a more peaceful view of the American colonies—to adopt "a more gentle mode of governing America." Reasserting that "this country had no right under heaven to tax the colonies," he warned the House that they must "repeal [America's] fears and her resentments, and you may then hope for her love and gratitude." "You may ravage," he said on May 30, 1777, "you cannot conquer. . . . You cannot conquer the Americans. . . . I might as well talk of driving them before me with this crutch." His last effort in the house, a few weeks before he died, was to continue his protest against the "dismemberment of this ancient and most noble monarchy."[50]

Enter Charles Townshend (1725-1767)

Into the power vacuum created when Grafton took over the ministry from the ailing Pitt stepped the colorful gadfly Charles Townshend, Chancellor of the Exchequer. Elected to Parliament in 1747, Townshend was "the delight and ornament" of the House of Commons—a brilliant man but also one unwilling to accommodate himself to others.

From 1749 on, Townshend occupied a variety of ministerial posts, but he never held a position of influence until 1766, when, upon Grafton's insistence, Pitt offered him the Exchequer. The ministry's disorganized character under Grafton afforded Townshend free rein. In the colonial question, he had long felt that Britain's best interests lay in tightening its controls over America. As a member of the Board of Trade in the early 1750s, he had advocated that salaries of royal colonial officials be drawn from a fund raised in America but immune to the whims of colonial assemblies. That he still harbored hopes for such changes in 1765 was clear in his staunch support of the Stamp Act. Although he favored repeal a year later, he did so only because violent American protest made enforcement impossible. Now, however, Townshend thought he saw a way to bring the Americans to heel in a manner they would accept. What is more, he was in a position to carry out his ideas.

In May 1767, without authorization from the ministry, Townshend presented Parliament with an outline for "improving the system of government in the colonies." Willing to "indulge" America in what he considered its foolish distinction between internal and external taxation, he proposed a tax on all imported lead, printer's paper, and tea. The revenue that would be derived from these taxes he planned to place in a fund for the payment of salaries of royally appointed officials in America. To facilitate the collection of these and other duties, a new Board of Customs Commissioners was to be stationed in the colonies.

Although most of the members of the ministry

agreed with Pitt that it was unwise to impose any tax on the colonies, Parliament on the whole was in the mood for Townshend's proposals. The recent affronts by New York and Massachusetts had left a bitter residue, and most members of Parliament shared the Chancellor's desire to demonstrate Parliament's "indubitable" right to tax British American subjects. Townshend's proposals also promised to compensate for the recent reduction in local land taxes. Predictably, the Townshend Acts were passed with ease.

A FARMER ANSWERS TOWNSHEND: JOHN DICKINSON (1732–1808)

It was soon evident that many Americans would not accept Townshend's distinction between external trade duties and internal taxation. The new duties represented a revenue-raising device, not regulation of trade. To raise revenues without their consent meant taxation without representation.

Among the first to wave the banner of colonial rights in this new crisis was John Dickinson of Philadelphia. In the fall of 1767 he published a series of letters in the *Pennsylvania Chronicle* under the title "Letters from a Pennsylvania Farmer." By winter, newspapers from New Hampshire to Georgia were publishing his serialized challenge to Parliament's right to pass the Townshend duties, and before long, colonists were describing him as that "judicious Farmer," the "Benefactor of Mankind," and the "American Pitt."

As a critic of British politics and policy, Dickinson was no neophyte. The son of a prosperous Delaware lawyer and landowner, he had studied law at London's Middle Temple, and in the course of his four-year stay had viewed first-hand the workings of the home government. British officials seemed to him a dissolute and self-interested lot, ready to sacrifice public welfare for their own profit. The ministers, he wrote home, were men who would "gratify every desire of Ambition and Power at the expense of truth, reason and their country."

Dickinson's jaundiced attitude toward Britain's decision-makers did not change when he returned to America to set up a law practice in Philadelphia. As a member of the Pennsylvania legislature in the early 1760s, he strongly opposed the movement headed by

*John Dickinson as "The Patriotic American Farmer,"
by James Smither, circa 1768.*

Benjamin Franklin to make Pennsylvania a royal colony—not because he approved of the Penn proprietors, but because he feared the change to royal authority would destroy the rights enjoyed by Pennsylvanians.

The Sugar and Stamp acts only increased Dickinson's hostility to Britain's authority. Urging peaceful defiance, he enthusiastically participated in the Stamp Act Congress where he played a pivotal role in drawing up the convention's Declaration of Rights and Privileges. Now in the "Letters" he again rose to the defense of American rights.

The colonists, wrote Dickinson, were the sole judges of whether or not a given financial measure constituted unlawful taxation of the colonies. But there were even worse dangers inherent in the Townshend Acts—especially where they involved salary reform.

Once salaries were free of local legislative control, the Farmer warned, officials would feel free to sacrifice local welfare in the pursuit of selfish ends. Governors who were no longer fearful of alienating assemblies would suffer no qualms in limiting the colonies' elective bodies to legislation "for the yoking of stray cattle."

Dickinson urged Americans to express their dissatisfaction with Britain "sedately." The cause of liberty is "a cause of too much dignity," he observed, "to be sullied by turbulence and tumult." One of the most effective ways to combat the Acts, he suggested, lay in non-importation, which would prevent America's "oppressors [from] reaping advantage from their oppression." [51]

Dickinson's hopes, however, lay in peaceful reconciliation of American and English differences. Bitter alienation between America and the mother country was not his goal. In 1769, he brooded,

How mournful a Reflection is it, that a just Regard for ourselves, must wound Great Britain, the Mother of brave, generous, humane Spirits, the chief Bulwark of Liberty on this Globe, and the blessed Seat of unspotted Religion. [52]

THE CIRCULAR LETTER

While the "Pennsylvania Farmer" fanned colonial indignation with his rustic dissertation on American rights, Sam Adams and his Whig cohorts hatched plans for a new protest. In a Circular Letter, the

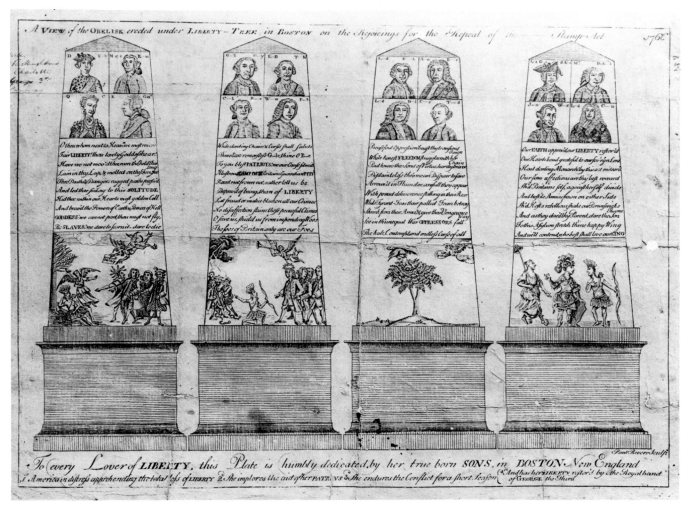

Views of the four sides of the obelisk erected in Boston upon news of the repeal of the Stamp Act. Engraving by Paul Revere, 1766.

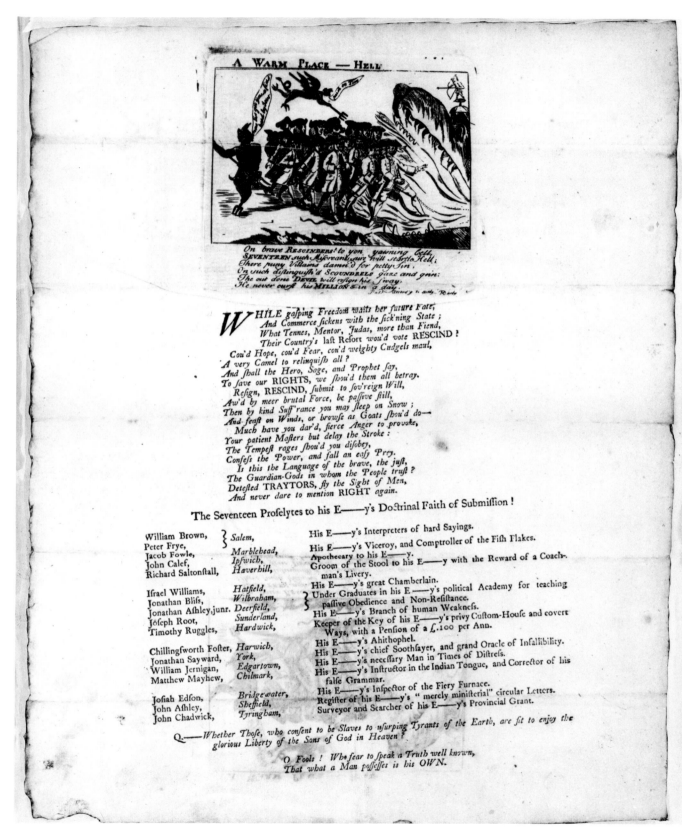

Broadside vilifying the 17 members of the Massachusetts House of Representatives who voted to rescind the House vote on February 11, 1768, to approve the Circular Letter. The flying devil in the illustration shouts "push on Tim" in reference to Timothy Ruggles, a conservative member.

Massachusetts Assembly urged other colonial legislatures to unite with it in informing the King of their collective hostility to the new duties.

Approval for the Letter did not come easily. Adams and his friends in the Assembly had done their best in the years since the stamp crisis to keep anti-British sentiments at a high pitch. Yet, they had lost strength in the recent elections. When the Circular Letter was first presented for a vote early in 1768, the Massachusetts legislature was in no mood to endorse it. But the Adams faction remained patient. Once many of the more conservative representatives left for their homes in the belief that the Assembly had completed its major business for the session, the Adams faction re-introduced its proposal. On February 11, 1768, the Assembly officially approved it. Without delay, the Circular Letter was drawn up and dispatched to the other twelve colonial assemblies for their consideration and approval.

WILLS HILL, LORD HILLSBOROUGH
(1718–1793)

Had Britain passed it off as an innocuous exercise in political rhetoric, the Circular Letter might have earned less attention in the colonial assemblies. But Lord Hillsborough, Britain's newly appointed Secretary of State for the colonies, was unable to shrug off what seemed to him to mark the beginning of an "unwarrantable Combination." While informing Pennsylvania proprietor Thomas Penn that the Letter was not only improper but illegal, he sent his own circular letter to American governors ordering all assemblies to ignore the Letter. If assemblies balked, they were to be prorogued.

Hillsborough was a man of little judgment, as George III later recognized. Benjamin Franklin described him as an amalgam of "Conceit, wrongheadedness, Obstinancy and Passion." Nowhere were Hillsborough's unbending traits more evident than on questions of American policy. As president of the Board of Trade from 1763 to 1766, and again from 1768 to 1772, when he combined this office with his duties as Secretary for the colonies, he was never willing to compromise his belief in the supremacy of Parliament. At one point during the stamp crisis he remarked to an acquaintance that "he would rather see every Man to 50 in America put to the sword than the

Wills Hill, Lord Hillsborough, by Allan Ramsay, 1742.

Stamp Act repealed." [53] His letter to the American governors in 1768 was simply one more manifestation of his inflexible determination to maintain British authority.

Ironically, it was this inflexibility that strengthened America's will to oppose British policy. In Maryland, for example, Assembly representatives drew up their petition to show that they could "not be intimidated . . . doing what we think is right." [54] Philadelphia citizens pushed the reluctant Pennsylvania Assembly to formulate a petition to King and Parliament as a revolt against Hillsborough's "ministerial mandate" which placed them under "the yoke" without allowing them to utter "one groan."

Hillsborough's challenge also inspired a new slogan for American protestors to rally popular opinion. In Boston and the neighboring towns of Newport and Providence, "number 92"—the majority by which the Massachusetts Assembly voted to defy the Secretary's rescinding order—quickly became a catchphrase. Fifteen of Boston's Sons of Liberty commissioned a bowl from Paul Revere celebrating the "Glorious 92."

The "Liberty Bowl" made by Paul Revere to honor the 92 members of the Massachusetts House of Representatives who voted not to rescind the Circular Letter.

The other side of the Liberty Bowl showing inscription and saluting John Wilkes and his North Briton *issue No. 45 wherein he attacked the King and Lord Bute.*

Non-Importation

Non-importation—a boycott of luxury goods—and the encouragement of home manufactures became the second step in the program of Boston's radicals. In October 1767, members of Boston's town meeting approved such a program and recommended it to citizens of neighboring towns. By the spring of 1768, more than twenty Massachusetts towns had agreed to follow the city's lead, as well as communities in Connecticut, Rhode Island, New York, and even distant South Carolina. Gradually, colonial-made homespun changed from a sign of poverty and humble social position to become a badge of honor and the symbol of America's endangered liberties. Spinning bees began to enjoy great vogue. In Newport, tailors offered reduced rates to anyone ordering clothes of locally made fabrics. Funerals, hitherto elaborate affairs requiring expensive imported mourning clothes and rings, became consciously ascetic occasions. When Christopher Gadsden appeared at his wife's funeral in blue homespun, the South Carolina *Gazette* applauded him for the "Patriotic example" he was setting. Rags were saved for paper manufacture, since paper was one of the most indispensable items subject to the Townshend duties. Harvard College demonstrated its concern for American rights by having all theses printed on paper inscribed "Made in New England."

This limited boycott soon proved insufficient. Through the winter of 1767 and 1768, Boston's merchants found themselves increasingly harassed by Board of Customs Commissioners who were stationed there to prevent circumvention of the Townshend duties. Stronger boycott measures were needed. On March 1, 1768, ninety-eight merchants appointed a committee to draw up a new non-importation agreement. Completed and approved at a merchants' meeting three days later, the new resolutions went well beyond the earlier town meeting agreement. Aside from absolute necessities such as salt and hemp, merchants voted to cease importing altogether for a period of one year. They also agreed to urge other towns to follow Boston's example.

JOHN ROWE (1715–1787)

Few subscribed to non-importation more enthusiastically than John Rowe. Rowe had emigrated to Boston from England in 1736 bearing a considerable inheritance from his father and had quickly established himself as a merchant of consequence. Prosperity and English ties, however, did not interfere with his practicality. When the Sugar Act threatened mercantile prosperity, he presided over the drafting of the protest of the Society for Encouraging Trade and Commerce. During the stamp crisis, he worked with Sam Adams to force the opening of the colony's courts.

The coming of the Townshend Acts again found Rowe in the forefront of protest. His days were filled with numerous meetings called to devise ways and means of implementing the city's boycott of English goods. On March 1, 1768, he was chairman of the committee to draw up the city's formal non-importation agreement. Once it was approved, Rowe remained faithful in his attendance at non-importation meetings which supervised enforcement. By the end of 1768, his reputation as a militant leader of Boston's protest had grown to such an extent that upon entering the British Coffee House one October afternoon, he heard himself accused of being a "Damn Incendiary" deserving of nothing less than being "hanged" in his "shoes."

This epithet was hardly to Rowe's liking. Although he continued to support non-importation throughout 1769, he became increasingly disenchanted with the militant intimidation that began to characterize the movement. By the spring of 1770, when Parliament repealed most of the Townshend Acts, removing all duties except the one on tea, the practical-minded merchant believed that the cause was won. By 1770, he was convinced that further agitation would only prove "prejudicial to the Merchants & Trade of the Town of Boston," and during that summer he disassociated himself from non-importation entirely.

THE PATRIOTS' THORN:
JOHN MEIN (? – ?)

Boston's Sons of Liberty described non-importation as a "*pacifik* method of recovering our lost liberties." Nevertheless, fear of violence was a key ingredient in forcing would-be importers to toe the mark. It was said that some opponents to non-importation slept with loaded pistols next to their pillows lest they find themselves visited during the night by Sam Adams's self-appointed guardians of the city's austerity program. In the spring of 1769, handbills listing eleven violators who should not be patronized by patriotic citizens were widely circulated throughout the city. For one violator, James McMasters, balking at non-importation meant being carted through Boston to a gallows where he was advised to quit the city. Even after being forced to flee to New York, violator Nathaniel Rogers did not escape the vendetta of Boston's non-importers. Their letter to the New York Sons of Liberty forced him out of that city too.

Of the violators, none inspired more hatred than John Mein. Having arrived in Boston from Scotland in 1765, Mein began his career in the New World as a bookseller. Within a few years he was engaged in printing American editions of English books and editing *The Boston Chronicle*. Whatever prosperity and comfort he enjoyed, however, came to an end with his fierce opposition to non-importation. By 1769, his defiance of the boycott and his bitter attacks on its enforcers not only ruined his book business, but inspired acts of vandalism. Worse still, two men suffered severe back-alley beatings as a result of their unfortunate resemblance to the vituperative Scot.

Mein, however, managed to even the score. Issue after issue of the *Chronicle* detailed how those "grave well-disposed Dons," who preached boycott, were at the same time violating it. Included in his list of venal hypocrites was John Hancock, who, Mein claimed, was "getting rich" from his dual role as boycott leader and violator. By the end of 1769, copies of Mein's exposés had so bred suspicions among non-importers in the city that the mutual trust upon which the movement's success depended began to weaken.

Mein's position in Boston became, however, impossible. To insure his safety against an openly hostile populace, he armed himself with a pistol. In November 1769, encountering a mob on his way to his lodgings, he drew his weapon in an effort to stave off the sticks and clubs brandished at him. Unfortunately, the gun accidentally went off, wounding a nearby soldier. Mein had no alternative but to flee. Disguised as a soldier, he sought refuge on an English ship which shortly carried him back to Britain.

Non-Importation Spreads

Boston's call for a united American front on non-importation quickly found enthusiastic support among vast numbers of citizens in other towns. By March 1769, all major ports with the exception of Portsmouth were participating in the movement, with more or less success.

On the whole, colonial trade with England fell substantially. Yet, every colony experienced dissension in implementing non-importation. Outright and secret violations were common. By 1770, many merchants and political activists found themselves at loggerheads over the question of whether, in light of increasing violations and pending repeal of the Townshend duties, the boycott should remain in force.

SOUTH CAROLINA:
WILLIAM HENRY DRAYTON (1742–1778)

To South Carolina planter William Henry Drayton, non-importation represented a violation of citizen rights. Drayton, the son of a patrician family related to royal officials in the colony—his uncle was Lieutenant Governor William Bull—opposed any challenge to the British establishment. When Charleston, under the leadership of Christopher Gadsden, drew up its non-importation agreement in 1769, Drayton attacked it violently and soon found himself embroiled in a newspaper war with Gadsden and his Sons of Liberty.

For Drayton, the most deplorable aspect of non-importation was the proscription of violators. Because the agreement to boycott was informal and voluntary, the non-importers, he claimed, did not have the right to blacklist or coerce those who refused to go along. To do so was as much a violation of personal rights as the Townshend Acts themselves. No group had the right to harm others who through exercise of their "free Wills" took issue with them.

Drayton fought a losing battle. By the beginning of 1770, he found it impossible to locate Charleston merchants willing to market his crops. After petitioning the legislature in vain to order the non-importers to desist from persecuting violators, he sailed to England to seek an appointment to South Carolina's Governor's Council. By 1774, however, bitter conflict with South Carolina's Council over its legislative powers and his failure to gain official approval for a lease on public lands turned him into an ardent critic of British policy.

PHILADELPHIA:
CHARLES THOMSON (1729–1824);
JOSEPH GALLOWAY (1731–1803)

Philadelphia was one of the last ports to adopt non-importation. Merchant Charles Thomson deplored the delay. Writing in 1768, he insisted that as long as the city's merchants continued to import, they risked *"destruction"* of their colony.

William Henry Drayton, engraving by Benoît Louis Prevost after a drawing from life by Pierre Eugène Du Simitière.

Joseph Galloway, Speaker of the Pennsylvania Assembly, did not like the Townshend Acts any more than Thomson. But he was more concerned with another scheme, the success of which, he feared, would be jeopardized by a local non-importation movement. Resentful of the power wielded by the Penns, Galloway like Benjamin Franklin agitated to replace the colony's proprietary regime with a royal government; thus, to lose royal goodwill by protesting the Townshend duties was the last thing Galloway wanted. When Dickinson's "Letters" first appeared, he quickly disclaimed them as "mere fluff! Fustian! Altogether stupid and inconsistent." Those in his colony taking up the call for non-importation he called "hot-headed" and "indiscreet." [55]

Galloway had not reckoned with Charles Thomson. His accusations that Philadelphia's merchants were indifferent to the welfare of their colony bore fruit. To

Galloway's distress and Thomson's delight, the city embarked in February 1769 on what was to be one of the best maintained boycotts on the Atlantic seaboard.

RHODE ISLAND:
AARON LOPEZ (1731–1782)

Aaron Lopez, a leading figure in Newport's Jewish community, did not like the Townshend duties but did not accept non-importation either. Having come to Rhode Island in 1752, after fleeing the Inquisition in Portugal, Lopez was just beginning to reach the height of mercantile prosperity in 1769. After years of poor markets and indebtedness, Lopez's efforts to find new markets and diversify his trade were finally being rewarded, and he did not care to sacrifice his economic progress by entering into a non-importation agreement.

Lopez's refusal to participate in Rhode Island's protests may have resulted from his feeling alienated by the colony's refusal to grant him citizenship in 1761. When, two years later, the Rhode Island Assembly formally limited citizenship to professed Christians, Lopez lost hope of ever sharing in the political decisions of his adopted community. A call for economic sacrifice in defense of individual rights under the circumstances must have seemed irrelevant to his own situation.

Lopez's reluctance to cooperate in non-importation aroused bitterness in Newport. His friend Ezra Stiles was especially mortified and hoped that Lopez's behavior would not reflect on Newport's patriotism. Although Lopez was never seriously attacked, boycotting merchants were incensed when they discovered that his cargoes were subject to only cursory inspection by British customs officials, while their much-reduced shipments underwent the most careful scrutiny.

NEW YORK:
ISAAC SEARS (1730–1786);
JOHN LAMB (1735–1800)

The first colonial city to follow Boston's lead, New York was the most successful in maintaining its non-importation agreement. Moderates, conservatives, and radicals alike gave enthusiastic support to the boycott. Long-standing conflict between the provincial council and Acting Governor Cadwallader Colden, the fact that many New York merchants were engaged in trade with the foreign West Indies, and economic unrest affecting all classes had made New Yorkers dissatisfied with the British regime. The dissenting elements—Dutch, French, Swedes, and other nationalities—were reacting strongly against the movement to create an Anglican episcopate in New York City. The province bore an unusually heavy military burden, made heavier by the Mutiny Act of 1765. And, finally, all this unrest and discontent were fused by the skillful efforts of some astute radical leaders, among whom Isaac Sears and John Lamb figured most prominently.

Leaders of New York's Sons of Liberty since the

John Lamb by the 19th-century engraver Joseph Napoleon Gimbrede after a miniature presumably painted from life.

beginning of the stamp crisis, Isaac Sears and John Lamb worked in tandem. Sears, a former privateer and now captain of a sloop that sailed between coastal and Caribbean ports, led the artisans and sailors who habituated the city's docks. John Lamb, an importer of wines, served as propagandist. Both had intimate connections among the affluent merchants of New York City as well as among the lower classes; thus they were able to move from merchant committees to mass meetings and mob activities with an easy efficiency. Taking over an earlier New York organization called "Liberty Boys," they transformed it into the Sons of Liberty. In 1765, they used the group to goad the leading merchants of the city into signing a non-importation agreement while urging the people to carry on business without using stamps. Their efforts contributed to Colden's decision not to enforce the Stamp Act, and to its repeal.

When the Townshend Acts were passed in 1767,

Augustus Henry Fitzroy, third Duke of Grafton, by Nathaniel Dance, date unknown.

New York acquiesced quietly, and for a year accepted the duties. In August 1768, however, the merchants, suffering from an economic depression caused by a British act making the colony's paper money useless, determined again on non-importation, fearful that the act would result in the loss of all their specie. With Lamb and Sears at their head, the Liberty Boys whipped up resentment against British policy. Liberty poles were erected throughout the city, which British soldiers quickly chopped down, much to the inhabitants' chagrin. On January 18, 1770, the mounting tensions climaxed in a riot—the Battle of Golden Hill, in which thirty or forty British soldiers were forced to use bayonets against New Yorkers armed with cutlasses and clubs.

Meanwhile, Lamb, the Liberty Boys' chief correspondent, pleaded with other towns and colonies to continue non-importation. As late as May 1770, when the boycott was all but over, he helped draft a letter to Philadelphia, urging merchants there to hold the line and to ignore rumors of boycott violations.

Sears and Lamb did not have their way. By mid-July New York merchants were sending orders to England. The defection of this most exemplary of the boycotting towns provided the deathblow to an already weakened movement. After venting their spleen against New York's "unaccountable duplicity," towns along the seaboard began resuming "business as usual."

Repeal of the Townshend Duties

AUGUSTUS HENRY FITZROY, DUKE OF GRAFTON (1735–1811)

By 1769, it was clear that the Townshend duties were not filling Britain's coffers as Townshend had hoped. Non-importation had also taken its toll on British merchants who, according to Barlow Trecothick's estimates, lost at least £700,000 in American orders in 1768. Together with news of colonial anger, these factors convinced Britian's decision-makers to rescind their colonial policy.

The man directing the first move for repeal was the Duke of Grafton, who now headed the ministry following William Pitt's untimely illness. Educated in

Advertisement published in a Philadelphia newspaper shortly after the New York merchants decided to break their non-importation agreement.

"the sound system of Locke," and politically bred in England's Whig circles, Grafton was devoted to the great statesman. "I should be willing to serve in any capacity," he once noted, ". . . for him I would take up the spade and mattock." [56] Like Pitt, Grafton opposed taxing the colonies without their consent. Although it was at his suggestion that Pitt had included Townshend in his ministry in 1766, he had not foreseen that Townshend would bypass the administration and win parliamentary approval for his plans for a colonial revenue.

Grafton was at a disadvantage, however. Immature politically, unambitious, and at times indolent to the point where his taste for sporting pleasures sometimes took precedence over affairs of state, he was incapable of winning a repeal policy on his own terms. Although his ministry agreed with him on the necessity for repeal, they refused to revoke all the Townshend duties, and insisted on leaving the tea tax in force as a symbol of Parliament's right to tax. To Grafton's further distress, the majority of the cabinet approved

Lord Hillsborough's letter to the colonies which warned Americans that removal of the duties should not "be taken" as a relinquishing of Britain's "legislative authority" in the colonies. As with the Stamp Act, Britain's policy-makers refused to accept America's constitutional arguments. Instead, they rubbed salt in the wound by reiterating the stand taken in the Declaratory Act.

For Grafton, the cabinet's repudiation of his conciliatory policy meant the end of his ministry. Realizing that he was unpopular with the King, who objected to his extra-marital philandering and other vices, as well as to his desire to placate the colonies, Grafton determined to withdraw from office "at the first favorable opportunity." The chance came early in 1770, when, deserted by many members of his cabinet, who looked to a recovered Pitt for leadership, he presented his resignation to the King. In the spring of 1770, a new ministry, headed by Lord North, guided through Parliament the repeal of the Townshend duties as proposed in Grafton's cabinet.

Bloodshed
on Boston Common

CHARLES PAXTON (1704–1788)

In the fall of 1767, the Board of Customs Commissioners arrived in Boston to administer their offices under the stipulations of the Townshend Acts. Unfortunately, their arrival coincided with Boston's traditionally raucous Pope Day, which commemorated the revelation of the Catholic plot to bomb Parliament. No sooner had they disembarked than they found themselves face to face with holiday marchers wearing banners inscribed, "Liberty, Property and no Commissioners."

Soon, the commissioners were the most "detested" men in Boston. Newspapers described them as degenerate pariahs plotting to extract colonial money to satisfy their insatiable appetite for *"luxury."* American ladies were warned to show their hostility by socially boycotting them.

Of the five commissioners, none was more vilified than Charles Paxton. Paxton was a native of Boston, and for many years had served with an iron fist as the port's surveyor of customs. An outraged mob in 1766 had hastened him out of the country after he had invaded a merchant's warehouse without a warrant. In England, he had urged the establishment of a Board of Commissioners in the colonies to oversee customs collecting, and now he had returned to his native city exercising official authority. He was received with deep-rooted hostility. On March 18, 1768, the anni-

versary of the repeal of the Stamp Act, Bostonians strung his effigy from the Liberty Tree. That night, Paxton's house was surrounded by a group of ominously silent protesters. He and his family passed two more harrowing nights while pranksters harassed the sleepless commissioner with catcalls and yells.

For the first six months, Paxton and the other commissioners stood their ground, going about their unpopular business of seizing goods. Nevertheless, they were not confident they could continue without aid. From early 1768 on, Paxton and his fellow Board members wrote alarmist letters to England and the naval commander at Halifax, pleading for armed forces to insure their safety. In May 1768, the battleship *Romney* and two armed sloops arrived from Halifax.

JOHN HANCOCK (1737–1793)

In reporting their woes to London, the commissioners especially blamed John Hancock for their deplorable situation. In their view, there was enough evidence to place him in irons and try him for royal treason.

Raised by his uncle Thomas Hancock, young John fell heir to a fortune of £70,000. With this, he assumed his position at the top of Massachusetts' mercantile hierarchy. By temperament a seeker of applause, Hancock's entry into politics was to a large extent inevitable. In May 1766, at Sam Adams's urging, the

Charles Paxton by John Cornish, 1751.

Boston town meeting elected him to the Assembly as a reward for his gift to the town of hogsheads of madeira to celebrate the repeal of the Stamp Act.

The Townshend Acts increased Hancock's prominence among Whig activists. Incensed at the thought of additional duties, and even more at the prospect of their strict enforcement by a Board of Customs Commissioners, he applied himself to undermining Britain's new customs schemes. Becoming the cornerstone of Boston's economic boycott, he urged other merchants to resist enforcement. He issued an ultimatum that he would "suffer" no officers "to go even on board of any of his London ships." In the spring of 1768, he declared that he would do his utmost to rid Boston of the commissioners "before Christmas."[1]

When customs officers boarded Hancock's ship *Lydia*—just arrived from London—the arrogant merchant did, indeed, make good his threat that no commissioners would inspect his cargoes. With ten of his strongest employees accompanying him, he boarded his ship and bodily carried the officers out of the hold and from the ship. After a court upheld his high-handed behavior on a technicality, Hancock grew bolder. When his ship *Liberty* arrived in port with a taxable cargo of foreign wines, he arranged to have the customs officer locked in a compartment far away from the goods. Once the wine was unloaded, the officer was freed, but not before he was warned to keep the story of his incarceration to himself if he valued his safety.

A month later, the officer sufficiently recovered his courage to report his experience on the *Liberty* to the Board of Customs. The commissioners were incensed. The time had come, they decided, to squelch Hancock. On June 10, a month after the illicit wine had disappeared into Boston's warehouses, the order went out to have the *Liberty* seized.

The Board quickly learned that to trifle with a Hancock ship was to take on a substantial part of the Boston populace. As sailors from the British man-of-war *Romney* cut the *Liberty* from its moorings and pulled it under the shadow of the battleship, they were pelted with stones and bricks. The crowd then turned on two British customs officers. Fistfuls of dirt and volleys of stones rained upon them. That evening the rioters moved through the streets wielding torches and clubs and breaking the windows of the customs officers' homes. Finally dragging a sailing vessel belonging to a customs official to within sight of Hancock's Beacon Hill mansion, they set it afire.

Although the mob did not regain the *Liberty*, their acts of violence served "sufficient notice" on the commissioners of the hazards now awaiting them in Boston's streets. The next week found them and their families safely ensconced on the *Romney*. From there, they retreated to fortified Castle William.

Reports were sent to London that Boston was ruled by "Rabble." Francis Bernard wrote Hillsborough that he feared the *Liberty* riot was but "a prelude" to still "further mischiefs." The commissioners at Castle William renewed their pleas for military forces. By the end of the summer, preparation for the transport of four thousand British troops to Boston was well under way.

JOSEPH WARREN (1741–1775)

Until early September, most Bostonians were not really certain that they were to be honored with military guests. Once certain of military occupation, however, the town began to seethe. A Whig writer in

The blockade of Boston and the landing of troops on Long Wharf. Watercolor by Christian Remick, 1768.

the *Boston Gazette* guaranteed that the appearance of His Majesty's soldiers would lead to more violence. "I have observed that mobs are represented as most hideous things," he commented. "I confess they ought not to be encouraged; but they have been sometimes useful. In a free Country I am afraid a standing Army rather occasions than prevent[s] them." [2]

While most Bostonians—even many of radical sympathies—fretted over this new portent of violence, Dr. Joseph Warren no doubt smiled approvingly. Described by Governor Bernard as one of the "Chiefs" among Boston's radicals, Warren was not an overnight convert. A constant foe of elitist rule from the days he had participated in Roxbury's democratic town meeting, he had long felt great antipathy for the Oliver-Hutchinson-Bernard clique.

Warren's gift for propaganda quickly proved an asset to Sam Adams's radicals. In 1766, Bernard's veto of Otis's election to the Assembly speakership stimulated him to compose some of the most ruthless public attacks ever made on a royal governor. In a letter to the *Boston Gazette* on this occasion, Warren accused the honorable Francis Bernard of "wantonly sacrific-[ing] the happiness of this Province" to his own vindictive passions. Not long afterward, he likened Bernard to Verres, the plundering governor of ancient Sicily. By 1768, Boston's "Cicero" had grown still bolder. In response to Bernard's veto of the Assembly appointment of six Whigs to the Governor's Council, he charged the Governor publicly with "malice." If American grievances could not be solved through relatively peaceful means, said Warren, then perhaps the sword was the only alternative. In town meetings

following the *Liberty* incident, his committee asserted that colonists were prepared to sacrifice "lives and fortunes" for the cause of American liberty.[3]

In September when the arrival of the troops became certain, Warren's threatening rhetoric turned into actual plans for revolt. His home became the site of a "small private meeting" that included Otis, Adams, and Hancock. According to Bernard's informants, plans were laid there for armed attack on Castle William. That some such scheme was under consideration became clear two days later at Boston's town meeting at Faneuil Hall when Warren and his friends turned the discussion to the question of home ordinance. Pointing at four hundred new muskets stored in the Hall, James Otis declared: "There are the arms; when an attempt is made against your liberties, they will be delivered: our declaration wants no further explication." With that, Boston's freeholders overwhelmingly approved the resolution to carry out the "good and wholesome law of this Province" requiring that every household contain "a well-fixed firelock musket, Accoutrement and Ammunition." [4]

The preparations for local rebellion died aborning. When a convention of representatives from Massachusetts towns gathered in Boston on September 22, convened at the urging of Sam Adams in defiance of Bernard's refusal to call the Assembly, delegates from outlying districts were in no mood to support the Boston conspiracy. Instead, while protesting the coming of troops and Bernard's refusal to reconvene the Assembly, members of the convention pledged obedience to the King and advised fellow colonists "to prevent . . . all tumults and disorders."

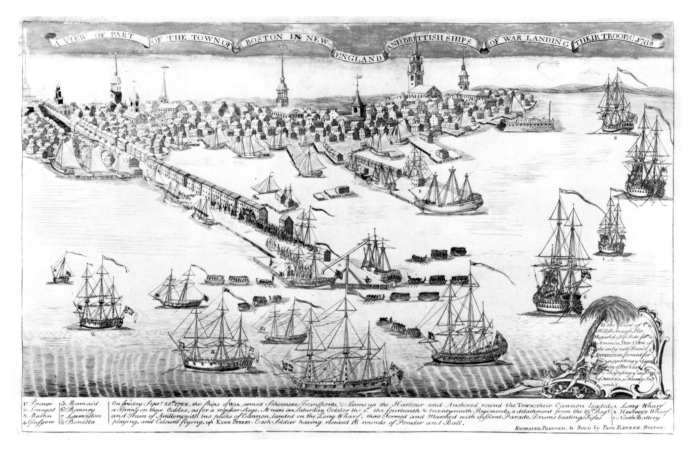

British troops landing in Boston in 1768. Engraving by Paul Revere.

Tension Mounts

Two British regiments arrived on October 1, two more in November. Bostonians lost little time in making their uniformed guests as uncomfortable as possible. Encouraged by Warren, Adams, and other Boston radicals, the townspeople determined to obstruct the quartering of the troops in the town. A New England winter spent in tents was what the soldiers deserved. When regimental commander Lieutenant Colonel William Dalrymple applied to Boston's selectmen for housing, he was cut off with the reply that the matter was no "cognisance" of theirs. The Colonel fared no better when he turned to the radical-dominated Governor's Council. Not until General Gage, Commander of North American troops, arrived from New York in October and demanded that the town accommodate his men, did the Council grudgingly grant the soldiers the use of the colony-owned Manufactory House.

As 1768 wore into the new year, brawling between soldiers and civilians became common. Radical publicists stirred the city with reports—factual and otherwise—of the latest affronts to the people of Boston by villainous Redcoats. According to the *Journal of the Times*, drunkenness, quarrels, thievery, and "beastly" proposals to the town's women were the recreational outlets of the King's troops. Even white hair and old age were no guarantee of female safety, according to the newspaper's editors, who wrote an account of how one uniformed "wretch" attacked an "aged" Bible-reading woman of "piety."

Adding still further to the soldiers' discomfort was Boston's brand of justice. "I don't suppose," Dalrymple complained in October 1769, "my men are without fault, but twenty of them have been knocked down in the streets and got up and scratched their heads and run to their Barracks and no more has been heard of it, whereas if one of the Inhabitants meets with no more than just a Kick for an Insult to a Soldier the Town is immediately in an Alarm and not one word the Soldier says in his justification can gain any credence."[5] This was frequently the case when soldiers found themselves before Whig Justice of the Peace Richard Dana. In fact, on one occasion, Dana instructed a jury to believe "Nothing" of what soldiers said in their own defense, "but Everything in the fullest" said against them. In cases involving theft, some of Boston's judges decided to resuscitate the long-forgotten law allowing the aggrieved to recover triple damages by indenting the convicted thief to the highest bidder.

A grenadier of the 29th Foot Regiment.

By August 1769, when Governor Bernard sailed for England, the tension between townsmen and troops had assumed a nightmarish quality. "I live in hourly dread of disturbance," Dalrymple reported to Gage toward the end of the summer.[6] In September, incensed by the reports of the Board of Customs Commissioners, in which he was cast as chief instigator of Boston's lawless behavior, James Otis strode into the British Coffee House to challenge Commissioner John Robinson to a duel. What began as a fistfight ended in a general mêlée, with Otis bleeding profusely from a blow to the head. The next month Ensign Ness was charged with assault and stealing firewood—falsely it turned out. When soldiers tried to prevent the local constable from arresting the junior officer, a mob began tossing brickbats and stones at the soldiers. In the shuffle, a soldier struck a townsman and it was only by leveling their bayonets that the soldiers succeeded in holding off the crowd.

By the new year, these and other incidents involving the troops were quickly moving to a climax. Sam Adams and his followers attempted to burn the house of a violator of non-importation. They also encouraged school-boy harassment of those who attempted to purchase imported goods. In February, the death of young Christopher Snider, at the hands of a customs officer who had opened fire on rock-throwing boys besieging his house, pushed Boston to the brink of rebellion. In the wake of Snider's funeral procession came cries to rid Boston of its British "Oppressors!" "Like the blood of the righteous Abel," declared the *Boston Gazette*, Snider's death cried for "Vengeance."

The Massacre

Exactly how it happened nobody could say for certain. Whatever the case, Boston was poised for the climactic civilian-soldier violence that broke out on Monday night, March 5, 1770. Although the question of premeditation was never settled, it was said that after soldiers and a group of ropemakers exchanged insults and blows on March 2, "many" in the town were looking forward to "fighting it out with the soldiers." According to a maid in the service of Thomas Hutchinson's sister, bells were to ring on March 5, to signal the moment when townsmen should converge on the soldiers. By the dawning of the fifth, rumors of a fight were rampant in town and barracks.

The day, however, remained peaceful. As the quarter moon rose over the city's snow-covered streets and soldiers took their stations at guard posts, it appeared as if the guards were going to pass a relatively tranquil evening. At the Customs House on King Street, Private Hugh White, walking his post, called to an acquaintance making his way home. Not far away, the captain of the day, Irish-born Thomas Preston, was quietly eating a late dinner at his quarters.

What began as a peaceful evening, however, soon began to erupt. On the walk fronting the Customs House, young Edward Garrick and his companion Bartholomew Broader began baiting sentry White with insults. Angered, the sentry swung his musket and struck Garrick on the side of the head. The noise of the scuffle attracted a crowd. It was not long before the sentry was surrounded by a crowd of fifty taunting him with catcalls of "lousey rascal" and "Lobster son of a bitch!" Now facing a shower of snowballs and chunks of ice as well as insults, the beleaguered White, after knocking fruitlessly at the Customs House door in search of refuge, began crying desperately for help.

Meanwhile, as the bell of Old Brick Church began to peel, townsmen gathered in other parts of the city. While a mob hurled insults at soldiers housed in Murray's Barracks on Brattle Street, a tall red-cloaked figure stirred another mob of some two hundred with harangues against the soldiers. At the end of the speech, the crowd ended their huzzahs with a promise to "do for the soldiers." The bulk of them turned toward the Customs House, where they were joined by the mob from Murray's Barracks. Shouts, bells, and running feet drew others. Young Samuel Gray, on being told that the bells signified an outbreak of fighting with soldiers, enthusiastically ran toward King Street shouting, "Damn their bloods." Crispus Attucks, a forty-year-old mulatto ex-slave, was eating his supper when he first heard the noise; upon finishing his meal, he went out, brandishing a cordwood stick. From still another quarter came Patrick Carr, a fiery young Irish émigré who scurried toward King Street from the home of his employer, breeches-maker Mr. Field.

As the crowd at the Customs House increased, Captain Preston, now at the main guardhouse, "walked up and down," trying to decide how to rescue White from his perilous situation. Finally, on his orders, seven men proceeded with him to King Street where they wended their way to White's side. Standing in front of his men, Preston yelled at the crowd to disperse. The mob returned his yells with insults, followed by taunts daring the soldiers to shoot. Finally, the inevitable happened. After being knocked down by a club-swinging townsman, Private Hugh Montgomery rose to his feet in rage, shouting, "Damn you, fire!" and fired his own gun. As the crowd began to move back from the Customs House, the other soldiers raised their guns for firing. Within seconds, five members of the crowd—Attucks, Carr, Gray, student mariner James Caldwell, and Samuel Maverick, an apprentice ivory-turner—lay dead or dying.

Boston Vindicated

JAMES BOWDOIN, II (1727–1790)

The cry for removal of the troops now turned into a roar. Townsmen crowded into Faneuil Hall the morning after the "Massacre" to hear Sam Adams condemn the "Bloody work in King's Street." In short order they approved plans for a committee to confront Lieutenant Governor Hutchinson with the declaration that "peace" and an end to "blood and carnage" could only be accomplished by "immediate removal of the troops." "The people in general," Whig Councillor Royall Tyler urged, "were resolved to have the troops removed . . . that, failing of other means, they were determined to effect their removal by force. . . ." Even Colonel Dalrymple felt that Castle William might be a better place for the troops who now seemed so "peculiarly obnoxious to the town." Hutchinson finally agreed to the move.[7]

While Dalrymple wrote a military version of the Massacre and Commissioner John Robinson gathered depositions blaming the town's radicals, Bostonians prepared their vindication. By the end of March, silversmith-engraver Paul Revere was advertising his famous engraving depicting the "Bloody Massacre perpetrated in King Street . . . by a party of the 29th Regt." Revere's graphic rendering, however, was hardly the proof of soldier guilt deemed necessary by Adams, Hancock, and the town's selectmen. They required a literary antidote to Robinson's and Dalrymple's efforts.

The task of writing a description of the episode was delegated to Councillor James Bowdoin, a multi-faceted man interested in science, trade, land speculation, fisheries, iron manufacturing, books, and the political life of the province. Bowdoin had always been on easy terms with the royal governors and conservative members of the Council, but when Governor Bernard arrived in 1760, he upset Bowdoin's hope of having his brother-in-law, George Scott, named governor. In 1767, Bowdoin's daughter married John Temple,

The Boston Massacre as engraved by Paul Revere, 1770.

James Bowdoin, II, by Robert Feke, 1748.

Surveyor-General of the Customs for Massachusetts and newly appointed member of the Board of Customs Commissioners. Temple was angry when he discovered that his post on the Board of Commissioners decreased rather than increased his authority, and blamed Governor Bernard for this diminution of responsibility. So did Bowdoin, and from that time on, he stood squarely with the Adams-led Whigs, becoming more and more "virulent" in promoting hostility throughout Boston for both the Board of Commissioners and the Townshend Acts. When Governor Bernard in 1770 vetoed Bowdoin's reelection to the Council, Bowdoin irrevocably aligned himself with Boston's Whigs.

It was with great ardor that Bowdoin now set about freeing Boston from any blame for the Massacre. He and his committee took ninety-six publicly sworn depositions from townsmen who had witnessed the outbreak on King Street and collated them into the "Short Narrative of the Horrid Massacre in Boston." A single deposition that suggested that the crowd on King Street had provoked the soldiers into firing was disposed of with a footnote stating that "no credit"

should "be given" to this witness. The rest of the "evidence" painted the town as innocence itself, and the riot victims as slaughtered martyrs.

Bowdoin added his own summary, claiming that the Massacre had not only been the soldiers' fault, but a plot as well. "There was a general combination among them [the soldiers]," he wrote, "to take vengeance on the town indiscriminately." [8]

Trial

For Captain Preston and his eight men, imprisoned since the night of the Massacre, their coming trial was not a happy prospect. Convinced that they had acted in self-defense, they could not help but feel apprehension after the grand jury charged them with murder. The soldiers knew that many had already judged them guilty. Preston was so certain of Boston's prejudices against him that he felt compelled to write General Gage asking him to apply his "influence" in "petitioning for His Majesty's royal pardon."

Although the indictments were made promptly, the actual trial took some time in coming, due largely to the procrastinations of Thomas Hutchinson. While the Whigs pressed for hasty trial—a group led by Sam Adams even marched into court to register its anger at further delay—Hutchinson found reasons for postponement, the most frequent being the ill-health of the judges who were to preside over the trial. Finally, on October 24, the Massachusetts Superior Court convened in Boston for the trial of Preston, to be followed by the trial of his men.

The Prosecution

Serving the prosecution for the Crown were Samuel Quincy and Robert Treat Paine. Actually the King's attorney, Jonathan Sewall, should have held this position; but because of his sympathy for the soldiers, Sewall decided to have nothing to do with the trial. After drawing up the soldiers' indictments, he washed his hands of the whole affair and disappeared from the city, swearing he would never appear in a Boston courtroom again. As Sewall's solicitor general, Quincy succeeded him. Whigs questioned the conservative Quincy's trustworthiness and willingness to construct a strong case against the soldiers. As a safeguard, they maneuvered the appointment of a special counsel more to their liking. Their man was Robert Treat Paine.

SAMUEL QUINCY (1734–1789)

Born in Braintree outside of Boston, reared in a prominent family, and educated at Harvard, Sam Quincy had many friends among Boston's radicals. His brother Josiah—then serving as a member of the soldiers' defense—was, in fact, a "spirited" defender of American "Liberty" and "Freedom." Samuel himself had been known to speak out against British policy during the Stamp and Townshend crises.

But Quincy had served under the conservative Sewall and he was known to take the safe path when faced with a political decision. As he later said to his sister, "I am but a Passenger, and must follow the fortunes of the day." [9] Despite his competence as a lawyer and his likeability—John Adams once described him as an "easy, social and benevolent com- panion"—Quincy had a tendency for self-deprecation. As a young man, he had confessed to John Adams that he would never make a significant mark in the law. Although admission to the bar evidently raised his self-esteem, he never became the assertive individual his brother was.

ROBERT TREAT PAINE (1731–1814)

Quincy's fellow prosecutor was Robert Treat Paine, whose sharp and sometimes flip humor was once described by John Adams as verging on the "impu- dent." The son of a minister-turned-merchant, he had spent the first few years of his adult career moving from one enterprise to another. Plagued by ill-health as well as the usual problems of a struggling lawyer, he doubted that he would ever realize success. "I have now neither Health enough for an active life," he told John Adams, "nor Knowledge enough for a sedentary one." [10] His move to Taunton in 1761 brought a change in his fortunes professionally as well as person-

Samuel Quincy by John Singleton Copley, circa 1767.

Robert Treat Paine by Edward Savage, begun in 1802.

ally. By 1770, he had settled down to a lucrative practice and happy marriage.

Although not a political ideologue, Paine, nevertheless, was well known for his opposition to British policy. Describing November 1, 1765, the date set for implementation of the Stamp Act, as that "Ill boded dreaded never to be forgotten" day, he led the struggle to force the courts in nearby Plymouth to proceed despite the lack of stamps. In 1768, he was a delegate to Sam Adams's abortive Massachusetts Convention. Yet, however respected his militancy, Boston's Whigs took no chances with their hand-picked prosecutor. Accompanying the letter notifying him of his appointment was a copy of Bowdoin's "Narrative" to put him into the proper "Spirit of the thing."

The Defense Lawyers

Whatever their politics, lawyers in Boston abhorred the thought of taking on the task of defending the soldiers, fearing for their safety as much as for their

Robert Auchmuty, attributed to Robert Feke, 1748.

future popularity. Nevertheless, by the end of March, the services of three lawyers—Robert Auchmuty, Josiah Quincy, and John Adams—had been secured. Later Sampson Blowers replaced Auchmuty on the defense.

Auchmuty's presence on the defense was no surprise in light of his loyalty to the colony's royal establishment. Nor was Blowers's, whose family had long been intimately connected with Hutchinson. In the case of Quincy and Adams, however, many townsmen were taken aback. As widely known for their Whig sympathies as for their legal talents, they now stood as traitors to the cause in the eyes of many radicals. "Good God!" Josiah, Sr., exclaimed. "Is it possible? I will not believe it." [11]

JOSIAH QUINCY, JR. (1744–1775)

Of Josiah Quincy, Jr., one Whig contemporary once observed: "He is a person of more than common powers, of sprightly genius, thorow [sic] acquaintance with the constitution and laws of the country, and a perfect friend to the principles of true liberty." [12] Actively opposed to Britain's imperial establishment since 1767, Quincy had to a large extent inherited his anti-British outlook from his wealthy merchant father, who had learned first-hand on a trip to London of England's deplorable ignorance of American conditions. Complementing this was a highly emotional temperament which John Adams once described as "impetuous and vehement."

When Quincy took his place among Boston's Whig publicists, his attacks on British policy were among the most virulent and eloquent. Only Sam Adams and perhaps Joseph Warren came close to equaling the venomously lucid pen he wielded. "Already the minions of power," he declared of Bernard and Hutchinson, "in fancy, fatten and grown wanton on the spoils of the land. . . . In the imaginary possession of lordships and dominions, these potentates and powers dare tell us that our only hope is to crouch, to cowl under, and to kiss the iron of oppression." [13]

It was not just his extraordinary gift for words that made Quincy an outstanding figure among the Whigs. It was also his advanced view of the Anglo-American conflict. "Blandishments will not fascinate us, nor will threats of 'halter' intimidate," he proclaimed in the fall of 1767. "For under God, we are determined, that wheresoever, whensoever, or how-

Josiah Quincy, Jr., by Gilbert Stuart, 1825.

remarked, "Council ought to be the very last thing that an accused Person should want in a free country." With that he offered his "assistance." [16]

Although sympathetic to Boston's radical faction and on easy terms with many of its members, including his cousin Samuel, Adams had often remained aloof from certain aspects of the colony's political protests. Adams became thoroughly committed to Whig ideals after hearing James Otis's spirited attack on the writs of assistance in 1761; however, he could not join in the rabble-rousing tactics of his political allies. Always distrustful of the "People" and the extremities to which they might go once stirred to "passion," he eschewed the heated rhetoric in which Warren and cousin Sam indulged. When Warren, in the midst of the Townshend crisis, pleaded with him to "harangue" a town meeting, he flatly refused, declaring, "That way madness lies." Instead, Adams limited his efforts in the colonial cause to abstract legal arguments and orderly petition. In the Stamp crisis, while abhorring the violence done to Hutchinson and

soever, we shall be called to make our exit, we will die freemen." [14]

If such statements were representative of his convictions, why did Quincy undertake the defense of the soldiers? Part of the answer lay simply in the fact that Quincy was a lawyer, trained in the ideals of English law. The soldiers, he wrote in response to his father's expression of shock, were *"not yet legally proved guilty"* and therefore were "entitled, by the laws of God and man, to all legal counsel and aid." This being the case, his "duty as a lawyer" obligated him to come to their assistance.[15]

JOHN ADAMS (1735–1826)

John Adams himself told how he came to defend the men whose very presence was "proof" enough for him of Britain's "determination . . . to subjugate Us." According to his account written more than thirty years later, the tearful pleas of a loyalist merchant on Preston's behalf convinced Adams to take the case. He

John Adams by Benjamin Blyth, circa 1766.

Oliver by the "Rabble," he employed himself in writing a tract citing historical precedents for the colonies' objections to Grenville's policies. In the Townshend protest, his chief contribution was his skillful courtroom defense of Hancock against charges resulting from the *Liberty* incident.

At the intervention of Sam Adams, who obviously did not hold it against his cousin for accepting the soldiers as clients, he was elected to the Assembly in June 1770. Recalling his reaction many years later, he remarked that it was only "a sense of duty" that caused him to accept this office which now promised to destroy all the "bright prospects" of his legal career toward which he had labored so hard. Yet it was not just election to the General Court that disturbed Adams in 1770—there was also the question of what his role in the forthcoming trial would do to his reputation.

The Trials

Preston's trial opened in late October. The first move was lost by the Whigs. For some inexplicable reason, the jury leaned heavily to the conservative side, consisting of a large number of men known for their staunch loyalty to the Crown. Indignant Whigs insisted that the jury was packed, but despite these allegations, the prosecution began constructing its case. The prosecution was well on its way to success when two witnesses precisely described Preston's appearance on the night of March 5, and then repeated his instructions to his soldiers, ordering them to open fire on the crowd. In his summation of prosecution testimony, Sam Quincy strengthened the case by citing precedents asserting that any "cruel act" done "voluntarily," whether planned in advance or the result of a split-second decision, constituted malice aforethought and was therefore punishable under the law.

As Quincy and Adams called their witnesses, the certainty of Preston's utterances to his men, so carefully established by the prosecution, was replaced by a picture of confusion—especially when Richard Palmes took the stand. The order to fire, Palmes swore, could not possibly have come from Preston, who at that instant was staring directly into Palmes's face just a few feet away. Adams increased the credibility of this "most material witness" by alluding

to Palmes's well-known Whig sympathies and the fact that he had little reason to protect the soldiers. The testimony of Crown witness Theodore Bliss, who claimed to have heard Preston order the firing, lost all credibility when an acquaintance testified that Bliss had told him shortly after the Massacre that he did not think Preston had given the order after all. The incriminating testimony by prosecution witnesses, Adams declared, resulted from the "passions" of the times rather than honest recall and thus, although given by normally honest men, was totally unreliable.

After Adams's summation, Paine did his best to rescue the case, but without success. When the jury returned to the courtroom on October 30, after three hours of deliberation, it reported a verdict of not guilty.

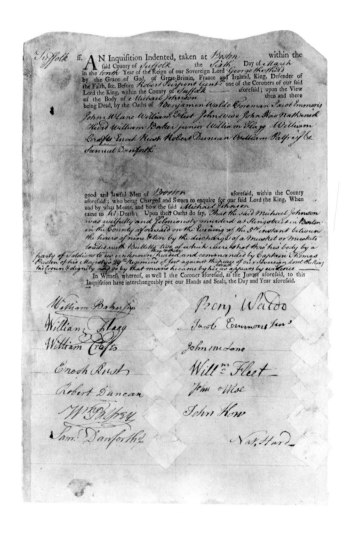

The coroner's report on the body of Crispus Attucks, alias Michael Johnson.

If acquittal brought joy to Preston, it boded poorly for his eight men who were now to be tried. For, if he had not given the order to fire, the soldiers must have fired on their own initiative and were therefore guilty of willful murder.

For a while it seemed that Paine and Sam Quincy would succeed in establishing the soldiers' enmity toward Boston and thus their guilt. Twelve-year-old John Appleton described how soldiers had cornered him in an alley and announced to the cowering lad, ". . . damn you, we'll kill you all." For Matthew Kilroy, identified as the one who shot Samuel Gray, Crown testimony proved particularly damaging. According to one witness, Kilroy said that "he would never miss an opportunity . . . to fire on the inhabitants and that he had wanted to have an opportunity ever since he landed." [17]

Adams and Josiah Quincy now brought on witnesses to demonstrate that crowd intimidation, not soldier hostility, had brought about the events on King Street. After warning the jury to exercise "caution" in reaching their decision, lest it prove a "stain" on "our humanity," Quincy brought on witness after witness who told of townsmen rushing to the Customs House, armed with sticks and clubs. In one instance, the court heard how "martyr" Crispus Attucks had picked up two clubs from a woodpile, giving one to a friend and keeping one for himself. Others reported seeing members of the crowd actually strike the soldiers. The high point for the defense came when Dr. John Jeffries, who had attended Massacre victim Patrick Carr, took the stand. According to Jeffries, Carr had confessed that the soldiers were provoked by the crowd. When asked by the doctor why he thought the soldiers had opened fire, the dying Carr replied that it was to "defend themselves."

After reminding the jury of the "snowballs, oyster shells [and] white brick sticks" the mob wielded, Adams summed up: ". . . I believe [the civilians] would not have borne one halfe of what the witnesses have sworn the soldiers bore, till they had shot down as many as were necessary to intimidate and disperse the rest." [18] Against such statements, Paine, "much fatigued and unwell," was no match. In fact, he even began his closing remarks admitting that he knew he had "the severe side of the question to conduct."

The jury agreed. After two hours of deliberation, the foreman declared six of the defendants not guilty. Matthew Kilroy, charged with killing Gray, and Hugh Montgomery, who had fired the first shot, were

Broadside utilizing a woodcut of the Boston Massacre, issued in 1772.

found guilty of manslaughter. But even they escaped with only token punishment when John Adams pleaded "benefit of clergy" on their behalf. The clerical penalty for manslaughter was a branding on the convicted man's thumb.

Although Sam Adams, under the name of "Vindex," railed at the miscarriage of justice in the *Boston Gazette*, most Bostonians, weary from the upheavals of the previous year, reacted passively to the results of the trials. So peaceful was Boston by the end of 1770, in fact, that even the hated Board of Customs Commissioners, just returned from Castle William where they had exiled themselves before the Massacre, experienced no "Insults" or "Molestation."

Quiet Rumblings

When the New York merchants agreed to break the non-importation agreement, they brought a temporary halt to the revolutionary movement that had been gathering momentum with the passage of the Townshend Acts and the spilling of blood on Boston Common. With the repeal of the Townshend duties in 1770, "political Lethargy" set in. "The Spirit of Patriotism seems expiring in America in general," radical leaders complained as they searched for issues that would reawaken the colonists' hostilities to the mother country.[1]

Prosperity marked these years. After 1770, British manufacturers provided luxury-loving Americans with the rich textiles and elegant coaches they had eschewed during the earlier boycott. Spinning wheels were put aside, as homespun became unfashionable. Everything, wrote a Philadelphian, "is as we would wish and nothing but some unhappy misunderstanding with the Mother Country can hurt us."[2] Conservative Tories toasted "Confusion to S. Adams and party"— and turned their attention to business, instead of taking advantage of the lull to build their own power structure. Governor Hutchinson of Massachusetts might warn them that they did not live "in the Commonwealth of Plato but in the dregs of Romulus," but, like their Whig opposition, they were too intent upon enjoying the prevailing harmony to prepare for future crises.

Colonists, however, could never remain completely free of politics. If they had no issue with Lord North's administration—which, indeed, was eager to prevent American affairs from disturbing parliamentary debates—they could find something to disturb them in provincial politics. Royal governors seldom agreed with the assemblies; assemblies were occasionally at odds with the people. Class distinctions, geographical divisions, religious controversies, and ethnic and racial variations disrupted the harmony of the domestic scene even when England kept its hands out of colonial affairs. In the friction that was created by the constant irritation of group against group lay the seeds of further dissatisfaction with British rule.

The Regulators in North Carolina, 1765-1771

In 1770, the finest "government house" in the land— the Governor's Palace—was completed in New Bern, North Carolina. Construction on it had begun in 1767 under the supervision of the London architect John Hawks, who had been brought by Governor Tryon from England specifically for the task. Its two main stories and two wings connecting with the main building by semicircular colonnades had involved the

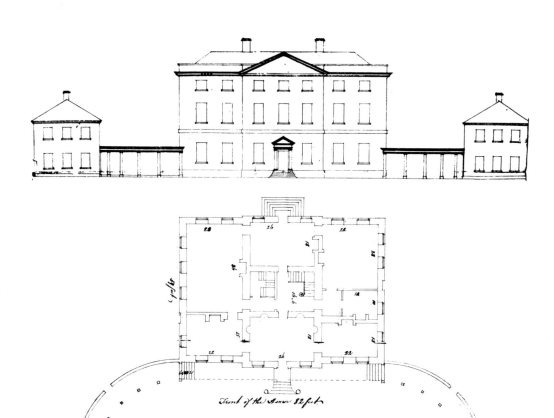

Drawing of the plan and elevation of the north front of the governor's palace in New Bern, North Carolina, by John Hawks, 1766.

expenditure of large sums of money, most of which had to be collected in higher taxes imposed upon the colony. But its planners thought that the cost was warranted by the symbolic role the Palace would play in North Carolina society. Above the vestibule door, in Latin, read the inscription, "A free and happy people, opposed to cruel tyrants, has given this edifice to virtue. May the house and its inmates, as an example for future ages, here cultivate the arts, order, justice, and the laws." [3]

To the settlers of the back country, the house was a waste of money. It was not, they believed, devoted to virtue, nor did they consider themselves a free and

happy people. They found the necessity to pay for the "unnecessary building" an odious burden and they refused to carry it. "We want no such House, nor will we pay for it," said the farmers of Orange County in 1768. "Good God, Gentlemen," exclaimed another group of back-country petitioners, "what will become of us when these demands come against us? Paper money we have none [;] Gold or Silver we can purchase none." [4]

The aristocratic leadership of the tidewater plantations, however, who were active in planning the Governor's Palace paid little attention to the cries of distress coming from these "poor Wretches." For years, they had enjoyed control of the province by limiting piedmont counties to two representatives each in the Assembly despite their large and increasing population. Tidewater control of the Assembly, in turn, gave the easterners control over recommendations made to the governor of provincial officers. Official position became the gift of the "sheriff and his bums" and no officers were chosen by popular vote. Multiple office-holding increased the viciousness of the system and made possible corruption and malpractice on a large scale. Against the extortions of the officials, the poor settlers had no defense.

The back-country settlers, however, were not easily intimidated. Bold emigrants from Ulster and Germany, these Protestant dissenters were shrewd and intelligent fighters. In 1759, they had rioted in Halifax County (N.C.) because of maladministration; in 1765, they had organized a rent riot, called "the war of Sugar Creek," in Mecklenburg County. By 1766, they began to organize even more efficiently to end the abuses under which they suffered. Adopting the name Regulators from an earlier movement in South Carolina, which had been organized to protect the people of the back country against the lawless Schofilites who were robbing and terrorizing them, the North Carolinians saw their organization as a similar people's movement designed to bring justice to the piedmont settlers.

"Regulator Advertisement Number 1," written by Hermon Husbands, called on the people of North Carolina to resist oppression by means of forcing court officials and assembly delegates to account for their expenditure of tax money at annual meetings with the settlers. The first meeting was to be held at Maddock's Mill in Orange County, a "place where there is no liquor." The Regulators, in calling this meeting, thought of themselves as Sons of Liberty and hoped to redeem the people "from tyranny."

HERMON HUSBANDS (1724–1795); EDMUND FANNING (1739–1818)

Born a Quaker, Hermon Husbands believed in the ideals of the Quaker faith. But as a result of a theological disagreement between himself and the church's leaders in Cecil County, Maryland, where he was born, Husbands was disciplined by the church and deprived of fellowship. In November 1755, he moved to North Carolina and soon began cultivating a grant of 640 acres on Deep River. By 1765, his holdings had extended to about 8,000 acres, and through his integrity and modesty he had earned the respect of his fellow settlers.

Husbands derived many of his political ideas from the writings of Benjamin Franklin in the Pennsylvania *Gazette*. He also read widely in other eighteenth-century publications, many of which were concerned with questions of a political and social nature relating to the rights of man. His various Regulator resolutions, and especially his narrative history of the Regulator uprising—*An Impartial Relation of the First Rise and Cause of the Recent Differences, in Publick Affairs, in the Province of North Carolina* (1770)—reflect these influences.

Husbands frequently found himself caught between his Quaker conscience—although he was not a pious man—and his worldly ambitions. On several occasions, this conflict made him hesitate to participate in acts of violence and when he was in danger, "shuffle, dodge, and lie." He much preferred to use the weapons of peaceful persuasion, and through the organization of public opinion, bring about the desired reforms.

After ten years in the colony, Husbands had become quite aware of the difficulties under which the farmers labored. It was his idea to have twelve representatives of the people meet with the officers of the county at Maddock's Mill in October 1766, to resolve their differences peacefully. He did not count on the refusal of Edmund Fanning, assemblyman from Orange County, to be "summoned to a mill" and "arraigned at the bar of the people's shallow understanding."

Edmund Fanning was a native of Long Island, New York, a graduate of Yale, and a client and friend of Governor William Tryon. The multiple offices he held in North Carolina reveal not only a successful career but suggest that he was truly a young man "on the make" and an "honest grafter." He was registrar of deeds, justice of the peace, colonel of the militia, assemblyman from Orange County, and leader of the "ring" in that county. From each of these offices, he extracted all that he could, and soon became enormously wealthy. He was, said the Regulators, a member of that group of "cursed, hungry Caterpillars, that will eat out the very Bowels of our Commonwealth if they are not pulled down from their Nests in

Edmund Fanning
by Thomas Goddard, date unknown.

a very short time." [5] The songs composed by the Regulators revealed the contempt in which Fanning was held by his largely illiterate neighbors:

> When Fanning first to Orange came
> He looked both pale and wan,
> An old patched coat upon his back
> An old mare he rode on.
>
> Both man and mare wa'nt worth five pounds
> As I've been often told,
> But by his civil robberies
> He's laced his coat with gold. [6]

When Fanning refused to attend the meeting called by "Regulator Advertisement Number 1," calling it insurrectionary and extralegal, the other officers also refused, and no conference took place. Similar conferences called for Anson, Granville, Halifax, and other piedmont counties also failed to materialize. By 1768, the area seethed with discontent, to some of which Husbands contributed through his pamphlets and exhortations. In April 1768, he formally organized his neighbors into a society called "The Regulation"—which he, however, never joined—and tied them to the organization with an oath. "We will pay no more taxes until we are satisfied they are agreeable to law and applied to the purposes therein mentioned," their platform insisted. [7]

Soon the back-country people were given the opportunity to test their oath. When the sheriff of Orange County, early in February 1769, posted at the Hillsboro Courthouse a notice indicating that he and his deputies were ready to collect taxes for that year, they refused to pay them. In response, the sheriff seized the horse, saddle, and bridle of a dissenting Hillsboro farmer. So important were horses to yeoman farmers of this area that the theft of one was commonly punished by death. The sheriff's act, then, seemed a deliberate provocation; to the settlers it represented simply another example of official thievery. On April 8, 1769, about seventy Regulators rode into Hillsboro, tied the sheriff to a tree, freed the horse, and as they were parting, fired a few random shots into the roof of the house of Edmund Fanning, who had sponsored the tax acts.

Wild rumors flew through the countryside that the war had begun, that the Governor had aroused the Indians who were coming to massacre the settlers, that the leaders of the Regulators had been arrested and hurried off to New Bern where they were to be tried and hanged, and that the Regulators were planning to march on Hillsboro to murder its inhabitants and burn the town. In this anxious situation, Fanning called upon the local militia to suppress "rioting and rebellion" and asked Governor Tryon to send aid. Now sympathy began to turn against the Regulators, and the fact that Fanning and his fellow officers were corrupt officials responsible for the uprising became buried under Fanning's assertion of the necessity to restore law and order.

As a Quaker who hated violence, Husbands took no part in this initial act of defiance, but remained at his plantation tending to his chores. Because he had been so active in initiating the Regulator movement, however, and had written what were considered incendiary pamphlets, he was arrested on charges of "inciting the populace to rebellion" and in September 1769 was tried along with the arrested leaders of the Hillsboro disturbance. Husbands was acquitted, but the other Regulators were not. Standing trial at the same time for taking excessive fees as registrar of deeds was

Edmund Fanning. Although he too was found guilty, his penalty was a fine of "one penny and costs." The Regulators had to await pardon from the Governor before they were released from prison. The obvious favoritism shown Fanning incensed the Regulators even more against officialdom.

In 1769, Husbands was elected to the legislature from Orange County, but Fanning was also chosen from Hillsboro, a "pocket borough" recently created by Tryon who was trying to get a friend into the legislature—or so the Regulators charged. Other Regulators were elected from Anson, Granville, and Halifax counties. They presented Regulator grievances to the Assembly, but four days after the first meeting, Governor Tryon dismissed the legislature and prevented any possible action. As the Regulator organization expanded, disorders continued, until finally the Assembly met once again to pass the Johnston Riot Act which attempted to impose stringent provisions on the farmers to prevent further rioting.

Husbands was expelled from the Assembly on trumped-up charges of libel and for not being "a credit to the Assembly." Jailed for libel in New Bern, Husbands was just released when a large group of Regulators began to march on the capital to rescue him and presumably to burn down the town. To meet the marching farmers, Tryon called out over fourteen hundred militiamen. Riding at their head, he encountered the militant settlers—approximately two thousand of them—at the Great Alamance Creek, a few miles west of Hillsboro. Many of the farmers had come along simply to present their cause to Governor Tryon, but when they sought an audience with him, he refused to confer until they laid down their arms and dispersed. He gave the farmers an hour in which to comply with his conditions. But

the ill-fated people seem not to have realized their position. . . . They had not the least idea of what a battle was, and when their envoy returned to report his failure [to see the Governor] and to advise them to go to their homes they stood stolidly in their places. . . . So unconscious were the men of their danger that they were engaged in wrestling matches, when an old soldier who happened to be among them advised them to look out for a volley. It was but a few minutes before the firing began. . . . All agree that [the first shot] came from the governor's side.[8]

The farmers took to the trees and "much annoyed the [militia] men who stood at the guns." When the artillery was unable to penetrate the foliage, Governor Tryon ordered his first line to advance and flush out "the rebels from their covering." At the advance of the militia, the Regulators fled, leaving behind their horses, provisions, and ammunition. Both sides lost nine men, but Tryon reported that the battle was "a signal and glorious victory . . . over the obstinate and infatuated rebels."[9]

Husbands had been present at the Alamance, but when it became clear that peaceful means had failed, he rode away before a shot was fired. Once the Regulators were crushed, however, the government named him one of the perpetrators of the uprising. Outlawed, and with a price on his head, Husbands fled, first to Maryland and then to Pennsylvania, where he spent the remainder of his life.

Fanning, too, left North Carolina. Accompanying Governor Tryon to New York where the Governor was transferred in 1770-71, he soon received the lucrative office of surrogate of the City of New York and surveyor-general of the Province. He served actively in the war in the British army, and died in England in 1818.

Twelve Regulators were tried for treason after the Battle of Alamance and all were convicted. Six were hanged and the rest pardoned. Within six weeks, over six thousand Regulators had accepted Tryon's offer of clemency and laid down their arms; many left North Carolina. All that remained of the Regulator movement were its songs, poems, and legends.

The Alamance battle was not "the first battle of the American Revolution," as it has been said. It marked the high point and end of the revolt of the western settlers against the oppressive laws of the eastern majority and corrupt local officials. Although the movement collapsed in 1771, the fight for justice in the back country continued until the Revolution. The fact that the corruption of colonial officials and a corrupt system were countenanced by a royally appointed governor made some of these back-country settlers ready to oppose British policy in 1776. The British were also associated with the wanton expenditure of good tax money on a luxurious "Palace," designed by an Englishman for an English governor. But the settlers were also bitter against the colonial planters of the eastern and northern counties who had usurped power in North Carolina. Their bitterness against all government created a climate of dissent particularly suitable for breeding revolutionary ideas and practices.

The Wilkes Fund Controversy, South Carolina, 1769-1775

In 1770, Parliament refused to seat John Wilkes, duly elected representative from the county of Middlesex. John Wilkes had been a thorn in Parliament's side since 1763, when he had issued *The North Briton No. 45*, a criticism of George III's speech from the Throne, suggesting that the King was covering up the lies of Lord Bute's ministry. His attack on the King so irritated George and his Court that Wilkes was arrested for seditious libel and later denied his parliamentary seat. As a result of his arrest and punishment, Wilkes became a *cause célèbre* for both Englishmen and Americans who saw him as a symbol of the fight they were waging for their constitutional liberties against the despotism of the King.

John Wilkes was a radical newspaper editor and writer who had been educated somewhat above his social station as a result of an early display of intelligence and capacity. Having married a wealthy heiress ten years his senior, with the proceeds of her estate he turned to the pursuit of fashionable vices while purchasing a seat in Parliament. In Parliament, he became a loyal supporter of Pitt and Pitt's brother-in-law, Lord Temple, through whom he hoped to obtain a lucrative and pleasant post either in Constantinople or Quebec. Disappointed, he attributed his failure to the malice of Lord Bute, who disapproved of Wilkes as much as Wilkes did of Bute's foreign policy and governmental ideas. His antagonism to Bute's government led him to purchase *The North Briton* and to use its pages for repeated jabs at the hapless minister; at one time he hinted at immoral relations between him and the Dowager Princess, while at another time, he mercilessly lampooned him.

Wilkes's arrest coincided with the wholesale dismissal of Whigs and their friends and dependents from government office by Lord Bute's Tory ministry. The two events convinced many Britons and Americans that George III and Lord Bute had taken despotic control over the government. When Wilkes's home was invaded by the King's messengers armed with a general warrant for the editor's arrest, it seemed clear to many Englishmen that their constitutional liberties were endangered. William Pitt saw the situation as involving the issues of freedom of the press and the illegality of general warrants. Wilkes, as a member of Parliament, should have been immune to arrest. Now "the personal freedom of every representative of the nation [was] at the mercy of His Majesty's Attorney-General," declared Pitt.[10]

When Wilkes was deprived of his parliamentary seat after being reelected by Middlesex County, another issue—the right of the electors to have a representative of their own choice seated in Parliament—focused on principles near to the colonists' own experiences.

In the colonies, the main surge of sentiment on behalf of Wilkes came between 1768 and 1770. It gathered strength from the fact that London merchants who supported Wilkes also supported the repeal of the Stamp Act. The Wilkes case continued to exacerbate feelings in South Carolina, however, long after 1770, when it became the center of an argument between the South Carolina Commons and the royal governor and Council over the right of the Commons to spend or to tax on its own authority for objects desired by the colony's inhabitants.

In 1769, a committee of "Supporters of the Bill of

John Wilkes by Robert Edge Pine, 1768.

Rights" was established in London to pay off Wilkes's many debts. To this committee, the Commons of the South Carolina legislature voted to contribute £1,500 sterling, for the "support . . . [of] the Just and Constitutional Rights and Liberties of the People of Great Britain and America."[11] Since the order of the treasurer was issued without the consent of the governor or Council, the Wilkes Fund, as it came to be called, became an object of concern to London officials, who threatened to remove the acting governor, William Bull, if he assented to such a measure, and the colony's treasurer if he issued money without the consent of the governor and Council.

WILLIAM BULL (1710–1791)

William Bull was born at Ashley Hall, South Carolina. His family had long been associated with South Carolina, his grandfather being prominent among its first settlers and his father, acting governor and lieutenant governor of the colony.

As Speaker of the House of Commons during the decade of the 1740s he had acted as chief spokesman for the representatives. Later, as lieutenant governor during the Stamp Act controversy, he had permitted the Commons to meet, understanding clearly that it would appoint delegates to the Stamp Act Congress and join with the other southern colonies in taking a stand against parliamentary taxation. When the Commons appropriated money to pay the expenses of the colony's delegates in New York, Lieutenant Governor Bull and the Council had allowed the appropriation bill to pass "sub silentio," as Bull remarked, rather than provoke a dispute about Commons' control over the treasury. This had been in clear violation of the Crown's stipulation to its governors that colonial treasuries could issue money only upon warrants signed by the governors.

The right of the South Carolina Commons to issue money from the treasury without the consent of the governor and the Council—a power that Commons had assumed during the 1740s and '50s—became the issue that set Bull against his fellow Carolinians. Although loyal to his native province, Bull took his position as a royal appointee seriously, and frequently found himself torn between colonial pride and English policy. His situation was made even more difficult by the fact that although he actually held the reins of office for long periods of time, he never possessed the

Wilkes and Liberty, *1763*.

full powers of governor. Three royal governors came and went during his tenure as lieutenant governor; but, lacking powerful patronage, Bull never received the promotion he so fully deserved. Now, in 1769, he discovered that his position was, indeed, weak.

When the Commons of the colony of South Carolina determined upon supporting Wilkes and the cause of civil liberties, Lieutenant Governor Bull became concerned and sent Lord Hillsborough a summary of the situation, explaining his inability to prevent the Commons from taking such a step. "The great religious and Civil indulgences granted by the Crown to encourage Adventurers to settle in America," he wrote, had made the colony more democratic than monarchical. "Since the late unhappy discontents and the universal extension of the Claims of the American Commons," he explained, the power of the South Carolina assembly had "risen to a great height." [12]

The imperial authorities were, of course, surprised to learn that the South Carolina Commons had acquired the power to spend money without the consent of the governor and the Council. Attorney General William DeGrey reported that the Commons could not constitutionally do so and furthermore, that it could not through usage change what was ordained by law. To prevent further abuses, Lord Hillsborough sent a new set of instructions to Bull in 1770 forcing him to veto all illegal efforts to get around the laws. Each time the Commons tried to pass a money bill that ignored the Governor's Instructions of 1770, it was dismissed. Meanwhile, the Council, deciding that the Commons could not spend money for purposes that did not directly concern the colony, challenged the Commons' decision to include an item in the annual tax bill to repay the Wilkes Fund grant to the treasury. The Commons' reply to the Council outlined the policy that it would unabatedly maintain for the next four years. Its report was written by leading members of South Carolina's ruling elite—among whom was the merchant Henry Laurens.

HENRY LAURENS (1724–1792); RALPH IZARD (1741/2–1804)

Henry Laurens was 160 miles away from Charleston when the Commons voted to appropriate money to the London "Supporters of the Bill of Rights." When he heard of the action, he was not pleased. "These Chaps will get a rap o' the knuckles for this," he is reported to have said critically. [13] Having experienced the consequences of mob violence when, during the Stamp Act crisis, an armed mob entered to search his Charleston home for stamps, he was not a friend of the activists. But Laurens was a defender of the rights of the Commons, which represented some of the most prominent and oldest families in the colony. He believed, he said, in an attitude of "constitutional stubbornness"; and when the Council refused to assent to a tax bill until the item reimbursing the treasurers for the Wilkes grant was erased, this attitude deter-

mined his presence on the Commons committee appointed to report on the Council's action.

Henry Laurens was the son of a wealthy Charleston businessman who saw that his son received every advantage in education and training befitting a young gentleman-merchant of his day, including a period in London for additional experience in the commercial world. A remarkably methodical man, Laurens was well prepared to become the leading merchant of Charleston. By the age of forty he had already acquired a large fortune and his interest had shifted from trade to the raising of rice and indigo and the management of several large plantations.

From 1757 until the Revolution, Henry Laurens was elected to the South Carolina Commons House regularly. Here he joined fellow planters and merchants Thomas Lynch, James Parsons, Christopher Gadsden, Thomas Ferguson, and Benjamin Dart to help spell out the constitutional issue that Carolinians saw at the heart of the controversy.

Carolinians were no novices at this kind of political conflict. Ten years before, they had confronted Governor Boone on the question of determining whether Commons could determine the eligibility of its representatives. The Stamp Act had clarified the issue even more, boiling it down to the right to be taxed by their own representatives. Laurens himself had experienced difficulties with royally appointed customs officers who had seized two of his vessels on very slight charges. Although he lost his case, he took advantage of the opportunity to challenge the corrupt judge in a pamphlet marked by sarcastic and abusive language. Now again, the authority of the Commons to handle the colony's money matters became his concern, for the right to spend also implied the right to tax. Laurens wrote that he would "rather forfeit my whole estate and be reduced to the necessity of working for my bread than to have these clauses in consequence of a *ministerial dictate* made parts of our tax bills." [14]

The committee's report, upon which the Commons based its reply to the Council's challenge, argued that it was no affront to His Majesty to contribute money for the support of constitutional rights, since His Majesty was "the great patron of the Liberty and Rights of all His Subjects." Since the Commons had always issued money from the treasury upon its own authority, without the consent of the governor or the Council, local practice and precedent rendered that right constitutional. If the Council insisted upon

Henry Laurens by Benoît Louis Prevost, 1777-1780.

determining money matters, then it ceased being merely advisory and became, instead, a legislative body, composed, however, of royal placemen rather than elected representatives. It was, said Laurens's committee, "seditious doctrine," to rule that ministers or a royally appointed Council could dictate "how a Money Bill shall be framed."[15]

While the Wilkes Fund grant was arousing consternation in London and while in Charleston the Council and the Commons were locked in an argument concerning the right to appropriate money, the wealthy and handsome Ralph Izard had his mind on personal affairs. Recently married to the lovely New York belle Alice DeLancey, his happy life at "The Elms"—the Carolina estate where he was born and which he inherited—had been interrupted by a family tragedy. His young brother-in-law from New York on a visit to his sister in Charleston had become involved in a quarrel with the enthusiastic rebel Dr.

Haley and had been killed in a duel. To remove themselves temporarily from the scene of the scandal, the young couple left for Europe. In 1771, the Izards were in London setting up permanent residence.

But the young Izard was not without loyalty to his native Carolina. In 1769, he had been as incensed against the Crown's intervention in Carolina's affairs as any rebellious Charlestonian. Now in London his enthusiasm did not abate. When approached in 1774 by Laurens to aid him and Arthur Lee in issuing a pamphlet to refute a publication of Attorney General Sir Egerton Leigh, which had asserted that the South Carolina Council was a legislative body and could properly intervene in money matters, he gladly gave economic and editorial help to the project. Although Arthur Lee wrote the *Answer to the Considerations on Certain Political Transactions of the Province of South Carolina*, we may be sure that the ideas he expressed represented the thinking of Laurens, Izard, and other South Carolinians of their position; they also indicate the gulf that existed between British constitutional thought and American.

Leigh's pamphlet had argued that the Constitution was "derivative and entirely flows from the Crown." Colonial assemblies owed their existence not to the natural right of freeholders to be represented, but to the King's pleasure. Traditional usage of the community—especially of "new Communities" and *"Infant Societies"*—carried no constitutional weight. The Commons, insisted Leigh, had no right to issue money on its sole authority, and the vote of a grant to the Wilkes Fund was "an unconstitutional and unwarrantable stretch of Power" which had to be checked by the Crown. The Council, on the other hand, derived its right to act as an upper house from the royal commission and instructions, and therefore could act as a legislative body.[16]

The *Answer* issued by Laurens, Izard, and Lee denied Leigh's assumptions and conclusions, and argued that the right to be represented was "inherent, not permissive." "The Rights and Privileges of the Commons House," Lee wrote, "spring from the Rights and Privileges of *British* Subjects, and are coeval with the Constitution. They were neither created, nor can they be abolished by the Crown." Precedent was "Part of the Constitution," which constantly underwent change and development rather than being fixed and unchangeable, as Leigh had contended. The vote of money to the Wilkes Fund was *"constitutional in its Mode, and laudable in its*

Intention," argued the three Carolinians, because "it was agreeable to the Usage and Practice, both ancient and modern, of the Commons House of Assembly in the Province of South Carolina."[17]

For four years, South Carolina was unable to pass a tax bill, because each time the Commons did so, it included in it a provision to repay the Treasurer for the money sent to the Wilkes Fund and ignored Hillsborough's 1770 Instructions to Lieutenant Governor Bull. Each time, the tax bill was vetoed, and the Assembly prorogued. As a result, government in South Carolina came almost to a halt. When unrest among the Indians on the southern frontier forced the Assembly to consider the need for defensive measures and the Council refused to pass a money bill providing for that defense because it included what they considered was an illegal provision, the Commons finally took matters into its own hands. It ordered its clerk to issue certificates of indebtedness to pay the accounts and promised to redeem the certificates once it had succeeded in passing a tax bill. The Council protested vigorously and Lieutenant Governor Bull prorogued the legislature. But all the people involved accepted the certificates as currency and thus permitted the Commons to avoid the issue.

Meanwhile, imperial authorities began to have second thoughts and urged Dartmouth, who had succeeded Hillsborough, to modify the controversial 1770 Instructions. A new and more amiable governor—Lord William Campbell—was appointed to replace Admiral Montagu. Upon Campbell's request, colonial officials omitted the Instructions so that the South Carolina representatives would "have no longer any pretence to say that they are not left at liberty to frame their Money Bills as they think fit."[18] By the time Campbell arrived in the colony in June 1774, conflict had broken out in Massachusetts and the larger question of American rights had been raised. The Wilkes Fund controversy paled in comparison.

The controversy, however, had brought South Carolina politicians to a fuller realization of the nature of the political challenges involved in Britain's new colonial policies, especially the question of the right of colonial assemblies to tax and legislate for their constituents. These were rights which American colonists had developed through practice over the decades, and Americans were not going to allow these hard-gained rights to be taken away. As Henry Laurens wrote,

the Representative Body of the People in Carolina, when regularly Assembled, have and ought to enjoy all the Rights and Privileges of a free People—or in other words—all the Rights and Privileges, as a Branch of the Legislature, which are held, enjoyed, and exercised by the House of Commons in Great Britain.[19]

For five years, the Wilkes Fund issue had aroused bitterness toward the British among Carolinians. Bitterly, they responded to a description of a statue of Lord Hillsborough, published in the *South Carolina Gazette* of September 6, 1773. The inscribed motto read, "Massachusetts is my wash-pot and South Carolina my Footstool." "What Shall We Say," wrote Henry Laurens in April 1774, "of the Injury done to a province by a Ministerial Mandate held over that province and totally Stagnating public business for four Years."[20] Aristocratic planters and merchants realized that their political life could never be secure while it was subject to politicians over whom they had no control and from whom they could expect no sympathy. As historian Jack Greene has written, "The Wilkes Fund controversy was the bridge to Revolution in South Carolina."

The People vs. the Proprietors: Maryland and the Fee Struggle, 1770-1773

On October 20, 1770, the old Tobacco Inspection Law of 1747 of the province of Maryland expired, and members of both houses of Maryland's legislature were intensely involved in arguing provisions for a new law. Each time the 1747 law had previously expired, its renewal had stimulated heated controversy, because it incorporated not only an inspection system necessary for crop control and the mode of payment for the tobacco, but also the amount of money that officials and clergymen could receive in payment for their services. Since officers of the colony and the clergy were not elected but were chosen by the proprietors of Maryland and their appointed governors—and profited from this patronage—they incurred the hostility of the landed gentry, lawyers, and small businessmen of Maryland, who sought to be politically self-govern-

Samuel Adams by John Singleton Copley, 1770-1772.

140

OPPOSITE PAGE:
Landon Carter,
attributed to
Charles Bridges,
date unknown.

RIGHT:
Charles Townshend
by Sir
Joshua Reynolds,
1764-1767.

ABOVE LEFT:
Mercy Otis Warren
by John Singleton Copley,
1761-1763.

ABOVE RIGHT:
Joseph Warren
by John Singleton Copley,
1765.

RIGHT:
Richard Clarke
(third from left)
and the Copley family
by John Singleton Copley,
1777.

OPPOSITE PAGE:
Abigail Smith Adams
by Benjamin Blyth,
circa 1766.

John Hancock by John Singleton Copley, 1750.

Ralph Izard and his wife, Alice DeLancey, by John Singleton Copley, 1775.

ing. They banded together loosely in what was called the "country party." Their power lay primarily in the House of Delegates, while the "court party," whose members held their authority from the proprietor, Lord Baltimore, was entrenched in the upper house. Here in the legislature the battle of the people of Maryland against the proprietary interests was waged. It was also waged against the governor, who represented the proprietary prerogative or power.

In 1770, the House of Delegates saw in the necessity to pass a new Inspection Law an opportunity "to clip fees and clergy incomes" which they believed were scandalously high. The upper house, of course, wished to secure the advantages it enjoyed as an official governing class. The Governor wished to assert proprietary power. The question became one of constitutional rights. The Delegates asserted that the Assembly, as the legal representative of the people, had the power to establish official fees. However, Governor Eden, who had just arrived in Maryland in 1769, insisted that he could do so by proclamation. Dismissing the legislature, he issued the Proclamation of November 26, 1770, ordering all officers who took fees to abide by the old inspection law and reiterating the conviction of the proprietors that the governor could govern with or without a legislature.

For three years, the irreconcilable views of the House of Delegates and the Governor prevented legislation in Maryland. Tobacco remained uninspected, and, therefore, could not be shipped from the

Governor Robert Eden by Charles Willson Peale, 1775.

Three of the most eminent of the "poets and writers" Dulany was so contemptuous of were William Paca, Samuel Chase, and Charles Carroll of Carrollton. All three men were members of the Sons of Liberty and delegates to the Assembly in Annapolis. Having been involved in a quarrel with the mother country against a system of taxation without the consent of the taxed, they had viewed the Stamp Act as an extension of the system they had been deploring for some time. Now they entered enthusiastically into the fight against the Governor's proclamation and against a poll tax that had been laid for the support of the clergy.

William Paca and Charles Carroll were members of wealthy families, well-entrenched politically and socially in the life of the colony. Samuel Chase's father was rector of St. Paul's Church in Baltimore. All three

colony. To meet the crisis, tobacco growers and buyers established extralegal associations to inspect tobacco awaiting shipment on the wharves on both sides of Chesapeake Bay. While they provided for voluntary inspections of tobacco crops, they became adept at organization and self-government and performed a real service for Maryland trade. Some small growers, however, feared that the power gained by the extralegal inspectors of tobacco would render them a dangerous faction, capable of setting controls over production and forcing the growers to submit to "club law."

WILLIAM PACA (1740–1799);
SAMUEL CHASE (1741–1811);
CHARLES CARROLL (1737–1832)

The fee struggle produced a flood of propaganda, newspaper articles, pamphlets. "Who," asked the younger Daniel Dulany, writing from London, "are all of these poets and writers that have started up among you all at once? As to some of the party disputes, I cannot help saying that I think they flavour very considerably of toddy." [21]

William Paca by Charles Willson Peale, 1772.

*Charles Carroll of Carrollton
by Sir Joshua Reynolds, 1763.*

Bennett Allen, be given two livings. Rumor had it that one living would be just enough to pay Allen's liquor bill. Since the proprietor had the right to make all clerical appointments, and since many Anglican clerics were given to excessive drinking and scandalous living, the parishioners and vestries felt the need to control these appointments. In the 1747 Tobacco Inspection Act, a limit of thirty pounds of tobacco from each parishioner had been placed on the incomes of the Anglican clergy. Now that that act had not been renewed, and no act passed to replace it because of the quarrels between the Governor and the legislature, the old 1702 law went into effect. Some clergymen began demanding also the establishment of an American bishopric, which added to the fury against the clergy felt by citizens of Maryland.

Since 1702 when the first Inspection Act was passed, Maryland had seen a heavy influx of dissenters. Together with Catholics such as Charles Carroll, these settlers strongly opposed the idea of a bishopric. Paca's

men were educated in the classics and law, although Carroll never pursued the law professionally. Paca and Chase met while students of law in Annapolis and their friendship continued throughout the years of revolutionary upheaval until Paca's death in 1799. Paca continued his education in 1762 at the Inner Temple, but returned to Annapolis in 1763 to practice his profession. In 1764, both young men became members of the Maryland legislature. Carroll did not return from his studies abroad until 1765, and not until 1771 did he begin to take a public role in Maryland affairs.

William Paca and Samuel Chase emerged into prominence in Maryland politics in 1772, when together with a third delegate, they argued in the pages of the *Maryland Gazette* against the legality of the Inspection Act of 1702 that provided each minister of the Established Church with forty pounds of tobacco from each parishioner. The question of the status of the clergy in Maryland had become an issue of great concern in the 1760s when Lord Baltimore, the proprietor, insisted that his friend, the clergyman

Samuel Chase by Charles Willson Peale, 1773.

and Chase's cause, then, was popular, for the religious issue was apparent in the whole tobacco fee problem. It became bound up with the question of the proper separation of powers that should obtain in government when the governor asserted his right to regulate the fees of civil officers by proclamation. Civil and religious freedom thus became the burden of the Carroll-Dulany debate that from January until July 1773, filled the pages of the *Maryland Gazette.*

Daniel Dulany, Maryland's able lawyer, defended Governor Eden's proclamation in terms of the proprietary prerogative and the role of the governor as representative of that prerogative. As "The First Citizen," Carroll answered with a spirited argument against the authority of the chief magistrate to interpose himself in a disagreement between the two houses of the legislature. "In a land of freedom, this arbitrary exertion of prerogative will not, must not, be endured." [22] Having given careful study to the writings of Montesquieu, Newton, and Locke, Carroll brought to his exercise in propaganda a large and liberal view of society and government. Especially was he convinced of the importance of the law in maintaining the political balance necessary to prevent arbitrary rule.

Carroll emerged from the debate as the intellectual leader of the radical element in Maryland. Bringing to his task a battery of historical and legalistic studies, he clarified the issue involved in the fee controversy as few others could, and from that time on, he became one of the most important figures in Maryland's revolutionary movement. When Chase and Paca joined the battle in a final letter to Dulany that was reprinted in London papers, leadership of the radical movement fell to the two men also; and the three together became a formidable triumvirate ready to lead Maryland into the Continental Congress and independence.

The Hutchinson-Oliver Letters, 1772

In the years immediately following the end of non-importation and the Boston Massacre trial, a quiet descended upon Bostonians as they went about their everyday affairs, interrupted only by the annual fiery and impassioned orations commemorating the slaughter on Boston Common. Radicals, such as Dr. Samuel Cooper, the political parson of Boston's liberal Brattle Street Church, and Sam Adams, sought in vain for an issue to rouse their compatriots to the defense of their rights and liberties against parliamentary abuse.

By the spring of 1772, the influence of the radical activists was at an ebb. Even when the colonists learned that the salaries of Governor Hutchinson and Lieutenant Governor Oliver would be paid by the Crown rather than by the legislature, Adams's attempts to alert the citizenry to "perfect Despotism" had no effect. His arguments that the mother country was abrogating the colonists' rights and destroying the checks and balances in their constitution went unheeded.

But when the Bostonians learned in September 1772 that the salaries of the Superior Court judges and other legal officials—many of them Hutchinson's relatives—would also be paid out of Crown revenues and no longer be subject to legislative control, they were more susceptible to Adams's persistent and adroit propaganda. So aroused, in fact, were the townspeople by this step that they immediately organized a Committee of Correspondence to inform the other towns in Massachusetts and the rest of the world of the usurpation of their rights. Within three months, over eighty local committees were formed throughout the province.

Unifying other towns to support future action against the Governor was a large step for the activists. Yet, they still lacked an injustice sufficiently blatant and outrageous to goad their fellow colonists to outright action against the chief officers of the province. In December 1772, Benjamin Franklin fortuitously supplied the issue in the shape of a small packet of letters he sent to Thomas Cushing, the Speaker of the House.

As London agent for the Massachusetts legislature, Franklin had been given the letters to help him in presenting the petitions of the colony to have the Governor and Lieutenant Governor removed from their offices because they were insensitive to the colony's welfare. The letters, he was told by their donor, were not to be published; they were merely to advise his American employers that the source of their troubles was not the British ministry but their own compatriots who were urging the administration to enact oppressive measures. The letters had been sent to Thomas Whately between 1767 and 1769 when he was a member of Parliament and secretary to Lord

Grenville. Among the correspondents were Thomas Hutchinson and Andrew Oliver. Governor Hutchinson had written that "there must be an abridgment of what are called English liberties"[23]; Oliver, lieutenant governor and secretary of the province, had suggested that the Crown's functionaries should be "in some measure independent" of the people. Other correspondents had suggested that a military presence in the colony would contribute to more efficient government.

Considering the letters to be "written by public officers to persons in public stations, on public affairs, and intended to procure public measures," Franklin did not hesitate to forward them. He did ask that they be shown only to a chosen few and that they not be published, although he must have realized that there was little likelihood of his instructions being obeyed.[24]

Cushing showed the letters to Sam Adams, Dr. Cooper, and others, and for a while Franklin's injunction of secrecy was observed—Adams merely began an intensive propaganda campaign in the press hinting

at their existence. Franklin had urged forbearance—a wait-and-see attitude, certain that the economic importance of the colonies to Britain would enable them to achieve all they wanted in time.

But he had been out of the country too long. Sam Adams and his men were the last ones to practice patience and prudence when they finally had their hands on an issue that would inflame the people. In a secret session of the Assembly in early June, the letters were read to the assembled delegates. Within a few days they appeared in the public press, with changes to make them sound more incriminating. Now that they were a matter of public knowledge, their contents were openly discussed in both houses of the legislature; the writers were declared traitors and the King was petitioned to remove the

combination of evil Men in this province, who have contemplated Measures and formd [sic] a Plan, to raise their own Fortunes and advance themselves to Posts of Power Honor & Profit, to the Destruction of the Character of the province, at the Expence of the Quiet of the Nation and to the annihilating of the Rights & Liberties of the American Colonies.[25]

SAMUEL COOPER (1725–1783)

One of the most popular ballads of the Revolutionary period described Parson Samuel Cooper simply but accurately:

> In politics he all the tricks
> Doth wonderfully ken.[26]

Admirers of the learned Doctor Cooper believed he was "enlight'ned from above"; but enemies, such as Chief Justice Peter Oliver, who had felt the wrath of a mob stirred up by the Parson's preachings, were not so kind. Oliver described him as "not deep in his profession, but very deep in the black Arts." "His tongue," complained Oliver, "was Butter and Oil, but under it was the Poison of Asps." Whatever the case, there is no question that in mid-eighteenth-century Boston the Reverend Doctor Samuel Cooper, pastor of the wealthy and liberal Brattle Street Church, was one of the most active protesters against British policies and one of the most ardent defenders of American liberties.[27]

Samuel Cooper was the son of a Congregational minister, the Reverend William Cooper, former pastor

The Reverend Samuel Cooper
by John Singleton Copley, 1769.

of the Brattle Street Church, and grandson of Thomas Cooper, one of its founders. A fine classical scholar, he was admired for his glittering orations and "sweet" manners. Although the more critical John Adams found his style "too flowery, too figurative . . . too labored," his congregation was charmed by his eloquence and wisdom—although some did admit that his knowledge "although very extensive, was very shallow." [28] Certainly, he was a man who possessed a powerful way with large audiences; in turn, he was listened to with respect by those who recognized his sincere commitment to the cause of liberty, both civil and ecclesiastical. "There is a close connection between civil liberty and true religion," preached "Silver-Tongued Sam"; "Tyrants are commonly equal enemies, to the religious and civil rights of mankind; and having enslaved the bodies of their subjects, they affect also to enslave their consciences." To such utterances, his aroused audience could only say "Amen." Supported in his politics by his brother William Cooper, who controlled the Boston town meeting, it was said that "the patronymic of the holy family [in Boston] was Cooper." [29]

In 1753, Samuel Cooper was appointed chaplain of the House of Representatives. In his prayers in the House or the Council, he so mixed politics and religion that "he became the moral validation of the policies of the Whigs." By 1754, he was taking an active part in the politics of revolution. Attacking a proposed provincial tax on wine and rum in an anonymous pamphlet called *The Crisis,* he called the bill's proponents "Bastards and not Sons" of the British constitution. Once such a tax was allowed, further taxes would follow, and liberty would be destroyed.

It was inevitable that the old Puritan Sam Adams and the liberal Congregational preacher should join forces. Both sought to recover an independent Massachusetts such as they believed had flourished under its original charter. Superficial in thought, activist in temperament, they did not attempt to find a solution to the problems of empire that British policy posed, but, instead, dreamed of restoring an idyllic democratic utopia that existed only in men's imaginations.

Cooper's activities in behalf of fomenting and maintaining discontent were far-ranging, from publishing articles in the *Boston Gazette* and *Independent Ledger* to writing letters to English Whigs describing, sometimes distortedly, the situation in America that required reform. During this period of political calm he was able to help Sam Adams keep the pot boiling by warning the people vaguely but ominously of coming threats to their liberties and of vicious plots being hatched.

Cooper, Adams, James Otis, and John Hancock would frequently meet at the parsonage "to cook up politics." At one of these meetings John Adams reported that Cooper remarked that "an ounce of mother wit is worth a pound of clergy," but that his position made him "an excellent hand to spread a rumor." Indeed, Cooper was in a strategic position for the spreading of rumors. Enjoying a voluminous correspondence with English Whigs and Benjamin Franklin in London, he was able to pass on ideas, fantasies, and facts to both sides and have them accepted on the assumption that he was knowledgeable and well informed. It was natural that Benjamin Franklin should think of Cooper, then, when he had to decide what to do with the Hutchinson-Oliver correspondence.

In his reply to Franklin, Cooper tried to justify the publication of the letters. He claimed that whatever "inconveniences" arose from having broken his promise to Franklin to keep the letters secret were compensated for by the knowledge that their publication contributed "to the security and the happiness of millions"; he tried to mitigate his deed by complimenting Franklin on his "honest Openness in this Affair, and noble Negligence of any Inconveniences that might arise to yourself in this essential Service to our injur'd Country." [30]

To the folks at home, however, Cooper appeared "much grieved at the consequence of the publication" of the letters. Most Bostonians believed his apologetic story that since the papers had come to the attention of so many individuals in Boston, it was deemed best to publish them for all to see for themselves.

Cooper's activities on behalf of the American cause did not stop here. Although it is only legendary that he put on feathers and paint to join the "Indians" in the Boston Tea Party, it is a matter of record that he wrote many of Hancock's speeches, including his Massacre oration, and he himself delivered a masterful oration against the Massachusetts Port Bill. So dangerous did he appear to British authorities, that General Gage was warned to watch out for him. In 1775, he actually had to flee Boston, not to return until after the British army had left the city.

In pamphlet form, the Hutchinson-Oliver letters were sent to the other American colonies where they created a sensation as they made their appearance in paper after paper. Although their inflammatory effect was short-lived, in Boston the successful handling of the propaganda inherent in the letters served to reunite and revitalize the radical leadership. The Boston Committee of Correspondence, which Sam Adams had formed in the fall of 1772 to inform the towns of Massachusetts and the rest of the world of the wrongs perpetrated on Massachusetts, became an effective political organization. The radicals regained control of the Massachusetts legislature, and when their rights were again threatened, the people of Boston were prepared to act effectively and expeditiously to thwart British decision-makers.

The Burning of the Gaspee, Rhode Island, 1772

In March 1772, Lieutenant William Dudingston and his crew sailed His Majesty's armed schooner *Gaspee* into the Narragansett Bay off the coast of Rhode Island in order to seize colonial ships entering the port carrying contraband cargo. "Haughty, insolent, and intolerant," Dudingston appeared more like a pirate than protector of the laws to Rhode Islanders whose livelihood came from the sea, and whose prosperity frequently depended on successful smuggling ventures. Dudingston was not a gentle officer. He "personally ill treat[ed] every Master and Merchant of the Vessels he boarded, stealing Sheep, Hogs, Poultry, &c. from the Farmers around the Bay, and cutting down their Fruit and other Trees for Fire Wood." No self-respecting Englishman, added the Rhode Islander who described the Lieutenant's activities in this way, could "patiently bear" such provoking behavior.[31]

By June, Rhode Islanders' patience had almost snapped. Merchants, whose vessels were being hounded by the *Gaspee*, farmers, whose crops and livestock were being despoiled to feed the crew, and small oyster fishermen were all up in arms against this latest attempt of the Royal Navy to control illicit trade in Rhode Island.

Rhode Islanders, who were used to independence as a result of the colony's liberal charter, were also accustomed to standing up to the Royal Navy. In 1764, they had fired upon a British man-of-war, *St. John*, and in 1769 had burned the English sloop *Liberty*, when these vessels had interfered in their trading practices. They were more than ready for the *Gaspee*, when the welcome news quickly spread around Providence that the ship had run aground off Namquit Point in Warwick while chasing a smuggler, and probably would not get free until after midnight.

Immediately, the merchant John Brown directed that eight of the largest longboats in the harbor be outfitted with muffled oars and brought to Fenner's Wharf. Just about the time when shops in Providence were closing, a drummer marched along Main Street informing the town's inhabitants of the *Gaspee*'s situation and inviting any "who felt a disposition to go and destroy that troublesome vessel" to meet in the evening at the public house across from the wharf. Among the sea captains who answered John Brown's call for help was Abraham Whipple, shipmaster for Nicholas Brown & Company.

JOHN BROWN (1736–1803); CAPTAIN ABRAHAM WHIPPLE (1733–1819)

John Brown was far more adventurous than his older brother Nicholas, who presided at the head of the Brown family's mercantile business. Establishing his own enterprise, which like his brother's depended on the forbidden but lucrative trade with the West Indies, the young John was extremely successful and enjoyed wide personal influence throughout Rhode Island. In the 1760s he had actively protested the Molasses, Sugar, and Stamp acts and was active in the Rhode Island Assembly promoting non-importation. Cocky self-assurance was his trademark—he had written in one of his schoolbooks when young, "John Brown the cleverest boy in Providence Town"—and his impetuous independence, as well as the threat to his prosperity posed by Lieutenant Dudingston, drove him to quick action on the night of June 9th when the *Gaspee* ran aground at the end of Namquit Point.[32]

John Brown not only instigated and outfitted the expedition against the *Gaspee*, but personally participated in it. Throughout the whole episode, his was the commanding voice that determined the successful resolution of the affair. It was Captain Abraham Whipple, however, whose knowledge of the Rhode Island coast and skillful seamanship were indispensable in such a venture.

Captain Abraham Whipple by Edward Savage, 1786.

Whipple was born in Providence and identified himself at an early age with Rhode Island's commercial life. He acquired some of his knowledge of navigation and accounting while engaged in privateering during the French and Indian War, and the rest while employed by Nicholas Brown in the West India trade.

On the night of June 9th, 1772, Whipple, along with Captain John B. Hopkins, took command of the fifty or more volunteers who had come to burn the detested British vessel. Silently rowing out to the helpless ship, the eight longboats came to within sixty yards of the *Gaspee* when a sentinel hailed, "Who comes there?" When Dudingston came to the starboard gunwale to investigate, Captain Whipple presumably answered, "I am the sheriff of the county of Kent, G—d d—n you. I have got a warrant to apprehend you, G—d d—n you; so surrender, G—d d—n you." While Captain Whipple spoke, his fellow crewman, Joseph Bucklin, reached for his gun and fired. "I have killed the rascal," exclaimed Bucklin— mistakenly, as it turned out, for Lieutenant Dudingston was merely wounded. The group boarded the *Gaspee* without opposition. Brown sent for a surgeon

to dress Dudingston's wound, searched the Lieutenant's papers for possible incriminating information, and sent the entire British crew to shore on small boats. The vessel was set on fire and burned.[33]

The success of the *Gaspee* incident added to Captain Whipple's reputation for bravery and seamanship. In 1775, he was made commodore of the Rhode Island fleet of two armed ships. Later becoming a captain in the Continental Navy, Captain Whipple was responsible for capturing the richest spoils of the war—more than a million dollars' worth of goods on board a fleet of East Indiamen.

The British government lost no time in responding to this offense against the Crown. Rhode Islanders had avoided punitive measures from London after two previous incidents involving attacks on British vessels, but this latest flagrant act of rebellion had to be met, if Great Britain were to retain any respect in the small colony of Rhode Island. "If the *Gaspee* rioters were not punished," wrote Thomas Hutchinson from Massachusetts, "the Friends to Government will despond

John Brown by Edward Greene Malbone, date unknown.

and give up all hopes of being able to withstand the Faction." [34]

Immediately, George III appointed a Royal Commission to examine the events and determine the persons responsible for the crime against the *Gaspee*. His intention was that they should be sent to England for trial. Rhode Islanders were incensed. Accustomed to political autonomy, citizens of the colony could not accept the idea of a Royal Commission investigating a local affair, or of alleged offenders being tried away from the scene of the crime. One of the rights of Englishmen which all colonists treasured was the right to be tried in the locality of the crime by one's own peers. Americans called the Commission a Court of Inquisition more horrible than anything that had ever occurred in Spain. Such a "Court of the Star Chamber" presented activists with another issue that would serve to revive colonial discontent with the mother country.

The Commissioners included Joseph Wanton, the elected governor of Rhode Island; Frederick Smythe, chief justice of New Jersey; Daniel Horsmanden, chief justice of New York; Peter Oliver, chief justice of Massachusetts; Robert Auchmuty, judge of the Vice-Admiralty Court in Boston; and Admiral John Montagu, Commander of the English fleet in Boston. The Commission was instructed to examine the behavior of the King's officers as well as that of the rebels, and they were to ask the local civil authorities of the colony to apprehend any suspects.

JOSEPH WANTON (1705–1790)

Joseph Wanton was a descendant of a long line of Rhode Island governors. From youth, he had assumed that he would continue the family tradition of taking a prominent place in the colony's political life, and had early identified himself with the powerful Hopkins faction in Rhode Island which urged self-government for the colony within the British empire.

Trained in shipbuilding, privateering, and mercantilistic pursuits, Wanton engaged in general merchandising with his two sons in Newport. Often, he found himself doing business with the Browns of Providence, who along with other Hopkins party men supported Wanton and helped forward his political career.

In 1739, Wanton was elected deputy collector of customs, and from that position, he rose to become governor of the colony in 1769. As governor, how-

Governor Joseph Wanton by an unidentified artist, date unknown.

ever, Wanton found politics not easy. He believed strongly in the "Charter Privileges" of Rhode Island, but he was bound to enforce British law. He sympathized with the American cause, but he also believed that the best way for the colony to preserve its rights and autonomy was to remain a part of the British empire. A popular governor, on the whole, until 1772, Wanton had protested Dudingston's arrival in the colony in strong terms to Admiral Montagu, and in fact had sent a copy of his protest to the Secretary of State in London. Wanton was loath to allow any British officer to diminish his authority within the colony, and he steadfastly insisted that he had the right to control any ship that came within his jurisdiction.

With the burning of the *Gaspee*, however, Wanton was placed in a difficult position. As governor, he had to issue a proclamation offering a reward for the arrest, or information leading to the arrest, of the men involved in the incident, but Wanton did not zealously pursue the matter. Rather, he wrote a letter describing the whole incident to Lord Hillsborough, pointing out the insults offered the inhabitants of his colony from officers who lacked "that temper, prudence, and discretion which persons entrusted with the execution of laws ought . . . to manifest." [35] When Admiral Montagu sent him a deposition made by Aaron Briggs, a Negro indentured servant, accusing John Brown and his brother Joseph of being the leaders in the affair, Wanton countered with four affidavits denying Briggs's presence at the scene and discrediting his statement.

Appointed to the "unconstitutional Court of Inquisition," Wanton again found himself with two loyalties. The Commissioners' lack of success, however, saved him from having to make an unpopular decision.

The Commissioners met with obstruction from all sides. None of the colonists seemed to have any recollection whatsoever of the affair or who might have been involved in it. The judges, finally, had to agree that there was not enough evidence to make any arrests, and adjourned. Daniel Horsmanden reported to the Earl of Dartmouth in England that Rhode Island was a "downright democracy," whose Governor is "entirely controlled by the populace." [36] Admiral Montagu concluded that news of the *Gaspee* affair had made the Bostonians "almost ripe for independence. . . ." [37] The Crown contented itself with promoting Lieutenant Dudingston to Captain.

News of the *Gaspee* affair spread very quickly. As a ballad sung in many taverns throughout the colonies, with the help of "spirits," its story roused men's minds from the lethargy into which they had fallen and turned their thoughts once again to bold adventures for the defense of their liberties:

> Seventeen hundred and seventy-two
> In Newport Harbor lay a crew,
> That played the parts of pirates there,
> The sons of freedom could not bear.
>
> That night about half after ten,
> Some Narragansett Indiamen,
>
> Being sixty-four, if I remember,
> Which made this stout coxcomb surrender;
> And what was best of all their tricks,
> They in his britch a ball did fix,
>
> And set the men upon the land,
> And burnt her up, we understand;
> Which thing provokes the King so high,
> He said those men shall surely die.
>
> So if he could but find them out,
> The hangman he'll employ, no doubt;

> For he's declared, in his passion,
> He'll have them tried a new fashion.
> Now for to find these people out
> King George has offered very stout,
> One thousand pounds to find out one
> That wounded William Dudingston.
> One thousand more he says he'll spare,
> For those who say they sheriffs were;
>
> One thousand more there doth remain
> For to find out the leader's name;
> Likewise five hundred pounds per man
> For any one of all the clan.
>
> But let him try his utmost skill,
> I'm apt to think he never will
> Find out any of those hearts of gold,
> Though he should offer fifty fold. [38]

RICHARD HENRY LEE AND THE VIRGINIA HOUSE OF BURGESSES

News of the *Gaspee* affair did not reach Virginia until January 1773. Many Virginians regarded New Englanders as troublesome Yankees, but the minds of Patrick Henry, Richard Henry Lee, Francis Lightfoot Lee, Dabney Carr, and Thomas Jefferson had traveled beyond provincial prejudices. The establishment of a Royal Commission with its threat to civil liberties dramatized their fears of British tyranny. It also made them aware, as Jefferson later wrote,

that the most urgent of all measures was that of coming to an understanding with all the other colonies to consider the British claims as a common cause to all, and to produce a unity of action: and for this purpose that a committee of correspondence in each colony would be the best instrument for intercommunication: and that their first measure would probably be to propose a meeting of deputies from every colony at some central place who should be charged with the direction of the measures which should be taken by all. [39]

The idea of committees of correspondence was not new. As early as 1768, Richard Henry Lee had conceived the idea of establishing committees for inter-colonial communication. He saw these as "leading to the union, and perfect understanding of each other, on which the political salvation of America so

Richard Henry Lee by Charles Willson Peale, 1795-1805.

eminently depends." [40] Lee had been elected to the House of Burgesses in 1758, at a time when the balance of power was gradually shifting from the more conservative older members to a new group of liberal young Whigs. As an outspoken critic of British rule, Lee became one of the leaders, along with Patrick Henry and Thomas Jefferson, of this group of young radicals.

The Lee family of Virginia was one of the wealthiest and most aristocratic families in a society saturated with bluebloods. Richard Henry's father, Thomas Lee, sired four sons, all of whom became important figures during the Anglo-American conflict. In the years preceding the War, there were six Lees serving in the House. The Lees had always sat in the Virginia House of Burgesses, so it was not unusual that Richard Henry decided to make politics his career after returning from legal studies in England.

Lee's evolution toward a radical position took several years, although he constantly maintained his liberalism. During these years, he gained the respect of many of the members of the House—and thus power and seniority—by speaking out against slavery, the

Stamp Act, and the Townshend duties. When news of the *Gaspee* Commission reached Virginia, Lee and his progressive friends met in a private room of the Raleigh Tavern to consult as to how they should act in the light of such a flagrant attack on American liberties. "Not thinking our old and leading members up to the point of forwardness and zeal which the times required," they plotted their plan for establishing colonial committees of correspondence. On March 12, under the prompting of Lee and his group of "Young Turks," Virginia's House of Burgesses passed resolutions to appoint a committee that would obtain information concerning parliamentary acts affecting the American colonists and that would maintain correspondence with the other colonies. Several old-line conservatives, as well as members of the more liberal, younger group were appointed to serve on the committee, and Peyton Randolph, Speaker of the House, was made chairman.

Lee's intention ". . . That every Colony on the Continent will adopt these Committees of correspondence and enquiry" was realized within the following year.[41] On May 8, the Rhode Island Assembly appointed its committee to inform the other colonies concerning the Commission's proceedings and "other acts." Twenty days later, Massachusetts "agreed to [the Virginia proposal] in the most ready and respectful manner," according to Samuel Cooper. The other colonies followed suit, and by February 8, 1774, each of them had taken a stand on the Virginia Resolves.[42]

The committees of correspondence proved to be effective revolutionary agents that solidified public sentiment and indicated the method by which united resistance to a common enemy could be created. Even the British Commission investigating the *Gaspee* affair was alarmed and is generally conceded to have moderated its investigation so as not to inflame the colonists into further and more drastic action. As Ezra Stiles noted in his *Diary,* "a Congress had been sure, if one person had been seized & carried off from Rhode Island." Stiles also suggested that instructions from England "contributed to letting the matter go off easily." [43]

With the failure of the Rhode Island Commission to take action, the movement toward a colonial meeting inherent in the Virginia Resolves slowed down. It would take another provocation, like the Tea Act of May 1773, to set in motion a new chain of events that ultimately would lead to the fulfillment of the intentions of the Virginia Resolves.

A Tempest over Tea

Tea—"harmless, necessary tea, which, with the harmless, necessary cat, made up the sweet content of the domestic hearth"—was the agent that unified the colonies, precipitated their opposition to Great Britain, and in the end, turned America into an independent nation of coffee drinkers.[1]

The tea situation should have been solely Britain's concern—not one to make the colonists react so violently. It started with the greed and irresponsibility of the proprietors and directors of the East India Company. Possessing extensive lands and military forces in India, the company monopolized the sale of tea to the British Empire. Its importance to England's economy was expressed by the King, who welcomed an arrangement that would "in some degree curb if not eradicate what otherways must render that trade the ruin instead of a source of restoring the finances of this country."[2] Since 1767, the company had helped restore the government's finances by an annual payment of £400,000. But the company was in a precarious position: although it occupied an "established place as a pillar of the London money market," its reputation on the European exchanges was as "a very fluctuating and gaming Stock." By 1772, as a result of disastrous management, it could no longer contribute money to the government's treasury. Seventeen million pounds of tea were stored in its London warehouses—unsold—and a debt of £1,300,000, mostly to the government, had to be met. The company was barely one step from bankruptcy.[3]

SIR GEORGE COLEBROOKE (1729–1809)

One member of the East India Company who did much to bring it to its precarious position was Sir George Colebrooke, son of a wealthy banker. Ambitious and not entirely scrupulous, Colebrooke was always seeking opportunities to extend his power, prestige, and pocketbook. His colleagues called him "a great Adventurer in . . . Articles of Speculation." At the height of the East India troubles, he was trying to corner the world market in alum.[4]

Colebrooke's position in Parliament, which he entered in 1754, made him extremely attractive to the East India management. In 1767, he was elected to the company's board of directors. His appointment as chairman in 1769 and again in 1772 put him in a powerful position for determining company affairs. Colebrooke and his supporters bought voting stock to be held just long enough to control company elections, guaranteeing to sell it back at a stipulated price. They assumed that the high dividends they voted would increase the stocks' value above the agreed resale price. In 1769, after such a ruse failed, one prominent figure in the company lost his fortune; Sir George Colebrooke only managed to squeak through.

The directors did not publicize the shaky state of the company's finances. Instead, they voted a large dividend in the fall of 1771 and another the following spring, knowing there would be insufficient money to meet obligations coming due. In June, partly as a result

William Pitt (seated at left), Charles Fox (standing center), and Lord North (seated at right) in the House of Lords, by James Sayer, not dated.

of East India Company speculations, a credit crisis hit London. In September, the company announced there would be no quarterly dividend and, a few days later, defaulted on its payment to the government. The Bank of England refused to renew an outstanding loan.

When Parliament met at the end of November 1772, the affairs of the East India Company constituted the chief topic of discussion. Colebrooke and the directorate of the company, sitting on seventeen million pounds of tea and facing bankruptcy, were willing to cooperate if the government would bail them out.

FREDERICK, LORD NORTH (1732–1792)

Frederick, Lord North, First Lord of the Treasury, Chancellor of the Exchequer, and chief spokesman for the ministry in the House of Commons, was aware of the financial distress of the East India Company and had been warned by the King that remedial action against the company was expected: "Any wavering now would be disgraceful to you and destruction to the public, but I know you too well to harbour such a thought." [5]

Appointed First Lord of the Treasury following Townshend's death, the aristocratic and charming Lord North had become prominent in Parliament as a leading advocate of the ministry. Loyal to the King, whom he strongly resembled, and highly regarded by London's financial leaders, North was unable to act decisively in critical times. His excessive caution and anxiety to please earned him the reputation of being the King's puppet, although he thought of himself—as did the King—as a national representative of the people, above faction and political party.

North proposed to get the East India Company out of its financial difficulties by making it subject to government regulation, giving it a substantial loan, and reducing the huge surplus of tea stockpiled in London warehouses. Although he encountered opposition in Parliament and from the company, North managed to get his Regulating Act through by mid-June 1773.

North hit upon what he considered a splendid plan to reduce the company's tea supply. By permitting the company to export the tea in their warehouses directly to America, duty free, it would bypass the middleman —the London merchant who bought the tea at auction for later distribution. Americans would be able to buy the tea cheaper than Englishmen could in England. Of course, Americans would still have to pay the three-pence-per-pound tax that North insisted be retained when the Townshend duties were repealed to sustain "that just right which I shall ever wish the mother country to possess, the right of taxing Americans." [6] This would allow the government to benefit from the increased sales of East India tea.

Benjamin Franklin, in London as agent for the Massachusetts House of Representatives, was indignant at the maintenance of the tea tax. Parliament believes, he wrote Thomas Cushing, "that three pence in a pound of tea, of which one does not drink perhaps ten pounds a year, is sufficient to overcome all the patriotism of an American." [7]

From the time of the Stamp Act crisis and the non-importation movement that had resulted in the repeal of the Townshend Acts, American activists had been looking for issues to unite the colonies once again in opposition to the Crown. In the Tea Act they

Frederick North, from the studio of Nathaniel Dance, 1767-1770.

The Philadelphia Story

HENRY DRINKER (1734–1809);
THOMAS WHARTON, SR. (1731/32–1782);
ABEL JAMES (1724–1809);
THOMAS MIFFLIN (1744–1800)

Henry Drinker, one of Philadelphia's consignees, was not convinced by the warnings of New Yorkers. He could not discern "that Spirit of opposition, which seem'd to govern formerly in the Case of the Stamp & Revenue Acts," and he was certain that "Men of property & weight" would support the landing of the tea.[9] As an importer who carried on an extensive trade with the West Indies and England, Drinker had maintained a firm stand against the Townshend duties, along with the other Quaker merchants Thomas Wharton, Sr., and Abel James. But like them, when

found new strength. Propagandists accused the mother country of bribing the colonists with cheap tea so they would overlook the tax that subverted Americans' rights. At the same time they alerted merchants and artisans to the dangers of monopoly: if the East India Company were allowed to enjoy exclusive rights to all tea sold in the colonies, it would only be a matter of time before monopolies on other commodities would be granted. Smugglers in New York and Philadelphia also were aroused, when they realized that they could not maintain their illicit trade if subsidized English tea sold at a lower price than smuggled Dutch tea.

Meanwhile, American merchants appointed by their London associates as consignees for the tea, looked forward to handsome profits—6 percent on £21,000. They expected trouble, but only from the smuggling interests. New York agents hoped the tea would land first in Philadelphia "because we have ten times the number of People interested in preventing it." They warned their Philadelphia friends that emissaries would probably be sent from New York to "infuse a malignant spirit among your Citizens." [8]

Henry Drinker, Jr., silhouette cut from memory by Joseph Sansom, c. 1791.

he realized that some merchants were breaking their promise to uphold the non-importation agreement, he resolved not to be "duped" again.

In mid-October 1773, Colonel William Bradford, publisher of *The Pennsylvania Journal*, stopped several Philadelphia citizens who were out for a stroll to suggest that they organize opposition to the landing of the English tea. On being reminded of the difficulty of arousing public sentiment, Bradford responded, "Leave that business to me. I will collect a few active spirits at my house tomorrow evening." And turning to Thomas Mifflin, a member of the Assembly, he said, "Do you be one of them, and we will soon set the city in motion." [10]

Thomas Mifflin was a man of action. Born into a prosperous Quaker merchant family active in public affairs, he favored a greater measure of colonial self-government—at least respecting trading rights. Even before graduating from the College of Philadelphia, he had defined his belief that "Power" is only "Right" when it is based upon "the hearty Consent of

Thomas and Sarah Morris Mifflin
by John Singleton Copley, 1773.

the Body of the People." Mifflin was a "sensible" and "agreeable" worker for causes, whether in the American Philosophical Society or the patriotic Sons of St. Tammany. As a representative from Philadelphia to the Pennsylvania Assembly, he had vehemently opposed the Stamp Act, organized the signing of the non-importation agreement, and now, in the fall of 1773, was speaking out against the Tea Act.

Mifflin's handbill signed *Scaevola* was published in the *Pennsylvania Journal*. Warning the people that the British were tricking them into paying the last remaining Townshend duty and that after the East India tea was successfully imported there would be a deluge of other products—all enjoying the privileges of monopoly—Mifflin's outburst helped provoke public protest from over six hundred people gathering at the State House on Saturday night, October 16th.

The meeting, Benjamin Rush recollected, was "conducted with prudence, spirit, and unanimity. . . ." Having assembled to warn the consignees to resign their commissions and to appoint a committee to obtain their resignations, the organizers also resolved that Parliament had no right to levy taxes on Americans without their consent. "To preserve even the Shadow of Liberty," they declared, every man owes a duty to his prosperity and his posterity to oppose "the ministerial Plan of governing America." Whoever aided in the unloading or sale of East India tea was "an Enemy to his Country." [11]

Thomas Wharton was the first of the tea agents to be approached. The merchant replied ambiguously, declaring that although he had not yet received his appointment as a dealer, he would not harm the tea nor do anything to "enslave America." But Henry Drinker and Abel James refused to resign commissions they had not yet received. They made it clear that they were determined to act "a part which we conceive becomes very good & honest Man circumstanced as we are, & truly desirous of preserving the peace & good order of the City & to prevent the evils which the mad and ungovernable conduct of some might be a means of bringing on us." [12] They were not going to suffer at the hands of the rabble as they had during non-importation. They would not forfeit profit for principle again.

When James's and Drinker's reply was read, "a Hiss was heard from divers in the Coffee House." [13] Thomas Wharton informed his brother Samuel in England that James and Drinker had not acted candidly with either their fellow consignees or the townspeople, and their conduct was "so ambiguous . . . as to render them dispised by their fellow Citizens." [14] James and Drinker, on the other hand, petulantly complained that Philadelphians read only matter that spoke of "Cursed Tea, Detested Tea, Rotten Tea &c. &c. with a Torrent of Abuse of the British Ministry, Parliament, India Company, American Tea Commissioners &c. &c." [15]

The Philadelphians agreed in their meetings to delay further action until the ship bearing the tea arrived. But before the *Polly* was sighted, another vessel arrived with the commissions from the East India Company. James and Drinker were still hoping for a compromise that would permit the tea to be landed and stored until the East India Company could petition Parliament to remove the tax—the only way, they thought, the company could ever sell its wares in America. On the day they received their commissions, they also received an ominous warning requesting that they "renounce all Pretension to execute" their commissions so "THAT WE MAY GOVERN OUR-SELVES ACCORDINGLY." Realizing that had they petitioned the governor for protection, "such a step would undoubtedly have made the Town too hot for us," they resigned. [16]

Philadelphians, still bent on preventing the tea from landing, printed a warning to Delaware River pilots, promising "Tar and Feathers will be his Portion, who pilots" the *Polly* into harbor. [17] The evening of Christmas Day, the *Polly* was sighted below Philadelphia where she anchored, the pilots not being willing to bring her into the harbor. The ship's captain was instructed to provision his ship and set sail immediately for England. Without unloading any of his cargo—including Thomas Wharton's splendid new carriage—he headed out to sea. Also on board was Gilbert Barkley, the last of the Philadelphia consignees. He arrived, resigned, and returned.

Invitation sent to John Dickinson to the meeting of the Society of St. Tammany at Philadelphia, May 1, 1773.

New York's Welcome

ABRAHAM LOTT (1726–1794);

HENRY WHITE (1732–1786);

BENJAMIN BOOTH (?–c. 1789)

In New York, much to the surprise of the tea agents, no mass meetings occurred. The opposition to the importation of East India tea came primarily from the smugglers, some of whom were men of influence in the city councils. But none of them were of the same caliber, as a historian of the period has observed, as the East India Company's three commissioned agents, who "were among the city's most distinguished citizens."

Abraham Lott had been "a merchant of reputation" for almost twenty years and was treasurer of the province and a member of the Governor's Council when he received his commission as tea agent. Henry White, too, was "a merchant of fortune" and served on the Council. Benjamin Booth was not as influential as Lott or White, but was recognized as a merchant of standing. All three men were members of the New York Chamber of Commerce, which White had helped found in 1768 partially to combat the Townshend Acts.

As soon as the three merchants received unofficial news of their appointments as tea agents at the end of September, they met to prepare for the expected opposition from the smugglers and the "considerable Mob" of dockworkers who followed them. Within days, a series of news articles appeared denouncing the Tea Act. These were quickly followed by a handbill, *Alarm No. 1*—the first of five—which advised the citizenry of the avarice of the East India Company and of the dangers of such a monopoly. Booth called the handbill "a dull labored piece" copied mostly from a history book and dismissed its significance.

Here, of course, Booth was mistaken. He and the other New York agents, thinking the tea tax had been suspended, ignored the opposition and insisted that the only issue was trade, and that the only Americans who were really concerned were the smugglers, "Men of such detestable characters, that the Merchants despise them and the common people avoid them." The agents decided that if asked to resign, they first would say that they had to await official instructions from the East India Company; if that failed, they would resign, but only if they were guaranteed that no one else would be allowed to sell English tea. Booth had no intention of sacrificing "our private property . . . to the Publick good." As for the threats of the Sons of Liberty, he was not seriously concerned.[18]

Lott was more realistic. If the tea arrived with the duty due in America, he was certain:

There will be no such thing as selling it, as the people would rather buy so much poison, than the tea with the duty thereon, calculated (they say) to enslave them and their posterity, and therefore are determined not to take what they call the nauseous draft.[19]

In mid-October 1773, William Smith, a member of the Governor's Council, commented in his diary, "A New Flame is apparently kindling in America . . . the Sons of Liberty & the Dutch Smugglers set up the Cry of Liberty. At New York it opened Wednesday the 7th with a Paper stiled the Alarm No. 1." Other handbills and articles from Philadelphia were circulated, "holding up the Factors as another Species of Stamp Masters, & penned to inspire Terror into those Traitors, & animate the Populace agt. them. Vertue

and Vice being thus united, I suppose we shall repeat all the Confusions of 1765 & 1766." [20]

Two days after Smith confided his fears to his diary, the radical leaders of New York—John Lamb, Isaac Sears, and Alexander McDougall—called a mass meeting to thank publicly those captains who had put principle before profit by refusing to carry the East India tea from London. The Tea Act gave these men the issue that revived the New York Sons of Liberty, dormant since the end of the non-importation boycott.

ALEXANDER McDOUGALL

(1732–1786)

Alexander McDougall was a man of the people, the son of a dairy farmer and pastor. He had gone to sea at sixteen and worked his way up, finally becoming a privateer during the French and Indian War. In 1763, he wooed and won a wealthy wife from the island of St. Croix, with whose fortune he was able to set himself up as a merchant and to indulge his predilection for politics. During the Townshend crisis he had boldly, although unsuccessfully, challenged Lamb and Sears for control of the Sons of Liberty. As a result Sears considered him a "rotten-hearted fellow." But in December 1769, he wrote an anonymous broadside protesting the Assembly's provision of funds for the quartering of British troops. This publication brought him great popularity and reconciled him with the other radical leaders. Signing himself "A Son of Liberty," McDougall had addressed his opus "To The Betrayed Inhabitants of the City and Colony of New York." The Assemblymen, he said, were "Minions of Tyranny and Despotism . . . indefatigable in laying every Snare that their malevolent and corrupt Hearts can suggest, to enslave a free People." New Yorkers must rouse themselves in opposition.[21] When the incensed Assembly and Lieutenant Governor offered a reward for the name of the scoundrel who wrote the alleged libel, the printer, promised legal immunity, stepped forth and named McDougall.

McDougall deliberately refused to pay bail, stating after he was sentenced, "I rejoice that I am the first to suffer for liberty since the commencement of our glorious struggle." [22] Three not very lonely months were spent in jail where the populace serenaded him with patriotic songs and visited him so often and in such great number that he had cards printed indicating his daily visiting hours. Released after his indictment

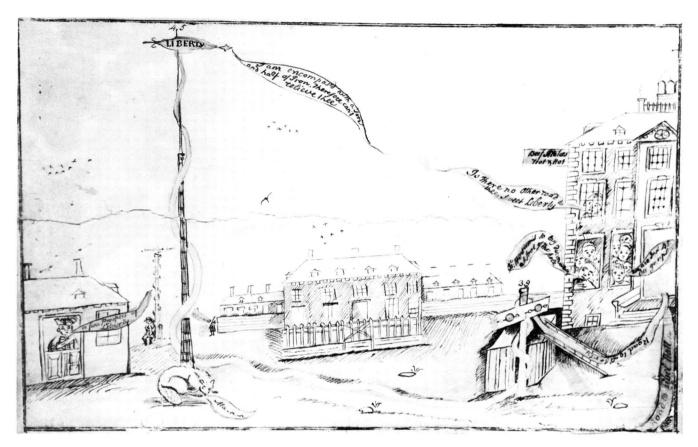

*Liberty Pole, the almshouse, the jail, and the Commons in
New York in 1770. Drawing by Pierre Eugène Du Simitière.*

by a grand jury, he was re-incarcerated for contempt by the Assembly the following December, but again released on a writ of habeas corpus. By spring, the case was dropped; but McDougall emerged from it the people's hero.

McDougall's oratorical skills lay dormant until the fall of 1773, when with Lamb and Sears, he once more tried to rouse the people to protect their rights and liberties with more "Alarms" and other broadsides. In late October, a mass meeting denounced the tea consignees as participating in "public robbery." It was followed by the appearance of a broadside warning the harbor pilots of dire consequences if they guided the ship bringing the tea to New York into port.

On November 25th, a committee was appointed to call upon the consignees demanding they resign their commissions. But Booth, Lott, and White, still not having officially heard from the East India Company, insisted they could not resign what they did not have. Their reply spurred the reorganization of the "Association of the Sons of Liberty of New York."

When the consignees at length received their commissions, they learned that the tea was indeed taxed, and the tax was payable in America upon its being landed. They promptly resigned their commissions and appealed to Governor Tryon to take the tea under his protection when it arrived, hoping to forestall damage to the tea until the spring when they planned to market it.

In mid-December, the Committee of the Association called a mass meeting which sent its delegation to the Governor demanding that the tea be returned untouched. Governor Tryon replied that, without using force, he would see that the tea was landed and stored, although "not an Ounce of it" would be delivered unless he received an order from the King and the consent of his own Council.

Fear of violence, however, prompted White to ask the Governor to send the tea ship back as soon as it was sighted. Anxious to retain his popularity and peace, the Governor secretly agreed and drafted a letter, advising the captain of the expected ship to return at once.

At the end of April, the tea ship *Nancy* was sighted

Alexander McDougall by John Ramage, circa 1790.

off Sandy Hook. The captain came into town, received the refusal of the consignees to take his cargo, and was allowed to provision his ship for the return voyage. He was then escorted by a band playing "God Save the King" to the wharf. He embarked for London with his cargo still in the hold.

Boston Tea-Men

THOMAS HUTCHINSON, JR. (1740–1811); ELISHA HUTCHINSON (1745–1825); RICHARD CLARKE (1711–1795)

Thomas Hutchinson, Jr., and his younger brother Elisha, sons of the Massachusetts Governor, had established a partnership in Boston as tea merchants

after graduating from Harvard College. Their first sizable order was one ton of the finest Bohea tea, which arrived—unfortunately for them—just before the non-importation agreement went into effect. They ignored the agreement as long as they could—as did other Boston merchants—and continued to import such necessities as tea and playing cards until public opprobrium forced them to stop. Even so, the minute the agreement expired in January 1770, the Hutchinsons went down to the warehouse where the tea had been stored and demanded the key. When told they would not be allowed to sell their supply until those other merchants who had agreed to non-importation had time to order and receive their goods, Elisha simply broke down the store, secreted the tea elsewhere, and sold it. Their father unsuccessfully interceded with the Council, in an attempt to denounce the non-importers as an illegal group. Finally, fearing the mob, he reluctantly decided that concession was the better part of nepotism, and instructed his sons to forfeit their tea and profits. The "inconsistent and dishonorable conduct" of the "TWO CHILDREN," as the townspeople called the brothers, did not improve their public image, nor did their appointment in the fall of 1773 as consignees for the East India Company.[23]

Just as unpopular as the House of Hutchinson was agent Richard Clarke, the Governor's nephew. Richard, too, was the son of a prosperous merchant, who improved the family fortune by extending his investments into manufacturing and mining enterprises. Although Clarke preferred to avoid getting entangled in politics, he frequently found himself serving on committees protesting excessive local taxation and the enforcement of the Sugar Act of 1764. But he opposed the Stamp Act riots and would not yield to non-importation until—like the Hutchinsons—forced to by public pressure.

None knew better than the Hutchinsons and Clarke that Boston had been imbibing taxed East India tea for years, and that Boston merchants were the first in the colonies to violate and then end non-importation. But the tea tax was not the real concern of Boston's radical leadership. What they resented were Hutchinson's political attitudes and the emphasis on profit at the expense of what they considered patriotism.

"The Safety of the Americans in my humble opinion depends upon their pursuing their wise Plan of Union in Principle & Conduct," Sam Adams wrote a friend that fall of 1773.[24] To retain that safety, it was necessary to "keep up a perpetual Watchfulness." Adams feared that the ministry in England would gull the colonists with minimal concessions. To arouse Americans from the general apathy brought about by three years of prosperity, the radicals needed a new issue. In August of 1773 they had learned of the Tea Act, but the only comment it had elicited in Adams's correspondence at the time was an expression of sympathy for the East India Company whose "sacred Charter Rights" were being mangled by the ministry. A month later, writing for the Boston Committee of Correspondence to committees in other colonies, Adams had obviously given more thought to the Act's implications; now the Tea Act represented "a fresh Instance of the temper & Design of the British Ministry," which was intent upon destroying colonial trade while increasing the mother country's revenue. "How necessary then," his letter concluded, "is it that Each Colony should take effectual methods to prevent this measure from having its designed Effects." The Bostonians' effort to do so appeared in articles and editorials in the *Boston Gazette* urging that the consignees be sent back to England with the tea.[25]

Richard Clarke in a detail from The Copley Family *by John Singleton Copley, 1777.*

THOMAS YOUNG (1731–1777)

Dr. Thomas Young had left his Albany home chagrined at the apathy of his fellow citizens during the Stamp Act. In Boston, he had sought—and found—a livelier field for his talents as doctor, political orator, and writer. A bold thinker, Dr. Young held daring religious as well as scientific beliefs. He was a Deist at a time when his neighbors were convinced Calvinists. Later, his radicalism was expressed in politics and particularly in his outspoken protests against the mother country's disregard of colonial rights. For seven years, his lively articles supported the designs of Boston activists, especially those of his good friends Dr. Joseph Warren, Dr. Benjamin Church, and Sam Adams.

During the year following his arrival in Boston, Young helped organize the North End Caucus, a powerful Whig club, and became its first president. In March 1771, he gave the first oration commemorating the Boston Massacre—a discourse on treason. When a member of the Roxbury town meeting said that Young should not be listened to because he was a profane and ungodly man, Sam Adams defended him as a man of "political integrity" and an "unwearied assertor of the rights of his countrymen."

In the summer of 1772, sensing a change of wind that might finally blow the complacent citizenry out of its doldrums, Young wrote: "We are brewing some things which will make some people's heads reel. . . . [The] ripeness for great enterprises advances slowly; but perhaps that is the best fruit which requires time to attain its perfection."[26] By the fall of 1773, Young was ready to exploit the arrival of the tea in Boston as an issue to rally the citizenry to action. As a further inducement, he offered free medical advice:

Tea is really a slow poison . . . [and is] said to be possessed of a corrosive quality, strong enough to injure the hands of workmen almost intolerable. . . . I have my self been rheumatically affected from my infancy, and in special at the annual changes of spring and autumn had defluxions on the jaws, teeth or other parts, till the Tea became politically poisoned, and then, however much I admired it, leaving it totally off I have gained a firmness of constitution unexperienced before from my infancy. My substitute is chamomile flowers.[27]

On the night of October 23rd, Young and his colleagues of the North End Caucus met at the Green Dragon Tavern. They voted to "oppose the vending of any Tea, sent by the East India Company to any part of the Continent, with our lives and fortunes." [28] Other Sons of Liberty, encouraged by the accounts from New York and Philadelphia, debated what to do with the tea when it arrived.

In the early hours of the morning of the first of November, Richard Clarke's family was "roused out of our sleep by a violent knocking at the door of our house" to receive a message: he and the other tea agents were "expected" to appear at the Liberty Tree at noon on the third "to make a public resignation of your commission." Public notices posted all over town indicated that the consignees would not only resign, but would publicly "swear" to return the tea to England immediately upon its arrival.[29]

At the behest of the North End Caucus, Drs. Warren, Church, and Young drafted the resolution demanding that the tea agents resign. On the morning of November 3rd, to the sound of church bells and the town crier, the citizenry was summoned to the Liberty Tree. Hundreds came—but not the consignees, although they had been warned, "fail not upon your peril." Gathered at Clarke's warehouse, the tea agents had no intention of responding to what they considered an illegal demand by an illegal body. Angered, the radicals at the Liberty Tree appointed a committee of nine led by William Molineux to call upon the consignees with the draft resolution.

WILLIAM MOLINEUX (1716–1774)

Molineux was not liked by conservative Bostonians. Considered to be like Young, a man "of no Principles and Infamous Character," he was as independent in his religious and political thinking as the impetuous doctor, and he possessed great skills in the art of rousing a mob to action. As the "first Leader of Dirty Matters," Molineux, with a mob behind him, confronted the tea consignees at Richard Clarke's warehouse. "I shall have nothing to do with you," Richard Clarke is said to have asserted. The mob, reported the newspapers, "irritated with the haughty manner with which the answer was said to be given, turned back and showed some marks of their resentment and then dispersed." [30] The next day, a Boston paper reprinted more news from Philadelphia and New York indicating that the protesters in those cities were determined to prevent the landing of the tea. Probably fearful of Pope Day mischief if they stayed in town, the

Francis Rotch by Miers, circa 1795.

Hutchinson sons fled to their country home on the outskirts of Boston.

On November 5th, a thousand Bostonians gathered at Faneuil Hall where they voted their approval of the Philadelphia Resolves and appointed John Hancock to lead a delegation to receive the tea agents' resignations. Again the consignees refused, using the same ploy adopted by the agents in New York and Philadelphia: they had no idea, they insisted, "what obligations, either of a moral or pecuniary nature [they] may be under," and until they had such information they could do nothing.[31]

On the 17th of November, a ship, carrying Richard Clarke's son Jonathan aboard, arrived bearing the news that three tea ships were coming down the channel. That night, while the Clarkes were celebrating the young man's homecoming, a mob descended on the house, shouting and breaking windows. A shot was fired from an upstairs window, but no one was hurt.

The impending arrival of the tea necessitated another town meeting. But again the consignees delayed submitting their resignations. Finally, unable to stall any longer, they requested protection from Governor Hutchinson and the Council. The Council refused to acknowledge authority in the matter or

166

yield to the Governor's pressure to safeguard the consignees' tea.

Anticipating violence, Richard Clarke fled to the protection of the harbor fort, Castle William. His sons offered the Selectmen a compromise: in exchange for protection, they promised that the tea would not be unloaded secretly, and as soon as formal instructions from the East India Company arrived, they would present further proposals.

On Saturday, November 28th, the *Dartmouth,* bearing 114 chests of tea, anchored in the outer harbor. As far as the Bostonians knew, this was the first tea ship to arrive in America—it was up to them to set the precedent. That it would be returned to London they had already decided; the question was how and when. They had only twenty days in which to accomplish their purpose, since the law provided that every ship entering port had to pay customs duties within that period or have its cargo seized. Once the cargo was landed, it could be legally sold. The radicals' anxiety was heightened by the knowledge that the town was running out of tea. The sooner it was returned, the better.

Sunday was no day of rest for Bostonians. The Sabbath notwithstanding, the Board of Selectmen met twice to hear the consignees' proposals, but none were made. When the merchant-controlled town meeting failed to gain the agents' resignations, the Boston Committee of Correspondence took over, inviting the committees and citizens of five nearby towns to join them. All avenues of legal appeal being exhausted, the people could only turn to mob action to effect their ends.

The next day Molineux was charged with asking the owner of the *Dartmouth,* Francis Rotch, not to enter the ship at the customs house till Tuesday, so that it might still be free to return to England with its cargo intact. Rotch agreed. Caught between the Governor and the radicals, he was fearful that at any time either one could destroy the cargo and the ship.

Early Monday morning, November 29th, the people of Boston were called to Faneuil Hall by the sound of church bells. There they heard Sam Adams propose that the tea be returned. The people voted approval, and then, because over five thousand had gathered, they moved to a larger hall. Rotch was advised that the people "had now the Power in their Hands" and that he must so inform the Governor in order to be allowed to take his vessel out of the harbor. In the meantime, the ship was moved to a townside wharf, where a

twenty-four-hour watch was stationed on board to keep the tea from being smuggled ashore or the ship from being moved.

At a mass meeting the next day, the tea agents, now safely ensconced at Castle William, sent word that they could not return the tea, but would store it until further instructions arrived from the London company. Shortly after this unsatisfactory answer was read to the meeting, a sheriff, sent by the Governor to tell the unlawful body to disperse, was greeted with "a loud and general hiss." Sensing the impasse, young John Singleton Copley, Richard Clarke's son-in-law, offered a compromise. If he brought the consignees to the meeting, would they be heard and their safety guaranteed? The vote was in the affirmative, and Copley was given two hours to execute his errand.

JOHN SINGLETON COPLEY (1738–1815)

Born a year after his parents emigrated from Ireland, Copley grew up along the Boston waterfront, where his widowed mother ran a tobacco shop. When he was

John Singleton Copley, self-portrait, 1769.

BOSTON, December 1, 1773.

At a Meeting of the PEOPLE of Boston, and the neighbouring Towns, at Faneuil-Hall, in said Boston, on Monday the 29th of November 1773, Nine o'Clock, A. M. and continued by Adjournment to the next Day; for the Purpose of consulting, advising and determining upon the most proper and effectual Method to prevent the unloading, receiving or vending the detestable TEA sent out by the East-India Company, Part of which being just arrived in this Harbour:

IN Order to proceed with due Regularity, it was moved that a Moderator be chosen, and

JONATHAN WILLIAMS, Esq;
Was then chosen Moderator of the Meeting.

A MOTION was made that as the Town of Boston had determined at a late Meeting legally assembled, that they would to the utmost of their Power prevent the landing of the Tea, the Question be put, Whether this Body are absolutely determined that the Tea now arrived in Capt. Hall shall be returned to the Place from whence it came at all Events. And the Question being accordingly put, it passed in the Affirmative. Nem. Con.

It appearing that the Hall could not contain the People assembled, it was Voted, that the Meeting be immediately Adjourned to the Old South Meeting-House, Leave having been obtained for this Purpose.

The People met at the Old South according to Adjournment.

A Motion was made, and the Question put, viz. Whether it is the firm Resolution of this Body that the Tea shall not only be sent back, but that no Duty shall be paid thereon; & pass'd in the Affirmative Nem. Con.

It was moved, that in order to give Time to the Consignees to consider and deliberate, before they sent in their Proposals to this Body, as they had given Reason to expect would have been done at the opening of the Meeting, there might be an Adjournment to Three o'Clock, P. M. and the Meeting was accordingly for that Purpose adjourned.

THREE o'Clock, P. M. met according to Adjournment.

A Motion was made, Whether the Tea now arrived in Captain Hall's Ship shall be sent back in the same Bottom—Pass'd in the Affirmative, Nem. Con.

Mr. Rotch the Owner of the Vessel being present, informed the Body that he should enter his Protest against their Proceedings.

It was then moved and voted, nem. con. That Mr. Rotch be directed not to enter this Tea; and that the Doing of it would be at his Peril.

Also Voted, That Captain Hall the Master of the Ship, be informed that at his Peril he is not to suffer any of the Tea brought by him, to be landed.

A Motion was made, That in Order for the Security of Captain Hall's Ship and Cargo, a Watch may be appointed—and it was Voted that a Watch be accordingly appointed to consist of 25 Men.

Capt. Edward Procter was appointed by the Body to be the Capt. of the Watch for this Night, and the Names were given in to the Moderator, of the Townsmen who were Volunteers on the Occasion.

It having been observed to the Body, that Governor Hutchinson had required the Justices of the Peace in this Town to meet and use their Endeavours to suppress any Routs or Riots, &c. of the People that might happen.—It was Moved and the Question put—Whether it be not the Sense of this Meeting, that the Governor's Conduct herein carries a design'd Reflection upon the People here met; and is solely calculated to serve the Views of Administration—Passed in the Affirmative, nem. con.

The People being informed by Col. Hancock, that Mr. Copley, Son-in Law to Mr. Clarke, Sen. had acquainted him that the Tea Consignees did not receive their Letters from London till last Evening, and were so dispersed, that they could not have a joint Meeting early enough to make their Proposals at the Time intended; and therefore were desirous of a further Space for that Purpose,

The Meeting out of great Tenderness to these Persons, and from a strong Desire to bring this Matter to a Conclusion, notwithstanding the Time they had hitherto expended upon them to no Purpose, were prevailed upon to adjourn to the next Morning Nine o'Clock.

TUESDAY Morning Nine o'Clock,
Met according to Adjournment.

THE long expected Proposals were at length brought into the Meeting, not directed to the Moderator, but to John Scollay, Esq; one of the Selectmen—It was however voted that the same should be read, and they are as follow, viz.

Monday, Nov. 29th, 1773.

SIR,

WE are sorry that we could not return to the Town satisfactory Answers to their two late Messages to us respecting the Teas; we beg Leave to acquaint the Gentlemen Selectmen that we have since received our Orders from the Honorable East-India Company.

We still retain a Disposition to do all in our Power to give Satisfaction to the Town, but as we understood from you and the other Gentlemen Selectmen at Mess. Clarkes Interview with you last Saturday, that this can be effected by nothing less than our sending back the Teas, we beg Leave to say, that this is utterly out of our Power to do, but we do now declare to you our Readiness to Store the Teas until we shall have Opportunity of writing to our Constituents and shall receive their further Orders respecting them; and we do most sincerely wish that the Town considering the unexpected Difficulties devolved upon us will be satisfied with what we now offer.

We are, SIR,

Your most humble Servants,
Tho. & Elisha Hutchinson,
Benja. Faneuil, jun. for Self and
Joshua Winslow, Esq;
Rich'd Clarke & Sons.

John Scollay, Esq;

Mr. Sheriff Greenleaf came into the Meeting, and begg'd Leave of the Moderator that a Letter he had received from the Governor, requiring him to read a Proclamation to the People here assembled might be read; and it was accordingly read. Whereupon it was moved, and the Question put, Whether the Sheriff should be permitted to read the Proclamation—which passed in the Affirmative, nem. con.

The Proclamation is as follows, viz.

Massachusets-Bay. } By the Governor.

To JONATHAN WILLIAMS, Esq; acting as Moderator of an Assembly of People in the Town of Boston, and to the People so assembled:

WHEREAS printed Notifications were on Monday the 29th Instant posted in divers Places in the Town of Boston and published in the News-Papers of that Day calling upon the People to assemble together for certain unlawful Purposes in such Notifications mentioned: And whereas great Numbers of People belonging to the Town of Boston, and divers others belonging to several other Towns in the Province, did assemble in the said Town of Boston, on the said Day, and did then and there proceed to chuse a Moderator, and to consult, debate and resolve upon Ways and Means for carrying such unlawful Purposes into Execution; openly violating, defying and setting at nought the good and wholsome Laws of the Province and the Constitution of Government under which they live: And whereas the People thus assembled did vote or agree to adjourn or continue their Meeting to this the 30th Instant, and great Numbers of them are again met or assembled together for the like Purposes in the said Town of Boston,

IN Faithfulness to my Trust and as His Majesty's Representative within the Province I am bound to bear Testimony against this Violation of the Laws and I warn exhort and require you and each of you thus unlawfully assembled forthwith to disperse and to surcease all further unlawful Proceedings at your utmost Peril.

Given under my Hand at Milton in the Province aforesaid the 30th Day of November 1773 and in the fourteenth Year of His Majesty's Reign.

By His Excellency's
Command, T. Hutchinson.

THO's FLUCKER, Secr'y.

And the same being read by the Sheriff, there was immediately after, a loud and very general Hiss.

A Motion was then made, and the Question put, Whether the Assembly would disperse and surcease all further Proceedings, according to the Governor's Requirement——It pass'd in the Negative, nem. con.

A Proposal of Mr. Copley was made, that in Case he could prevail with the Mess. Clarkes to come into this Meeting, the Question might now be put, Whether they should be treated with Civility while in the Meeting, though they might be of different Sentiments with this Body; and their Persons be safe until their Return to the Place from whence they should come—And the Question being accordingly put, passed in the Affirmative, Nem. Con.

Another Motion of Mr. Copley's was put, Whether two Hours shall be given him, which also passed in the Affirmative.

Adjourn'd to Two o'Clock, P. M.

TWO o'Clock P. M. met according to Adjournment.

A Motion was made and passed, that Mr. Rotch and Capt. Hall be desired to give their Attendance.

Mr. Rotch appeared, and upon a Motion made the Question was put, Whether it is the firm Resolution of this Body, that the Tea brought by Capt. Hall shall be returned by Mr. Rotch to England in the Bottom in which it came; and whether they accordingly now require it—The which passed in the Affirmative, Nem. Con.

Mr. Rotch then informed the Meeting that he should protest against the whole Proceedings as he had done against the Proceedings on Yesterday, but that tho' the returning the Tea is an involuntary Act in him, he yet considers himself as under a Necessity to do it, and shall therefore comply with the Requirement of this Body.

Capt. Hall being present was forbid to aid or assist in unloading the Tea at his Peril, and ordered that if he continues Master of the Vessel, he carry the same back to London; who reply'd he should comply with these Requirements.

Upon a Motion, Resolved, That John Rowe, Esq; Owner of Part of Capt. Bruce's Ship expected with Tea, as also Mr. Timmins, Factor for Capt. Coffin's Brig, be desired to attend.

Mr. Ezekiel Cheever was appointed Captain of the Watch for this Night, and a sufficient Number of Volunteers gave in their Names for that Service.

VOTED, That the Captain of this Watch be desired to make out a List of the Watch for the next Night, and so each Captain of the Watch for the following Nights until the Vessels leave the Harbour.

Upon a Motion made, Voted, that in Case it should happen that the Watch should be any Ways molested in the Night, while on Duty, they give the Alarm to the Inhabitants by the tolling of the Bells—and that if any Thing happens in the Day Time, the Alarm be by ringing of the Bells.

VOTED, That six Persons be appointed to be in Readiness to give due Notice to the Country Towns when they shall be required so to do, upon any important Occasion. And six Persons were accordingly chosen for that Purpose.

John Rowe, Esq; attended, and was informed that Mr. Rotch had engaged that his Vessel should carry back the Tea she bro't in the same Bottom, & that it was the Expectation of this Body that he does the same by the Tea expected in Capt. Bruce; whereupon he reply'd that the Ship was under the Care of the said Master, but that he would use his utmost Endeavour, that it should go back as required by this Body, and that he would give immediate Advice of the Arrival of said Ship.

VOTED, That it is the Sense of this Body that Capt. Bruce shall on his Arrival strictly conform to the Votes passed respecting Capt. Hall's Vessel, as tho' they had been all passed in Reference to Capt. Bruce's Ship.

Mr. Timmins appeared and informed that Capt. Coffin's Brig expected with Tea was owned in Nantucket, he gave his Word of Honor that no Tea should be landed while she was under his Care, nor touched by any one untill the Owner's Arrival.

It was then Voted, That what Mr. Rowe and Mr. Timmins had offered was satisfactory to the Body.

Mr. Copley returned and acquainted the Body, that as he had been obliged to go to the Castle, he hoped that if he had exceeded the Time allowed him they would consider the Difficulty of a Passage by Water at this Season as his Apology: He then further acquainted the Body, that he had seen all the Consignees, and tho' he had convinced them that they might attend this Meeting with safety, and had used his utmost Endeavours to prevail upon them to give Satisfaction to the Body; they acquainted him, that believing nothing would be satisfactory short of re-shipping the Tea, which was out of their Power, they thought it best not to appear, but would renew their Proposal of storing the Tea, and submitting the same to the Inspection of a Committee, and that they could go no further, without incurring their own Ruin; but as they had not been active in introducing the Tea, they should do nothing to obstruct the People in their Procedure with the same.

It was then moved, and the Question put, Whether the return made by Mr. Copley from the Consignees, be in the least Degree satisfactory to this Body, & passed in the Negative. Nem. Con.

Whereas a Number of Merchants in this Province have inadvertently imported Tea from Great Britain, while it is subject to the Payment of a Duty imposed upon it by an Act of the British Parliament for the Purpose of raising a Revenue in America, and appropriating the same without the Consent of those who are required to pay it:

RESOLVED, That in thus importing said Tea, they have justly incurr'd the Displeasure of our Brethren in the other Colonies.

And Resolved further, That if any Person or Persons shall hereafter import Tea from Great-Britain, or if any Master or Masters of any Vessel or Vessels in Great-Britain shall take the same on Board to be imported to this Place, until the said unrighteous Act shall be repeal'd, he or they shall be deem'd by this Body an Enemy to his Country; and we will prevent the Landing and Sale of the same, and the Payment of any Duty thereon. And we will effect the Return thereof to the Place from whence it shall come.

RESOLVED, That the foregoing Vote be printed and sent to England, and all the Sea-Ports in this Province.

Upon a Motion made, Voted, That fair Copies be taken of the whole Proceedings of this Meeting, and transmitted to New-York & Philadelphia, And that Mr. SAMUEL ADAMS,
Hon. JOHN HANCOCK, Esq;
WILLIAM PHILLIPS, Esq;
JOHN ROWE, Esq;
JONATHAN WILLIAMS, Esq;
Be a Committee to transmit the same.

Voted, That it is the Determination of this Body, to carry their Votes and Resolutions into Execution, at the Risque of their Lives and Property.

Voted, That the Committee of Correspondence for this Town, be desired to take Care that every other Vessel with Tea that arrives in this Harbour, have a proper Watch appointed for her — Also Voted, That those Persons who are desirous of making a Part of these Nightly Watches, be desired to give in their Names at Messieurs Edes and Gill's Printing-Office.

Voted, That our Brethren in the Country be desired to afford their Assistance upon the first Notice given; especially if such Notice be given upon the Arrival of Captain Loring, in Messieurs Clarkes' Brigantine.

Voted, That those of this Body who belong to the Town of Boston do return their Thanks to their Brethren who have come from the neighbouring Towns, for their Countenance and Union with this Body in this Exigence of our Affairs.

VOTED, That the Thanks of this Meeting be given to JONATHAN WILLIAMS, Esq; for his good services as Moderator.

VOTED, That this Meeting be Dissolved —— And it was accordingly Dissolved.

Printed by EDES and GILL, 1773.

Broadside announcing the results of the Faneuil Hall meeting of November 29, 1773.

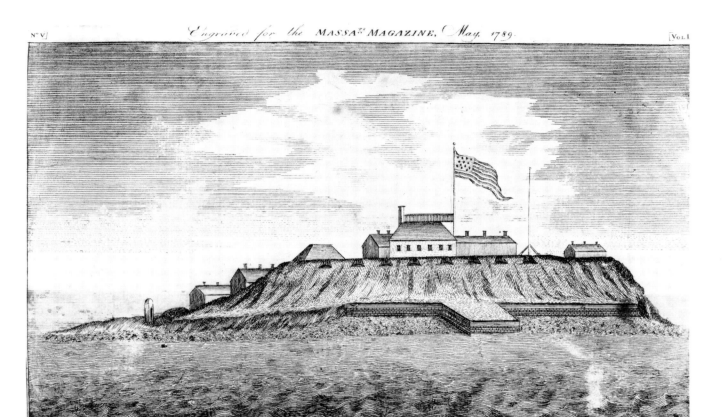

A North View of CASTLE WILLIAM *in the* HARBOUR *of* BOSTON.

Castle William in Boston harbor as it appeared late in the 18th century.

ten, his mother married the engraver Peter Pelham, and for three years—until Pelham died—young Copley enjoyed his only art training. By the time he was fifteen, he was already receiving commissions, and by 1766, on the basis of a portrait sent to Benjamin West for exhibition in London, he was elected Fellow of the Society of Artists of Great Britain. By 1773, Copley, as a result of his lively insight and mastery of the art of realistic portraiture, was earning a handsome living in America. Having married the daughter of one of Boston's merchant princes, he now owned a fine farm and splendid home on Beacon Hill. "I am in as good business as the poverty of this place will admit," he wrote. "I make as much as if I were a Raphael or a Correggio; and at three hundred guineas a year, my present income is equal to nine hundred a year in London." [32]

Politically neutral, Copley was the perfect man to mediate between the consignees and the town. While he sought out the tea agents, the meeting summoned the owners, or their representatives, of the other tea ships, to receive their pledges to return the tea when it arrived. Most promised to do so. Ship owner John Rowe admitted he "was very sorry he had any Tea on Board." The crowd was pleased they had won a "Tory." Rowe, skilled at running both with the hares and the hounds, confided to his diary: "I staid some time at the Meeting & was Chose a Committee Man much against my will but I dare not say a word." [33]

Copley returned late—and alone. He tried "every argument my thoughts could suggest" to persuade the mob not to take drastic action. The consignees, he said, had to abide by their arrangements with the tea company or else face ruin. They had not come in person not because they feared for their safety, but because they saw no point in telling the people in person they could not accede to their demands. They were not in collusion with Governor Hutchinson, and, in fact, had not seen him that day. Finally, Copley reported, the tea agents would not object if the townspeople arranged for the return of the tea, but they could not legally do so themselves. The meeting voted the reply unsatisfactory and agreed once more to carry out their resolution at the "risque of their Lives and Property." Before adjourning, they arranged for news of their gathering to be sent to London, Massachusetts port towns, Philadelphia, and New York, and for the townspeople to sign up for continuous watches aboard the tea ships. At the end of the meeting, John Hancock said: "My Fellow Countrymen, we have now put our Hands to the Plough and Wo Be to him that shrinks or looks back." [34]

ABIGAIL ADAMS (1744–1818); MERCY OTIS WARREN (1728–1814)

Although only men were permitted to serve in regulating the affairs of the colony, women were not without either voice or influence in political matters. Three years earlier the women of Boston had signed a pledge against the consumption of English tea, substituting instead a concoction made from raspberry leaves called "balsamic hyperion." They were prepared to do their part again to protect their rights and liberties.

Both Abigail Adams and Mercy Warren were married to men involved in public affairs. Both were women of intellectual attainments, and both shared their husbands' political involvement and philosophies.

Abigail was the daughter of William Smith, a Congregational minister, and Elizabeth Quincy of Weymouth. She had married John Adams despite the disapproval of her mother's family and her father's congregation, who thought the young lawyer not worthy of a daughter descended from "so many of the shining lights of the Coloney." The first ten years of her marriage were spent moving back and forth from their Braintree farm to Boston townhouses, as John became more involved in colonial affairs and as his legal reputation grew. During these years, Abigail bore him five children, one of whom died in infancy, and competently managed the affairs of the home and the farm during her husband's forced absences practicing law in neighboring towns.

Happily for her, Abigail was much more than the household manager. A cheerful person with an eager, alert intelligence, she provided constant support and comfort to her husband as he argued his political principles in the local press and formulated legal documents sustaining colonial rights against the mother country. But she fought a losing battle in her several attempts to win his good offices for the cause of women's rights.

Abigail Adams's close friend, Mercy Otis Warren of Barnstable, has been called "perhaps the most remarkable woman who lived in the days of the American Revolution." [35] Though both women supported and influenced their husbands, Mrs. Warren exerted a wider influence on the movement against the mother country through her close association with the radical leadership and through her political writings.

Mercy's father, Colonel James Otis, Sr., the presiding judge of the district court, was active in local Whig affairs. His home was always the center of local political discussions, at which his children were welcome guests. Mercy's older brother James strongly influenced her early years, and after his mental breakdown, she tried to continue his political work with her pen.

Mercy Otis had married her brother's good friend, James Warren, a merchant and farmer, who also served in the colonial legislature. Warren's home became a political club and meeting place for Boston activists. It was most likely at the Warren fireside that Sam Adams and his host discussed the forming of a Committee of Correspondence in October 1772—discussions in which Mercy took an important part.

With Abigail Adams, Mercy exchanged information on the education of their children, advising her friend that she was teaching her sons that the "love of *truth*" was the most important principle in life. For her pleasure, she turned always to "the book and the pen." Encouraged in the composition of political satire by her husband and John Adams, she wrote her first literary drama in the spring of 1772, which was published anonymously in the *Massachusetts Spy*. Entitled "The Adulateur: A Tragedy: as It Is Now Acted in Upper Servia," it cast Thomas Hutchinson as the arch villain Rapatio, her brother as Brutus, and Sam Adams as Cassius. The next year, the *Boston Gazette* published "The Defeat," another attack on Hutchinson. Believing that Providence had endowed Mercy "with Powers for the good of the World, which . . . would be criminal to neglect," John Adams suggested to James Warren that his wife celebrate "the late frolic among the sea nymphs"—the Boston Tea Party. Three months later, Mercy Otis Warren published "The Squabble of the Sea Nymphs." [36]

The Boston Tea Party

Though still recovering from a severe fever, Mrs. Adams felt obligated to inform Mercy of the events taking place in Boston since the arrival of the tea ships.

You Madam are so sincere a Lover of your Country, and so Hearty a mourner in all her misfortunes that it will greatly aggravate your anxiety to hear how much she is now oppressed and insulted. . . .

. . . The Tea that bainfull weed is arrived. Great and I hope Effectual opposition has been made to the landing of it. . . . The proceedings of our Citizens have been United, Spirited and firm. The flame is kindled and like Lightning it catches from Soul to Soul. Great will be the devastation if not timely quenched or allayed by some more Lenient Measures.

Altho the mind is shocked at the Thought of shedding Humane Blood, more Especially the Blood of our Country-men, and a civil War is of all Wars, the most dreadfull Such is the present Spirit that prevails, that if once they are made desperate Many, very Many of our Heroes will spend their lives in the cause, With the Speach of Cato in their Mouths, "What a Pitty it is, that we can dye but once to save our Country."

"Tender plants must bend but when Government is grown to Strength like some old oak rough with its armed bark, it yealds not to the tug, but only Nods and turns to sullen State."

Such is the present Situation of affairs that I tremble when I think what may be the direfull concequences. . . . My Heart beats at every Whistle I hear. . . .[37]

On December 13, the *Boston Gazette* published a letter from Philadelphians that not too subtly chided their brothers in the North for inaction: "All that we fear is, that you will shrink at Boston. May God Give you virtue enough to save the liberties of your country!"[38] In the same issue an article signaled the end of the radicals' patience with Rotch's procrastina-tions—there would be another mass meeting to hear him explain why he had not yet returned his ship to England.

At the meeting on the fourteenth, Rotch was instructed to apply immediately to the customs house for clearance. Out he went and back he came, with the message that he must return the next day, after the officials had consulted. A committee was appointed to accompany him, and the meeting adjourned until the morning of the sixteenth—the last day before the tea would be landed.

At ten that morning, a cold and rainy day, seven thousand people gathered at the Old South Meeting House. Rotch appeared to report that he could not obtain a pass from the customs officials. He was instructed to go to Governor Hutchinson at his Milton residence and obtain permission for his ship to sail. Hutchinson, however, had no anticipation of trouble: "there being so many men of property active at their meetings," he wrote, who knew they would have to pay out of their own pockets for any damage done. Therefore, he refused to endorse any "violation" of the trade acts.[39]

By the time Rotch returned, the people had unani-mously voted that the tea should not be landed. Hearing him report that Hutchinson had refused to let his tea-laden ship depart, they cried for the mob to act. "I heard an hideous Yelling in the Street . . ." a witness reported, "as of an Hundred People, some imitating the Powaws of Indians and others the Whistle of Boatswain, which was answered by some few in the House."[40]

Amid shouts and cheering, Sam Adams dismissed the crowd. "This meeting can do nothing more to save the country," he announced; and the gallery, recog-nizing this as the signal for action, shouted back "Boston Harbor a tea-pot tonight!" and "Hurrah for Griffin's Wharf!"[41] The events that followed had all been prearranged. The plan called for disguise to prevent recognition and later punishment of the participants; an orderly dispatch of the tea, with no harm done to any other property or any person; and silence, except for the giving of orders which was done in a "jargon . . . unintelligible to all but themselves."

The organizers of the Tea Party included the respectable people of the town: over fifteen merchants and almost fifty artisans. Their uninvited but welcome guests were mostly apprentices, passersby, and some who had come from as far as Maine determined to dump tea. A number were members of the volunteer watch and knew the vessels well.

Members of the political Long Room Club met in the parlor at Edes & Gill, publishers of the *Boston Gazette,* the afternoon of the Tea Party. Donning Indian makeup and blankets, they waited until dark. Up on Fort Hill, a number met in a store to prepare for the night's work. In houses along one street, others, too, made ready. In one house, David, Thomas, Nathaniel, and Josiah Bradlee, and their brother-in-law, John Fulton, put on garments they had hidden for several days. Across the way, Samuel Fenno and John

The BOSTONIAN'S Paying the EXCISE-MAN, or TARRING & FEATHERING

Plate I.

London. Printed for Rob.ᵗ Sayer & J. Bennett, Map & Printsellers N.º 53, Fleet Street, as the Act directs 31 Oct.ʳ 1774.

Crane made their preparations. Others met at the home of James Brewer, a pump- and blockmaker who had stood guard on the *Dartmouth*, to blacken their faces with burnt cork. Richard Hunnewell, a Son of Liberty who also had guarded the *Dartmouth*, took his two teenage sons down to the wharf. John Russell and Thomas Moore smeared lampblack and red ochre on their faces and went forth. Ebenezer Stevens, with about seventy-five other men, went directly from the Old South Meeting House to the wharf, stopping to paint his face at a shop along the way. Joseph Eyres, housewright, Thomas Chase, distiller, Samuel Peck, cooper, and Adam Collson, leather dresser, also showed up.

The notorious shoemaker Ebenezer McIntosh, whose accomplishments earned him the title of "first Captain-General of Liberty Tree," was on the scene the night of the Tea Party. "It was my chickens that did the job," he told listeners years later.[42]

Housewright Thomas Crafts, one of McIntosh's "chickens" and a member of the St. Andres Masonic Lodge, disguised his apprentice, Amos Lincoln, and then, dropping to his knees in prayer for his success and safety, sent him down to the wharf to do his duty. Quite a number of apprentices, however, participated on their own initiative. Peter Slater's master had locked him in his room, but the lad escaped, stopping first at a blacksmith's shop for the necessary anointing. The Scottish-born James Swan, an apprentice in a counting house and already the author of anti-slavery pamphlets, disguised himself along with other apprentices living in his boarding house. Sixteen-year-old Joshua Wyeth, a journeyman blacksmith, and his friends smeared their faces with soot and grease. Garbed in rags and resembling "devils from the bottomless pit," they were amused at "making so large a cup of tea for the fishes."[43]

Robert Sessions ran down to the wharf without disguise. "Everything was as light as day, by the means of lamps and torches," he recalled; "a pin might be seen lying on the wharf."[44]

Samuel Sprague, a journeyman mason on his way to

The brutal treatment of John Malcomb, Commissioner of Customs at Boston, for trying to collect customs duties. Mezzotint, 1774.

court his future bride, saw the mob and hurried after them. He stopped only to dig his hand into a stovepipe chimney and blacken his face with soot. Dr. Elisha Story was the son of the Registrar of the Court of Admiralty, whose office had been broken into and papers burned during the Stamp Act crisis. Yet, the young doctor, a Son of Liberty, had taken the first watch on the *Dartmouth*. Late in the afternoon of the Tea Party, he again met his companions in a distillery to help prepare their disguises.

One man, hearing the commotion, interrupted his tea-drinking at home but could get no farther than the meeting-house porch, where he encountered a band of men "cloath'd in Blankets with heads muffled, and copper color'd countenances, being each arm'd with a hatchet or axe, and a pair of pistols." Wanting no part of what sounded like "the inhabitants of the infernal regions . . . broke loose," he turned about and "went contentedly home and finished my tea."[45]

In falling rain, hundreds of blanketed "Mohawks"

OPPOSITE PAGE:
John Malcomb, Commissioner of Customs at Boston, tarred and feathered and forced to drink tea for attempting to collect customs duties. Mezzotint attributed to Philip Dawe, 1774.

The Boston Tea Party by Johann Ramberg,
probably 1784.

marched down to Griffin's Wharf. Quietly, they boarded the *Dartmouth* and demanded the keys from Captain Hall. Warning him and the customs officials to stay clear, they descended into the hold, brought up the tea chests, hacked them open, and dumped the cargo overboard. John Crane was the sole casualty of the night, knocked unconscious by a derrick used to hoist the tea. His friends interrupted their labors to stow the body under a pile of shavings in a nearby carpenter's shop. When they returned, the man presumed dead, a stocky, heavy-set lad, was dazed but conscious.

It took three hours to dispose of 342 chests of tea worth £18,000. When the rain stopped and the bright moonlight revealed clumps of tea in the water, some Bostonians attempted to collect the floating contraband. John Hooten and his buddies, seeing one such scavenger, upset the man's boat and his ill-gotten cargo, in the shallow water. Care was taken that no tea was taken off the ships. One who tried to stuff some into his coat pocket was stripped and given "a coat of mud, with a severe bruising into the bargain." [46]

Small deposits of tea clung to the shoes and clothing of some of the men when they returned to their homes late that night. "We have only been making a little salt-water tea," Joseph Pearse Palmer told his wife. William Russell, a schoolteacher, carefully emptied his shoes over the fire. Sweeping the tea that dropped from her husband's boots, Josiah Wheeler's wife refused to "touch the cursed stuff." Thomas Melville, a Princeton graduate, who had just returned from a health cure in Scotland and had joined his fellow members of the Long Room Club down at the wharf, preserved a vial of tea from that eventful night which was retained by his descendants, including the writer Herman Melville.

"The next day," reported a Tory paper, "joy appeared in almost every countenance, some on occasion of the destruction of the tea, others on account of the quietness with which it was effected." [47]

PAUL REVERE (1735–1818)

One of those on Griffin's Wharf that night was Paul Revere. Described by contemporaries as "cool in thought, ardent in action," he was a natural-born leader of the artisan class, and one who could provide easy communication with other radical leaders of greater education and higher class status. Not an orator, he preferred the stylus and the political caricature for stirring the people to a defense of their rights.

Revere's father had come to Boston as a young boy, a victim of the Huguenot persecution in France, and had been indentured to a highly skilled gold- and silversmith. By the time his first son was born, Apollos de Revoire had anglicized his name so "that the Bumpkins [should] pronounce it easier." Young Paul learned his father's trade and developed his talents to become one of the best silversmiths in the colonies.

During the hard times in the mid-1760s, Revere had few commissions in his shop and turned to engraving a book of psalm tunes. Soon, he developed great skill as an engraver on copper, which he used to satirize the British and memorialize the heroism of Boston's radicals.

In every action plotted to prevent the landing of the East India tea, Revere was involved, whether it meant acting as emissary to the committees of correspondence of nearby towns, standing guard in the first watch on the *Dartmouth,* or blackening his face and donning a disguise to help dump the tea. He was scarcely home from the Tea Party when he was selected to carry "the Glorious Intelligence" to New York and Philadelphia. In his saddle bags he carried a letter announcing that Bostonians

are in a perfect jubilee. Not a Tory in the whole community can find the least fault with our proceedings. . . . The spirit of the people through the country is to be described by no terms in my power. Their conduct last night surprised the admiral and English gentlemen, who observed that these were not a mob of disorderly rabble, (as they have been reported,) but men of sense, coolness and intrepidity.[48]

The report was not exaggerated. After all the tea was dumped, and the keys returned to the ship captains, the men swept the decks clean and went home peacefully. Hutchinson had already abdicated his authority as governor, knowing he could expect no support from the officials. Had he used military force, he was certain it would have "brought on a greater convulsion than there was any danger of in 1770."[49]

Revere was gone eleven days, returning on December 27th with the news that the colonists in New York and Philadelphia would stand firm against the landing of the tea when it arrived in their ports. The Boston Tea Party had, according to Revere, united New

York, causing Governor Tryon to make "a Virtue of Necessity" by promising to return the tea as soon as it arrived. While Revere was on the road, the taverns rang with an account of his heroics:

Rally Mohawks! bring out your axes,
And tell King George we'll pay no taxes
    On his foreign tea;
His threats are vain, and vain to think
To force our girls and wives to drink
    His vile Bohea!
Then rally boys, and hasten on
To meet our chiefs at the Green Dragon.

Our Warren's there, and bold Revere,
With hands to do, and words to cheer,
    For liberty and laws;
Our country's "braves" and firm defenders
Shall ne'er be left by true North-Enders
    Fighting Freedom's cause!
Then rally boys, and hasten on
To meet our chiefs at the Green Dragon.[50]

The day after Revere returned, Sam Adams wrote James Warren, fixing the blame for the Tea Party on "our Enemies" whose "Obstinacy" had left the colonists with no alternative to safeguard their rights. The

Chinese tea chest said to have been emptied at the Boston Tea Party.

Boston Committee of Correspondence began to renew contacts with others in New England as well as in New York and Philadelphia. "The Ministry could not have devised a more effectual Measure to unite the Colonies. . . . Old Jealousies are removed, and perfect Harmony subsists between them," Adams wrote.[51]

John Adams learned of the Tea Party on his way home from the court at Plymouth. That night, in his diary, he remarked first on the deed, which he thought necessary given the circumstances, and then on the probable consequences:

This is the most magnificent Movement of all. There is a Dignity, a Majesty, a Sublimity in this last Effort of the Patriots that I greatly admire. The People should never rise without doing something to be remembered,—something notable & striking. This Destruction of the Tea is so bold, so daring, so firm, intrepid, & inflexible, and it must have so important Consequences, and so lasting, that I cannot but consider it as an Epocha in History. . . .

What Measures will the Ministry take in Consequence of this? Will y^y resent it? Will y^y dare to resent it? Will y^y punish us? how? By quartering Troops upon us? By Annulling our Charter? by laying on more duties? by restraining our Trade? by sacrifice of Individuals? or how?[52]

Paul Revere by John Singleton Copley, 1768-1770.

ALEXANDER WEDDERBURN (1733–1805), FIRST BARON LOUGHBOROUGH (in 1780) AND FIRST EARL OF ROSSLYN (1801)

In a letter to Thomas Cushing, Speaker of the Massachusetts Assembly, Ben Franklin, agent for Massachusetts, observed: "I suppose we have never had since we are a people, so few friends in Britain. . . . The violent destruction of the tea seems to have united all parties here against our province. . . ."[53] None knew better than he: in late January he had been excoriated by Alexander Wedderburn, the solicitor-general, before the Privy Council for his role in the affair involving the Hutchinson-Oliver letters. "Men will watch him with a jealous eye," Wedderburn had ranted. "They will hide their papers from him and lock up their escritoires." Franklin, he had quipped, "will henceforth esteem it a libel to be called a 'man of letters.' "[54]

Wedderburn's attack on Franklin had been stimulated not merely by disclosure of the letters' contents, but by the recently arrived news of Boston's Tea

Party. Wedderburn, a politician governed by an unrelenting ambition to advance, had been for a long time antagonistic toward the colonies. But his plan to attack Franklin and the petition from the Massachusetts Bay was motivated more by the desire to ingratiate himself with Lord North and the King than to create a colonial crisis. Having switched parties three times within two years, Wedderburn finally had won a position in Lord North's administration as solicitor-general, chancellor to the Queen, and a member of the Privy Council. Now he wished to solidify his gains.

Franklin, on his part, was "less concerned about censure, when I am satisfied that I act right." Censure was scarcely the word for what Franklin was forced to endure at a hearing on the petition on the 29th of January. Thirty-five privy councillors and a group of interested bystanders, including Burke, Jeremy Bentham, and Joseph Priestley, crowded into the room. During the entire proceeding, the sixty-nine-year-old Franklin stood alone, his head resting on one hand, "his countenance as immovable as if his features had been made of wood," as Priestley observed.[55]

It was not for himself, but for the colonies, that

Franklin grieved, fearful of what must result when they were no longer allowed to have their petitions receive a fair hearing. "Grievances cannot be redressed unless they are known," he wrote, "and they cannot be known but through complaints and petitions. . . . But where complaining is a crime, hope becomes despair." [56] The aftermath was immediate. The next day Franklin was deprived of his position as Deputy Postmaster General of North America.

In his letter to Cushing, written two weeks after the hearing, Franklin warned, "It is not likely . . . that the session will pass over without some proceeding relating to us." There was no evidence yet of what was planned nor was he certain if there would be direct legal action against any individuals, although he knew visitors from America had been interrogated, and there was "some intention of seizing persons, and perhaps of sending them hither." [57]

The ministry planned a two-pronged attack to "secure the Dependence of the Colonies on the Mother Country": prosecution of the individuals responsible for the Tea Party and punishment of the

Alexander Wedderburn by Mather Brown, date unknown.

town and colony. Wedderburn, however, faced a dilemma. Although he considered the Tea Party a treasonable act, he could not conduct a trial without knowing the identity of the defendants or having at hand sufficient evidence. Thus, the ministry, determined to punish the colonies rather than persuade them, turned to Parliament with a bill to close the port of Boston, the lifeline of Massachusetts Bay.

JOHN POWNALL (c. 1725–1795)

The man who suggested the drastic measure was John Pownall, Secretary of the Board of Trade and first Undersecretary of State in the American Department. Pownall had risen to his position of power through luck, perseverance, and political sensitivity. Because his superior, Lord Dartmouth, knew little about American affairs, Pownall was able to influence him to adopt a strict colonial policy, something he had favored since 1763. In the summer of 1773, he plotted to increase the authority of the governor of Massachusetts as a first step toward bringing the recalcitrant colony into line. When news of the Tea Party reached ministerial ears, Pownall urged that the port of Boston be closed by law. Once the matter of punishment was turned over to Parliament, there was little doubt that it would attempt to settle once and for all its legislative sovereignty in regulating American affairs.

The Boston Port Bill was presented by Lord North to the House of Commons the second week of March. It was intended, as was the other legislation North said would soon follow, to allow the King to end the "present disturbances in America . . . [and] to secure the just dependence of the colonies on the Crown of Great Britain." Since "Boston had been the ringleader in all the riots," North declared, "We must punish, controul [sic] or yield to them." [58]

The bill would close the port of Boston to all shipping until the East India Company and the concerned revenue officers were compensated, and the King had decided it was safe for it to be reopened. The customs officers would be removed to Marblehead in the port of Salem. Only military stores and coastal vessels carrying food and fuel would be allowed to enter, provided they had been searched by customs officers. North assumed that the bill could be easily enforced with only a few ships and a few regiments stationed in Boston. He anticipated that the other colonial ports, far from protesting the punishment,

John Pownall's engraved bookplate.

would welcome the opportunity to enjoy the trade denied Boston.

By the end of the month, the bill had passed both Houses of Parliament and had received the royal assent. A few days before its final enactment, North presented the Bill for Regulating the Government of Massachusetts Bay. It was clear, he said, that there was "something radically wrong" in the present charter, that "an executive power was wanting." The bill he proposed would "purge the constitution of all its crudities"—that is, it would greatly enhance the powers of the Crown, through its agent, the governor, by severely curtailing the power of the people.[59] The governor would appoint the Council (the upper house of the legislature), as well as sheriffs, judges, and the attorney general. Except for allowing an annual gathering for electing officers, the governor could prohibit all town meetings, which the ministry believed provided forums for insurrection, and his decision would no longer be subject to the Council's veto.

Juries would no longer be elected, but appointed by the sheriff.

The bill was introduced formally in the middle of April and enacted within a month along with a third bill, the Impartial Administration of Justice Act. The intent of this latter measure was to provide legal protection to His Majesty's officers: any indictment for a capital offense committed in the line of duty—quelling a riot or collecting revenue—could be tried in England, if the governor thought the defendant could not obtain a fair trial in Massachusetts. The last of the so-called Coercive Acts, enacted in early June, simply extended the provisions of the 1765–1766 quartering acts, allowing the troops to be billeted in private dwellings.

Although the Boston Port Bill was clearly punitive, the ministry considered the other measures as redressing a constitutional imbalance and insuring sufficient military authority to enforce the rights of Parliament. Each of the measures was passed swiftly, but not before old friends of America in the House of Commons registered their protests against the excessive reaction of their fellow members.

WILLIAM DOWDESWELL (1721–1775); EDMUND BURKE (1729–1797)

The day Lord North asked leave to introduce the Boston Port Bill, William Dowdeswell complained of "the present hasty, ill-digested mode of proceeding." Long accustomed to speaking against Tory measures, he had gained prominence as a leader of the Whigs. In 1765, he became Rockingham's Chancellor of the Exchequer, upon which appointment the waspish Walpole wrote:

. . . he was fit for nothing else. Heavy, slow, methodical without clearness, a butt for ridicule, unused in every graceful art, and a stranger to men and courts, he was only esteemed by the few to whom he was personally known.[60]

Walpole, however, conceded Dowdeswell's disinterest, his lack of concern for personal aggrandizement. The promotion of trade at home and with the colonies was his principal goal. His approach was never doctrinaire, but always pragmatic. Parliament's right to tax the colonies he considered an insoluble issue and so he avoided it, just as he avoided making distinctions between internal and external taxes. Instead, he

Edmund Burke by James Barry, 1774.

of his party in urging that only the malefactors, not the innocent citizens of Boston, be punished. If Hutchinson had not tried to stop the riot, why punish others for the same failure? The Boston Port Bill was being pushed through Parliament when what was required, so he and his colleagues felt, was a full review of American-British relations.

Edmund Burke had first appeared in public life as a literary man who enjoyed entrée to London's intellectual and artistic society. Having served as secretary to various influential political figures, he soon became a political force on his own, especially after 1766 when he became a member of Parliament. Burke was a realist: "Principles should be subordinate to government," he said. In keeping with this belief, he favored the repeal of the Stamp Act because of the difficulty in administering it; however, he voted for the Declaratory Act because it established the principle of parliamentary supremacy.

Townshend duties he believed were a mistake: "You will never see a shilling from America," he

attempted to solve all issues as they arose on an objective and practical basis. The repeal of the Townshend duties, thus, was justified because they were harmful to British manufacturing and colonial trade.

When debate began on the Coercive Acts, Dowdeswell wondered why only Boston should be punished; other towns had refused to land the tea but were not threatened with penalties. And why was Boston denied the right to defend itself? In his speech against the bill altering the Massachusetts charter, he asked that his colleagues "recollect yourselves in a cool, dispassionate manner, and look upon Americans as your children" whose "ill humour and disposition" might have been caused by "the petulant obstinacy of a foolish parent." The only part of the bill that Dowdeswell favored was the provision for the removal of Governor Hutchinson.[61]

The consensus among the majority of British Whigs was that the punishment inherent in the Boston Port Bill fit the crime, but that the other measures were excessive. Edmund Burke, who had served Rockingham as private secretary, joined others

William Dowdeswell's engraved bookplate.

Covent-garden, Feb. 9. 1774

Sir,

The report of the lords of the comittee, upon the address of sent by Dr. Franklin, house of representatives, with the royal approbation of it, will shew you the temper of the present times, of whose violence, injuries, & improvidence I can foresee no end, altho' their chief conductors are thro' fear of consequences, I believe, unwilling to come to imediate extremities; but you are sensible that when passion & power unite in support of errors & wrongs their future operations are often unknown even to their authors — for my own part I continue my endeavours to check this torrent of folly & madness, going on day & night with my intended vindication of the & the various difficulties of the work rights of the colonies as fast as these troublesome avocations will permit

Altho' the right of petition evidently includes the right of supporting it, the chief ministers seem unwilling to grant or refuse a hearing in maintenance of my own.

I am with great Esteem & regard
Sir
your most obedient
humble servant
W Bollan

The Honble Ja. Bowdoin Esqr.

Letter from William Bollan to James Bowdoin, II, February 9, 1774.

predicted. Several years later, urging reconciliation with the American colonies, he urged that Parliament be guided not by legal theory but by "humanity, reason, and justice." [62]

Burke's position was echoed by other members of Parliament who shared his and Dowdeswell's pragmatic approach to political problems. Colonel Barré warned: "You have stimulated discontent into disaffection, and you are now goading that disaffection into rebellion." He supported the first measure though he thought it "a bad way of doing what was right," but the later measures were persecutory and would result in violence: "Instead of sending them the olive branch, you have sent the naked sword. By the olive branch I mean a repeal of all the late laws, fruitless to you, and oppressive to them." [63]

On April 19th, Rose-Fuller, a Jamaican planter and member of Parliament, proposed that the tea duty, the last of the Townshend taxes, be removed in order to soften the sting of the Coercive Acts. If both were maintained, the result would surely be rebellion, he warned. To this proposal, Charles Cornwall, a lesser official in the ministry, objected. Parliament must now assert its "authority," he insisted; "such a pusillanimous timidity in repealing this tax, merely because . . . [the colonists] object to it" would profit Parliament nothing.[64] If Parliament gave in on this issue, insisted Cornwall, it would find itself giving in on everything else, and thus lose the opportunity to tax the colonies when the need was urgent. Cornwall's principal criticism of the Whig policy was that conciliation, far from satisfying the colonists, only resulted in continual violence and vandalism; coercion in the guise of reform was required to make the colonists obedient.

Since the stamp tax was repealed under a Whig ministry, Edmund Burke could not let Cornwall's speech pass unanswered. The colonists, he argued, had not demanded further concessions when the stamp tax was repealed; they would not do so if the tea duty were repealed. It was only when "departing from the maxims of [the Stamp Act] repeal," he reminded his colleagues, "you revised the scheme of taxation, and thereby filled the minds of the colonists with . . . all sorts of apprehensions, then it was that they quarrelled with the old taxes, as well as the new; then it was, and not till then, that they questioned all the parts of your legislative power; and by the battery of such questions have shaken the solid structure of this empire to its deepest foundations." [65]

Quoting the preamble to the Townshend Act, Burke reminded his fellow members that its purpose was to raise revenue for the administration of the colonies.

Now where is the revenue which is to do all these mighty things? Five sixths repealed—abandoned—sunk—gone—lost for ever. Does the poor solitary tea duty support the purposes of this preamble? Is not the supply there stated as effectually abandoned as if the tea duty had perished in the general wreck? Here, Mr. Speaker, is a precious mockery—a preamble without an act—taxes granted in order to be repealed—and the reasons of the grant still carefully kept up! This is raising a revenue in America! This is preserving dignity in England! If you repeal this tax in compliance with the motion, I readily admit that you lose this fair preamble. Estimate your loss in it. The object of the Act is gone already; and all you suffer is the purging of the statutebook of the opprobrium of an empty, absurd, and false recital.[66]

Burke's conclusion was clear. Get rid of this tax—"a tax of sophistry, a tax of pedantry, a tax of disputation, a tax of war and rebellion, a tax for anything but benefit to the imposers, or satisfaction to the subject." [67]

Burke believed—as Dowdeswell had also inferred—that Britain's imperial policy went wrong when she began to tax the colonies, not for legitimate commercial purposes, but for revenue. Parliament, he said, does indeed have the power to tax, but in practice that power must be used in a limited way—as "an instrument of empire," not "as a means of supply." If asked, the colonists would tax themselves; but "Tyranny is a poor provider." Having lost the "profit" promised by the Townshend Acts, now he suggested, "let us get rid of the odium." He knew, he concluded, that his defense of American privileges would not lead to his own personal preferment. Nonetheless, the policy of the Rockingham administration in repealing the onerous stamp tax was the most honorable and judicious policy to follow. "Until you come back to that system," he concluded, "there will be no peace for England." [68]

WILLIAM BOLLAN (c. 1710–1782); ARTHUR LEE (1740–1792)

Two principal arguments against the passage of the Coercive Acts were that no evidence existed against the town of Boston itself and that the colonists had been denied the legal right to be heard in their own defense. William Bollan, agent for the Council of the Province of Massachusetts Bay, and Arthur Lee, an American living in London, both petitioned the House of Commons for a hearing in defense of their countrymen.

Almost all of Bollan's professional life had been spent serving Massachusetts. As a young lawyer in the colony, he had served as counselor for Harvard College, adviser for the Episcopal Church, and King's Advocate-General with the duty of prosecuting violators of the Acts of Trade. From 1745 to 1748, he lived in England while recovering the £200,000 owed the colony for its participation in Governor Shirley's Louisbourg expedition.

His success recommended him for continued service as the colony's agent in London until 1762 when his employment was terminated. The necessity to lobby against the Townshend Acts brought him back into Massachusetts' service, and from 1770 on, Bollan labored hard for his constituents. Cooperating with

Arthur Lee by Charles Willson Peale, 1785.

Ben Franklin, the Assembly's agent, Bollan tried to intercede on Franklin's behalf when the Privy Council deprived Franklin of his position as Deputy Postmaster General because of his publication of the Hutchinson-Oliver letters. Of Wedderburn's castigation of Franklin in that affair, Bollan wrote that "his reproaches appear[ed] to me incompatible with the principles of law, truth, justice, propriety & humanity." [69]

Arthur Lee was also in attendance that day, as Franklin's attorney. He was to become Franklin's replacement as Massachusetts Assembly agent when Franklin retired. The ambitious Lee had been waiting impatiently for the appointment for years. The previous spring he had written to Sam Adams: "Dr. Franklin frequently assures me, that he shall sail for Philadelphia in a few weeks; but I believe he will not quit us till he is gathered to his fathers." [70]

A fourth-generation Virginian of a famous family, Lee received a medical degree from the University of Edinburgh in 1764, but practiced medicine for only a few years before returning to London to study law and engage in politics. In several series of letters, signed with an assortment of pseudonyms, he defended the rights and privileges of his fellow Americans. As "Monitor," he warned the colonists of the evil designs of the British upon their privileges and liberties. As "Junius Americanus," he advised the British that their well-being was directly connected with the Americans' struggle to preserve their rights. His aim was a Bill of Rights for Americans that he hoped the British would regard as mutually beneficial.

Lee's political letters received wide publication in America, and he was highly regarded as an effective defender of his homeland. His reward was his appointment as agent for Virginia and, in 1770, surrogate for Franklin. Sam Adams informed Lee that he knew of no one "in London who has the liberties of America more warmly at heart, or is more able to vindicate them than yourself." [71] Lee also received letters from Joseph Warren and the Boston Committee of Correspondence, all hoping that he could "penetrate the Egyptian darkness" in London, as Warren put it, and get Massachusetts a fair hearing with respect to the dumping of the tea.

In February 1774, Lee wrote Sam Adams, "Be prepared . . . to meet some particular stroke of revenge during this session of parliament; and instead of thinking to prevent it, contrive the means of frustrating its effect." By early April he wrote his brother, Richard Henry Lee, in Virginia of the intent of the Coercive Acts and suggested, as the only means "to save our liberties from shipwreck," the calling of a colonial congress and a united embargo against all trade with Britain for a year. Unless such action was taken, "you may depend upon it, that if they find the chains can be easily imposed, they will make them heavy, and rivet them fast." [72] In the same letter, Lee remarked upon the unsuccessful petition of the Americans to be heard against the enactment of the Boston Port Bill. He had himself written a petition for "native Americans" living in England on behalf of the Bostonians. These frail documents were, as Franklin pointed out, not petitions at all but *Remonstrances and Protests.* However, with the exception of a not too sympathetic press, they were the only recourse the Americans in London had to make their voices heard.

The prevailing attitude in Parliament and in the ministry was that the Americans knew they had acted wrongly and they would therefore accept their punishment. Thus, it was not necessary to hear their statements.

Bollan rejected such assumptions. He ran himself ragged calling upon members of Parliament, desperately pleading that he be recognized as the spokesman for Massachusetts Bay. Although denied a hearing by the Privy Council, he was finally promised that his plea would be heard in the House of Commons just before final passage of the Boston Port Bill. But when formal permission was requested after "a short, but warm debate," it was denied on the grounds that since Bollan only represented a part of the legislature rather than the whole, he, in effect, represented no one. Of this spurious logic, Burke remarked, "We are resolved not to hear the only person we *can* hear; but are mighty ready to hear anyone else." [73]

In the House of Commons, Burke was determined to inform his colleagues of the substance of Bollan's intended remarks. The resistance in America to the importation of goods taxed by Parliament, he reported, was universal and not restricted to Boston alone. Furthermore, it was conducted not by a childlike rabble, but by "men of the first rank and opulent fortune" and "with the utmost decency." [74]

A petition written by Arthur Lee and signed by twenty-nine native Americans residing in London was finally heard. Briefly it observed that the Bostonians were being denied their natural and inalienable rights by being deprived of an opportunity to be heard in their own defense. It deplored the presumption that

The BOSTONIANS in DISTRESS.

London Printed for R. Sayer & J. Bennett, Map & Printsellers N°53 Fleet Street, as the Act directs 19 Nov 1774.

Mezzotint satirizing the blockade of Boston after the tea party, 1774.

the law was not impartially administered in America, giving as an example the trial of Captain Preston and his soldiers at the time of the Boston Massacre. It was for the East India Company, Lee added, not Parliament, to prosecute the wrongdoers in Boston. But Lee's appeal was ignored.

A similar petition from much the same group of Americans was heard in the House of Lords, as was Bollan's. The "Natives of America" unsuccessfully petitioned the King not to assent to this unprecedented legislation. In late April, Dowdeswell asked that the Acts not be passed until a defense arrived from Massachusetts. He was as unsuccessful as were the Americans in London, who, in early May, penned another plea, beseeching Parliament not to consign them to "a state of slavery," nor to "drive them to the last resources of despair." [75]

Liberty and Catholics

It took only three months for British legislators to frame, debate, pass, and submit for royal approval the four Coercive Acts. A fifth bill, which appeared before Parliament on May 2, had been much longer in preparation. Representing the matured thinking of the men who ran the western section of the Department of the Secretary of State for the colonies, the Quebec Act had taken over two years to write and involved many recommendations, arguments, compromises. In some ways a sincere effort to solve a difficult and complicated problem in government, the Quebec Act was generous if judged by the practices of the times, and certainly humane. But its introduction at this crucial moment proved to be one of the most serious errors committed by British lawmakers since the ill-advised Stamp Act of 1765. For if the Coercive Acts made open rebellion in America inevitable, the Quebec Act inflamed passions even more, convincing the colonists that the British government had no concern at all for their welfare. The man responsible for drafting and sponsoring the bill in Parliament was William Legge, the second Earl of Dartmouth, Secretary of State for the colonies.

WILLIAM LEGGE, LORD DARTMOUTH (1731–1801)

Although Benjamin Franklin believed that Lord Dartmouth was "a truly good man . . . [who] wishes sincerely a good understanding with the colonies," many other Americans at home and resident in London held him in "utter contempt." The pious Dartmouth maintained such a strong attachment to Methodism that he acquired the nickname "the Psalmsinger," but Arthur Lee believed his "affected meekness of temper" covered a "weak mind, or hypocritical heart."[1]

Actually, Dartmouth was inclined to favor the American cause. His liberal point of view with respect to colonial taxation was well known among Americans, and so his appointment as Secretary of State for the colonies raised expectations among them that here was an official sympathetic to their welfare. But Dartmouth had accepted his office reluctantly. He would have much preferred to spend his time improving his estates, visiting his numerous relatives, acquiring paintings for his large art collection, or engaging in philanthropic and religious activities. As Lord North's stepbrother and close friend, he had accepted his post as a duty to help North strengthen Grafton's weak and disorganized ministry; but he knew little about colonial affairs and was inclined to accept the views of more experienced officials such as John Pownall. Thus, the hopes that Dartmouth's appointment was a harbinger of future harmonious relations between the colonies and the mother country were bound to be disappointed.

One of the most important tasks facing the new Secretary was the determination of a policy for

William Legge, second Earl of Dartmouth,
by Thomas Gainsborough.

Quebec, which had posed complex problems for British ministries since its formal acquisition in 1763. Soon after taking office, in September 1772, Dartmouth wrote to the lieutenant governor of Quebec that the Privy Council was at the moment considering "everything that concerns the state of Quebec with regard as well to its civil as to its ecclesiastical constitution." [2] In August 1773, Dartmouth received from the Lord Chancellor a number of papers referring to Quebec, with the Lord Chancellor's expression of hope that they would "enable his Lordship to form a plan of government for that province to be laid before Parliament. . . ." [3] The attorney general of Quebec, Francis Maseres, who was anxious that the province's government be settled soon, suggested that Dartmouth prepare a bill that could be presented to Parliament at the beginning of the next session.

The Quebec Act, then, was conceived and framed before the Boston Tea Party and the coercive policy that it provoked. In fact, it has been suggested that it might have become law sooner than it actually did if the crisis in Boston had not forced British legislators to

set it aside while they turned their minds to the more pressing concern of punishing Boston's wrongdoers. But certainly Lord North and others who were consulted about the question—including William Knox—had in mind the troublesome condition of the older American colonies as well as the colonists' disregard of the restraints to settlement included in the Proclamation of 1763. Emigration of families to the banks of the Ohio had proceeded at a rapid pace after 1763, despite the provisions of the Proclamation prohibiting settlement in the territory beyond the Appalachian chain. Such an influx of people threatened, wrote one official, a "great many inconveniences" and especially irritated the Indians. It was feared that such remote settlements would become "the asylum of the lawless and the repair of the most licentious inhabitants" of the American colonies. [4]

Dartmouth's foremost aim in formulating the Quebec Act was to provide such a civil government as to discourage settlers from entering the new territories. Nothing could discourage such settlement better than the establishment of non-representative government over the whole area, including the "province of the Ohio and the Mississippi," and the continuation of French law and landholding practices, which insured the maintenance of a feudal system.

Even more galling to potential British settlers of the new territories was that provision of the Act which not only tolerated Roman Catholicism in the newly acquired territories but contributed to the maintenance of its establishment. Long before the Tea Party, Lord Dartmouth had expressed his belief that such toleration was essential "to conciliate their [the Canadians'] affections and to create that attachment to and dependence on the British government upon which the safety and prosperity of the colony depend." [5] Thus, much to the disgust of militant Protestants, the Act allowed for the collection of tithes for the support of the Catholic Church. Colonel Barré called the measure "Popish from the beginning to the end."

Dartmouth could not see where he had gone astray. The Quebec Act satisfied, he believed, "nearly 100,000 peaceable, loyal subjects" who appreciated the retention of French legal procedures and enjoyed the opportunity to carry on their religious faith according to custom. His provisions for the collection of tithes and the establishment of a Catholic bishop in Quebec were, in his mind, reasonable solutions to a local problem taken "in the most anxious good wishes for its [Quebec's] welfare and prosperity." [6]

GENERAL JAMES MURRAY (1719?–1794);
SIR GUY CARLETON,
FIRST LORD DORCHESTER (1724–1808)

The French Canadians, according to Governor James Murray, constituted "a strong, healthy race, plain in their dress, virtuous in their morals, and temperate in their living." Although ignorant and superstitious— and particularly prejudiced against the British conquerors whom they had been taught to fear—they had been able to accept the conquering armies with "a harmony unexampled even at home." All that was required to maintain their loyalty, both Murray and Sir Guy Carleton believed, was reassurance as to the preservation of their religious beliefs and practices. "Perhaps the bravest and best race upon the globe," wrote Murray in 1764, "a race, who, could they be indulged with a few privileges which the laws of England deny to Roman Catholics at home, would soon become the most faithful and useful set of men in the American empire." They would, added Carleton three years later, serve the British "with as much valor, with more zeal, and more military knowledge for America than the regular troops of France that were joined with them." [7]

Murray and Carleton, the first two British governors of Quebec, were evaluating a conquered people. The British had permitted the French Canadians to emigrate back to France, thus ridding the country of many disaffected members of the French governing classes. Those who remained were not only submissive, but anxious to cooperate with the British in order to maintain some of their former power. These were the French Canadians of whom the two governors were speaking; they constituted primarily the upper classes—the *noblesse* or *gentilhommes* and clergy. Of the feelings of the peasantry, or *habitants*, Murray and Carleton knew little.

Carleton's and Murray's opinions reflected their military background. Murray had served nearly twenty years as a commissioned officer before he was given command over a brigade at the siege of Louisbourg in 1758. He had served under Wolfe as commander of the left wing of the British army in the battle on the Plains of Abraham, which had resulted in the surrender of the city of Quebec; and he was also present at the surrender of Montreal. In 1760, he was appointed governor of Quebec, and when the peace treaty of 1763 formally ceded Canada to Great Britain, he became governor of Canada.

Carleton, too, rose in the ranks of the British army, so that by the time he came to participate in the government of conquered Quebec, he had reached the rank of colonel and was accustomed to associating with British officers and those members of the noblesse who shared his values.

While under control of the French *seigneurs* and clergy, the habitants were indeed submissive. Poor, ignorant, and politically powerless, they accepted their lot with a patience ingrained in them for generations. But, as the position of the seigneur changed under the new regime, the docility and humility described by their British conquerors also underwent change. Assured that the British were not going to break up their communities and families, as they had done in 1755 to the Acadians, the habitants began to resent the compulsory powers exercised by the legal and religious establishments. Although not quite ready for self-gov-

This Sr. Is the Meaning of the Quebec Act—1774.

A View of the Thames *by Samuel Scott, 1772.*

ernment, they were fast learning how to use English techniques and procedures in their elections—even ways to use "bribery and corruption."

Murray had sensed the Canadians' capacity for independent political action, reporting in 1762 that the people "do not submit as tamely to the yoke, and under sanction of the capitulation [which had required them to pay their customary dues to the Church] they every day take an opportunity to dispute the tithes with their curés." Murray's report included a few petitions from the people indicating that they opposed a religious establishment "with compulsory powers." [8]

Carleton, too, realized the changed nature of the Canadians, who resented being deprived of office-holding privileges. He discouraged petitions to the King, knowing that there would not be a "Canadian from one extremity of the province to the other that would not sign or set his mark to such a petition." [9]

Carleton disliked the English residents of Quebec and Montreal, and was unwilling to listen to their plea that Quebec be made in the fullest sense a British possession. This small but radically articulate group

disliked French law, wished to discourage the use of the French language, hated the existent hierarchy, and was deeply offended by Catholicism. Carleton believed them infected with the "mutinous" views causing so much difficulty in Britain's other colonies. Believing that the French Canadians were a "populous and long-established colony" permanently entrenched in Canada and that they would remain a majority, he advocated that their customs, both legal and ecclesiastical, be maintained.

THE BRITISH OPPOSITION: CHARLES PRATT, LORD CAMDEN (1714–1794); CHARLES JAMES FOX (1749–1806)

For nine days, the House of Commons debated the Quebec Act. Presented by Lord North, the bill was favored by most members of Parliament, who shared the belief of Attorney General Edward Thurlow that whatever law would make the Canadians happy should be given them. It would be tyrannous, he said, to impose an alien law on a conquered French people. As for the English who went to live in Canada, they must accept the laws of the land.

A vocal minority was unwilling to accept Thurlow's justification for the bill. Rather than viewing it as a liberal act reflecting English generosity, they saw it, as did Colonel Barré, as a "monstrous production of tyranny, injustice, and arbitrary power." Barré suspected that behind the bill lay a malicious intent—"to raise a Popish army to serve in the colonies." Ahead lay terrible consequences: "it carries in its breast," he suggested, "something that squints and looks dangerous to the inhabitants of our other colonies." From this time on, Barré warned, "all hope of peace in America will be destroyed."[10]

The former governor of Florida, George Johnstone, opposed the bill because it lacked a provision for an elected assembly. "The great maxim to be learned from a history of our colonization is to let men manage their own affairs," he insisted. Johnstone and Barré were joined by Edmund Burke and his cousin William, who asserted that the French in Quebec would be freer in a system based on English law rather than French "slavery." If tyranny were established in Canada, it would sooner or later "come home to England." Canada, warned Edmund Burke, "will become a dangerous instrument in the hands of those who wish to destroy English liberty in every part of our possessions."[11]

A view across the Thames of Westminster Hall, by William Marlow, 1770.

Guy Carleton, first Lord Dorchester,
by an unidentified artist, date unknown.

William Pitt, Lord Chatham, agreed with Burke that the bill promised further harassment of the American colonists. A "most cruel, oppressive, and odious" measure, he called it, designed to antagonize all Americans. In Lord Shelburne's opinion, the ministry's design in formulating such a bill was to undermine the freedom of the Protestant colonies by means of a "Popish army."

Among the most vehement opponents of the Quebec Act in Parliament were Charles Pratt, Lord Camden, and Charles James Fox, son of Lord Holland, former Secretary of State and Commons leader.

In 1765, Charles Pratt, now Baron Camden, entered the House of Lords. Described by Horace Walpole as "steady, warm, sullen, stained with no reproach, and a uniform Whig," Pratt had earned a reputation for careful decisions that were based upon a fine knowledge of the British constitution.

Lord Camden's first speech to the House of Lords reflected this concern: he condemned the Stamp Act as unconstitutional. Later, arguing against the Declaratory Act, he maintained that taxation without representation was robbery. During Chatham's second administration and during Grafton's, Camden held the position of Lord Chancellor. Embarrassed by being part of an administration whose policies he disapproved of, he remained silent, speaking out only after Chatham returned to the House of Lords. He then resumed his former role as watchdog of the constitution.

Between 1772 and 1774, Camden took little part in public affairs. When, however, the North ministry put into effect a policy that was fast forcing Americans into revolution, he found his old anger returning. The constitutional issue provoked by the Quebec Act was clear: the French Canadians were being deprived of an elected assembly and of their rights as British subjects. The minority of Englishmen in Canada was also being deprived of natural rights. With no provision for future representative government, the Act undermined one of the most important of British liberties.

Lord Camden also opposed the Act's provision to extend the boundaries of Quebec to include the interior settlements of all the old English colonies. He saw this, as he said in his bill to repeal the Quebec Act, as an attempt "to prevent [the colonies'] further progress." It was, he insisted, a "chinese wall, against the further extension of civil liberty and the Protestant religion." [12]

Charles James Fox, who has been described as "hard, bold, and ready," resigned from North's ministry in 1772 because of his opposition to a proposed Royal Marriage Bill, which the King wanted passed in order to restrict marriages made by members of his household. Joining Burke in opposing the bill, Fox identified himself from that time on with the Opposition party. Now took place, as Lord John Russell has written, "the real commencement of Mr. Fox's political career." [13]

Fox's attack on the Quebec Act grew out of his belief that the entire program offered by the North administration for the governing of the colonies could only divide the British Empire. Compounded, as Fox put it, "of violence and weakness," he believed that the program would "irritate the minds of the people" but not correct the difficulties that had created the situation.[14] "It is not right," said Fox, "for this country to originate and establish a constitution, in which there is not a spark or semblance of liberty." Quebec's was "a perfectly despotic government, contrary to the genius and spirit of the British constitution." The Act reinforced this "love of despotism" and conveyed "a settled design to enslave the people of America, very unbecoming this country." America, Fox insisted, must be governed not by force, but "by affection and interest."[15]

Fox's criticism of the Quebec Act rested largely on the absence of an elected assembly, which to him spelled "military government." He saw no difficulty in allowing Roman Catholics self-rule, nor did he fear the establishment of the Catholic Church and religious toleration.

His and others' opposition to the Act carried little weight with Parliament. The bill passed in the Commons by a vote of 56 to 21, and in the House of Lords 26 to 7. On June 22, 1774, the royal assent was given to the Quebec Act by a King only slightly troubled by his vows to uphold the Protestant faith in the British Empire.

That day London witnessed a display of protest more typical of cities on the other side of the Atlantic. Hatred of Roman Catholicism ran high in the city. On June 22, the Lord Mayor accompanied by the aldermen and 150 common councillors, robed and decorated with the symbols of office, marched in procession to St. James' Palace to urge George III to veto the bill. Crowds lined London's streets to watch the procession. Word ran through the watching throngs that the march was a protest against the machinations of the "idolatrous and bloody" Roman Church being established in Canada against the interests of "true worship." George III refused to answer the petition of the protesters. Later that day, however, when he went

France offers the keys of Quebec to Britannia. Detail of an engraving by James Hulet.

down to Westminster, he was met by an angry mob with "hisses, groans, and the cry of No Popery!" [16]

At Westminster, George III gave formal assent to the Quebec Act, declaring that "it was founded on the clearest principles of justice and humanity" and would promote the happiness of his Canadian subjects.

JEAN OLIVER BRIAND,
BISHOP OF QUEBEC (1715–1794)

When Carleton returned to Canada in 1775, with the bill for governing Quebec in hand, he was welcomed warmly by the French Canadians. In particular, the clergy led by Bishop Briand were delighted with his appointment to the governorship. They regarded him, as they said in their welcoming address, as "protector of our laws and religious liberties." [17]

Abbé Briand had come over to New France many years before—in 1741—after having been ordained a priest in 1739. When the Cathedral Chapter of Quebec in 1766 searched for a bishop acceptable to the

Charles Pratt, Lord Camden,
by Richard Cosway, date unknown.

British government to occupy the vacancy in that province, it turned to him for this highest religious post. Briand was known as being "well disposed to British rule" as well as a "thorough and conscientious churchman." [18] Possessing little sense of humor, he treasured his piety and thought of himself as a loyal servant of God and the Crown.

When the American colonists heard of Briand's elevation to the Quebec episcopate in 1772, their reaction was intense. The opposition of Protestant Americans to the establishment of an Anglican bishop in the thirteen colonies was based on their hatred of those elements within the English Church which smacked of "popish superstitions" and hierarchical control of their Protestant liberties. They viewed the establishment of a Roman bishop in Quebec as a harbinger not only of British intentions to establish the English Church in the colonies, but of its popish intentions as well. The *Connecticut Journal* on June 12, 1772, voiced their fears when it reported Briand's consecration and noted that it presupposed a secret agreement between Rome and Westminster. By November, the *Journal* was publishing the story that at the Bishop's consecration, the Heavens reacted so violently that "the affrighted spectators, conscious of their idolatry and the propriety of Divine Vengeance, cried out as it were with one voice, *Eviva il Protestantismo.*" [19]

The Quebec Act solidified Americans' suspicions of British colonial policy. The *Massachusetts Spy* reported in September 1774, that the Act was so favored by Catholics that Lord North had been named Commissioner of Supply to the College of Jesuits; Edmund Burke, the Professor of Oratory at the University of Padua; and the Archbishop of Canterbury, the new Pope. In the October 1774 issue of the *Royal American Magazine*, Paul Revere published an engraving as its frontispiece entitled "The Mitred Minuet," showing four bishops in pairs, their hands clasped at right angles so as to form a cross, dancing about the Quebec Bill at their feet. Looking on—seemingly with satisfaction—were the King, Lord North, and Lord Bute, while in the background, forming a semicircle, sat the audience of Lords Temporal. In Pennsylvania, the *Packet* asserted that in signing the Quebec Act, George III had broken his coronation vows, and therefore should be removed from his throne. John Adams wrote to his wife that Catholicism was "the worst tyranny that the genius of Toryism ever

*Charles James Fox (left)
with Edmund Burke
by Thomas Hickey,
date unknown.*

invented."[20] And all Americans, who for generations had been conditioned to hate Catholicism with a vengeance, agreed with him, for they saw in the bill "establishing popery and tyranny" the beginning of a policy destructive of the principles of a free constitution and the rights and liberties of the people. If they were more moderate than the radical Sam Adams, who was later accused by Brooks Adams of using the Quebec Act "as a goad wherewith to inflame the dying Puritan fanaticism," they still were sufficiently under the influence of a Protestant clergy, whether liberal or orthodox, who preached the identification of religious and civil liberty so that "if one falls it is not to be expected that the other will continue"—as the Reverend Charles Turner warned in 1773.[21] The fact that Quebec was denied an elected legislature (the Act provided for an appointed governor and council possessing legislative powers) added fuel to the existing fear that popery represented a curtailment of civil liberties. The Coercive Acts and the Quebec Act, wrote Gurdon Saltonstall to Silas Deane, were designed to "abridge American Liberty" in preparation for "the alteration of the British Constitutions at home and abroad." Because the Quebec Act included the western settlements along the Ohio River and Great Lakes as part of the Quebec province, it was seen as "a bridle on the northern colonies," preventing them from expansion into these rich areas.[22]

One of the most eloquent voices raised in America to warn the colonies of the menace of the arbitrary government being established on its frontiers was that of seventeen-year-old Alexander Hamilton, already assuming his position as a forceful political thinker dedicated to the formation and development of a strong American nation.

ALEXANDER HAMILTON (1757–1804)

Born in the British colony of Nevis, one of the Leeward Islands, Alexander Hamilton was of Scottish

Alexander Hamilton, pastel by James Sharples, date unknown.

and French Huguenot birth. Virtually an orphan by the age of eleven, he worked in a general store in Christianstadt on the island of St. Kitts until 1772, when, through the generosity of his aunts and prominent islanders who recognized his ability, he was sent to New York for an education. In the autumn of 1773, he entered King's College (now Columbia University), and almost immediately became active in the affairs of his newly adopted colony. An excellent and diligent student, Hamilton enjoyed a congenial social life with his schoolmates and members of New York's upper-class society, to whom he had carried letters of introduction. He helped organize a club for mutual improvement in debating and public speaking, and soon became the club's leader, outshining all. The subjects debated were, of course, the topics of the day, and these were full of political interest: the tax on tea, the Boston Tea Party, the Acts to govern the colony of Massachusetts. There seems to be little question that Alexander's sympathies were with the colonies. The planters and merchants of the West Indies had also resented British mercantilistic restrictions and had formed their own bands of Sons of Liberty to oppose the Stamp Act. Hamilton's anti-British friends in St. Kitts vicariously participated in the events exploding in the colonies farther north. When Hamilton traveled to New York, he brought with him not only ambition, but an anti-British bias that was to shape the direction of his ambition.

Hamilton's first effort on behalf of American rights was an essay accepted by *Holt's Journal* called "Defence of the Destruction of the Tea." This was followed by a series of similar articles, all published in *Holt's*. When the Port of Boston was closed during the summer of 1774, New Yorkers called a mass meeting to protest the outrageous act. Gathering on July 6th at the "Fields," where City Hall Park is now located, the Sons of Liberty mingled with rough sailors, mechanics, apprentices, merchants, students, and other "patriots." One after another, fiery speakers mounted the platform to urge non-importation and strong opposition. When the crowd refused to disperse, Hamilton's club elevated him to the speaker's platform, and the young Alexander eloquently addressed the seething masses.

From this beginning, Hamilton went on to even more influential tasks. While continuing his studies diligently, he found time to justify the activities of the Continental Congress in a far-reaching pamphlet that

The Mitred Minuet *by an unidentified artist, published in* London Magazine, *July 1774.*

combined a moderate radicalism with economic nationalism, and moved from the rights of man to a call for home manufactures. A year after the Quebec Act was passed, Hamilton published his "Remarks on the Quebec Bill," that generally but eloquently summarized the American response to an odious measure.

Hamilton's appeal in his "Remarks . . ." was frankly directed to the radical and religious prejudices of the colonists. The Quebec Act, he declared, "develops the dark designs of the ministry more fully than any thing they have done." The ministry's purpose? The answer was clear—"the subjugation of the colonies, and afterward that of Great Britain itself." Catholicism represented a "great engine" of arbitrary power, which would support the despotism of the King and his ministry in exchange for favors granted. Once left to the mercies of a triumphant

popery, Protestants would be forced to yield, and soon the lands of the Ohio would be filled with "innumerable hosts" of Catholics who would block the advance and progress of the Protestant colonists.[23]

Yet, once having discharged his religious antagonisms, Hamilton revealed the clear logic that later was to mark his state papers. Making a distinction between toleration of Catholicism and its establishment, he pointed out that the former, depending upon *voluntary* support, could be successfully encouraged; but once the collection of tithes was recognized by law, the Church became permanently established and "the free agency of the people" was destroyed. Hamilton insisted that "the privilege of worshipping the Deity in the manner his conscience dictates" constituted the "dearest" liberty a Protestant Englishman could enjoy. The loss of this precious gift could not be permitted.[24]

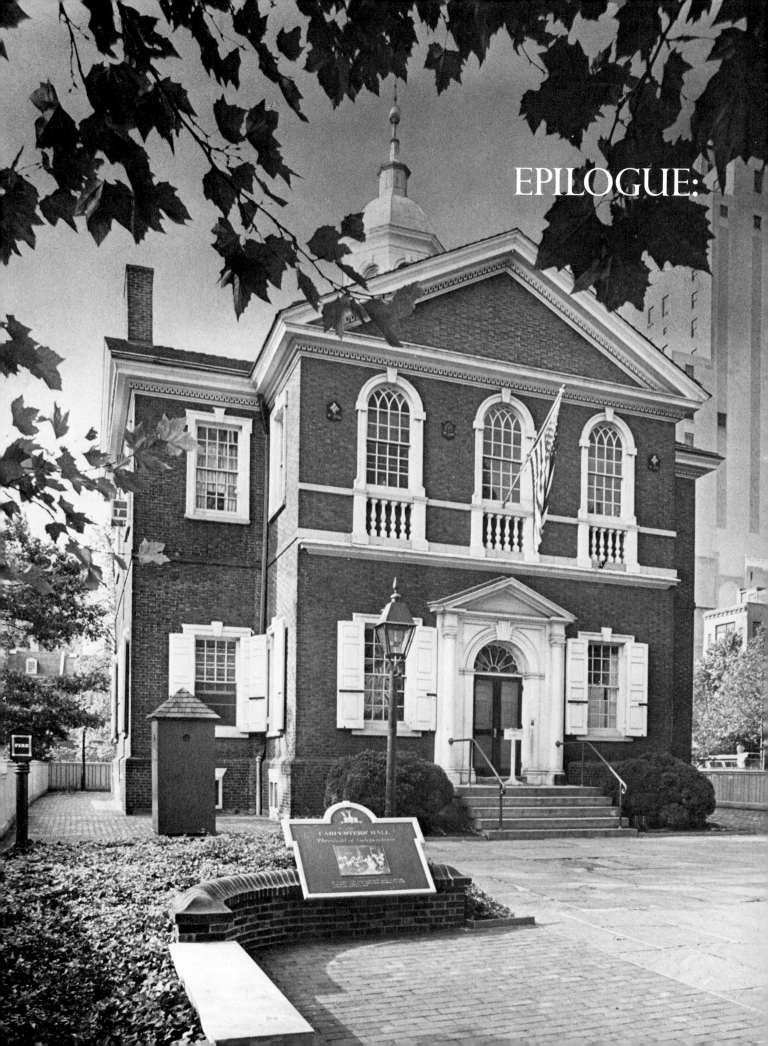

EPILOGUE:

Continental Congress, 1774

While Alexander Hamilton painted the melodramatic image of the Inquisition burning Protestants on Boston Common, an assembly of Americans had already convened to protest formally the Quebec Act, the Boston Port Bill, the Massachusetts Government Act, and the other coercive measures that marked 1774 as a year of crisis. From 1772 to 1774, the colonies had been moving toward intercolonial cooperation. Sam Adams had begun the process with his personal organization of informal committees of correspondence within the Massachusetts towns and Boston, a local network which he utilized for spreading propaganda, and which he hoped eventually to extend to other colonies. In 1773, the Virginia House of Burgesses had appointed a committee to communicate with the other colonies, clearly intending it to lead to a formal system of intercolonial cooperation. Now with the threat implicit in the Boston Port Bill, intercolonial cooperation became a recognizable necessity.

When the Boston Committee of Correspondence received word of the Port Bill, it immediately sent a circular letter to all the colonies calling for suspension of trade between Britain and America. Most of the colonial leaders received Boston's suggestion approvingly, except those in New York and Philadelphia. New York merchants had no desire to stop trade, but they also wished to keep the popular movement under their own control. Appointing a Committee of Fifty-one, they suggested instead that "a congress of deputies from the colonies in general" should be "assembled without delay, and some unanimous resolution formed in this fatal emergency . . . for the security of our common rights." [1]

Philadelphia merchants were as unenthusiastic as New Yorkers about stopping trade. A boycott, they insisted, was a last resort. Instead, they too believed that a congress of deputies was the best way to procure "relief for our suffering brethren" and to obtain "redress of American grievances." [2]

The most forceful support of Boston came from Virginia. On May 22, 1774, Paul Revere and other express riders came riding into Williamsburg bearing Massachusetts' call for help. Among the dismayed legislators who responded sympathetically was Thomas Jefferson, who had just arrived from Monticello to attend a session of the legislature.

THOMAS JEFFERSON (1743–1826)

To Jefferson, the Boston Port Bill spelled the "utter ruin" of a great commercial city. Something of a drastic nature had to be done to "alarm" popular attention to this new offense of the King and Parliament. The only thing dramatic enough to do this was a day of general fasting and prayer. Searching the records through the night for old forms and proclamations, he discovered that not since 1755, when war with France threatened, had such a day been called for in Virginia. Now, as Jefferson wrote, he and his friends "cooked up a resolution . . . for a day of fasting, humiliation, and prayer to implore heaven to avert from us the evils of civil war, to inspire us with firmness in support of our rights, and to turn the hearts of the King and Parliament to moderation and justice." [3]

The following day, Jefferson and other radical Burgesses approached the pious treasurer of the colony, Robert Carter Nicholas, and asked him to introduce the resolution into the House. It passed unanimously, and immediately Governor Dunmore dissolved the Assembly, claiming that its resolution reflected unfavorably upon the King and Parliament. Marching to Raleigh Tavern, Jefferson and eighty-nine fellow Burgesses organized a permanent association and ordered the colony's Committee of Correspondence to inform other colonial committees of Virginia's proclaimed day of fasting, declaring "that an attack made on one of our sister colonies is an attack made on all British America and threatens ruin to the rights of all." The rump assembly went even further: it called for all the colonies to meet in congress "at such place, annually, as should be convenient to direct from time to time the measures required by the general interest." [4]

Jefferson left Williamsburg after the meeting, but the rest of the Assembly attended prayer ceremonies at Bruton Church on June 1st, the day the Boston Port Bill was to take effect. Shops closed throughout the colony, flags hung at half mast, muffled church bells rang in funereal tones, and the churches filled with sympathetic worshipers and angry preachers. "The effect of that day," Jefferson later wrote, "through the whole colony, was like a shock of electricity, arousing every man and placing him erect and solidly on his center." [5]

The idea of calling for a day of fasting and prayer was Jefferson's first important political decision. Up to this time, although a member of the House of Burgesses since 1769, he had been more literary and scholarly in his pursuits. His studies in history and law had, however, prepared him for taking a place among Virginia's "Young Turks." Always interested in the practical application of knowledge to human affairs, he

pursued studies that would illuminate problems of men in government and society. That he did so, "never fearing to follow truth and reason to whatever results they led, and bearding every authority which stood in their way," testifies to his independence of mind and boldness of judgment. [6] By the time the dispute with Great Britain had reached a serious juncture, he had arrived at an intellectual maturity that would redound favorably to the cause of the American colonies.

Toward the end of July, the freeholders of Albemarle County reelected Jefferson to represent them in the House of Burgesses. Since, however, the Governor had again put off a meeting of the Burgesses, hoping to prevent radical action, the determined members of the Assembly decided to meet unofficially in Williamsburg in August to determine their representation and role in the intercolonial congress they had been instrumental in calling. On the way to Williamsburg, Jefferson was stricken with dysentery and was forced to return to Monticello. As a result, he was not chosen to be a delegate to the convention in Philadelphia.

The members of the Virginia delegation, headed by Peyton Randolph, were all older than Jefferson, and more generally regarded as "glowing patriots." They included George Washington, Richard Bland, Benjamin Harrison, Edmund Pendleton, and Patrick Henry, along with Jefferson's friend Richard Henry Lee. Unable to be present at the Williamsburg meeting, and certainly unable to attend the Philadelphia congress, Jefferson resorted to the pen—which, indeed, constituted his strength. Two copies of his paper were sent to the Congress, which when read was applauded, though not officially approved. It was, claimed the conservative majority, "too bold for the present state of things." Without his knowledge, it was printed in Williamsburg, appearing as *A Summary View of the Rights of British America,* reprinted in Philadelphia, and twice reprinted in England. It was more widely read than any other of Jefferson's writings except the Declaration of Independence and became one of the most important revolutionary pamphlets published during this period. As he later assessed his work, "If it had any merit, it was that of first taking our true ground, and that which was afterwards assumed and maintained." [7]

Jefferson's arguments in *Summary View* were based upon the assumption that the colonists possessed natural rights, which were theirs historically as well as philosophically. The ancestors of British Americans had been free once in England, and had a natural right to emigrate and establish a society and laws of their

Thomas Jefferson by Mather Brown, 1786.

own. The conquest and settlement of America had been made wholly at the expense of the individual colonists—"for themselves they fought, for themselves they conquered, and for themselves alone they have the right to hold." Once having arrived, the settlers had adopted "that system of laws under which they had hitherto lived in the mother country" and had submitted "to the same common Sovereign, who was thereby made the central link connecting the several parts of the empire thus newly multiplied." The early charters embodied the compact between the King and the colonists—but the charters were not royal gifts, as the British believed. They were, Jefferson insisted, restrictions on royal power. Since free trade was a natural right of the colonists, parliamentary regulations of trade were really void. Parliament's acts of oppression against the colonies formed, he said, "a connected chain of parliamentary usurpation." The measures against Boston were "acts of power, assumed by a body of men, foreign to our constitutions, and unacknowledged by our laws." [8]

Jefferson conceived of himself as spokesman for a free people. Kings were, and ought to be, "the servants, not the proprietors of the people." Disclaim-

ing any thought of independence or rebellion, he insisted that all that the Americans sought was "union on a generous plan," a plan that included the right to trade in markets of the colonists' own choice, and to be taxed by their own representatives. The legislatures of the "states" of America were fully equal to the legislature, or Parliament, of Great Britain. "The God who gave us life," wrote Jefferson, "gave us liberty at the same time; the hand of force may destroy, but cannot disjoin them." [9]

If Jefferson's views were too radical for the Continental Congress to adopt, they were not out of step with the sentiments of the popular leaders. Patrick Henry, Richard Henry Lee, Sam Adams, and John Adams shared Jefferson's extreme view, and at the Continental Congress formed a powerful team that became known as the "Lee-Adams Junto." As for more conservative leaders, such as Joseph Galloway of Pennsylvania, they did not welcome Jefferson's plea for colonial autonomy. They preferred to "define American rights, and explicitly and dutifully to petition for the remedy which would redress the grievances justly complained of." "Tamer statements were preferred," Jefferson wrote, "and, I believe, wisely preferred; the leap I proposed being too long, as yet, for the mass of our citizens." [10] The conservatives won the day, and during its first session, the Continental Congress did not declare the autonomy of the colonies.

Actually, in 1774, the assembled delegates hardly considered the possibility of independence. What they hoped to get was recognition of their sovereignty in certain fundamental areas through a reform of the British imperial system. In 1774, however, Parliament was unwilling to grant the colonists that measure of autonomy. Convinced that the American leaders were set on rebellion, they refused to compromise with traitors. Few Englishmen really recognized the deep dissatisfactions that existed in America with the role Americans were forced to play within the Empire. They believed that most colonists were happy enough with their British connection to want to avoid fighting. Moreover, many Englishmen believed that the colonists would not fight. They were, the Earl of Sandwich assured Parliament, "raw, undisciplined, cowardly men. . . . The very sound of a cannon would carry them off . . . as fast as their feet could carry them." [11] Under such circumstances, England would never make concessions.

The calling of the Continental Congress did more to unite Americans than any other event. Until the passage of the Coercive Acts, the revolutionary movement had been most active in the seaport towns, whose inhabitants were directly involved in a stamp tax, Townshend duties, the corruption and greed of customs officials. The Coercive Acts affected a larger range of Americans, posing to their liberties threats which before had seemed too vague to be believed. The response of small towns such as Farmington or Windham, Connecticut, to Boston's plight was as great as the response from ports such as Charleston or Baltimore. From all over the colonies, Boston received aid. Corn, sheep, money, clothing came pouring into the city from communities throughout settled America, many of which had initially disapproved of the violence to property perpetrated by the Tea Party.

By September 1774, all the colonies had expressed their opposition to the British Parliament. The fifty-six delegates from twelve colonies (Georgia had been unable to send representatives) who assembled in Carpenters' Hall in Philadelphia represented the determination of a large colonial element to resist the Coercive Acts as "the attempts of a wicked administration to enslave America." In its "Declaration of Colonial Rights and Grievances," the Congress asked for a rescinding of all the acts involving the American economy that had been passed since 1763. Organizing themselves into a Continental Association, they once again declared a boycott on British imports and proposed to enforce that boycott by extralegal groups established throughout the colonies. "Government is dissolved," Patrick Henry proclaimed. A new government had to take its place. Since, as Henry said, "the Distinctions between Virginians, Pennsylvanians, New Yorkers, and New Englanders" no longer existed, the only government that could logically take the place of the British had to be "American." [12]

During the months that followed, the extralegal groups established by the Continental Congress became extralegal governing bodies. Frequently acting through the provincial committee, in many instances they supplanted royal officials as the effective government. As they expanded their powers to include the gathering of munitions and the training of militia, they also became military governments, merely waiting for the outbreak of hostilities before entirely taking over colonial government.

The Continental Congress was the first step toward the Revolutionary War, and the first step toward a united America.

NOTES

INTRODUCTION

1. Quoted in J. Thomas Flexner, *George Washington: The Forge of Experience*, Boston, 1965, p. 56.

2. *Ibid.*, p. 89 and 89n.

3. *Ibid.*, p. 133.

4. *Ibid.*, p. 134.

5. Samuel Eliot Morison, *The Oxford History of the American People*, New York, 1965, p. 164.

6. Flexner, *George Washington*, pp. 175-176.

CHAPTER I

1. *Gentleman's Magazine*, Vol. 31 (September 1761), pp. 414-415.

2. *Ibid.*

3. Lewis Namier, *Personalities and Powers*, London, 1957, pp. 49-50.

4. Quoted in J. H. Plumb, *The First Four Georges*, London, 1956, p. 83.

5. Quoted in J. S. Watson, *The Reign of George III*, Oxford, 1960, p. 5.

6. Quoted from the *Massachusetts Gazette*, June 4, 1761, no. 2970.

7. C. W. Colby, "Chatham, 1708-1908," *American Historical Review*, Vol. 14 (1909), p. 725.

8. Quoted from Horace Walpole, *Memoirs of the Reign of George II*, Vol. 3, London, 1846, p. 84.

9. Quoted in Watson, *Reign of George III*, p. 4.

10. Quoted from Romney Sedgwick, ed., *Letters from George III to Lord Bute, 1756-1766*, London, 1939, p. xlvi.

11. *Ibid.*, p. xlv.

CHAPTER II

1. Quoted in Lawrence Henry Gipson, *The Coming of the Revolution, 1763-1775*, New York, 1954, p. 32.

2. Mrs. Napier Higgins, *The Bernards of Abington and Nether Winchendon*, London, 1903, p. 217.

3. Quoted from *Otis Papers II*, p. 56, in John J. Waters and John A. Schutz, "Patterns of Massachusetts Colonial Politics: The Writs of Assistance and the Rivalry between the Otis and Hutchinson Families," *William & Mary Quarterly*, Vol. 24 (October 1967), p. 559n.

4. G. B. Warden, *Boston, 1689-1776*, Boston, 1970, p. 150.

5. Higgins, *The Bernards*, p. 224.

6. Quoted in Gipson, *Coming of the Revolution*, p. 34.

7. Edmund and Helen Morgan, *The Stamp Act Crisis*, Chapel Hill, 1953, p. 208.

8. Clifford K. Shipton, *Sibley's Harvard Graduates*, Vol. 11, Boston, 1937-1970, p. 249.

9. Quoted in Clifford K. Shipton, "James Otis and the Writs of Assistance," *Proceedings of the Bostonian Society* (January 1961), p. 21.

10. Quoted in C. F. Adams, ed., *The Works of John Adams*, Vol. 2, Boston, 1856, p. 521.

11. *Ibid.*

12. Quoted in William Tudor, *Life of James Otis*, New York, 1970, pp. 63f, and Adams, *Works*, Vol. 2, Boston, 1856, pp. 521-523.

13. Tudor, *Life of James Otis*, p. 60.

14. Quoted in Shipton, "James Otis," p. 323.

15. John Adams, *Diary and Autobiography*, Vol. 1, L. H. Butterfield, ed., Cambridge, Mass., 1962, p. 55.

16. Adams, *Works*, Vol. 2, p. 67.

17. Quoted in Bernard Bailyn, ed., *Pamphlets of the American Revolution, 1750-1776*, Cambridge, Mass., 1965, p. 485.

18. Quoted in Adams, *Works*, Vol. 10, p. 286.

19. Oxenbridge Thacher to Benjamin Prat (1762), quoted in Shipton, *Sibley's Harvard Graduates* Vol. 10, p. 325.

20. From "Substance of Mr. Gridley's Argument before the Superior Court in favor of Writs of Assistance," *James Hawley Papers*, quoted in John J. Waters, *The Otis Family*, Chapel Hill, 1968, p. 122.

21. Quoted from Ezra Stiles, *Itineraries*, F. B. Dexter, ed., New York, 1901, p. 444.

22. Quoted in Ann Maury, ed., *Memoirs of a Huguenot Family*, New York, 1853, p. 380.

23. *Ibid.*

24. Quoted in Bernhard Knollenberg, *Origin of the American Revolution*, New York, 1961, pp. 54-55.

25. John Camm to Mrs. McClurg, July 24, 1766, in *William & Mary Quarterly Historical Papers*, Vol. 2 (1893-1894), pp. 337-338.

26. Quoted in Clinton Rossiter, *Seedtime of the Republic*, New York, 1953, p. 259.

27. Richard Bland, "The Colonel Dismounted," quoted in Bailyn, *Pamphlets of the American Revolution*, pp. 297-298.

28. Quoted in Rossiter, *Seedtime of the Republic*, p. 261.

29. Bland quoted in Bailyn, *Pamphlets of the American Revolution*, p. 298.

30. Quoted in Merrill Jensen, *Founding of a Nation*, New York, 1968, p. 102.

31. Quoted in Maury, *Memoirs of a Huguenot Family*, p. 402.

32. Quoted in William W. Henry, *Life, Letters, and Correspondence of Patrick Henry*, Vol. 1, New York, 1891, pp. 39-41.

33. Quoted in Jack P. Greene, "The Gadsden Election Controversy," *Mississippi Valley Historical Review*, Vol. 46 (1959), p. 472.

34. *Ibid.*, p. 476.

35. *Ibid.*, p. 477.

36. *Ibid.*, p. 488.

CHAPTER III

1. Quoted in John C. Miller, *Sam Adams: Pioneer in Propaganda*, Stanford, 1936, p. 50.

2. Quoted in David H. Corkran, *The Cherokee Frontier, Conflict and Survival, 1740-1762*, Norman, Oklahoma, 1962, p. 96.

3. *Ibid.*

4. *Ibid.*, pp. 150-151.

5. Quoted in Samuel G. Drake, *Biography and History of the Indians of North America*, Boston, 1848, p. 35.

6. Quoted in Corkran, *Cherokee Frontier*, p. 184.

7. *Ibid.*, p. 193.

8. Quoted in Howard Peckham, *Pontiac and the Indian Uprising*, New York, 1970, p. 119.

9. *Ibid.*, pp. 119ff.

10. *Gentleman's Magazine* (December 1763), pp. 617-618.

11. Quoted in Peckham, *Pontiac and the Indian Uprising*, p. 120.

12. Quoted in *ibid.*, p. 296.

13. Quoted in Lawrence Henry Gipson, *The Triumphant Empire: New Responsibilities within the Enlarged Empire*, New York, 1968, p. 93.

14. Quoted in Francis Russell, "Oh Amherst, Brave Amherst," *American Heritage*, Vol. 12 (December 1960), p. 91.

15. *Ibid.*

16. Quoted in Francis Russell, "Father to the Six Nations," *American Heritage*, Vol. 10 (April 1965), p. 84.

17. Quoted in Allan Nevins, ed., *Ponteach or the Savages of America* by Robert Rogers, New York, 1914, p. 45.

18. *Gentleman's Magazine*, Vol. 35 (January 1765), p. 7.

19. Quoted in Dale Van Every, *Forth to the Wilderness: The First American Frontier, 1754-1774*, New York, 1961, p. 177.

20. Quoted in Samuel Eliot Morison, *The Oxford History of the American People*, New York, 1965, pp. 196-197.

21. Quoted in Jack M. Sosin, *The North American Interior in British Colonial Policy, 1760-1775*, Bloomington, Indiana, 1957, p. 161.

22. *The Paxton Papers*, in James E. Crowley, "The Paxton Disturbance," *Pennsylvania History*, Vol. 37 (1970), p. 323.

23. "Fragments of a Journal Kept by Samuel Foulke," *Pennsylvania Magazine of History and Biography*, Vol. 5 (1881), p. 73.

24. Benjamin Franklin to Richard Jackson, February 1, 1764, in *Letters and Papers of Benjamin Franklin and Richard Jackson, 1753-1785*, Carl Van Doren, ed., Philadelphia, 1947, p. 140.

25. Benjamin Franklin, "A Narrative of the Late Massacres in Lancaster County" (1764), in *Franklin Papers*, Vol. 11, Leonard W. Labaree, ed., New Haven, 1967, p. 65.

26. *Ibid.*

27. Benjamin Franklin to Richard Jackson, February 11, 1764. Quoted from Van Doren, *Letters and Papers*, p. 141.

28. ". . . Journal Kept by Samuel Foulke," p. 73.

29. *Ibid.*

30. Quoted in Van Doren, *Letters and Papers*, p. 311.

31. *Ibid.*, pp. 315-316.

32. *Ibid.*, p. 314.

CHAPTER IV

1. *Grenville Papers*, Vol. 3, p. 106; quoted in *Dictionary of National Biography*, Vol. 8, London, 1964, p. 558.

2. Quoted in Lord Albemarle, *Memoirs of the Marquis of Rockingham*, Vol. 2, London, 1852, p. 50.

3. Quoted in Edmund and Helen Morgan, *The Stamp Act Crisis*, Chapel Hill, 1953, p. 21.

4. Quoted in Ella Lonn, *Colonial Agents of the Southern Colonies*, Chapel Hill, 1945, p. 358.

5. Quoted in Lawrence Henry Gipson, *Triumphant Empire, Thunder Clouds Gather in the West*, New York, 1961, p. 267.

6. *Ibid.*, pp. 272-273.

7. Quoted in Lawrence Henry Gipson, "The Great Debate in the Committee of the Whole House of Commons on the Stamp Act, 1766, as reported by Nathaniel Ryder," *Pennsylvania Magazine of History and Biography*, Vol. 86 (January 1962), p. 19.

8. Quoted in Morgan, *Stamp Act Crisis*, p. 247.

9. Quoted in Bernard Bailyn, ed., *Pamphlets of the American Revolution, 1750-1776*, Cambridge, Massachusetts, 1965, p. 527.

10. Quoted in David S. Lovejoy, *Rhode Island Politics*, Providence, 1958, p. 50.

11. Jack P. Greene, ed., *The Diary of Colonel Landon Carter of Sabine Hall, 1752-1778*, Charlottesville, 1965, p. 11.

12. *Ibid.*, p. 37.

13. *Ibid.*

14. Quoted in V. C. Jones, "Patrick Henry: A Personality Profile," *American History Illustrated*, Vol. 3 (January 1969), p. 16.

15. Quoted in Morgan, *Stamp Act Crisis*, pp. 94-95.

16. C. F. Adams, ed., *The Works of John Adams*, Vol. 10, Boston, 1856, p. 287; and John C. Miller, *Sam Adams: Pioneer in Propaganda*, Stanford, 1936, p. 57.

17. Quoted in Clifford K. Shipton, *Sibley's Harvard Graduates*, Vol. 7, Boston, 1937-1970, p. 394.

18. *Ibid.*, p. 396.

19. Quoted in Morgan, *Stamp Act Crisis*, p. 138.

20. Quoted in Miller, *Sam Adams*, p. 67.

21. *Boston Gazette*, February 28, 1763, September 16, 1765; quoted in *ibid.*, p. 58.

22. *Ibid.*, p. 18.

23. *Ibid.*, p. 45.

24. Aubrey C. Land, *The Dulanys of Maryland*, Baltimore, 1968, p. 251.

25. Quoted in Moses Coit Tyler, *Literary History of the American Revolution*, New York, 1897, p. 105.

26. Land, *Dulanys of Maryland*, 265.

27. Edmund Morgan, *The Gentle Puritan*, New Haven, 1962, p. 227.

28. *Ibid.*, p. 178.

29. *Ibid.*, pp. 176, 178.

30. *Ibid.*, pp. 222-223.

31. *Ibid.*, p. 224.

32. Quoted in Shipton, *Sibley's Harvard Graduates*, Vol. 12, p. 84.

33. Quoted in William Tudor, *Life of James Otis*, New York, 1970, pp. 144-145.

34. Shipton, *Sibley's Harvard Graduates*, Vol. 11, p. 461.

35. *Ibid.*, pp. 464-465.

36. Jonathan Mayhew, "The Snare Broken," Boston, 1776; quoted in *ibid.*, p. 467.

37. *Ibid.*

38. Quoted in Tudor, *Life of James Otis*, p. 146.

39. Quoted in Morgan, *Stamp Act Crisis*, p. 104.

40. Quoted in Shipton, *Sibley's Harvard Graduates*, Vol. 11, p. 207.

41. Correspondence of General Thomas Gage. Quoted in Morgan, *Stamp Act Crisis*, p. 105.

42. Quoted in Appleton, *Cyclopedia of American Biography*, Vol. 4, New York, 1887, p. 128.

43. Charles W. Colby, "Chatham, 1708-1908," *American Historical Review*, Vol. 14 (July 1909), p. 729.

44. Philip Guedalla, *Fathers of the Revolution*, New York and London, 1926, p. 110.

45. *Ibid.*, p. 114.

46. William Pitt, "Speech in Reply to Grenville, House of Commons, 14 January, 1766," in *The Debate on the American Revolution, 1761-1783, A Sourcebook*, Max Beloff, ed., pp. 100-105.

47. *Works of Edmund Burke*, Vol. 2 (1815), p. 420; quoted in *Dictionary of National Biography*, Vol. 15, London, 1964, p. 1246.

48. Lord Chesterfield to his son, August 1, 1776, *Letters and Works of the Earl of Chesterfield*, Vol. 4, London, 1774; reprinted, 1845-1853, p. 427, in *ibid.*, p. 1247

49. Guedalla, *Fathers of the Revolution*, p. 119.

50. Francis Thackeray, *History of the Earl of Chatham, II*, London, 1827, pp. 311-314; quoted in *Dictionary of National Biography*, Vol. 15, p. 1249.

51. David L. Jacobson, *John Dickinson and the Revolution in Pennsylvania, 1764-1776*, Berkeley, 1965, pp. 49-51.

52. Quoted in Miller, *Sam Adams*, p. 200.

53. Horace Walpole, *Memoires of the Reign of George III*, Vol. 1, London and Philadelphia, 1845, p. 80.

54. Charles A. Barker, *Background of the Revolution in Maryland*, New Haven 1967, p. 317.

55. Quoted in Jacobson, *John Dickinson*, p. 63.

56. Quoted in J. C. Long, *Mr. Pitt and America's Birthright*, New York, 1940, p. 459.

CHAPTER V

1. Oliver Dickerson, *The Navigation Acts and the American Revolution*, Philadelphia, 1951, pp. 235-236.

2. Quoted in Hiller Zobel, *The Boston Massacre*, New York, 1970, p. 89.

3. John C. Cary, *Joseph Warren: Physician, Politician, Patriot*, Urbana, Illinois, 1961, p. 61.

4. Quoted in John C. Miller, *Sam Adams: Pioneer in Propaganda*, Stanford, 1936, pp. 150-151.

5. Quoted in John C. Miller, *Origins of the American Revolution*, Boston, 1943, p. 295.

6. Quoted in John Shy, *Toward Lexington: The Role of the British Army in the Coming of the Revolution*, Princeton, 1965, p. 313.

7. Zobel, *Boston Massacre*, p. 207.

8. Quoted in Clifford K. Shipton, *Sibley's Harvard Graduates*, Vol. 11, Boston, 1937-1970, p. 528.

9. *Ibid.*, Vol. 13, p. 483.

10. John Adams, *Diary and Autobiography*, Vol. 1, Lyman H. Butterfield, ed., Cambridge, Massachusetts, 1962, p. 51.

11. Josiah Quincy, *Memoir of the Life of Josiah Quincy*, Boston, 1825, p. 35.

12. Charles Chauncy to John Temple (in London), September 13, 1774. "Bowdoin and Temple Papers," *Massachusetts Historical Society Collections*, 6th series, Vol. 9 (1897), p. 375.

13. Quoted in Shipton, *Sibley's Harvard Graduates*, Vol. 13, p. 480.

14. Quincy, *Memoir of Josiah Quincy*, pp. 13-14.

15. *Ibid.*, p. 36.

16. John Adams, *Diary and Autobiography*, Vol. 3, p. 293.

17. Zobel, *Boston Massacre*, p. 275.

18. *Ibid.*, p. 290.

CHAPTER VI

1. John C. Miller, *Origins of the American Revolution*, Boston, 1943, p. 315.

2. *Ibid.*, p. 316.

3. Hugh T. Lefler and Albert R. Newsome, *The History of a Southern State, North Carolina*, Chapel Hill, 1954, p. 166.

4. A. T. Dill, *Governor Tryon and His Palace*, Chapel Hill, 1955, p. 132.

5. John H. Wheeler, *Historical Sketches of North Carolina*, Baltimore, 1964, p. 302.

6. Dill, *Governer Tryon*, p. 129.

7. Wheeler, *Historical Sketches*, p. 55.

8. *Colonial Records, X*, pp. 1019-1022, in John S. Bassett, "The Regulators of North Carolina, 1765-1771," *Annual Report of the American Historical Association* (1894), p. 203.

9. Lefler and Newsome, *History of a Southern State*, p. 176.

10. J. C. Long, *Mr. Pitt and America's Birthright*, New York, 1940, p. 415.

11. David Duncan Wallace, *South Carolina: A Short History, 1520-1948*, Columbia, South Carolina, 1951, p. 244.

12. Quoted in Jack P. Greene, "Bridge to Revolution: The Wilkes Fund Controversy in South Carolina, 1769-1775," *Journal of Southern History*, Vol. 29 (1963), pp. 21-22, 24.

13. David Duncan Wallace, *The Life of Henry Laurens*, New York, 1969, p. 167.

14. *Ibid.*, p. 172.

15. Quoted in Jack P. Greene, *The Quest for Power*, Chapel Hill, 1963, pp. 406, 407.

16. Greene, "Bridge to Revolution," p. 46.

17. *Ibid.*, p. 47.

18. *Ibid.*, p. 49.

19. *Ibid.*, p. 51.

20. *Ibid.*, p. 52.

21. Quoted in Charles A. Barker, *Background of the Revolution in Maryland*, New Haven, 1969, p. 351.

22. *Ibid.*, p. 355.

23. Quoted in Carl Van Doren, *Benjamin Franklin*, New York, 1964, p. 445.

24. Jared Sparks, ed., *The Works of Benjamin Franklin*, Vol. 4, Boston, 1840, p. 435.

25. H. A. Cushing, ed., *The Writings of Samuel Adams*, Vol. 3, New York, 1907, pp. 46-47.

26. "Ballad of the Boston Ministers," quoted in Clifford K. Shipton, *Sibley's Harvard Graduates*, Vol. 11, Boston, 1937-1970, p. 203.

27. *Ibid.*

28. *Ibid.*, p. 195.

29. "A Sermon Preached in the Audience of His Honour Spencer Phips, Boston, 1756," quoted in *ibid.*, p. 197.

30. December 17, 1773, quoted in *ibid.*, p. 203.

31. Miller, *Origins of the American Revolution*, p. 326.

32. James B. Hedges, *The Browns of Providence Plantation, Colonial Years*, Cambridge, Massachusetts, 1952, p. 14.

33. There are variations on this story. This one is taken from the report of Ephraim Bowen in *The Documentary History of the Destruction of the Gaspee*, William R. Staples, ed., Providence, 1845, pp. 8-9.

34. Quoted in Miller, *Origins of the American Revolution*, p. 327.

35. Joseph Wanton to Lord Hillsborough, June 16, 1772. Quoted in *ibid.*, p. 16.

36. Quoted in David S. Lovejoy, *Rhode Island Politics*, Providence, 1958, p. 165.

37. Quoted in Miller, *Origins of the American Revolution*, p. 329.

38. Anonymous broadside, 1772; quoted in Staples, *Destruction of the Gaspee*, pp. 55-56.

39. Quoted in E. I. Miller, "The Virginia Committee of Correspondence of 1773-1775," *William & Mary Quarterly*, Vol. 22 (1965), p. 100.

40. James Curtis Ballagh, ed., *Letters of Richard Henry Lee*, Vol. 1, New York, 1911, p. 84.

41. *Ibid.*

42. Quoted in Eugene Wulsin, "The Political Consequences of the Burning of the *Gaspee*," *Rhode Island History*, Vol. 3 (January 1944), p. 58.

43. Ezra Stiles, *Diary*, Vol. 1, F. B. Dexter, ed., New York, 1901, pp. 384-385.

CHAPTER VII

1. Agnes Repplier, *To Think of Tea!*, Boston, 1932, p. 101.

2. George III to Lord North, May 3, 1773, in *The Correspondence of George III*, W. Bodham Donne, ed., Vol. 1, London, 1867, p. 480.

3. Quoted in *The Encyclopedia Britannica*, Vol. 7, Chicago, 1966, p. 878; and Lucy Sutherland, *The East India Company and 18th Century Politics*, London, 1952, p. 141.

4. Sutherland, *East India Company*, p. 242.

5. George III to Lord North, November 25, 1772, in Donne, *Correspondence of George III*, Vol. 1, p. 113.

6. Quoted in John C. Miller, *Origins of the American Revolution*, Boston, 1943, p. 244.

7. Benjamin Franklin to Thomas Cushing, June 4, 1773. *The Works of Benjamin Franklin*, Vol. 8, Jared Sparks, ed., Boston, 1840, p. 49.

8. Benjamin Booth to James and Drinker, October 4, 1773. Quoted in Thomas B. Taylor, "The Philadelphia Counterpart," *Friends Bulletin*, Vol. 2 (November 1908), pp. 94-95.

9. James and Drinker to Pigon and Booth, October 5 and 7, 1773. *Ibid.*, pp. 95-97.

10. Benjamin Rush to John Adams, August 14, 1809. *The Letters of Benjamin Rush*, Vol. 2, Lyman H. Butterfield, ed., Princeton, 1951, pp. 1013-1014.

11. "Philadelphia Resolves," *Friends Bulletin*, Vol. 2 (November 1908), pp. 103-104.

12. James and Drinker to Pigon and Booth, October 19, 1773. *Friends Bulletin*, p. 102.

13. *Ibid.*

14. Thomas Wharton to Samuel Wharton, January 1, 1774. *Pennsylvania Magazine of History and Biography*, Vol. 33 (1909), p. 324.

15. James and Drinker to Pigon and Booth, November 30, 1773. *Friends Bulletin*, Vol. 3 (February 1909), p. 28.

16. James and Drinker to Pigon and Booth, December 7, 1773. *Ibid.*, p. 35.

17. Quoted in Taylor, "The Philadelphia Counterpart," p. 48.

18. Benjamin Booth to James and Drinker, August 4, 1773. *Friends Bulletin*, Vol. 2 (November 1908), pp. 101, 107.

19. Quoted in Francis S. Drake, *Tea Leaves*, Detroit, 1970, pp. 269-271.

20. Quoted in William H. W. Sabine, ed., *Historical Memoirs of William Smith*, New York, 1956, p. 156.

21. Quoted in Thomas Jones, *History of New York during the Revolutionary War*, New York, 1879, p. 426.

22. Quoted in *National Cyclopedia of American Biography*, Vol. 11, New York, 1898, p. 542.

23. Quoted in Clifford K. Shipton, *Sibley's Harvard Graduates*, Vol. 15, Boston, 1937-1970, p. 291.

24. Sam Adams to Joseph Hawley, October 13, 1773. Quoted from *The Writings of Samuel Adams*, Vol. 3, H. A. Cushing, ed., New York, 1907, p. 62.

25. Committee of Correspondence of Massachusetts to Other Committees of Correspondence, October 21, 1773. Quoted, *ibid.*, p. 67.

26. Quoted in Merrill Jensen, *Founding of a Nation*, New York, 1968, p. 414.

27. *Boston Evening Post*, October 25, 1773. Quoted in Henry H. Edes, "Memoir of Thomas Young, 1731-1777," *Colonial Society of Massachusetts Publications*, Vol. 11 (December 1906), p. 33.

28. Quoted in Richard Brown, *Revolutionary Politics in Massachusetts*, Cambridge, Massachusetts, 1970, p. 156.

29. Richard Clarke to A. Dupuis, November 17, 1773. Quoted in Drake, *Tea Leaves*, p. 282.

30. *The Boston Gazette and the Evening Post*, November 8, 1773. Quoted in Jensen, *Founding of a Nation*, pp. 449-450.

31. Quoted in Drake, *Tea Leaves*, p. 289.

32. Quoted in Frank W. Bayley, *Five Colonial Artists of New England*, Boston, 1929, p. 142.

33. November 3, 1773. *The Diary and Letters of John Rowe*, Anne Rowe Cunningham, ed., New York, 1969, p. 256.

34. Quoted in L. F. S. Upton, "Proceedings of Ye Body Respecting the Tea," *William & Mary Quarterly*, Vol. 22 (April 1965), p. 296.

35. Elizabeth F. Ellet, *The Women of the American Revolution*, New York, 1969, p. 74.

36. Quoted in Katherine Anthony, *First Lady of the Revolution: The Life of Mercy Otis Warren*, Garden City, New York, 1958, p. 95.

37. Abigail Adams to Mercy Otis Warren. *Adams Family Correspondence*, Vol. 1, Lyman H. Butterfield, ed., Cambridge, Massachusetts, 1963, pp. 88-89.

38. Quoted in Richard Frothingham, *Life and Times of Joseph Warren*, Boston, 1865, p. 267.

39. Hutchinson to Maudit. Quoted in "Tea Party Anniversary," *Massachusetts Historical Society Proceedings*, Vol. 13 (December 1873), p. 170.

40. Quoted in Upton, "Proceedings . . . Respecting the Tea," p. 298.

41. Quoted in Drake, *Tea Leaves*, p. 64, and Benjamin W. Labaree, *The Boston Tea Party*, New York, 1964, p. 141.

42. Quoted in Drake, *Tea Leaves*, p. 127.

43. *Ibid.*, pp. 71-72.

44. *Ibid.*, pp. 79-80.

45. John Andrews to William Barrell, December 18, 1773. "Letters of John Andrews," *Massachusetts Historical Society Proceedings* (1864-1865), p. 326.

46. *Ibid.*

47. *Massachusetts Gazette*, December 23, 1770. Quoted in "Tea Party Anniversary," pp. 171-172.

48. Quoted in Elbridge H. Goss, *The Life of Colonel Paul Revere*, Vol. 1, Boston, 1891, p. 131.

49. Thomas Hutchinson, *History of Massachusetts Bay*, Vol. 3, Lawrence S. Mayo, ed., Cambridge, Massachusetts, 1936, p. 313.

50. Quoted in Goss, *Life of Colonel Paul Revere*, p. 128.

51. Sam Adams to James Warren, December 28, 1773. "Warren-Adams Letters," *Massachusetts Historical Society Collections* (1917), pp. 20-21.

52. John Adams, *Diary*, December 17, 1773. Quoted in "Tea Party Anniversary," pp. 191-192.

53. Quoted in Merrill Jensen, ed., *English Historical Documents*, Vol. 9, New York, 1964, p. 771.

54. Quoted in Miller, *Origins of the American Revolution*, p. 333.

55. Quoted in J. Campbell, *Lives of the Lord Chancellors of England*, Vol. 7, New York, 1875, p. 305.

56. Benjamin Franklin to Thomas Cushing, February 15, 1774. *The Works of Benjamin Franklin*, Vol. 8, Jared Sparks, ed., Boston, 1840, pp. 112-113.

57. *Ibid.*, p. 114.

58. Quoted in *The Parliamentary History of England, 1771, 1774*, Vol. 17, T. C. Hansard, ed., London, 1813, pp. 1163-1167.

59. *Ibid.*, pp. 1192-1193.

60. Quoted in *Dictionary of National Biography*, Vol. 5, London, 1964, p. 1290.

61. Quoted from Hansard, *Parliamentary History of England*, p. 1198.

62. Quoted in *Dictionary of National Biography*, Vol. 3, pp. 348-349.

63. Quoted in Hansard, *Parliamentary History of England*, pp. 1203, 1202, 1206.

64. *Ibid.*, p. 1214.

65. *Ibid.*, p. 1218.

66. *Ibid.*, pp. 1220-1221.

67. *Ibid.*, p. 1223.

68. *Ibid.*, pp. 1267-1269.

69. September 1, 1773. Quoted in Malcolm Freiberg, "William Bollan, Agent of Massachusetts," *Bulletin of Boston Public Library* (February-June, 1948), p. 217.

70. Arthur Lee to Sam Adams, June 11, 1773. Richard Henry Lee, *The Life of Arthur Lee*, Vol. 1, Freeport, New York, 1969, p. 232.

71. H. A. Cushing, ed., *Writings of Samuel Adams*, Vol. 3, p. 73.

72. February 8, 1774. Richard Henry Lee, *Life of Arthur Lee*, Vol. 1, pp. 242 and 271.

73. Quoted in Freiberg, "William Bollan," p. 215.

74. Quoted from Hansard, *Parliamentary History of England*, p. 1182.

75. *Ibid.*, p. 1300.

CHAPTER VIII

1. Richard Henry Lee, *The Life of Arthur Lee*, Vol. 1, Freeport, New York, 1969, pp. 238, 256-257.

2. B. P. Bargar, *Lord Dartmouth and the American Revolution*, Columbia, South Carolina, 1965, p. 119.

3. *Ibid.*, p. 120.

4. *Ibid.*, p. 123.

5. *Ibid.*, p. 127.

6. *Ibid.*, p. 129.

7. Quoted in Victor Coffin, "Province of Quebec and the Early American Revolution," *University of Wisconsin Bulletin: Economics, Political Science and History Series*, Vol. 1 (1896), pp. 282-283.

8. *Ibid.*, pp. 284-285.

9. *Ibid.*, p. 291.

10. Quoted in Chester Martin, *Empire and Commonwealth*, Oxford, 1929, pp. 131-132.

11. T. C. Hansard, ed., *The Parliamentary History of England, 1771-1774*, Vol. 17, London, 1813, pp. 656-657, 681, 734, 742, 1402-1404.

12. Quoted in Clarence W. Alvord, *The Mississippi Valley in British Politics*, Vol. 2, New York, 1959, p. 244.

13. Lord John Russell, ed., *Memorials and Correspondence of Charles James Fox*, Vol. 1, London, 1853-57; reprinted, New York, 1970, p. 102.

14. Lord John Russell, *The Life and Times of Charles James Fox*, Vol. 1, London, 1853-57; reprinted, New York, 1970, p. 64.

15. Quoted in Martin, *Empire and Commonwealth*, pp. 130-131.

16. *New York Journal*, August 25, 1774. Quoted in Charles Henry Metzger, *The Quebec Act: A Primary Cause of the American Revolution*, New York, 1936, p. 43.

17. *Ibid.*, p. 55n.

18. Samuel K. Wilson, "Bishop Briand and the American Revolution," *The Catholic Historical Review*, Vol. 19 (July 1933), p. 136.

19. November 30, 1772. *Ibid.*, p. 137.

20. September 26, 1774. C. F. Adams, ed., *The Works of John Adams*, Vol. 3, Boston, 1856, pp. 449-450.

21. Quoted in C. H. Van Tyne, "The Influence of the Clergy, and of Religious and Sectarian Forces, on the American Revolution," *The American Historical Review*, Vol. 19 (1913-1914), p. 55.

22. *Silas Deane Papers, Collections of the New-York Historical Society*, Vol. 19 (1886), p. 4.

23. Alexander Hamilton, "Remarks on the Quebec Bill," June 15, 1775, in *The Works of Alexander Hamilton*, Vol. 1, Henry Cabot Lodge, ed., New York, 1885-1904, pp. 184-185, 190-191, 193f.

24. *Ibid.*

EPILOGUE

1. Merrill Jensen, ed. *English Historical Documents*, Vol. 9, New York, 1964, pp. 141A, 790.

2. *Ibid.*

3. Thomas Fleming, *The Man from Monticello*, New York, 1969, p. 27.

4. *Ibid.*, p. 28.

5. *Ibid.*

6. Dumas Malone, *Jefferson the Virginian*, Boston, 1948, p. 174.

7. *Ibid.*, p. 182.

8. Thomas Jefferson, "A Summary View of the Rights of British America," in *The Debate on the American Revolution, 1761-1783, A Sourcebook*, Max Beloff, ed., New York, 1965, pp. 159-177.

9. *Ibid.*

10. John Braeman, *The Road to Independence, A Documentary History of the Causes of the American Revolution, 1763-1776*, New York, 1963, p. 220.

11. Quoted in Benjamin W. Labaree, *The Road to Independence, 1763-1776*, New York, 1964, p. 59.

12. Quoted in Lawrence Henry Gipson, *The Triumphant Empire: Britain Sails Into the Storm*, New York, 1965, p. 244.

LIST OF ILLUSTRATIONS

with Curatorial Acknowledgments and Notes

In assembling the portraits and related materials included in this catalogue, we are most grateful to the historical societies, libraries, museums, and individuals whose names appear below.

In Great Britain, we are particularly indebted to His Grace the Duke of Richmond and Gordon; the Marquess of Bute; the Marquess of Camden; the Earl of Dartmouth; the Earl of Dunmore; the Earl Fitzwilliam; Lord Northbourne; Lord Savile; Lord Thurlow; Sir John Johnson; Sir Geoffrey Agnew; Captain Richard Dobbs of Castle Dobbs, Northern Ireland; John Kerslake and Sara Wimbush of the National Portrait Gallery, London; Robin Hutchison of the National Portrait Gallery of Scotland; James White of the National Gallery of Ireland; Sir Oliver Millar, Keeper of the Queen's Works of Art; Richard Walker, Keeper of the Palace of Westminster; E. St. John Gore of the National Trust; Peter Wilson of Sotheby & Company, Ltd.; Paul Jordan, Archaeology and History Unit, BBC Television. We are also beholden to the American Ambassador to Great Britain, Walter Annenberg, for so graciously providing an office in the American Embassy for our man in London, Richard Kenin.

In the United States, we are grateful to John Alden of the Boston Public Library, Rare Book Room; Mrs. Ropes Cabot of the Bostonian Society; Malcolm Freiberg of the Massachusetts Historical Society; James J. Heslin of the New-York Historical Society; Sinclair Hitchings of the Boston Public Library Print Department; Milton Kaplan of the Library of Congress; the late Helen G. McCormack and J. Russell MacBeth of the Gibbes Art Gallery; Stephanie Munsing of the Library Company of Philadelphia; Caroline Rollins of the Yale University Art Gallery; Mildred Steinbach and Helen Sanger of the Frick Art Reference Library; Nada Saporiti of the Metropolitan Museum of Art; Mrs. Graham P. Teller of the Society for the Preservation of New England Antiquities.

Robert G. Stewart, Curator

INTRODUCTION

PAGE 14

William Shirley (1694-1771) by Thomas Hudson (1701-1779). Oil on canvas, 50 x 40, 1750. This portrait was painted when Governor Shirley was on leave from his gubernatorial post in London from 1749 to 1753 at which time he was appointed a member of the commission sitting in Paris to determine the boundary line between French North America and New England.

Collection of Mrs. Cornelia King Marsh. Photo: Frick Art Reference Library

PAGE 15

Lieutenant-General Sir William Pepperrell The Victor of Louisbourg (1696-1759) by John Smibert (1688-1751). Oil on canvas, 96 x 56, 1747. This portrait is one of a group of portraits painted by Smibert to commemorate the heroic Massachusetts expedition against Louisbourg. The poor proportions of the figure may have resulted from Smibert's failing eyesight and the necessity to have the work finished by another hand — probably Smibert's nephew.

Essex Institute, Salem, Massachusetts

PAGE 16

A View of the Landing the New England Forces in ye Expedition against Cape Breton, 1745. Engraving, 14¼ x 20¼, drawn by J. Stevens and engraved by Brooks, published by John Bowles and Carrington Bowles, London, after 1746.

The John Carter Brown Library

PAGE 17

Defeat and Death of General Braddock in North America. Drawn by Dodd and engraved by Edmund Scott for William Augustus Russel's *A New and Authentic History of England* . . . , published in London in 1781.

The John Carter Brown Library

PAGE 17

James Wolfe by George Townshend (1724-1807), first Marquis Townshend. Watercolor on paper, 6 x 5⅞, 1759, inscribed: to/ Isaac Barré/ from his friend/ Geo: Townshend. (The two-line note at the top was penciled on in 1864.)

McCord Museum, McGill University, Montreal

PAGE 18

Last page from a fragment of General Edward Braddock's Orderly Book used on his last campaign.

Manuscript Division, Library of Congress

PAGE 19

"A View of the Taking of Quebeck by the English Forces Commanded by Genl. Wolfe Sep:13th. 1759." Engraving published in the *London Magazine*, 1760.

Library of Congress

PAGE 20

Quebec, The Capital of New-France by Thomas Johnston. Engraving, 7 x 8¾, Boston, 1759. Although based on an inset in an earlier map printed in Paris, this engraving is considered the earliest printed American view of the Canadian capital.

American Antiquarian Society

PAGE 21

Britons Behold the Best of Kings by Nathaniel Hurd (1730-1770). Engraving, 3¾ x 5, Boston, 1762.

American Antiquarian Society

CHAPTER I

PAGE 24

St. Edward's Crown, from the collection of Crown Jewels kept in the Tower of London. The Crown was made for the coronation of Charles II in 1660, and was worn by British kings at their coronation thereafter.

Photo: Crown Copyright, by permission of the Controller of Her Britannic Majesty's Stationery Office

PAGE 25

Edward Augustus (1739-1767), Duke of York, with the future George III (1738-1820), by Richard Wilson (1714-1782). Oil on canvas, 56 x 62, c. 1751.

National Portrait Gallery, London

PAGE 26

Transfer-printed mug manufactured in Liverpool by J. Sadler. The likeness of Pitt was transfer printed from a T. Billinge engraving of the Hoare canvas of 1756.

City of Liverpool Museums

PAGE 27

Miniature glass boot, probably of English manufacture and of the third quarter of the 18th century.

Victoria and Albert Museum. Photo: Crown Copyright

PAGE 28

John Bull's House sett in Flames. Engraving, 11 x 13½. Published September 2, 1762. Bute flees while Pitt and his friends put out the fire Bute has started.

Courtesy of the Trustees of the British Museum

PAGE 29

The Times, Plate 1 by William Hogarth (1697-1764). Engraving, 8⁹/₁₆ x 11⅝, published September 7, 1762.

Rosenwald Collection, National Gallery of Art

CHAPTER II

PAGE 32

Sir Francis Bernard (1712-1779) by John Singleton Copley (1738-1815). Oil on canvas, 29 x 24, 1767. The Governor's portrait was painted in Boston and hung in Harvard Hall where the French emigrant artist Du Simitière reported seeing it in 1767.

Collection of Christ Church College, Oxford. Presented by Bernard's son in 1789

PAGES 33 AND 34

Recto and verso of a manuscript draft of a writ of assistance in the hand of Thomas Hutchinson, December 1761.

John Adams Papers, Massachusetts Historical Society. Photos: George M. Cushing

PAGE 36

Proclamation broadside, 16 x 13, printed in Boston by John Draper in 1761.

American Antiquarian Society

PAGE 37

Thomas Hutchinson (1711-1780), by Edward Truman (working in 1741). Oil on canvas, 28¼ x 23½, 1741.

Massachusetts Historical Society. Photo: George M. Cushing

PAGE 40

Title page of Oxenbridge Thacher's pamphlet, *The Sentiments of a British American*, published in Boston by Edes & Gill, 1764.

Harvard College Library

PAGE 43

Tobacco merchants on an American wharf. Vignette of the Joshua Fry and Peter Jefferson map of Virginia and Maryland published in London, 1751.

Map Division, Library of Congress

PAGE 44

The Wren Building of the College of William and Mary, Williamsburg, Virginia. First built in 1697, the building was heavily restored after fires in 1705 and 1859.

Photo: Colonial Williamsburg

PAGE 45

Title page of Richard Bland's pamphlet, *The Colonel Dismounted: or the Rector Vindicated*, printed in Williamsburg by Joseph Royle, 1764.

American Antiquarian Society

PAGE 47

Peter Lyons (1734-1809) by Thomas Sully (1783-1872). Oil on canvas, 33 x 29, 1806.

Collection of the Supreme Court of the Commonwealth of Virginia. Photo: Cook Collection. Valentine Museum

CHAPTER III

PAGE 52

Wampum belt, 21½ inches long, sent by Governor Denny of Pennsylvania to the Indians of the Ohio Valley in 1756. The design, representing the Governor and an Indian, is meant to say, "I have laid a nice smooth road for you and want all to come who can."

Museum of the American Indian, Heye Foundation

PAGE 53

The Cherokee Embassy to England, 1730 by Isaac Basire (1704-1768). Engraving, 18 x 22, 1730.

The South Caroliniana Library, University of South Carolina

PAGE 54

William Lyttelton (1724-1808) by Sir Joshua Reynolds (1723-1792). Oil on canvas, 29½ x 24½, date unknown.

Collection of Viscount Cobham, Hagley Hall. Photo: Courtauld Institute of Art

PAGE 57

Manuscript *Map of the Cherokee Country* by John Stuart, Superintendent of Indian Affairs for the Southern District. Ink on paper, approximately 14¼ x 25, circa 1760.

Courtesy of the Trustees of the British Museum

PAGE 58

No. 43. A South View of Crown Point. Pencil, ink, and watercolor, 10⅜ x 15¹⁵/₁₆, 1759. The watercolor was done on the site by Thomas Davies, one of Amherst's officers.

Division of Prints and Photographs, Library of Congress

PAGE 59

Sir William Johnson (1715-1774) by an unidentified artist. Oil on canvas, 30 x 25 inches.

Collection of Mr. Leavett-Shenley, The Holt, Upham, England. Photo: Copyright, *Country Life*

PAGE 60

Obverse and reverse of a medal of George III of the type given to American Indians. Silver, diameter 2⅜, 1766.

American Numismatics Society

PAGE 61

Treaty on parchment with red wax seals, 16 x 24¼, 1765. The document is signed by both William and Guy Johnson and bears the pictograph signatures of nine Indian representatives.

Museum of the American Indian, Heye Foundation

PAGE 62

Testimonial certificate engraved by Henry Dawkins for Sir William Johnson, 1770. The original plate in the possession of the New-York Historical Society measures 9½ x 9¼. This reproduction was made from one of 50 restrikes printed in 1946.

The New-York Historical Society

PAGE 63

Robert Rogers (1731-1795) by Johann Martin Will (dates unknown). Engraving in mezzotint, 16 x 8, published in London by Thomas Martin, 1776. This is an imaginary likeness.

Courtesy of the Trustees of the British Museum. Photo: John R. Freeman & Co.

PAGE 63

Henry Bouquet (1719-1765) by John Wollaston (c. 1710-c. 1767). Oil on canvas, 30 x 25, c. 1760.

Historical Society of Pennsylvania

PAGE 64

"The Indians giving a Talk to Colonel Bouquet . . . Oct. 1764." Engraving by Charles Grignon (dates unknown) after a drawing by Benjamin West (1738-1820), from Bouquet's *Historical Account of the Expedition against the Ohio Indians*, London, 1766.

Library of Congress

PAGE 65

George Washington (1732-1799) by Charles Willson Peale (1741-1827). Oil on canvas, 50½ x 41½, 1772. This earliest known likeness of Washington shows him in the uniform of the Virginia militia. The paper in his pocket is inscribed "Order of March."

Collection of Washington and Lee University

PAGE 66

George III (1738-1820) by Allan Ramsay (1713-1784). Oil on canvas, 95 x 61¼, 1761. This painting is one of several replicas of the life portrait which hangs in Buckingham Palace and shows the King in his coronation robes.

Colonial Williamsburg

PAGE 67

John Stuart (1713-1792), third Earl of Bute, by Sir Joshua Reynolds (1723-1792). Oil on canvas, 93¼ x 57, date unknown.

Collection of the National Portrait Gallery, London

PAGE 68

William Pitt (1708-1778), later first Earl of Chatham, by William Hoare (1706-1792). Oil on canvas, 49¾ x 39½, 1754. This portrait was painted while Pitt was a member of the House of Commons.

Museum of Art, Carnegie Institute, Pittsburgh

PAGE 69

James Otis (1725-1783) by Joseph Blackburn (working 1752-1778). Oil on canvas, 29½ x 25¼, 1755. Dated in the year that Otis married Ruth Cunningham, daughter of a wealthy Boston merchant, the painting was probably done as a wedding portrait.

Collection of Mrs. Carlos Hepp. Transparency: Geoffrey Clements

PAGE 69

Christopher Gadsden (1724-1805) by Jeremiah Theus (1719-1774). Oil on canvas, 50 x 40, date unknown.

Collection of George D. Shore, Jr. Transparency: Colorama Studios

PAGE 69

Patrick Henry (1736-1799) by Lawrence Sully (1769-1804). Watercolor on ivory, 2½ x 2, 1795. Painted in the year Washington offered Henry both the positions of Secretary of State and Chief Justice — he refused both.

Collection of Amherst College

PAGE 70

Benjamin Franklin (1706-1790) by Mason Chamberlin (d. 1787). Oil on paper on panel, 49 x 39, 1762. The portrait was commissioned by Philip Ludwell, II, a Virginian living in Westminster, England, and was painted there just prior to Franklin's return to the colonies. Franklin had been in England since 1757 on business concerning the Pennsylvania Assembly's grievance against the Penn family's claim to exemption from taxation.

Philadelphia Museum of Art, The Mr. and Mrs. Wharton Sinkler Collection. Transparency: Alfred S. Wyatt

PAGE 71

Cunne Shote (dates unknown), also known as Oconostota, by Francis Parsons (working 1762-1783). Oil on canvas, 36½ x 29½, 1762. When James MacArdell (c. 1710-1765) engraved this portrait in mezzotint shortly after it was painted, he identified the sitter as Cunne Shote. This version of the name may have been a corruption of the Cherokee "Cunni Chote," or "Turkey of Chote," a name very close to that of one of the Cherokees who is labeled "Stalking Turkey" on the ballad broadside published during the Indians' visit.

Thomas Gilcrease Institute of American History and Art

PAGE 72

Sir Jeffery Amherst (1717-1797), later first Baron Amherst, by Sir Joshua Reynolds (1723-1792). Oil on canvas, 49½ x 39½, 1765. On his armor Amherst wears the ribbon and star of the Order of the Bath. The background shows his troops in canoes on the way to the successful siege of Montreal in 1760.

Collection of Amherst College

PAGE 73

A New Map of the British Dominions in North America . . . settled by Proclamation, October 7th, 1763. Engraved by Thomas Kitchin in London for inclusion in the Annual Register for 1763.

Library of Congress

PAGE 74

Charles Wyndham (1710-1763), Earl of Egremont, by William Hoare (1706-1792). Oil on canvas, size not available, date unknown.

National Trust, Petworth Collection. Photo: Courtauld Institute of Art

PAGE 75

William Petty (1737-1805), Earl of Shelburne, by Jean Laurent Mosnier (1734/35-1808). Oil on canvas, 30 x 25, 1791.

Collection of the Marquess of Lansdowne. Photo: Tom Scott

PAGE 76

John Penn (1729-1795) by Richard Brompton (1734-1782). Oil on canvas, 35½ x 31, 1773. Upon receiving news of the death of his father in April 1771, John Penn left Philadelphia for England, where he remained until 1773. In August of that year, he returned to Pennsylvania as governor in his own right.

Collection of C. Anthony Barnes. Photo: Paul Laib

PAGE 77

The German Bleeds & bears ye Furs by an unidentified artist. Engraving, 7⅛ x 9⅞, published in Philadelphia, 1764. Franklin is at the left with Joseph Fox between his legs. Israel Pemberton rides the back of a Scotch-Irishman while an Indian rides the back of a German whom Pemberton leads by his nose.

The Library Company of Philadelphia

PAGE 78

The Paxton Expedition, Inscribed to the Author of the Farce, by HD, by Henry Dawkins. Engraving, 13¹¹/₁₆ x 7⁵/₁₆, 1764. This is the earliest known exterior view of any part of Philadelphia and shows the square in front of the Court House at Second and Market streets.

The Library Company of Philadelphia

CHAPTER IV

PAGE 82

The Deplorable State of America. Etching, 12¾ x 7¼, published in London, 1765. Britannia offers the Stamp Tax in the form of Pandora's box to America, pictured as an Indian. America appeals to the goddess of wisdom, Minerva, who advises America to "Take it Not." Liberty, lying prostrate at Britannia's feet, is oppressed by a thistle, the symbol of Lord Bute, attached to the tail of a serpent, the symbol of treachery. Mercury, symbolizing trade, abandons America reluctantly, while a strong wind blows against the tree dedicated "To Liberty." The boot, addressed by the King of France, represents Lord Bute, who is being offered a full purse to let his "banefull Influence be poured down upon them."

Courtesy of the Trustees of the British Museum

PAGE 83

The Deplorable State of America. Etching, 10⅛ x 14¾, published in Boston, November 1, 1765. The note at the top of the print, in the hand of Pierre Eugène Du Simitière, who originally collected the print, reads: "The Original Print done in Boston by Jo. S. Copley." This is the only known impression.

The symbolism of the print parallels that of the cartoon published in March 1765, in London (p. 82), but in many ways is an improvement on the original.

The Library Company of Philadelphia

PAGE 85

Jared Ingersoll (1722-1781) by an unidentified artist. Oil on canvas, size not available, date unknown.

Collection of C. Jared Ingersoll. Photo: Society for the Preservation of New England Antiquities

PAGE 86

Test impressions of the Stamp Act dies intended for use in the American colonies.

Courtesy of the Board of Inland Revenue Library, London

PAGE 87

The so-called "tombstone" issue of *The Pennsylvania Journal and Weekly Advertiser*, October 31, 1765.

The Historical Society of Pennsylvania

PAGE 88

Martin Howard (c. 1730-1781) by John Singleton Copley (1738-1815). Oil on canvas, 49½ x 39¾, 1767. Howard is wearing his robes as Chief Justice of North Carolina, a position to which he was appointed in 1767. The portrait was undoubtedly painted in Boston where he stopped on his return from England and where he married Abigail Greenleaf on August 26, 1767.

Collection of Social Law Library, Boston

PAGE 90

Andrew Oliver (1706-1774) by John Singleton Copley (1738-1815). Oil on copper, oval, 1¾ x 1½, circa 1758. This miniature portrait was painted two years after

Oliver was named Secretary of the Province of Massachusetts in 1756.

Collection of Andrew Oliver

PAGE 92

Daniel Dulany (1722-1797), attributed to John Wollaston (c. 1710-1767). Oil on canvas, 50 x 40, painted probably between 1753 and 1757. Dulany is portrayed in the judiciary robes he was entitled to wear as a member of the Maryland bar.

Collection of R. H. Dulany Randolph. Photo: Frick Art Reference Library

PAGE 95

Jonathan Mayhew (1720-1766), attributed to John Greenwood (1727-1792). Oil on canvas, 29½ x 22¾, circa 1750. Mayhew is shown in the robes of a Congregational clergyman.

Collection of the Congregational House, Boston

PAGE 98

Thomas McKean (1734-1827), attributed to Charles Willson Peale (1741-1827). Oil on canvas, 27¼ x 22, date unknown. Peale painted McKean about a half-dozen times between 1776 and 1797. This portrait may have been painted in 1791.

National Portrait Gallery, Smithsonian Institution, Washington, D.C.

PAGE 99

Obverse and reverse of the William Pitt Token, actual diameter, 17½ mm. Some numismatic authorities believe the token to have been produced by the engraver and seal cutter James Smither (?-1797) who worked in Philadelphia from 1768 to 1778.

City of Liverpool Museums

PAGE 100

Broadside, 13 x 8, announcing the first arrival of news of the repeal of the Stamp Act, issued jointly by the Boston newspaper publishers: Drapers, Edes & Gill, Green & Russell, and Fleets, in Boston, 1766.

American Antiquarian Society

PAGE 102

The Patriotic American Farmer by James Smither (?-1797). Engraving, 10⅜ x 7¼, published in Philadelphia, circa 1768.

The Library Company of Philadelphia

PAGE 103

A View of the Obelisk erected under Liberty-Tree in Boston on the Rejoicings for the Repeal of the _____ Stamp-Act, 1766, by Paul Revere (1735-1818). Engraving, 9⅜ x 13¼, 1766. The figures are: (1) the Duke of York, the Marquis of Rockingham, Queen Caroline, and George III; (2) General Conway, Lord T__n, Colonel Barré, William Pitt; (3) Lord Dartmouth, A__n B__r, Lord Dowdeswell, Charles Townshend; (4) Lord George Sackville, Mr. DeBerdt, John Watts, and Lord Camden.

American Antiquarian Society

PAGE 104

A Warm Place — Hell. Broadside, 13¾ x 8, published probably by Edes & Gill in Boston, 1768. The engraving at the top of the sheet is the work of Paul Revere. This is the only known copy of the broadside.

Sheffield City Libraries, Sheffield, England

PAGE 105

Wills Hill (1718-1793), Viscount Kilwarlin and Earl of Hillsborough, Lord Harwich, later Viscount Fairford and first Marquess of Downshire, by Allan Ramsay (1713-1784). Oil on canvas, 1742.

Collection of the Marquess of Downshire. Photo: National Portrait Gallery, London

PAGE 106

The "Liberty Bowl" by Paul Revere, silver, 5½ inches high, 1768.

Museum of Fine Arts, Boston, Publication Subscription, Francis Bartlett Fund

PAGE 108

William Henry Drayton (1742-1778) by Benoît Louis Prevost (c. 1735–1804 or 1809). Engraving, 7¼ x 5³/₃₂, after a drawing from life by Pierre Eugène Du Simitière (1736-1784). Du Simitière came to the colonies in 1765; by 1768, if not before, he had settled in Philadelphia, where he died.

Metropolitan Museum of Art. Bequest of Charles Allen Munn, 1924

PAGE 109

John Lamb (1735-1800) by Joseph Napoleon Gimbrede (1820-?) after a miniature by an unidentified artist. Frontispiece in *Memoir of the Life and Times of General John Lamb* by Isaac Q. Leake, Albany, N.Y., 1850. The miniature was owned in 1903 by Mrs. Kate Lamb Prentiss and is now unlocated.

PAGE 110

Augustus Henry Fitzroy (1735-1811), third Duke of Grafton, by Sir Nathaniel Dance (1734-1811). Oil on canvas, 34 x 28, date unknown.

Collection of the Duke of Grafton. Photo: Courtesy of the Courtauld Institute of Art

PAGE 111

Advertisement clipped from an unidentified Philadelphia newspaper.

The Library Company of Philadelphia

CHAPTER V

PAGE 114

Charles Paxton (1704-1788), by John Cornish (dates unknown). Oil on canvas, 24 x 20, 1751. The portrait was painted in England although Cornish has sometimes erroneously been called American.

American Antiquarian Society

PAGE 115

Perspective View of the Blockade of Boston by Christian Remick. Watercolor, 27½ x 9¾, 1768.

Massachusetts Historical Society

PAGE 116

A View of Part of the Town of Boston in New England and British Ships of War Landing Their Troops: 1768 by Paul Revere. Engraving, 10⅛ x 15⅞, 1770. It is believed that Christian Remick may have designed and drawn this print for Revere who first advertised it for sale in the *Boston Gazette*, April 16, 1770. The mutilated copper plate from which it was printed is in the office of the Massachusetts Archives.

The Henry Francis du Pont Winterthur Museum

PAGE 117

Grenadier of the 29th Foot, by an 18th-century English artist. Engraving, bound in a volume entitled *Uniforms of the Infantry 1798*.

Prince Consort's Library, Aldershot, England

PAGE 119

The Bloody Massacre perpetuated in King-Street by Paul Revere. Handcolored engraving, 9⅝ x 8⅝, State II, 1770. Revere surreptitiously copied his design from a drawing by Henry Pelham (1749-1806) and rushed his version into print ahead of his competitor, first advertising its availability on March 26, 1770. This engraving has been called the "cornerstone" of any fine collection of American prints.

Metropolitan Museum of Art. Gift of Mrs. Russell Sage, 1910

PAGE 120

James Bowdoin, II (1727-1790), by Robert Feke (1706/10–before 1767). Oil on canvas, 50 x 40, 1748. The portrait may have been commissioned to mark Bowdoin's marriage to Elizabeth Erving in 1748.

Bowdoin College Museum of Art

PAGE 121

Samuel Quincy (1734-1789) by John Singleton Copley. Oil on canvas, 35½ x 28¼, circa 1767. The sitter, a member of the Massachusetts bar, is pictured in his legal robes.

Museum of Fine Arts, Boston. Bequest of Miss G. W. Treadwell

PAGE 121

Robert Treat Paine (1731-1814) by Edward Savage (1761-1817). Oil on canvas, 26⅜ x 22³/₁₆. The painting was commenced in 1802 and was incomplete at the artist's death. It was completed by John Coles, Jr. (1780-?), in 1822.

Collection of John B. Paine, Jr., on loan to the Massachusetts Historical Society

PAGE 122

Robert Auchmuty (?-1788), attributed to Robert Feke. Oil on canvas, 30 x 25, 1748.

Collection of Amherst College

PAGE 123

Josiah Quincy, Jr. (1744-1775), by Gilbert Stuart (1755-1828). Oil on canvas, 35½ x 27½, 1825. Quincy was lost at sea returning from England in 1775. Stuart painted the portrait 50 years later after studying family portraits and prints, and the result was considered a good likeness by those who knew Quincy.

Collection of Edmund Quincy. Photo: Frick Art Reference Library

PAGE 123

John Adams (1735-1826) by Benjamin Blyth (circa 1746 — after 1786). Pastel on paper, 23 x 17½, circa 1766. This portrait is one of a pair with one of Abigail Adams (reproduced as a color plate).

Massachusetts Historical Society

PAGE 123

The original coroner's jury report on the body of Crispus Attucks, who is referred to in the body of the document as Michael Johnson. It is dated March 6, 1770, the day after the incident in King Street.

The Bostonian Society

PAGE 125

A Monumental Inscription. Broadside, 19½ x 11⅞, issued by Isaiah Thomas, Boston, 1772. In the broadside the reader is asked to recall the massacre when considering the release from prison of a customs official, Ebenezer Richardson, who was found guilty of killing a young man who was a member of a mob outside his door. The woodcut is based upon Revere's engraving of 1770.

American Antiquarian Society

CHAPTER VI

PAGE 128

Manuscript drawing of the plan and elevation of the north front of Governor Tryon's palace in New Bern, North Carolina, by John Hawks, 1766.

The New-York Historical Society

PAGE 130

Edmund Fanning (1739-1818) by Thomas Goddard (active 1779-1788). Watercolor on ivory, 2⅞ x 2⅜, date unknown. Painted in his uniform as Lieutenant Colonel of the King's American Regiment of Foot.

Collection of Captain W. C. Wickham

PAGE 132

John Wilkes (1727-1797) by Robert Edge Pine (c. 1720-1788). Oil on canvas, 50 x 40, 1768. Painted during the time when Wilkes's popularity with the common people of England was increasing as a result of his appeal of his prison sentence and fine for libel.

Palace of Westminster. Crown copyright photo

PAGE 133

Wilkes and Liberty. Ballad broadside, 11½ x 7. Published in London in 1763.

Courtesy of the Trustees of the British Museum

PAGE 135

Henry Laurens (1724-1792) by Benoît Louis Prevost (c.

1735–1804 or 1809) after Pierre Eugene Du Simitière (1736-1784). Engraving, 7¹/₁₆ x 5⅛. Probably executed between 1777-1780 when Laurens was a member of the Continental Congress.

Collection of the Metropolitan Museum of Art. Bequest of Charles Allen Munn, 1924

PAGE 137

Samuel Adams (1722-1803) by John Singleton Copley (1738-1815). Oil on canvas, 50 x 40¼, 1770-1772. Adams is shown as he confronted Governor Hutchinson during legal proceedings after the Boston Massacre. He points to a document inscribed "Charter of Willm & Ma(ry) to Massachusetts" and holds a paper inscribed "Instructions of/Town Boston."

Collection of the City of Boston, on deposit at the Museum of Fine Arts, Boston

PAGE 138

Isaac Barré (1726-1802) by Gilbert Stuart (1755-1828). Oil on canvas, 30 x 25, 1785. Barré along with Lord St. Vincent and the Duke of Northumberland, learning of the artist's pecuniary embarrassments, offered to sit for their portraits and pay half the fee in advance, a practice the artist continued for the rest of his career.

Collection of Mr. and Mrs. Paul Mellon

PAGE 138

John Dickinson (1732-1808) by Charles Willson Peale (1741-1827). Oil on canvas, 49 x 39, 1770. The portrait was commissioned by Edmond Jennings of London and painted in the year that Dickinson was returned to the Pennsylvania Legislature as a result of his increased popularity as author of *Letters of a Pennsylvania Farmer*.

The Historical Society of Pennsylvania

PAGE 138

George Grenville (1712-1770) by Joshua Reynolds (1723-1792). Oil on canvas, 52 x 40, 1764-1767. Painted in the robes of first Lord of the Treasury and Chancellor of the Exchequer.

National Trust for Historic Preservation, Petworth, England

PAGE 139

Ezra Stiles (1749-1819) by Samuel King (1748/49-1819). Oil on canvas, 33½ x 27½, 1771. Writing in his diary during August 1771, the sitter explains in great detail the symbolism of the various emblems painted in the picture

and concludes by stating, "These Emblems are more descriptive of my Mind, than the Effigies of my Face."

Yale University Art Gallery

PAGE 140

Landon Carter (1710-1778) attributed to Charles Bridges (working in Virginia 1740-1746). Oil on canvas, 50 x 40, date unknown.

Collection of the Rev. T. Dabney Wellford and R. Carter Wellford. Transparency: Thomas L. Williams.

PAGE 141

Charles Townshend (1725-1767) by Sir Joshua Reynolds (1723-1792). Oil on canvas, 60 x 40, 1764-1767. Portrayed in the robes of Chancellor of the Exchequer.

Collection of The Marquess Townshend of Raynham

PAGE 142

Mercy Otis Warren (1728-1814) by John Singleton Copley (1738-1827). Oil on canvas, 51¼ x 41, 1761-1763.

Museum of Fine Arts, Boston. Bequest of Winslow Warren, 31.212

PAGE 142

Joseph Warren (1741-1775) by John Singleton Copley (1738-1815). Oil on canvas, 50 x 40, circa 1765. The drawings of a human skull under the sitter's arm are an illusion to his medical profession.

Museum of Fine Arts, Boston. Gift of Buckminster Brown, M.D., through Church M. Matthews, Jr., Trustee

PAGE 142

Richard Clarke (1711-1795) (third from left) and the Copley family by John Singleton Copley (1738-1815). Oil on canvas, 90⅜ x 72½, 1777. Clarke, like his son-in-law Copley, left Boston for England at the outbreak of the Revolution and never returned. The large family conversation piece was painted there.

National Gallery of Art, Washington, D.C., Andrew W. Mellon Collection

PAGE 143

Abigail Smith Adams (1744-1818) by Benjamin Blyth (circa 1746-after 1786). Pastel on paper, 23 x 17½, circa 1766. Probably drawn during a visit to Salem in 1766, this portrait is a companion to one of her husband John.

Massachusetts Historical Society. Transparency: George M. Cushing

PAGE 144

John Hancock (1736/37-1793) by John Singleton Copley (1738-1815). Oil on canvas, 49½ x 40½, 1765. In 1764, at age 27, Hancock inherited the entire fortune of his wealthy merchant uncle, Thomas Hancock. This portrait was painted the following year.

Collection of the City of Boston, on deposit at the Museum of Fine Arts, Boston

PAGE 145

Ralph Izard (1741/2-1804) by John Singleton Copley (1738-1815). Oil on canvas, 88½ x 69, 1775. After his marriage to Alice DeLancey, Izard lived in London. This portrait was painted when the couple was in Rome and Copley was studying there.

Collection of Museum of Fine Arts, Boston, Edward Ingersoll Browne Fund

PAGE 146

Sir Robert Eden (1741-1784), first Baronet of Maryland, by Charles Willson Peale (1741-1827). Watercolor on ivory, 1½ x 1½, 1775. Peale painted the now unlocated full-length portrait of Eden at Annapolis. The miniature is a replica with an altered costume.

Collection of Sir John Eden, Bt., M.P. Photo: A. C. Cooper Ltd.

PAGE 146

William Paca (1740-1799) by Charles Willson Peale (1741-1827). Oil on canvas, 87 x 57, 1772. Peale wrote of this portrait: ". . . the action is resting on a pedestal on which I have introduced the bust of Tully [Cicero, Marcus Tullius]. In the distance is a view of his [Paca's] summer house."

Collection of the Peabody Institute, on loan to the Maryland Historical Society. Photo: Frick Art Reference Library

PAGE 147

Charles Carroll of Carrollton (1737-1832) by Sir Joshua Reynolds (1723-1792). Oil on canvas, 30¼ x 25¼, c. 1763. Painted while Carroll was a student in England.

Collection of Mr. and Mrs. Paul Mellon

PAGE 147

Samuel Chase (1741-1811) by Charles Willson Peale (1741-1827). Oil on canvas, 50 x 36½, 1773. The volumes in the lower left-hand corner represent the influence of the political theorists Locke and Sidney on the young lawyer.

Collection of Maryland Historical Society

PAGE 149

Samuel Cooper (1725-1783) by John Singleton Copley (1738-1815). Oil on canvas, 27 x 21, 1769.

Collection of the Emerson Association. Photo: Frick Art Reference Library

PAGE 152

John Brown (1736-1803) by Edward Greene Malbone (1771-1807). Watercolor on ivory, 3³/₁₆ x 2½, date unknown.

Collection of the New-York Historical Society

PAGE 152

Abraham Whipple (1733-1819) by Edward Savage (1761-1817). Oil on canvas, 78 x 54, 1786. The seascape in the background probably is meant to depict Whipple's capture and burning of the H.M.S. Gaspee.

Collection of U.S. Naval Academy. Gift of Mr. and Mrs. John Nicholas Brown

PAGE 153

Joseph Wanton (1705-1780) by an unknown artist. Oil on canvas, 30 x 25, date unknown. Wanton was one of the original members of the Redwood Library.

Collection of the Redwood Library and Athenaeum

PAGE 155

Richard Henry Lee (1732-1794) by Charles Willson Peale (1741-1827). Oil on canvas, 30 x 25, 1795-1805. Replica of Peale's 1784 portrait of Lee painted when Lee was elected president of the Continental Congress.

Collection of Duncan Lee. Photo: Frick Art Reference Library

CHAPTER VII

PAGE 158

Cicero in Catilinain by James Sayer (1748-1823). Drawing, 14 x 12, not dated.

Department of the Environment, London. Crown Copyright Reserved

PAGE 159

Frederick North (1732-1792), later second Earl of Guilford, better known as Lord North. From the studio of Nathaniel Dance (1735-1811). Oil on canvas, 49¼ x 29½, 1767-1770. North is shown in the robes of the

Chancellor of the Exchequer, a post which he held from October 7, 1767, until January 1770.

National Portrait Gallery, London

PAGE 159

Henry Drinker, Jr. (1734-1809), in a silhouette said to have been cut from memory by Joseph Sansom (dates unknown), approximately 3 inches high, circa 1791. It is said to represent the sitter at age 57.

Photo: Courtesy The Quaker Collection, Haverford College Library

PAGE 160

Thomas (1744-1800) and Sarah Morris Mifflin (1747?-1790) by John Singleton Copley (1738-1815). Oil on canvas, 61½ x 48, 1773. Painted while the couple was visiting in Boston, the portrait shows a thoroughly domestic scene. Mrs. Mifflin works a fringe loom.

The Historical Society of Pennsylvania

PAGE 161

Printed invitation to a meeting of the Society of St. Tammany to be held in Philadelphia, May 1, 1773. The reverse bears a written inscription addressing the invitation to John Dickinson.

The Library Company of Philadelphia

PAGE 163

Liberty Pole, the almshouse, the jail, and the Commons in New York in 1770. Drawing by Pierre Eugène Du Simitière.

New York was among the first of the colonies to adopt the Liberty Pole as a political symbol of freedom and as a meeting place for those who espoused the revolutionary cause. The "Road to Liberty" is shown as a ribbon which winds past the jail, over the pillory, and up the Liberty Pole which is encased in iron to prevent the British from cutting it down. On the left, a Son of Liberty stands in Hampden Hall, the group's headquarters.

The Library Company of Philadelphia

PAGE 164

Alexander McDougall (1732-1786) by John Ramage (c. 1748-1802). Watercolor on ivory, 1⁹/₁₆ x 1⅛, probably painted circa 1790.

New-York Historical Society

PAGE 165

Richard Clarke (1711-1795) by John Singleton Copley (1738-1815). Oil on canvas, 90⅜ x 72½, 1777, detail from *The Copley Family*. Clarke, like his son-in-law Copley, left Boston for England at the outbreak of the Revolution and never returned. The large family conversation piece was painted there.

National Gallery of Art, Washington, D.C., Andrew W. Mellon Collection

PAGE 166

Francis Rotch (?-1822) by Miers (dates unknown). Watercolor on plaster, 3½ x 2¾, circa 1795. The artist is known only by his last name. His studio was on the Strand, London.

The Bostonian Society

PAGE 167

John Singleton Copley (1738-1815), self-portrait. Pastel on paper, 23¾ x 17½, 1769.

The Henry Francis du Pont Winterthur Museum

PAGE 168

Broadside printed in Boston by Edes & Gill two days after the first of two meetings held at Faneuil Hall to decide the fate of tea in Boston harbor. Published December 1, 1773. This is one of four known copies of the broadside.

The John Carter Brown Library

PAGE 169

A North View of Castle William in the Harbour of Boston. Engraving by an unidentified artist in the *Massachusetts Magazine*, May 1789.

Library of Congress

PAGE 172

The Bostonian's Paying the Excise-man, or Tarring & Feathering, attributed to Philip Dawe (working in London 1750-1785). Mezzotint, 13½ x 9¾. In the background is the earliest known depiction of the Boston Tea Party. Published in London by Sayer & Bennett, October 1774.

The John Carter Brown Library

PAGE 173

A New Method of Macarony Making, as practised at Boston in North America. Published in London for Carrington Bowles, by an unidentified engraver. Mezzotint, 14 x 10, 1774. Macarony was an 18th-century name for a dandy.

The John Carter Brown Library

PAGE 174

The Boston Tea Party by Johann Ramberg (1763-1840). Drawing, 4⁵/₃₂ x 2¹⁹/₃₂, probably 1784. This appears to be the drawing for Plate 5 in *Allegemeines Historisches* published in Berlin in 1784.

The Metropolitan Museum of Art. Bequest of Charles Allen Munn, 1924

PAGE 175

Chinese tea chest, 18th century.

On loan from the Boston Tea Party Chapter, DAR, to the Daughters of the American Revolution Museum, Washington, D.C.

PAGE 176

Paul Revere (1735-1818) by John Singleton Copley (1738-1815). Oil on canvas, 35 x 28½, 1768-1770.

Museum of Fine Arts, Boston. Gift of the Revere Family

PAGE 177

Alexander Wedderburn (1733-1805), later Baron Loughborough and Earl of Rosslyn, by Mather Brown (1761-1831). Oil on canvas, 49½ x 39½, date unknown. The sitter is portrayed in the robes of Lord Chancellor.

Scottish National Portrait Gallery

PAGE 178

John Pownall's bookplate. Engraving by an unidentified artist, 18th century.

Courtesy of the Trustees of the British Museum

PAGE 179

Edmund Burke (1729-1797) by James Barry (1741-1806). Oil on canvas, 49¾ x 38¾, 1774. The portrait was exhibited at the Royal Academy in 1774 when Burke was urging the repeal of the tea duty.

National Gallery of Ireland

PAGE 179

William Dowdeswell's bookplate. Engraving by an unidentified artist, 18th century.

Courtesy of the Trustees of the British Museum

PAGE 180

Letter from William Bollan to James Bowdoin, II, dated at Covent Garden, London, February 19, 1774. The letter is in the hand of a secretary and has been annotated and signed by Bollan.

The letter reads: "The report of the lords of the committee, upon the address of house of representatives, with the royal approbation sent by Dr. Franklin, will shew you the temper of the present times, of whose violence, injuries, & improvidence I can foresee no end, altho' their chief conductors are thro' fear of consequences, I believe, unwilling to come to immediate extremities; but you are sensible that when passion & power unite in support of errors & wrongs their future operations are often unknown even to their authors — for my own part I continue my endeavours to check this torrent of folly & madness, going on day & night with my intended vindication of the rights of the colonies as fast as these troublesome avocations & the various difficulties of the work will permit.

"Although the rights of petition evidently includes the right of supporting it, the chief ministers seem unwilling to grant or refuse a hearing in maintenance of my own."

Massachusetts Historical Society.

PAGE 182

Arthur Lee (1740-1792) by Charles Willson Peale (1741-1827). Oil on canvas, 23 x 19, 1785. Painted when Lee was one of the Commissioners to sign the treaty of Amity and Commerce between Great Britain and America.

Collection of Independence Hall

PAGE 183

The Bostonians in Distress, attributed to Philip Dawe. Mezzotint, 13⅜ x 9, published by Sayer and Bennett, London, 1774.

The John Carter Brown Library

CHAPTER VIII

PAGE 186

William Legge (1731-1801), second Earl of Dartmouth, by Thomas Gainsborough (1727-1788). Oil on canvas, 42 x 36, c. 1769.

Collection of Lord Dartmouth

PAGE 187

This Sr. Is the Meaning of the Quebec Act — 1774. Mezzotint, size unknown. Published August 17, 1774, by Francis Adams.

Here two senile members of the old ministry attempt to explain the Quebec Act to one another as a woman looks on. It appears to be a satire on Lord Mansfield, who wears the tall wig, and the Earl of Sandwich, whose wife was notorious for supervising his conversations.

Courtesy of the Trustees of the British Museum

PAGE 188

A View of the Thames by Samuel Scott (1703-1772). Oil on canvas, 40 x 26½, 1772. At the end of the bridge at left is Westminster Hall, the meeting place of Parliament.

Colonial Williamsburg

PAGE 189

A view across the Thames of Westminster Hall, the seat of Parliament, by William Marlow (1740-1813). Oil on canvas, size unknown, 1770.

Collection of the Palace of Westminster. Copyright reserved by H. M. the Queen

PAGE 190

Guy Carleton (1724-1808), later Knight of the Bath and first Lord Dorchester, by an unidentified artist. Oil on canvas, size and date unknown.

Collection of The Earl and Countess Malmesbury. Photo: Ulster Museum

PAGE 191

ENG[L]AND'S TRIUMPH OVER FRANCE. . . . Detail of an engraving by James Hulet (?-1771). Published to commemorate the capture of Louisbourg in July 1758 and the surrender of Quebec to the English in 1759.

Public Archives of Canada

PAGE 192

Charles Pratt (1714-1794), Baron Camden, later Earl of Camden, by Richard Cosway (1740-1821). Oil on canvas, 30 x 25, date unknown.

Collection of Colonel M. C. Percival-Price. Photo: Belfort Museum and Art Gallery

PAGE 193

"Edmund Burke in Conversation with his Friend Charles James Fox" by Thomas Hickey (1741-1824). Oil on canvas, 31 x 23, date unknown.

National Gallery of Ireland

PAGE 194

Alexander Hamilton (1755/7-1804) by James Sharples (1751?-1811). Pastel, 5⅛ x 4⅞, date unknown.

Collection of the National Portrait Gallery, Smithsonian Institution

PAGE 195

The Mitred Minuet. Engraving, 3¹¹/₁₆ x 6⅜, published in *London Magazine*, July 1774. It was this cartoon which Paul Revere pirated almost line for line from the *Royal American Magazine* of October 1774.

Four bishops dance around the Quebec Bill directed by Lord North on the left who points at the dance. Lord Bute in Highland dress stands next to him. A devil flies above, pointing at North and implying the source of his inspiration for the bill. The bishops cross hands to show their approbation and countenance of the bill.

Courtesy of the Trustees of the British Museum

EPILOGUE

PAGE 196

Carpenter's Hall, Philadelphia, begun in 1770 and still incomplete when the Continental Congress convened there. The leading Philadelphia master carpenter and architect of the period, Robert Smith (circa 1722-1777), may have been the designer of the building.

Photo: Independence National Historical Park

PAGE 199

Thomas Jefferson (1743-1826) by Mather Brown (1761-1831). Oil on canvas, 35¾ x 28, 1786. This earliest known likeness of Jefferson was painted as an exchange present for a portrait of John Adams. The Brown portrait of Adams was completed two years later.

Collection of Charles Francis Adams

BIBLIOGRAPHY

with Historian's Acknowledgments

From the late 1770s when Mercy Otis Warren first took pen in hand to write her narrative of the *History of the Rise, Progress, and Termination of the American Revolution* (1805) to the present efforts of Bicentennial observers, the War for American Independence has fascinated historians. Each generation has read into the events of that conflict its own ideals and aspirations; each school of historical interpretation has applied its special analytic techniques in order to understand its causation; each historian has approached it from his own angle of vision. As a result, the literature on the American Revolution is voluminous, frequently contradictory, and of great variation in scope and quality. It has been impossible to encompass it all for this study.

Our problem was intensified by the fact that we were as much concerned with biography as we were with the crucial events and crises that set individuals' minds in the direction of rebellion. The biographical literature from the period of the American Revolution is almost as vast and various as the narrative and interpretive. Therefore, we have had to select from the mass of publications those volumes and articles that best served our purpose: to make the story of the pre-Revolutionary years come alive through portraits in paint and in words of the men and women who were involved either as decision-makers, spokesmen, activists, or bystanders. The selective bibliography given below reflects this purpose. To the authors of these many books and articles, we are very grateful.

For help in a complicated research project, we would like to acknowledge the assistance of Barbara Bares, Ellen Clain-Stefanelli, Kem Knapp, and Carolyn Walthall. Judith King, Marilyn Hughes, and Éloise P. Harvey carefully read and typed many drafts of the manuscript. Russell Bourne, Wayne Barrett, and Linda Landis gave editorial assistance for which we are grateful. The entire National Portrait Gallery Staff has been helpful and sympathetic throughout our preparations. We are grateful to Beverly J. Cox, Coordinator of Exhibitions, Jon Freshour, Registrar, and Suzanne Jenkins, Assistant Registrar. The NPG/NCFA Library Staff — especially William Walker, Librarian, and Joyce Chisley — deserve our special thanks for their help and cooperation.

Lillian B. Miller, Historian

GENERAL

ADAMS, JAMES T. *Revolutionary New England*, Vol. 2. New York, 1968.

ALDEN, JOHN RICHARD. *The South in the Revolution, 1763-1789.* Baton Rouge, Louisiana, 1962.

ALVORD, CLARENCE W. *The Mississippi Valley in British Politics*, Vol. 2. New York, 1959.

BAILYN, BERNARD. *The Ideological Origins of the American Revolution.* Cambridge, Massachusetts, 1967.

BAILYN, BERNARD, ed. *Pamphlets of the American Revolution, 1750-1776*, Vol. 1. Cambridge, Massachusetts, 1965.

BALDWIN, ALICE. *The New England Clergy and the American Revolution.* New York, 1965.

BARKER, CHARLES A. *The Background of the Revolution in Maryland.* New Haven, Connecticut, 1967.

BARROW, THOMAS C. *Trade and Empire: The British Customs Service in Colonial America, 1660-1775.* Cambridge, Massachusetts, 1967.

BECKER, CARL L. *The History of Political Parties in the Province of New York, 1760-1776.* Madison, Wisconsin, 1909.

BEER, GEORGE L. *British Colonial Policy, 1754-65.* New York, 1907.

BELOFF, MAX, ed. *The Debate on the American Revolution, 1761-1783, A Sourcebook.* London, 1949.

BRAEMAN, JOHN. *The Road to Independence. A Documentary History of the Causes of the American Revolution: 1763-1776.* New York, 1963.

BRIDENBAUGH, CARL. *Mitre and Sceptre, 1689-1775.* London, 1962.

BROWN, RICHARD D. *Revolutionary Politics in Massachusetts.* Cambridge, Massachusetts, 1970.

CLARK, DORA M. *The Rise of the British Treasury.* New Haven, Connecticut, 1960.

COLBURN, H. TREVOR, ed. *The Colonial Experience.* Boston, Massachusetts, 1966.

DAVIDSON, PHILIP. *Propaganda and the American Revolution.* Chapel Hill, North Carolina, 1941.

DEXTER, FRANKLIN B. *Biographical Sketches of the Graduates of Yale College*, Vols. 1 and 2. New York, 1885-1896.

DICKERSON, O. M. *The Navigation Acts and the American Revolution.* Philadelphia, Pennsylvania, 1951.

DOWDY, CLIFFORD. *The Golden Age: A Climate for Greatness, Virginia, 1732-1775.* Boston, Massachusetts, 1970.

FORD, WORTHINGTON C., comp. *British Officers Serving in America, 1754-1774.* Boston, Massachusetts, 1894.

Gentlemen's Magazine, 1761-1765.

GIPSON, LAWRENCE H. *The British Empire Before the American Revolution*, Vols. 6-12. New York, 1965.

GIPSON, LAWRENCE H. *The Coming of the Revolution, 1763-1775.* New York, 1954.

GOODWIN, A. *The American and French Revolutions, 1763-93*, Vol. 8. Cambridge, England, 1965.

GREENE, E. B. *The Revolutionary Generation, 1763-1790.* New York, 1943.

GREENE, JACK P. *The Quest for Power: The Lower Houses of Assembly in the Southern Royal Colonies, 1689-1776.* Chapel Hill, North Carolina, 1963.

GUTTRIDGE, G. H. *English Whiggism and the American Revolution.* Berkeley and Los Angeles, California, 1942.

HARRINGTON, VIRGINIA D. *The New York Merchant on the Eve of the Revolution.* New York, 1935.

HAWKE, DAVID. *The Colonial Experience.* Indianapolis, Indiana, 1966.

HAWKE, DAVID, ed. *U.S. Colonial History, Readings, and Documents.* New York, 1966.

HINKHOUSE, FRED JUNKIN. *The Preliminaries of the American Revolution as Seen in the English Press, 1763-1775.* New York, 1926.

HOOKER, RICHARD J. "The American Revolution Seen Through a Wine Glass," *William & Mary Quarterly*, Vol. 2 (1954), pp. 52-77.

JAMESON, F. J. *The American Revolution Considered as a Social Movement.* Princeton, New Jersey, 1926.

JENSEN, MERRILL, ed. *English Historical Documents.* New York, 1964.

JENSON, MERRILL. *The Founding of a Nation. A History of the American Revolution, 1763-1776.* New York, 1968.

JONES, E. ALFRED. *The Loyalists of Massachusetts.* London, 1930.

KNOLLENBERG, BERNHARD. *Origin of the American Revolution, 1759-1766.* New York, 1961.

LABAREE, BENJAMIN W. *The Road to Independence, 1763-1776.* New York, 1964.

LINCOLN, CHARLES H. *The Revolutionary Movement in Pennsylvania, 1760-1766.* Philadelphia, Pennsylvania, 1901.

LOVEJOY, DAVID S. *Rhode Island Politics and the American Revolution.* Providence, Rhode Island, 1958.

MAIN, JACKSON TURNER. *The Upper House in Revolutionary America, 1763-1788.* Madison and Milwaukee, Wisconsin, 1967.

MALRAUX, ANDRÉ. *The Miracle of England.* New York, 1937.

MILLER, JOHN C. *Origins of the American Revolution.* Boston, Massachusetts, 1943.

MORGAN, EDMUND S., ed. *The American Revolution: Two Centuries of Interpretation.* Englewood Cliffs, New Jersey, 1965.

MORGAN, EDMUND S. *The Birth of the Republic, 1763-89.* Chicago, Illinois, 1956.

MORISON, SAMUEL ELIOT. *Oxford History of the American People.* New York, 1965.

MORTON, RICHARD L. *Colonial Virginia.* Chapel Hill, North Carolina, 1960.

NAMIER, LEWIS B. *England in the Age of the American Revolution.* London, 1930.

NAMIER, LEWIS B. *Personalities and Powers.* London, 1955.

PITKIN, TIMOTHY. *A Political and Civil History of the United States of America.* New Haven, Connecticut, 1828.

PLUMB, J. H. *England in the Eighteenth Century.* Middlesex, England, 1955.

RITCHESON, CHARLES R. *British Politics and the American Revolution.* Norman, Oklahoma, 1954.

ROSSITER, CLINTON. *Seedtime of the Republic.* New York, 1953.

SCHARF, JOHN THOMAS. *History of Maryland,* 3 vols. Hatboro, Pennsylvania, 1897.

SCHLESINGER, ARTHUR M. *Colonial Merchants and the American Revolution, 1763-1776.* New York, 1939.

SCHLESINGER, ARTHUR M. *Prelude to Independence. The Newspaper War on Britain, 1764-1776.* New York, 1957-1966.

SIMKINS, FRANCIS BUTLER. *A History of the South.* New York, 1965.

SIRMANS, EUGENE. *Colonial South Carolina. A Political History, 1663-1763.* Williamsburg, Virginia, 1966.

SOSIN, JACK M. *Agents and Merchants: British Colonial Policy and the Origins of the American Revolution, 1763-1775.* Lincoln, Nebraska, 1965.

SOSIN, JACK M. *The Revolutionary Frontier, 1763-1783.* New York, 1967.

SOSIN, JACK M. *Whitehall and the Wilderness. The Middle West in British Colonial Policy, 1760-1775.* Lincoln, Nebraska, 1961.

THOMSON, MARK A. *The Secretaries of State, 1681-1782.* Oxford, England, 1932.

TREVELYAN, GEORGE OTTO. *The American Revolution, Part I, 1766-1776.* New York, 1899.

TYLER, MOSES COIT. *Literary History of the American Revolution, 1763-1783.* New York, 1897.

UBBELOHDE, CARL W., JR. *The Vice-Admiralty Courts in the American Revolution.* Chapel Hill, North Carolina, 1959.

VALENTINE, ALAN. *The British Establishment, 1760-1784.* Norman, Oklahoma, 1970.

VAN TYNE, C. H. *The Causes of the War of Independence.* New York, 1922.

VAN TYNE, C. H. "The Influence of the Clergy, and of Religious and Sectarian Forces, On the American Revolution," *The American Historical Review,* Vol. 19 (October 1913-July 1914), pp. 44-64.

WERTENBAKER, THOMAS J. *Give Me Liberty: The Struggle for Self-Government in Virginia.* Philadelphia, Pennsylvania, 1958.

WILSON, JAMES G. *The Memorial History of the City of New York,* Vol 2. New York, 1892.

WINSTANLEY, D. A. *Personal and Party Government.* Cambridge, England, 1910.

INTRODUCTION

AMBLER, CHARLES HENRY. *George Washington and the West.* New York, 1971.

FLEXNER, J. THOMAS. *George Washington: The Forge of Experience, 1732-1775.* Boston, Massachusetts, 1965.

FREEMAN, DOUGLAS S. *George Washington: A Biography.* New York, 1948.

CHAPTER I

BARNES, DONALD G. *George III and William Pitt, 1783-1806.* Stanford, California, 1939.

BROOKE, JOHN. *The Chatham Administration, 1766-1768.* London, 1956

BROOKE, JOHN. *King George III.* London, 1972.

BUTTERFIELD, HERBERT. *George III and the Historians.* London, 1957.

COLBY, CHARLES W. "Chatham, 1708-1908," *The American Historical Review*, Vol. 14, No. 4 (July 1909), pp. 723-730.

DONNE, W. BODHAM, ed. *The Correspondence of King George the Third, 1768-1783*, Vol. 1. London, 1867.

GREEN, V. H. H. *The Hanoverians, 1714-1815.* London, 1948.

GUEDALLA, PHILIP. *Fathers of the Revolution.* New York and London, 1926.

HALL, HERBERT. "Chatham's Colonial Policy," *The American Historical Review*, Vol. 5 (October 1899-July 1900), pp. 659-679.

KIMBALL, GERTRUDE S. *Correspondence of William Pitt.* New York, 1906.

LONG, J. C. *Mr. Pitt and America's Birthright.* New York, 1940.

LOVAT-FRASER, J. A. *John Stuart Earl of Bute.* Cambridge, England, 1912.

MACALPINE, I., and HUNTER, R. *George the Third and the Mad Business.* New York, 1970.

MACALPINE, I., and HUNTER, R. "Porphyria and King George III," *Scientific American*, Vol. 22 (July 1969), pp. 38-46.

NAMIER, LEWIS. *The Structure of Politics at the Accession of George III.* London, 1957.

PARES, RICHARD. *King George III and the Politicians.* Oxford, England, 1953.

PLUMB, J. H. *Chatham.* Hamden, Connecticut, 1965.

PLUMB, J. H. *The First Four Georges.* London, 1956.

PLUMB, J. H. "Our Last King," *American Heritage*, Vol. 11 (June 1960).

ROBERTSON, CHARLES G. *Chatham and the British Empire.* London, 1946.

RUVILLE, ALBERT VON. *William Pitt Earl of Chatham*, 3 vols. New York, 1907. Tr. by J. J. Chayter in reprinted edition.

SEDGWICK, ROMNEY, ed. *Letters from George III to Lord Bute, 1756-1766.* London, 1939.

SELLERS, CHARLES COLEMAN, "Virginia's Great Allegory of William Pitt," *William & Mary Quarterly*, Vol. 9 (January 1952), pp. 58-66.

WALPOLE, HORACE. *Memoirs of Reign of George II*, 3 vols. London, 1846.

WATSON, J. S. *The Reign of George III.* Oxford, England, 1960.

WILLIAMS, BASIL. *The Life of William Pitt*, 2 vols. New York, 1913.

WINSTANLEY, D. A. *Lord Chatham and the Whig Opposition.* London, 1966.

CHAPTER II

ADAMS, C. F., ed. *The Works of John Adams*, Vol. 2. Boston, Massachusetts, 1856.

BARRY, RICHARD. *Mr. Rutledge of South Carolina.* New York, 1942.

BOWEN, CATHERINE DRINKER. "Lord of the Law," *American Heritage*, Vol. 8, No. 4 (June 1957).

BRENNAN, ELLEN E. "James Otis: Recreant and Patriot," *The New England Quarterly*, Vol. 12 (1939), pp. 691-715.

BRENNAN, ELLEN E. *Plural Office-Holding in Massachusetts, 1760-1780.* Chapel Hill, North Carolina, 1945.

BULLOCK, HELEN. "A Dissertation on Education in the form of a letter from James Maury to Robert Jackson, July 17, 1762," *Albemarle County Historical Society Papers*, Vol. 2 (1941-42), pp. 36-39.

CHAPIN, H. M. *Privateering in King George's War, 1739-1748.* Providence, Rhode Island, 1928.

DEXTER, FRANKLIN B. *Extracts from the Itineraries and Other Miscellanies of Ezra Stiles.* New Haven, Connecticut, 1916.

ECKENRODE, HAMILTON J. *The Revolution in Virginia.* New York, 1916.

GREENE, JACK. "The Gadsden Election Controversy and the Revolutionary Movement in South Carolina," *Mississippi Valley Historical Review*, Vol. 46 (1959), pp. 469-492.

GRIGSBY, HUGH BLAIR. *The Virginia Convention of 1776*, a discourse delivered before the Virginia Alpha chapter of the Phi Beta Kappa Society, Williamsburg, July 3, 1855. Richmond, 1855; reprinted, New York, 1969.

GRINNELL, FRANK WASHBURN. "James Otis and His Influence as a Constructive Thinker," *Proceedings of the Bostonian Society and Report of the Annual Meeting, January 21, 1936*, Boston, Massachusetts, 1936, pp. 31-50.

HENRY, WILLIAM WIRT. *Patrick Henry, Life, Correspondence, and Speeches.* New York, 1891.

HIGGINS, MRS. NAPIER. *The Bernards of Abington and Nether Winchendon*, Vols. 1 and 2. London, 1903.

HILLARD, GEORGE STILLMAN. "Christopher Gadsden," *Pennsylvania Magazine of History and Biography*, Vol. 3 (1879), pp. 186-189.

HOSMER, J. K. *The Life of Thomas Hutchinson.* Boston, Massachusetts, 1896.

HUTCHINSON, PETER ORLANDO, comp. *The Diary and Letters of His Excellency Thomas Hutchinson, Esq.*, Vol. 1. London, 1883-1886.

JONES, E. A. *The Loyalists of Massachusetts.* London, 1930.

JONES, V. C. "Patrick Henry: A Personality Profile," *American History Illustrated*, Vol. 3 (January 1969), pp. 13-22.

KOONTZ, L. K. *Virginia Frontier, 1754-1763.* Baltimore, Maryland, 1925.

(The) Letters of Governor Hutchinson & Lt. Governor Oliver, &c. Boston, Massachusetts, 1773.

MAURY, ANN, ed. *Memoirs of a Huguenot Family.* New York, 1853.

MAYO, LAWRENCE SHAW, ed. *The History of the Colony and Province of Massachusetts Bay by Mr. Hutchinson, late governor of that province*, Vol. 3. Cambridge, Massachusetts, 1936.

MAYS, DAVID J. "Peter Lyons," *Proceedings of the Thirty-Seventh Annual Meeting: The Virginia State Bar Association.* Richmond, Virginia, 1926.

MEADE, ROBERT D. *Patrick Henry.* Philadelphia, Pennsylvania, 1969.

MEADE, WILLIAM. *Old Churches, Ministers, and Families of Virginia*, Vol. 1. Philadelphia, Pennsylvania, 1857; reprinted, Baltimore, Maryland, 1966.

MORRIS, RICHARD B. "Then and there the Child Independence was Born," *American Heritage*, Vol. 13, No. 2 (February 1962).

MULLET, C. F., ed. *Some Political Writings of James Otis.* University of Missouri, 1929.

NAMIER, L. B. "Charles Garth and his Connexions," *The English Historical Review*, Vol. 54 (July 1939).

NELSON, WILLIAM H. *The American Tory.* Oxford, England, 1961.

"Original Letters — Letter from the Rev. John Camm to Mrs. McClurg," *William & Mary Quarterly Historical Papers*, Vol. 2 (1893-94), New York, 1966, pp. 334ff.

OTIS, JAMES. *Considerations on Behalf of the Colonists in a Letter to a Noble Lord.* London, 1765.

"The Parson's Cause," *William & Mary Quarterly*, Vol. 20 (1912), pp. 172-173.

SCOTT, A. P. "Constitutional Aspects of the Parsons' Cause," *Political Science Quarterly*, Vol. 31 (1916), pp. 558-577.

SHIPTON, CLIFFORD KENYON. "James Otis and the Writs of Assistance," *Proceedings of the Bostonian Society*, January 1961, Boston, Massachusetts, 1961, pp. 17-25.

"SKETCH OF JOHN CAMM," *William & Mary Quarterly*, Vol. 19 (1910-11), pp. 28-30.

STAPLES, HANNAH THACHER OTIS. "Honorable James Otis," *Journal of American History*, Vol. 4 (1910), pp. 261-272.

THACHER, OXENBRIDGE. *Sentiments of a British-American, occasioned by an Act to lay Certain Duties in the British Colonies and Plantations.* Boston, Massachusetts, 1764.

TUDOR, WILLIAM. *The Life of James Otis.* New York, 1970.

TYLER, LYON G. "Descendants of John Camm, President of William and Mary College," *William & Mary Quarterly*, Vol. 1 (1865), pp. 61ff.

TYLER, MOSES C. *Patrick Henry.* New York, 1966.

WALSH, RICHARD. *Charleston's Sons of Liberty: A Study of the Artisans, 1763-1789.* Columbia, South Carolina, 1959.

WALSH, RICHARD. "Christopher Gadsden: Radical or Conservative Revolutionary?" *South Carolina Historical Magazine*, Vol. 63 (October 1962), pp. 195-203.

WALSH, RICHARD, ed. *The Writings of Christopher Gadsden.* Columbia, South Carolina, 1966.

WARDEN, G. B. *Boston, 1689-1776.* Boston, Massachusetts, 1970.

WATERS, JOHN J. *The Otis Family in Provincial and Revolutionary Massachusetts.* Chapel Hill, North Carolina, 1968.

WATERS, JOHN J., and SCHUTZ, JOHN A. "Patterns of Massachusetts Colonial Politics: The Writs of Assistance and the Rivalry between the Otis and Hutchinson Families," *William & Mary Quarterly*, Vol 24, No. 4 (October 1967), pp. 543-567.

WEIR, ROBERT M. "A Most Important Epocha — The Coming of the Revolution in South Carolina," *Tricentennial Booklet*, No. 5. Columbia, South Carolina, 1970.

WILLIAMS, FRANCIS LEIGH. *Matthew Fontaine Maury, Scientist of the Sea.* New Brunswick, New Jersey, 1963.

WIRT, WILLIAM. *The Life and Character of Patrick Henry.* Philadelphia, Pennsylvania, 1845.

CHAPTER III

ALDEN, JOHN R. *John Stuart and the Southern Colonial Frontier.* New York, 1966.

CORKRAN, DAVID H. *The Cherokee Frontiers, Conflict and Survival, 1740-1762.* Norman, Oklahoma, 1962.

CROWLEY, JAMES E. "The Paxton Disturbance and Ideas of Order in Pennsylvania Politics," *Pennsylvania History,* Vol. 37 (1970), pp. 317-339.

CUMMINGS, HUBERTIS M. "The Paxton Killings," *Journal of Presbyterian History,* Vol. 44 (December 1966).

DARLINGTON, MARY C. *History of Col. Henry Bouquet and the Western Frontier.* Privately printed, 1920.

DES COGNETS, LOUIS. *Amherst and Canada.* Princeton, New Jersey, 1962.

DRAKE, SAMUEL G. *Biography & History of the Indians of North America.* Books IV and V, Boston, 1848.

FARRAND, MAX. "The Indian Boundary Line," *American Historical Review,* Vol. 10 (1905).

FAY, BERNARD. *Franklin, The Apostle of Modern Times.* Boston, Massachusetts, 1929.

FITZMAURICE, LORD. *Life of William, Earl of Shelburne.* London, 1943.

"FRAGMENTS OF A JOURNAL KEPT BY SAMUEL FOULKE," *Pennsylvania Magazine of History and Biography,* Vol. 5 (1881), pp. 64-73.

HANNA, WILLIAM S. *Benjamin Franklin and Pennsylvania Politics.* Stanford, California, 1964.

HINDLE, BROOKE. "The March of the Paxton Boys," *The William & Mary Quarterly,* Vol. 3 (October 1946), pp. 461-486.

HODGE, FREDERICK W. *American Indians North of Mexico.* Washington, 1907.

HUMPHREYS, R. A. "Lord Shelburne and the Proclamation of 1763," *The English Historical Review,* Vol. 49 (April 1934), pp. 241-264.

JACOBS, WILBUR R., ed. *The Paxton Riots and the Frontier Theory.* Chicago, Illinois, 1967.

JACOBS, WILBUR R. *Wilderness Politics and Indian Gifts: The Northern Colonial Frontier, 1738-1763.* Lincoln, Nebraska, 1966.

JENKINS, HOWARD M. "The Family of William Penn," *Pennsylvania Magazine of History and Biography,* Vols. 20-23 (1899).

LABAREE, LEONARD W., and others, eds. *The Papers of Benjamin Franklin,* Vol. 11. New Haven, Connecticut, 1967.

MACLEOD, WILLIAM CHRISTIE. *The American Indian Frontier.* London, 1968.

METZGER, CHARLES. "An Appraisal of Shelburne's Western Policy," *Mid-America,* Vol. 19 (July 1937), pp. 169-181.

NORRIS, JOHN. *Shelburne and Reform.* London, 1963.

PARKMAN, FRANCIS. *The Conspiracy of Pontiac and the Indian War,* Vol. 2. Boston, Massachusetts, 1874.

PARTON, JAMES. *Life and Times of Benjamin Franklin,* Vol. 1. New York, 1864.

PECKHAM, HOWARD. *Pontiac and the Indian Uprising.* New York, 1970.

POUND, ARTHUR. *The Penns of Pennsylvania.* New York, 1932.

POUND, ARTHUR, and DAY, RICHARD. *Johnson of the Mohawks.* New York, 1930.

ROGERS, ROBERT. *Ponteach or the Savages of America.* Introduction and Biography by Allan Nevins. New York, 1914.

RUSSELL, FRANCIS. "Father to the Six Nations," *American Heritage,* Vol. 10 (April 1959).

RUSSELL, FRANCIS. "Oh Amherst, Brave Amherst . . ." *American Heritage,* Vol. 12, No. 1 (December 1960).

SOSIN, JACK M. *The North American Interior in British Colonial Policy, 1760-1775.* Bloomington, Indiana, 1957.

VAN DOREN, CARL. *Benjamin Franklin.* New York, 1964.

VAN DOREN, CARL, ed. *Letters & Papers of Benjamin Franklin and Richard Jackson, 1753-1785.* Philadelphia, Pennsylvania, 1947.

VAN EVERY, DALE. *Forth to the Wilderness: The First American Frontier, 1754-1774.* New York, 1961.

CHAPTER IV

ALDEN, JOHN E. "John Mein: Scourge of the Patriots," *Colonial Society of Massachusetts Publications,* Vol. 34 (February 1942), pp. 571-599.

ALMON, JOHN, comp. *A collection of interesting, authentic papers, relative to the dispute between Great Britain and America; showing the causes and progress of that misunderstanding from 1764-1775.* London, 1777.

ANDERSON, GEORGE P. "Ebenezer Mackintosh: Stamp Rioter and Patriot," *Colonial Society of Massachusetts Publications*, Vol. 26 (1924-1926), pp. 15-64.

ANSON, WILLIAM R., ed. *Autobiography and Political Correspondence of Augustus Henry, Third Duke of Grafton.* London, 1898.

APPLETON, MARGUERITE. "The Agents of the New England Colonies in the Revolutionary Period," *New England Quarterly*, Vol. 6 (1933), pp. 371-387.

BALDWIN, ERNEST. "Joseph Galloway, the Loyalist Politician," *Pennsylvania Magazine of History and Biography*, Vol. 26 (1902), pp. 161-191, 289-321, 417-442.

BARROW, THOMAS C. "Background to the Grenville Program, 1757-1763," *William & Mary Quarterly*, Vol. 22 (January 1965), pp. 93-104.

BARROW, THOMAS C., ed. "A Project for Imperial Reform: 'Hints Respecting the Settlement of Our American Provinces,' 1763, by William Knox," *William & Mary Quarterly*, Vol. 24 (January 1967), pp. 108-126.

BARRY, RICHARD. *Mr. Rutledge in South Carolina.* New York, 1942.

BASYE, A. H. "The Secretary of State for the Colonies, 1768-1782," *The American Historical Review*, Vol. 28 (October 1922), pp. 13-23.

BIGELOW, BRUCE. "Aaron Lopez, Colonial Merchant of Newport," *New England Quarterly*, Vol. 4 (1931), pp. 757-776.

BOND, BEVERLEY W., Jr. "The Colonial Agent as a Popular Representative," *Political Science Quarterly*, Vol. 35 (September 1920), pp. 372-392.

BRUNHOUSE, R. L. "The Effect of the Townshend Acts in Pennsylvania," *Pennsylvania Magazine of History and Biography*, Vol. 54 (October 1930), pp. 355-373.

BURNS, JAMES. *The Colonial Agents of New England.* Washington, D.C., 1935.

"The Case of the Good Intent," *Maryland Historical Magazine*, Vol. 3 (1908).

CONNOLLY, JAMES C. "The Stamp Act and New Jersey's Opposition to It," *New Jersey Historical Society Proceedings*, Vol. 9 (April 1924), pp. 137-150.

CROSS, ARTHUR. *The Anglican Episcopate and the American Colonies.* New York, 1902.

CUNNINGHAM, ANNE ROWE, ed. *Letters and Diary of John Rowe.* New York, 1969.

CUSHING, H. A., ed. *The Writings of Samuel Adams*, Vol. 3. New York, 1907.

DABNEY, WILLIAM, and DARGAN, MARION. *William Henry Drayton and the American Revolution.* Albuquerque, New Mexico, 1962.

DAWSON, HENRY B. *The Sons of Liberty in New York.* New York, 1969.

DECKER, MALCOM. *Brink of Revolution: New York in Crisis.* New York, 1964.

ERICSON, F. J. "Contemporary British Opposition to the Stamp Act, 1764-1765," *Michigan Academy of Science, Arts and Letters Papers*, Vol. 29 (1943), pp. 489-505.

FOSTER, WILLIAM. *Stephen Hopkins, Rhode Island Statesman.* Providence, Rhode Island, 1884.

GIDDENS, PAUL H. "Maryland and the Stamp Act Controversy," *Maryland Historical Magazine*, Vol. 27 (June 1932), pp. 79-98.

GIPSON, LAWRENCE H. "The Great Debate in the Committee of the Whole House of Commons on the Stamp Act, 1776, as Reported by Nathaniel Ryder," *Pennsylvania Magazine of History and Biography*, Vol. 86 (January 1962), pp. 10-41.

GIPSON, LAWRENCE. *Jared Ingersoll: A Study of American Loyalism.* New Haven, Connecticut, 1920.

GREENE, JACK P., ed. *The Diary of Landon Carter of Sabine Hall, 1752-1778.* Charlottesville, Virginia, 1965.

GREENE, JACK P. "Landon Carter and Pistole Fee Dispute," *William & Mary Quarterly*, Vol. 14 (1957), pp. 66-69.

GREENE, JACK P., ed. " 'Not to be Governed or Taxed but by Our Representatives' by Landon Carter," *Virginia Magazine of History and Biography*, Vol. 76 (July 1968), pp. 261-300.

GREENE, JACK P., and JELLISON, RICHARD M. "The Currency Act of 1764 in Imperial-Colonial Relations, 1764-1776," *William & Mary Quarterly*, Vol. 18 (October 1961), pp. 485-518.

GROCE, GEORGE. *William Samuel Johnson.* New York, 1937.

GUTTRIDGE, GEORGE HERBERT. *The Early Career of Lord Rockingham, 1730-1765.* Berkeley, California, 1952.

HOSMER, JAMES K. *Samuel Adams.* Boston, Massachusetts, 1898.

JACOBSON, DAVID L. *John Dickinson and the Revolution in Pennsylvania, 1764-1776.* Berkeley, California, 1965.

KAMMEN, MICHAEL. "The Colonial Agents, English Politics and the American Revolution," *William & Mary Quarterly*, Vol. 22 (April 1965), pp. 244-263.

KAMMEN, MICHAEL. *A Rope of Sand: The Colonial Agents, British Politics and the American Revolution*. Ithaca, New York, 1968.

KIMBALL, GERTRUDE. *Providence in Colonial Times*. New York, 1972.

LAND, AUBREY C. *The Dulanys of Maryland*. Baltimore, Maryland, 1968.

LAPRADE, WILLIAM T. "The Stamp Act in British Politics," *The American Historical Review*, Vol. 35 (July 1930), pp. 735-757.

LATROBE, JOHN. "Biographical Sketch of Daniel Dulany," *Pennsylvania Magazine of History and Biography*, Vol. 3 (1879), pp. 1-10.

LEAKE, I. Q. *Memoir of the Life and Times of General John Lamb*. New York, 1850.

LONN, ELLA. *Colonial Agents of the Southern Colonies*. Chapel Hill, North Carolina, 1945.

MARCUS, JACOB. *Colonial American Jews*, Vol. 3. Detroit, Michigan, 1970.

MARTIN, C. H. K. "The Stamp Act of 1765 (II)," *Discovery* (March 1920), pp. 52-54, 74-77.

MAYO, LAWRENCE, ed. *The History of the Colony and Province of Massachusetts Bay by Mr. Hutchinson, late governor of that province*. Cambridge, Massachusetts, 1936.

MILLER, E. J. "The Virginia Legislature and the Stamp Act," *William & Mary Quarterly*, Vol. 21 (1912-1913), pp. 233-248.

MILLER, JOHN C. *Sam Adams: Pioneer in Propaganda*. Stanford, California, 1936.

MORGAN, EDMUND S. *The Gentle Puritan: A Life of Ezra Stiles, 1727-1795*. New Haven, Connecticut, 1962.

MORGAN, EDMUND S., ed. *Prologue to Revolution; Sources and Documents on the Stamp Act Crisis, 1764-1766*. Chapel Hill, North Carolina, 1959.

MORGAN, EDMUND AND HELEN. *The Stamp Act Crisis*. Chapel Hill, North Carolina, 1953.

NAMIER, LEWIS. *Charles Townshend, His Character and Career*. Cambridge, England, 1959.

NAMIER, LEWIS, AND BROOKE, JOHN. *Charles Townshend*. London, 1964.

SELLERS, LEILA. *Charleston Business on the Eve of the American Revolution*. New York, 1970.

SPECTOR, MARGARET M. *The American Department of the British Government, 1768-1782*. New York, 1940.

SPENCER, RICHARD HENRY. "Honorable Daniel Dulany, 1722-1797," *Maryland Historical Magazine*, Vol. 13 (1918), pp. 143-160.

"Stamp Act Papers. (From the Society's Collection)," *Maryland Historical Magazine*, Vol. 6 (1911).

STEVENS, JOHN AUSTIN, ed. *Colonial Records of the New York Chamber of Commerce, 1768-1784*. New York, 1971.

STEVENS, JOHN AUSTIN. "The Stamp Act in New York," *The Magazine of American History*, Vol. 1 (June 1877), pp. 337-371.

STILLE, CHARLES J. *The Life and Times of John Dickinson, 1732-1808*. Philadelphia, Pennsylvania, 1891.

THOMAS, GEORGE, EARL OF ALBEMARLE. *Memoirs of the Marquis of Rockingham and His Contemporaries*. London, 1852.

WATSON, D. H. "Barlow Trecothick," *British Association of American Studies Bulletin* (October 1960 and April 1961), pp. 36-49.

WICKWIRE, F. B. *British Subministers and Colonial America, 1763-1783*. Princeton, New Jersey, 1966.

WICKWIRE, FRANKLIN B. "King's Friends, Civil Servants, or Politicians," *The American Historical Review*, Vol. 71 (October 1965), pp. 18-42.

WINSOR, JUSTIN, ed. *Narrative and Critical History of America*, Vol. 6. Boston and New York, 1884-1889.

ZIMMERMAN, JOHN. "Charles Thomson, the Sam Adams of Philadelphia," *Mississippi Valley Historical Review*, Vol. 45 (1958), pp. 464-480.

CHAPTER V

ALLAN, HERBERT. *John Hancock, Patriot in Purple*. New York, 1948.

ANDREWS, CHARLES M. "The Boston Merchants and the Non-Importation Movement," *Publications of the Colonial Society of Massachusetts*, Vol. 19 (1916-1917), pp. 159-259.

"The Bowdoin and Temple Papers," *Massachusetts Historical Society Collections*, 6th series, Vol. 9 (1897).

BUTTERFIELD, L. H., ed. *The Diary and Autobiography of John Adams*. Cambridge, Massachusetts, 1962.

CARY, JOHN C. *Joseph Warren: Physician, Politician, Patriot*. Urbana, Illinois, 1961.

CLARK, DORA MAE. "The American Board of Customs, 1769-1783," *The American Historical Review*, Vol. 45 (July 1940), pp. 777-806.

DICKERSON, OLIVER, ed. *Boston Under Military Rule (1768-1769) As Revealed in a Journal of the Times*. New York, 1970.

DONOVAN, FRANK. *The John Adams Papers*. New York, 1965.

FLEMING, THOMAS. "Verdicts of History; I: The Boston Massacre," *American Heritage*, Vol. 18, No. 1 (December 1966).

FROTHINGHAM, RICHARD. *Life and Times of Joseph Warren*. Boston, Massachusetts, 1865.

HART, A. B. *Commonwealth History of Massachusetts*, Vol. 2. New York, 1966.

MILLER, JOHN C. *Sam Adams: Pioneer in Propaganda*. Stanford, California, 1936.

MOORE, J. B. "Memoir of James Bowdoin," *American Quarterly Register*, Vol. 14 (November 1841), pp. 152-155.

QUINCY, JOSIAH, JR. *Memoir of the Life of Josiah Quincy, Jr. of Massachusetts*. Boston, Massachusetts, 1825.

SHY, JOHN. *Toward Lexington: The Role of the British Army in the Coming of the American Revolution*. Princeton, New Jersey, 1965.

SMITH, PAGE. *John Adams*. Garden City, New York, 1962.

WINTHROP, ROBERT. *Washington, Bowdoin, and Franklin*. Boston, Massachusetts, 1876.

ZOBEL, HILLER. *The Boston Massacre*. New York, 1970.

CHAPTER VI

ALLEN, GARDNER W. *A Naval History of the American Revolution*, Vol. 1. Williamstown, Massachusetts, 1970.

ANDREWS, MATTHEW PAGE. *Virginia, the Old Dominion*. Richmond, Virginia, 1949.

ASHE, SAMUEL A. *Biographical History of North Carolina from Colonial Times to the Present*, Vol. 1. Greensboro, North Carolina, 1905.

BALLAGH, JAMES CURTIS, ed. *The Letters of Richard Henry Lee*, Vol. 1. New York, 1911.

BASSETT, JOHN S. "The Regulators of North Carolina (1765-1771)," *Annual Report of the American Historical Association, 1894*, Vol. 1 (1895), pp. 141-212.

DEAS, ANNE IZARD, ed. *Correspondence of Mr. Ralph Izard of South Carolina*, Vol. 1. New York, 1844.

DEXTER, FRANKLIN B., ed. *The Literary Diary of Ezra Stiles*, Vol. 1. New York, 1901.

Diary and Letters of his Excellency Thomas Hutchinson, Vol. 1. Boston, Massachusetts, 1884.

DILL, A. T. *Governor Tryon and His Palace*. Chapel Hill, North Carolina, 1955.

GREENE, JACK P. "Bridge to Revolution: The Wilkes Fund Controversy in South Carolina, 1769-1775," *The Journal of Southern History*, Vol. 39 (February 1963), pp. 19-52.

HEDGES, JAMES B. *The Browns of Providence Plantations, Colonial Years*. Cambridge, Massachusetts, 1952.

HENDERSON, ARCHIBALD. "The Origin of the Regulation in North Carolina," *The American Historical Review*, Vol. 21 (January 1916), pp. 320-332.

HOLT, W. STULL. "Charles Carroll, Barrister: The Man," *Maryland Historical Magazine*, Vol. 31 (1936), pp. 112-126.

HOSMER, JAMES K. *The Life of Thomas Hutchinson*. Boston, Massachusetts, 1896.

HUTCHINSON, THOMAS. *Letters of Governor Hutchinson & Lt. Governor Oliver, etc. Printed at Boston & Remarks Thereon, with the Assembly's Address, & Proceedings of the House of Lords Together with the Substance of Mr. Wedderburn's Speech Relative to those Letters*. London, 1774.

KENNEDY, JOHN PENDLETON, ed. *Journals of the House of Burgesses of Virginia, 1773-1776*. Richmond, Virginia, 1905-1909.

LAND, AUBREY C. *The Dulanys of Maryland*. Baltimore, Maryland, 1955.

LEAKE, JAMES MILLER. "The Virginia Committee System and the American Revolution," *Johns Hopkins University Studies in Historical and Political Science*. Series 35, No. 1. Baltimore, Maryland, 1917.

LEE, RICHARD HENRY. *Life of Arthur Lee*, 2 vols. New York, 1829.

LEFLER, HUGH TALMADGE, and NEWSOME, ALBERT RAY. *The History of a Southern State, North Carolina*. Chapel Hill, North Carolina, 1954.

LESLIE, WILLIAM R. "The *Gaspee* Affair: A Study of its Constitutional Significance," *The Mississippi Valley Historical Review*, Vol. 39 (September 1952), pp. 233-256.

LYNAH, MARY-ELIZABETH. "Ralph Izard and Alice de Lancy," *Americana Illustrated*, Vol. 28 (January 1934 and December 1934), pp. 486-497.

MAYO, LAWRENCE, ed. *The History of the Colony and Province of Massachusetts Bay by Mr. Hutchinson, later governor of that province.* Cambridge, Massachusetts, 1936.

MILLER, E. I. "The Virginia Committee of Correspondence of 1773-75," *The William & Mary Quarterly*, Vol. 22 (1965), pp. 99-113.

PARTON, JAMES. *Life and Times of Benjamin Franklin.* New York, 1864.

RAMSAY, DAVID. *The History of South Carolina*, 2 Vols. Charleston, South Carolina, 1809.

RANDALL, HENRY S. *The Life of Thomas Jefferson*, Vol. 1. New York, 1858.

SILVERMAN, ALBERT. "William Paca, Signer, Governor, Jurist," *Maryland Historical Magazine*, Vol. 37 (March 1942), pp. 1-25.

SPARKS, JARED. *Franklin's Works*, Vol. 4. Boston, Massachusetts, 1840.

STAPLES, WILLIAM R., ed. *The Documentary History of the Destruction of the Gaspee.* Providence, Rhode Island, 1845.

STRAWSER, NEIL. "Samuel Chase and the Annapolis Paper War," *Maryland Historical Magazine*, Vol. 57 (September 1962), pp. 177-194.

VAN DOREN, CARL. *Benjamin Franklin.* New York, 1965.

WALLACE, DAVID D. *The Life of Henry Laurens.* New York, 1969.

WALLACE, DAVID D. *South Carolina: A Short History 1520-1948.* Columbia, South Carolina, 1951.

WHEELER, JOHN H. *Historical Sketches of North Carolina.* Baltimore, Maryland, 1964.

WINTHROP, R. C. *Massachusetts Historical Society Proceedings*, Vol. 16 (1878).

WULSIN, EUGENE. "The Political Consequences of the Burning of the *Gaspee*," *Rhode Island History*, Vol. 3 (January – April 1944), pp. 1-11, 55-64.

CHAPTER VII

ADAMS, C. F., ed. *Familiar Letters of John Adams and His Wife Abigail Adams During the Revolution.* New York, 1876.

ANDERSON, GEORGE P. "Ebenezer Mackintosh: Stamp Act Rioter and Patriot" *The Colonial Society of Massachusetts Publications*, Vol. 26 (1924-1926), pp. 15-64.

ANTHONY, KATHERINE. *First Lady of the Revolution: The Life of Mercy Otis Warren.* Garden City, New York, 1958.

BAYLEY, FRANK W. *Five Colonial Artists of New England.* Boston, Massachusetts, 1929.

BUTTERFIELD, L. H., ed. *Adams Family Correspondence*, Vol. 1. Cambridge, Massachusetts, 1963.

BUTTERFIELD, L. H., ed. *The Letters of Benjamin Rush*, Vol. 2. Princeton, New Jersey, 1951.

CAMPBELL, J. *Lives of the Lord Chancellors of England*, Vol. 7. New York, 1875.

CONE, CARL. *Burke and the Nature of Politics.* Lexington, Kentucky, 1957.

CUNNINGHAM, ANNE ROWE, ed. *Diary and Letters of John Rowe.* New York, 1969.

"Diary for 1773 to the end of 1774 of Mr. Thomas Newell, Boston," *Proceedings of the Massachusetts Historical Society*, Vol. 15 (1876-77), pp. 334-364.

DRAKE, FRANCIS S. *Tea Leaves: Being a Collection of Letters and Documents relating to the Shipment of Tea to the American colonies in the Year 1773, by the East India Company.* Detroit, Michigan, 1970.

EDES, HENRY H. "Memoir of Dr. Thomas Young, 1731-1777," *Colonial Society of Massachusetts Publications*, Vol. 11 (December 1906), pp. 2-54.

"Effects of the Non-Importation Agreement in Philadelphia, 1769-1770," *Pennsylvania Magazine of History and Biography*, Vol. 14 (April 1890), pp. 41-45.

ELLET, ELIZABETH F. *The Women of the American Revolution*, Vols. 1 and 2. New York, 1969.

FORBES, ESTHER. *Paul Revere: The World He Lived In.* Boston, Massachusetts, 1942.

FORCE, PETER, comp. *American Archives, Fourth Series, containing a Documentary History of the English Colonies in North America From . . . March 7, 1774 to the Declaration of Independence by the United States*, Vol. 1. New York, 1972.

FREIBERG, MALCOLM. "William Bollan, Agent of Massachusetts," *Bulletin of the Boston Public Library* (February–June 1948), pp. 43-54, 90-100, 135-146, 168-182, 212-220.

FRITZ, JEAN. *Cast for a Revolution.* Boston, Massachusetts, 1972.

FROTHINGHAM, RICHARD. *Life and Times of Joseph Warren*. Boston, Massachusetts, 1865.

GOSS, ELBRIDGE H. *The Life of Colonel Paul Revere*, Vol. 1. Boston, Massachusetts, 1891.

GRISWOLD, WESLEY S. *The Night the Revolution Began: The Boston Tea Party, 1773*. Brattleboro, Vermont, 1972.

GUEDALLA, PHILIP. *Fathers of the Revolution*. New York, 1926.

HANSARD, T. C. *The Parliamentary History of England, 1771-1774*, Vol. 17. London, 1813.

HUTCHINSON, PETER O., ed. *The Diary and Letters of Thomas Hutchinson*, Vol. 1. New York, 1971.

JENSEN, ARTHUR L. *The Maritime Commerce of Colonial Philadelphia*. Madison, Wisconsin, 1963.

"John Boyle's Journal of Occurrences in Boston, 1759-1778," *The New England Historical and Genealogical Register*, Vol. 84 (October 1930), pp. 366-373*ff*.

JONES, THOMAS. *History of New York During the Revolutionary War*. New York, 1879.

LABAREE, BENJAMIN W. *The Boston Tea Party*. New York, 1964.

LEE, RICHARD HENRY. *The Life of Arthur Lee*, 2 vols. Freeport, New York, 1969.

"Letter from a Committee of Merchants in Philadelphia to the Committee of Merchants in London, 1769," *Pennsylvania Magazine of History and Biography*, Vol. 27 (1903), pp. 84-87.

Letters and Papers of John Singleton Copley and Henry Pelham, 1739-1776. New York, 1970.

"Letters of John Andrews," *Massachusetts Historical Society Proceedings*, Vol. 8 (1864-65).

MAYO, LAWRENCE SHAW, ed. *The History of the Province of Massachusetts Bay, by Mr. Hutchinson, late governor of that province*, Vol. 3. Cambridge, Massachusetts, 1936.

MEYERSON, JOEL D. "The Private Revolution of William Bollan," *New England Quarterly*, Vol. 41 (December 1968), pp. 536-550.

MILLER, JOHN C. *Sam Adams: Pioneer in Propaganda*. Stanford, California, 1936.

"Observations Upon the Consumption of Teas in North America by Samuel Wharton (letter of January, 1773 to East India Co.)," *Pennsylvania Magazine of History and Biography*, Vol. 25 (April 1901), pp. 139-141.

"A Philadelphia Tea Party Letter," *Bulletin of Friends Historical Society of Philadelphia*, Vol. 10 (May 1921), pp. 67-70.

REPPLIER, AGNES. *To Think of Tea!* Boston, Massachusetts, 1932.

RIGGS, A. R. "Arthur Lee, A Radical Virginian in London, 1768-1776," *Virginia Magazine of History and Biography*, Vol. 78 (1970), pp. 268-280.

ROSSMAN, KENNETH R. *Thomas Mifflin and the Politics of the American Revolution*. Chapel Hill, North Carolina, 1952.

SABINE, WILLIAM H. W., ed. *Historical Memoirs of William Smith*. New York, 1956.

SCHLESINGER, ARTHUR M. "Politics, Propaganda, and the Philadelphia Press, 1767-1770," *Pennsylvania Magazine of History and Biography*, Vol. 60 (October 1936), pp. 309-322.

SCHLESINGER, ARTHUR M. "The Uprising Against the East India Company," *Political Science Quarterly*, Vol. 32 (March 1917), pp. 60-79.

"Selections from the Letterbooks of Thomas Wharton of Philadelphia, 1773-1783," *Pennsylvania Magazine of History and Biography*, Vol. 33 (1909), pp. 319-339, 432-453, and Vol. 34 (1910), pp. 41-61.

SOSIN, JACK M. "The Massachusetts Acts of 1774: Coercive or Preventive?" *Huntington Library Quarterly*, Vol. 26 (May 1963), pp. 235-252.

SPARKS, JARED, ed. *The Works of Benjamin Franklin*, Vols. 4 and 8. Boston, Massachusetts, 1840.

SPECTOR, MARGARET. *The American Department of the British Government, 1769-1782*. New York, 1940.

STEBBINS, CALVIN. "Edmund Burke: His Services as Agent in the Province of New York," *American Antiquarian Society*, Vol. 9 (October 1893), pp. 89-101.

STEVENS, JOHN AUSTIN, *Colonial Records of New York Chamber of Commerce, 1768-1784*. New York, 1867.

STEVENS, JOHN AUSTIN. "Henry White and His Family," *The Magazine of American History* (December 1877), pp. 727-733.

STONE, FREDERICK D. "How the Landing of Tea Was Opposed in Philadelphia by Colonel William Bradford and Others in 1773," *Pennsylvania Magazine of History and Biography*, Vol. 15 (1891), pp. 385-393.

SUTHERLAND, LUCY S. *East India Company in 18th Century Politics*. London, 1952.

SUTHERLAND, STUART L. "Sir George Colebrooke's World Corner in Alum, 1771-1773," *Economic History*, Vol. 3 (February 1936), pp. 237-258.

TAYLOR, THOMAS B. "The Philadelphia Counterpart of

the Boston Tea Party," *Bulletin of Friends Historical Society of Pennsylvania*, Vol. 2 (November 1908), pp. 86-110, and Vol. 3 (February 1909), pp. 21-49.

"Tea Party Anniversary," *Proceedings of the Massachusetts Historical Society*, Vol. 13 (December 1873), pp. 151-216.

THATCHER, BENJAMIN B., ed. *Traits of the Tea Party: Being a Memoir of George R. T. Hewes*. New York, 1835.

THOMAS, GEORGE, EARL OF ALBEMARLE, ed. *Memoirs of the Marquis of Rockingham and His Contemporaries*, Vol. 1. London, 1857.

UPTON, L. F. S. "Proceedings of Ye Body Respecting the Tea," *William & Mary Quarterly*, Vol. 22 (April 1965), pp. 287-300.

VALENTINE, ALAN. *Lord North*, Vol. 1. Norman, Oklahoma, 1967.

VAN DOREN, CARL. *Benjamin Franklin*. New York, 1938.

"Warren-Adams Letters," *Massachusetts Historical Society Collections*, Vol. 72 (1917).

WHARTON, ANNE H. "Wharton Family," *Pennsylvania Magazine of History and Biography*, Vol. 1 (1877), pp. 329, 455-457.

WICKWIRE, FRANKLIN B. *British Subministers and Colonial America, 1763-1783*. Princeton, New Jersey, 1966.

WICKWIRE, FRANKLIN B. "John Pownall and British Colonial Policy," *William & Mary Quarterly*, Vol. 20 (October 1963), pp. 543-554.

CHAPTER VIII

BARGAR, B. P. *Lord Dartmouth and the American Revolution*. Columbia, South Carolina, 1965.

BROUGHAM, LORD HENRY. *Historical Sketches of Statesmen Who Flourished in the Time of George III*, Vol. 1. Philadelphia, Pennsylvania, 1854.

BROWN, WELDON A. *Empire or Independence: A Study in the Failure of Reconciliation, 1774-1783*. Pineville, Louisiana, 1941.

BURT, ALFRED L. *The Old Province of Quebec*. Minneapolis, Minnesota, 1933.

CAVENDISH, HENRY. "Government of Canada," *Debates of the House of Commons in 1774 on the Quebec Act*. Edited by J. Wright. London, 1839.

COFFIN, VICTOR. "Province of Quebec and the Early American Revolution: A Study in English-American Colonial History," *University of Wisconsin Bulletin: Economics, Political Science, and History Series*, Vol. 1 (1896), pp. 275-562.

COUPLAND, REGINALD. *The American Revolution and the British Empire*. New York, 1930.

COUPLAND, REGINALD. *The Quebec Act. A Study in Statesmanship*. Oxford, England, 1925.

EILES, HENRY S. *Lord Chancellor Camden and His Family*. London, 1934.

FORCE, PETER, comp. *American Archives. Fourth Series, containing a Documentary History of the English Colonies in North America From . . . March 7, 1774 to the Declaration of Independence by the United States*, Vol. 1. New York, 1972.

FOSS, EDWARD. *The Judges of England; with Sketches of Their Lives . . . Vol. III, 1714-1820*. London, 1864.

GARRAGHAN, GILBERT J. "The Ecclesiastical Rule of Old Quebec in Mid-America," *The Catholic Historical Review*, Vol. 19 (April 1933).

LODGE, HENRY CABOT, ed. *The Works of Alexander Hamilton*. New York, 1885-1904.

MARTIN, CHESTER. *Empire and Commonwealth. Studies in Government and Self-Government in Canada*. Oxford, England, 1929.

METZGER, CHARLES HENRY. *The Quebec Act: A Primary Cause of the American Revolution*. United States Catholic Historical Society, Monograph Series, Vol. 16. New York, 1936.

PENN, JOHN. "Letters of Governor John Penn to Lovly Juliana Penn, 1774," *Pennsylvania Magazine of History and Biography*, Vol. 31 (1907), pp. 232-236.

REED, JOSEPH. *Life and Correspondence of Joseph Reed*, Vol. 1. Philadelphia, Pennsylvania, 1847.

RUSSELL, LORD JOHN. *The Life and Times of Charles James Fox*, Vol. 1. London, 1859.

RUSSELL, LORD JOHN, ed. *Memorials and Correspondence of Charles James Fox*, Vol. 1. London, 1853-1857; reprinted, New York, 1970.

SCHACHNER, NATHAN. *Alexander Hamilton*. New York, 1957.

Silas Deane Papers. Collections of the New-York Historical Society, Vol. 19 (1896).

THOMAS, GEORGE, EARL OF ALBEMARLE, ed. *Memoirs of the Marquis of Rockingham and His Contemporaries*, 2 vols. London, 1852.

WILSON, SAMUEL K. "Bishop Briand and the American Revolution," *The Catholic Historical Review*, Vol. 19 (July 1933).

WRONG, GEORGE M. *Canada and the American Revolution*. New York, 1935.

EPILOGUE

FLEMING, THOMAS. *The Man from Monticello: An Intimate Life of Thomas Jefferson*. New York, 1969.

MALONE, DUMAS. *Jefferson the Virginian*. Boston, Massachusetts, 1948.

ENCYCLOPEDIAS

BOATNER, MARK MAYO. *Encyclopedia of the American Revolution*. New York, 1966.

JOHNSON, ALLAN, ed. *Dictionary of American Biography*, Vols. 1-10. New York, 1927.

JOHNSON, ROSSITER, ed. *The Twentieth Century Biographical Dictionary of Notable Americans*, Vols. 1-10. Boston, Massachusetts, 1904.

LOSSING, B. J. *Biographical Sketches of the Signers of the Declaration of American Independence*. Glendale, New York, 1970.

The National Cyclopedia of American Biography, Vols. 1-53. New York, 1898.

SABINE, LORENZO. *Biographical Sketches of Loyalists of the American Revolution*, 2 vols. Port Washington, New York, 1966.

SANDERSON, JOHN. *Biography of the Signers of the Declaration of Independence*, Vols. 1-9. Philadelphia, Pennsylvania, 1823.

SHIPTON, CLIFFORD K. *Sibley's Harvard Graduates*, Vols. 5-15. Boston, Massachusetts, 1937-1970.

STEPHEN, SIR LESLIE, and LEE, SIR SIDNEY, eds. *The Dictionary of National Biography*, Vols. 1-21. London, 1964.

WILSON, JAMES G., and FISKE, JOHN, eds. *Appleton's Cyclopedia of American Biography*, Vols. 1-6. New York, 1887.

INDEX

A

Abercromby, Lord, 60
Abraham, Plains of, *19*, 21
Adams, Abigail Smith, *143*, 170-171
Adams, John, 21, 122, *123*, 170, 176
  Bland described by, 45
  at Boston Massacre trial, 123-125
  Cooper described by, 150
  Otis comment by, 39
  Paine (R. T.) described by, 121
  Quincy (Sam) described by, 121
  Ruggles characterized by, 96
  Sewall characterized by, 35
  Thacher described by, 40
  writs of assistance trial comments by,
    38, 39
Adams, Sam, 39, 95, 96, 98, 103, 106,
    107, 115, 116, 117, 118, 120, 122,
    123, 124, 125, 127, *137*, 148, 149,
    150, 151, 164-165, 167, 170, 171,
    175, 176, 182
  Circular Letter by, 103-105
  father of, 92
  political activities of, 91-93
Alamance, Battle of, 131
American Revolution, 13, 21, 26
Amherst, Jeffery, 72
  attitude of toward Indians, 56, 57-59,
    62-63
  Crown Point attack by, 60

Andros, Governor, 35
Articles of Friendship and Commerce,
  52
Attakullaculla, role of in Cherokee
  affairs, 52, *53*, 55
Attucks, Crispus, 118, 125
  coroner's report on, *124*
Auchmuty, Robert, *122*, 153
Avery, John, 92

B

Baltimore, Lord, 145
Barkley, Gilbert, 161
Barré, Isaac, 87, 100, *138*, 181, 186, 189
  Stamp Act opposed by, 85
Belcher, Governor, 92
Bernard, Francis, *32*, 35, 38, 39, 41, 90,
    96, 114, 117, 120
  characterization of, 122
  Mayhew characterized by, 95
  proclamation by, *36*
  Warren described by, 115
  Warren's attacks on, 115
Bill for regulating the government of
  Massachusetts Bay, 178
Bland, Richard, 45-46, 89, 198
  pamphlet by, *45*
Bliss, Theodore, 124

Bloody Run, Battle of, 61
Blowers, Sampson, 122
Bollan, William, 181-182, 183
  letter written by, *180*
Boone, Thomas,
  Commons House authority tested by,
    48-49, 134
Booth, Benjamin, 161, 162, 163
Boston, blockade of, *115*
Boston Massacre, 117-*119*, 120, 183
  broadside concerning, *125*
  trial following the, 120-125, 148
Boston Port Bill, 177, 178, 179, 183, 197,
  198
Boston Tea Party, 171-*174*, 175-177, 186
  harbor blockade following, *183*
  tea chest said to have been emptied at,
    175
Bouquet, Colonel, 18, 61-*63*
  meeting of, with Indians, *64*
Bowdoin, James, 95, *120*
  Boston Massacre report by, 118-120
Braddock, Edward, 15, 16
  death of, *17*
  Orderly Book of, *18*
Bradford, William, 160
Bradlee brothers, 171
Briand, Jean Oliver, 192
Briggs, Aaron, 154
British Parliament, theory of colonial
  subordination to, 82, 84, 88, 100,
  102

British policies
    concerning American colonies, 51,
        105, 136
    toward Indians, 64
British troops landing in Boston, *116*
    See also Military occupation
Broader, Bartholomew, 118
Brown, John, 151-*152*
Brown, Joseph, 154
Brown, Nicholas, 151, 152
Bucklin, Joseph, 152
Bull, John, house of, in flames, *28*
Bull, William, 55
    problems of, as Lieutenant Governor
        (S.C.), 133-134, 136
Burke, Edmund, *179*, 181, 183, 189-190,
    193
    Pitt's cabinet criticized by, 101
Burnaby, Andrew, colonies
    characterized by, 51
Burnet, Governor, 35
Bushy Run, Indian defeat at, 63
Bute, Lord, 26, 27-29, 64, 73, 81, 84, 91,
    132
    glass boot satirizing, 27

           C

Caldwell, James, 118
Camden, Lord. *See* Pratt, Charles
Camm, John, 43-45
    pamphlets by, 45
Campbell, Lord William, 136
Carleton, Guy, 187-188, *190*, 192
Carpenter's Hall, Philadelphia, *196*, 200
Carr, Dabney, 154
Carr, Patrick, 118, 125
Carroll, Charles, 146, *147*, 148
Carter, Landon, 89, *140*
    Stamp Act protests by, 89-90
cartoons
    Deplorable State of America, *82-83*
Cary, Archibald, 89
Castle William, 114, 115, 118, 125, 167,
    169
"Caucus Club," 92
charters, colonial, 84
    Connecticut, 83
    Rhode Island, 83, 88, 94, 153
Chase, Samuel, 146, *147*, 148
Chase, Thomas, 92, 173
Chatham, Lord. *See* Pitt, William

Chauncy, Charles, Gridley characterized
    by, 41
Cherokee country, map of, *57*
Cherokees, treaties between Britain and,
    51-52, 55
Cherokee wars, 51-55, *56*
Chesterfield, Lord, Pitt criticized by,
    101
Chew, Benjamin, 76
Church, Benjamin, 165, 166
Circular Letter, 103, 105
    broadside concerning the, *104*
Clarke, Jonathan, 166
Clarke, Richard, *142*, 164, *165*, 166, 167
Claus, Daniel, 15
Coercive Acts, 178, 179, 181, 183, 185,
    194, 200
Colby, C. W., Pitt characterized by, 26
Colden, Cadwallader, 109-110
Colebrooke, Sir George, 157-158
colonial rights, Barré defense of, 85, 87
colonial settlement, restriction of, 64, 75
colonial subordination to British
    Parliament, theory of, 82, 84
Colonies, Rights of the, Examined, 88
Committee of Correspondence,
    Boston, 151, 165, 167, 170, 197
    Massachusetts, 148
    in Virginia, 89, 154-155
Connecticut Susquehanna Land
    Company, Barré tribute from, 87
Continental Congress, 148, 199-200
    Second, 79
Cooper, Samuel, 148-*149*, 150, 155
Copley, John Singleton, *167*, 169
Copley family, *142*
Cornwall, Charles, 181
Corymore, Captain, 54
Crafts, Thomas, 92, 173
Crown Point, 16, 17
    attacks on, 60
    English camp at, *58*
Cushing, Thomas, 148, 149, 158
Customs Commissioners, Board of, 113,
    114, 117, 120, 125

           D

Dalrymple, William, 116-117, 118
Dana, Richard, 117
Dart, Benjamin, 134
Dartmouth, Lord, 185, *186*

Declaration of Independence, 10, 46, 79,
    198
Declaratory Act, 100, 111, 179, 190
DeGrey, William, 134
DeLancey, Alice (Mrs. Ralph Izard), *145*
Demere, Raymond, 54
Dickinson, John, 79, *102*-103, *138*
    invitation sent to, *161*
    "Letters" by, 102, 108
Dinwiddie, Robert, 13, 18
Dowdeswell, William, 178-179, 181, 183
    bookplate of, *179*
Drayton, William Henry, *108*
    non-importation opposed by, 108
Drinker, Henry, *159*, 160-161
Dudingston, William, 151, 152, 153, 154
Dudley, Governor, 35
Dulany, Daniel, *92*, 146, 148
    tax pamphlet by, 93

           E

East India Company, 157-161, 163, 164,
    165, 166, 167, 177, 183
Eden, Robert, 145-*146*, 148
Edes, Benjamin, 92
Egremont, Lord, 64, 73, *74*
Ellis, Henry, 74, 83

           F

Faneuil Hall, 115, 118, 166
    broadside about meeting in, *168*
    fire in, 35
Fanning, Edmund, 129, *130*, 131
Fauquier, Francis, 44
    Camm described by, 43
Ferguson, Thomas, 134
Field, John, 92
Fitch, Governor (Conn.), 84
Fitzroy, Augustus Henry. *See* Grafton,
    Duke of
Fleming, John, 89
Forbes, John, 18, 53, 54, 62
Fort
    Detroit, 56, 61
    Duquesne, 17, 18, 53, 58, 62
    Loudon, 54, 55
    Necessity, surrender of, 13, 14
    Niagara, 17

Ontario, 56
Pitt, 56
Stanwix, Treaty of, 60
Ticonderoga, 16, 58, 60
William Henry, 17
Foulke, Samuel, 79
Fox, Charles James, *158*, 190, *193*
Franklin, Benjamin, *70*, 76, 87, 108, 129, 148, 149, 159, 176-177, 182
   antagonism between Governor Penn and, 79
   Hillsborough characterized by, 105
   Hutchinson-Oliver letters released by, 148, 150
   satire of, 77
French and Indian War, 13, 19, 51, 56, 58, 59, 84, 85, 152

G

Gadsden, Christopher, 106, 134
   election of, challenged, 48-49, *69*
Gage, Thomas, 59, 61, 116-117, 150
   Stamp Act Congress delegates characterized by, 97
Galloway, Joseph, 76, 108-109, 199
Garrick, Edward, 118
Gaspee, burning of the, 151-154, *155*
George II, 13, 14, 25, 26, 27, 52, 55
   death of, 32
George III, 9, *21*, *25*, 27, 28, *66*, 81, 99, 100, 105, 132, 153, 191, 192
   characterization of, 23-26
   coronation of, 23
   crown worn by, *24*
   Franklin's opinion of, 79
   medal of, *60*
Georgia, 82
   Council, 83, 84
Gibson, James, 75
"Glorious 92," 105
Golden Hill, Battle of, 110
Grafton, Duke of, 109, 185, 190
   attitude of toward Townshend duties, 110-111
   as prime minister, 101
Grant, James, 55
Gray, Samuel, 118, 125
Great Awakening, 92
"Great Commoner, the." *See* Pitt, William

Great Meadows, Washington at, 13, 14, 15
Greene, Jack, comment by, on Wilkes Fund, 136
grenadier, *117*
Grenville, George, 64, 73, 74, 98, 100, *138*, 149
   as Chancellor of the Exchequer, 81-82
   economic policies of, 81-84, 99, 124
   fall of, 99
   as Secretary of State, 81
   Walpole's opinion of, 81
Gridley, Jeremiah, 38
   at writs of assistance trial, 38, 41

H

Haley, Dr., 135
Halifax, Lord, 61, 73, 74
Hamilton, Alexander, *194*-195, 197
Hancock, John, 95, 107, 115, 118, *144*, 166, 170
   reaction of, to Stamp Act, 91, 92, 114
   Townshend Acts opposed by, 114
Hardy, Josiah, 94
Harrison, Benjamin, 89, 198
Hawks, John, 127
Henry, John, 47
Henry, Patrick, *69*, 154-155, 198, 200
   in House of Burgesses, 90
   as lawyer in Maury "salary" case, 46-48
Hill, Wills. *See* Hillsborough, Lord
Hillsborough, Lord (Hill, Wills), *105*, 136, 153
   characterized by Franklin, 105
   reaction of, to Adams's Circular Letter, 105, 111
   Wilkes Fund ruling by, 133-134, 136
Hood, Zachariah, 91
Hopkins, John B., 152
Hopkins, Samuel, Stamp Act protest led by, 87-88
Horsmanden, Daniel, 153, 154
Howard, Martin, *88*, 94
Hughes, John, stamp distributor, 87
Husbands, Hermon, 129, 130, 131
Hutchinson, Elisha, 164, 166
Hutchinson-Oliver correspondence, 150, 176, 182
Hutchinson, Thomas, 35, 38, 40, 118, 120, 122, 125, 148, 149, 152,

164-166, 169, 171, 175, 179
   characterization of, 122
   exile of, 39
   home of, destroyed, 91, 92, 95, 124
   Mayhew characterized by, 95
   at writs of assistance trial, 39, 41
   as a young man, *37*-38

I

Impartial Administration of Justice Act, 178
Indian policy, British, 56, 64
Indians
   Conestoga, 75, 76
   land taken from, 51, 60
   testimonial certificate for, *62*
   western, rebellion of, 56, 59, 60
   See also Paxton Riots
Ingersoll, Jared, 84-*85*, 87, 97
Izard, Ralph, *145*
   collaboration of, with Laurens, 135

J

James, Abel, 159, 160-161
Jefferson, Thomas, 46, 90, 154, 155, 197-*199*
Jeffries, John, 125
Johnson, Augustus, 94
Johnson, Sir William, 16-17, *59*, 61, 64
   Crown Point expedition of, 60
   Pontiac's meeting with, 56, 60
   relationship of, with Six Nations, 59
   treaty between Indians and, *60*
Johnson Riot Act, 131
Johnstone, George, 189

K

Kilroy, Matthew, 125
Knox, William, 82-83, 84, 186

L

Lamb, John, *109*-110, 162, 163

Land Bank, 92
Laurens, Henry, *135*, 136
    tax ruling by, 134-135
Lee, Arthur, 181, *182*, 183
    collaboration of, with Laurens, 135
Lee, Francis Lightfoot, 154
Lee, Richard Henry, 89, *155*, 198
    Committees of Correspondence
        created by, 154-155
    reaction of, to Stamp Act, 90
Legge, William. *See* Dartmouth, Lord
Leigh, Sir Egerton, pamphlet by, 135
Letter of a Gentleman at Halifax (Howard),
    88
Liberty Bowl by Paul Revere, *106*
Liberty Boys, New York's, 110
Liberty riot, 114, 115
Liberty Tree, 91, 113, 166
Little Carpenter. *See* Attakullaculla
Lopez, Aaron, 109
Lott, Abraham, 161-162, *163*
Loudon, Earl of, 17, 31, 41, 60
Louisbourg, 58, 182
    seige of, *15, 16*
Lowndes, Rawlins, 49
"Loyall Nine," 92
Lynch, Thomas, 134
Lyons, Peter, as lawyer in Maury
    "salary" case, 47
Lyttelton, William, *54-55*

M

Malcomb, John, brutal treatment of,
    172-173
Maryland, fee struggle in, 136, 145-146
Maury, James
    Jefferson tutored by, 46
    salary suit by, 46-48
    Virginia plantation conditions
        described by, 42
Maverick, Samuel, 118
Mayhew, Jonathan, *95*
    Stamp Act denounced by, 95-96
McDougall, Alexander, 162-*164*
McIntosh, Ebenezer, 92, 173
McKean, Thomas, Stamp Act Congress
    delegate, 97-*98*
Mein, John, non-importation violator,
    107
Mercer, George, 91
Meserve, George, 91

Mifflin, Sarah Morris, *160*
Mifflin, Thomas, *160*
military occupation in Boston, 114-115,
    116-118
    See also Boston Massacre
"Mitred Minuet, The," 192, *195*
Moffat, Thomas, 94
Molasses Act of 1733, 31, 151
Molineux, William, 166, 167
Montagu, John, 136, 153, 154
Montgomery, Hugh, 118, 125
Morgan, Edmund S., Hutchinson
    described by, 37
Murray, James, 187-188
Mutiny Act, 100
    of 1765, 109

N

Namier, Lewis, George III characterized
    by, 24
Ness, Ensign, 117
"Newport Junto," 88
    Otis's description of, 88
New York, 102
    non-importation in, 109
    in 1770, *163*
Nicholas, Robert Carter, 198
Nicholson, Governor (S.C.), 48
non-importation agreements, 98, 103,
    106-110, 127, 148, 164
    newspaper ad relating to, *111*
    violators of, 107, 117
North America, map of, published after
    the Proclamation of 1763, *73*
North, Lord, 111, 127, *158-159*, 177,
    185, 186, 188

O

Oconostota, Cherokee warrior, 54-55, *71*
Ogden, Robert, 97
Ohio Company, 13
Oliver, Andrew, stamp distributor, *90*,
    148, 149
    home of, vandalized, 91, 92, 124
Oliver-Hutchinson-Bernard clique, 115
Oliver, Peter, 149, 153
    Cooper described by, 149

Otis, Harrison Gray, 95
Otis, James, Jr., 10, 32, 38-39, *69*, 92,
    93, 95, 96, 115, 117
    last days of, 39-40
    Newport Junto characterized by, 88
    writs of assistance denounced by, 10,
        123
    at writs of assistance trial, 38-39, 41
Otis, James, Sr., 38
Otis, Samuel Allyne, 35

P

Paca, William, *146*-148
Paine, Robert Treat, 95, 120, *121*
    at Boston Massacre trial, 124-125
Palmes, Richard, 124
pamphlets, 45
    Franklin's, 77
    Hopkins's, 88
    on taxation, 84
Parsons' Cause, 42, 43, 46, 90
Parsons, James, 134
Paxton, Charles, customs commissioner,
    113, *114*
Paxton Band, Philadelphia's preparations
    to repel the, *78*
Paxton Riots, 75-76, 79
Peale, Charles Willson, 19
Pelham, Peter, 169
Pemberton, Israel, satire of, 77
Pendleton, Edmund, 89, 198
Penn, John, 76, 77
    antagonism between Franklin and, 79
Penn, Thomas, 105
Penn, William, descendants of, 78
Pennsylvania, 102
Pennsylvania Assembly, dispute
    between Proprietors and, 78-79
"Pennsylvania Farmer, Letters from a"
    (Dickinson), 102, 108
Pennsylvania Journal and Weekly Advertiser
    closing announcement of, 87
Pepperrell, William, *15, 16*
Petty, William. *See* Shelburne, Lord
Philadelphia, non-importation in,
    108-109
Pitt, William, *21, 26-29, 58, 68, 73,* 81,
    100, 110-111, 132, *158,* 190
    attitude of, toward America, 101, 102
    Stamp Act denounced by, 93, 99
    token saluting, *99*

Plumb, J. H., quoted on court of George III, 26
Pontiac, Ottawa chief, revolt of, 56-57, 58, 60, 62, 64, 75, 81
Pownall, John, 32, 74, 177, 185
  bookplate of, *178*
Pownall, Thomas, 35
Pratt, Charles, 190, *192*
Preston, Thomas, 118, 120
  trial of, 124-125, 183
Proclamation of November 26, 1770, 145
Proclamation of 1763, 60, 74-75, 186
  map of North America published after, *73*
Proprietors, 102
  dispute between Pennsylvania Assembly and, 78-79

Q

Quartering Act, Britain's, 41
Quebec, *20*
  keys of, offered to Britannia by France, *191*
Quebec Act, 75, 185-*187*, 188, 190-194, 197
Quincy, Josiah, Jr., 92, 121, *122*
  at Boston Massacre trial, 125
Quincy, Samuel, 120, *121*
  at Boston Massacre trial, 124-125

R

Randolph, Peyton, 89, 155, 198
Regulating Act, 158
Regulators (N.C.), 129-131
revenue-raising, 102
Revere, Paul, 95, 118, 174-175, *176*, 197
  Liberty Bowl made by, *106*
  "Mitred Minuet," published by, *192*
Rhode Island, 83
  charter of, 88, 94
  citizenship limitations in, 109
  Stamp Act reaction in, 87-88
Robinson, John, 39, 118
Rockingham, Marquis of, *100*
Rogers, Robert, 60-61, *63*
Romney, the, 113, 114
Rose-Fuller, 181
Rotch, Francis, *166*, 167, 171

Rowe, John, 106-107
Ruggles, Timothy, delegate to Stamp Act Congress, 96-97, 98
Rush, Benjamin, 160
Rutledge, John, 49, 96

S

St. Edward's Crown, *24*
Scott, George, 119
Sears, Isaac, 109-110, 162, 163
Seven Years' War, 13, 27, 81
Sewall, Jonathan, 120
Sewall, Stephen, 35, 95
Shelburne, Lord, 64, 73-75, 85, 190
Shirley, William, *14*, 16, 17, 182
Shote, Cunne. *See* Oconostota
Shute, Governor, 35
Six Nations, Sir William Johnson's relations with, 59
Smith, Matthew, 75
Smith, William, 162
Smythe, Frederick, 153
Snider, Christopher, 117
Sons of Liberty, 85
  Boston's, 105, 107
  Gadsden's, 108
  New York's, 107, 110, 162, 163
  North Carolina's, 129
South Carolina
  Commons House authority in, 48-49, 54
  Governor's Council of, 108
Spencer, George, 31
Stamp Act, 41, 46, 82, 84, 102, 110, 111, 122, 123, 134, 155, 158, 160, 164, 165
  colonial reaction to, 87-96
  newspaper suspension due to, *87*
  opposition to, 85
  Townshend support of, 101
  unenforceability of, 98
Stamp Act Congress, 90, 96-98, 102, 133
Stamp Act repeal, 113
  broadside celebrating, *100*
  favored by Burke, 179
  Hillsborough's attitude toward, 105
  obelisk celebrating, *103*
  support of, by Wilkes, 132
stamp distributors, threats to, 91
stamps, British, for colonial use, *86*
Stewart, Lazarus, 75

Stiles, Ezra, 109, *139*, 155
  Stamp Act denounced by, 93-94
Stuart, John, 54, 55, 64, 67
  map of Cherokee country by, *57*
Stuart, John. *See* Bute, Lord
Sugar Act
  Grenville's, 88, 89, 102, 106
  of 1764, 82, 93, 164
Sugar Creek (N.C.), war of, 129

T

taxation, 84
  rights of, 88, 90, 101, 102, 111, 136
  without representation, 102
taxes, 46
  determination of, 88
  See also Stamp Act
Tea Act of May 1773, 155, 158, 162, 165
Temple, John, 119-120
Temple, Lord, 132
Thacher, Oxenbridge, 32, 38, 40-41
  pamphlet by, *40*
  Virginians praised by, 89, 90
Thames, The, *188*
Thomson, Charles, 108-109
Thurlow, Edward, 189
Times, The, Hogarth cartoon in, *29*
Tobacco Inspection Acts, 136, 147
tobacco merchants, *43*
Townshend Acts, 46, 102, 108, 110, 113, 114, 120, 123-124, 127, 158, 162, 181, 182
  repeal of, 107
Townshend, Charles, 111, *141*
  attitude of, toward America, 101-102
  death of, 158
  Stamp Act defended by, 85, 101
Townshend duties, 106, 107, 108, 109, 110, 127, 155, 158, 159, 160, 179
  repeal of, 111
trade, 102
  colonial, with England, 107
  West Indies, 109, 151, 152
Trade and Commerce, Society for Encouraging, 106
Treaty of Aix-la-Chapelle, 15
Treaty of Fort Stanwix, 60
Trecothick, Barlow, 100, 110
Trott, George, 92
Tryon, William, 127, 129-131, 163, 175
Turner, Charles, 193

Two-Penny Acts, 42, 44, 45, 46, 47
Tyler, Royall, 118

V

Villiers, Coulon de, 13
Virginia, rights asserted by, 89-90
Virginia Resolves, 155

W

Waldegrave, Lord, 24
Walpole, Horace, 26, 27, 178
    Egremont described by, 64
    Grenville characterized by, 81
Walpole, Robert, 26
wampum belt, *52*
Wanton, Joseph, *153*

Warden, G. B., quoted on conditions in
    Boston, 35
Warren, James, 170
Warren, Joseph, 92, 115, 116, 122, 123,
    142, 165, 166
Warren, Mercy Otis, *142*, 170-171
Washington, George, 16, 19, 62, *65*, 198
    description of, 13-14
    at Fort Necessity, 13, 14
    at Great Meadows, 13, 14
    as a military commander, 17-18
Watson-Wentworth, Charles. *See*
    Rockingham, Marquis of
Webster, Noah, Johnson characterized
    by, 97
Wedderburn, Alexander, 176-*177*, 182
West, Benjamin, 169
Westminster Hall, *189*
Wharton, Thomas, Sr., 159, 160, 161
Whately, Thomas, 82, 84, 85, 148
    release of letters sent to, 148-149
Whipple, Abraham, 151-*152*
White, Henry, 161-162, 163

White, Hugh, 118
Whitefield, George, 92
Wilkes Fund, 133, 134, 135, 136
Wilkes, John, *132*-133
    Stamp Act repeal supported by, 132
Wilkes and Liberty, *133*
Willing, Thomas, 76
Winthrop, John, 95
Wolfe, James, *17*, *21*, 58, 74, 85
Wren Building, College of William and
    Mary, *44*
Writs of assistance, 10, 31-32, *33-34*, 35,
    38-39, 41, 123
Wyndham, Charles. *See* Egremont, Lord
Wythe, George, 89

Y

York, Duke of (Edward Augustus), 24,
    25
Young, Thomas, 165, 166